Contents

Selling Forest Environmental Services

Selling Forest Environmental Services

Market-based Mechanisms for Conservation and Development

Edited by

Stefano Pagiola,
Joshua Bishop,
and
Natasha Landell-Mills

Earthscan Publications Limited
London • Sterling, VA

First published in the UK and USA in 2002
by Earthscan Publications Ltd

ISBN: 1 85383 888 8 paperback
        1 85383 889 6 hardback

Typesetting by JS Typesetting Ltd, Wellingborough, Northants
Printed and bound in the UK by Creative Print and Design (Wales), Ebbw Vale
Cover design by Danny Gillespie

For a full list of publications please contact:

Earthscan Publications Ltd
120 Pentonville Road, London, N1 9JN, UK
Tel: +44 (0)20 7278 0433
Fax: +44 (0)20 7278 1142
Email: earthinfo@earthscan.co.uk
Web: **www.earthscan.co.uk**

22883 Quicksilver Drive, Sterling, VA 20166-2012, USA

Earthscan is an editorially independent subsidiary of Kogan Page Ltd and publishes in
association with WWF-UK and the International Institute for Environment and
Development

A catalogue record for this book is available from the British Library

Library of Congress Cataloging-in-Publication Data

Selling forest environmental services : market-based mechanisms for conservation and
development / edited by Stefano Pagiola, Joshua Bishop, and Natasha Landell-Mills.
        p.cm
    Includes bibliographical references.
    ISBN 1-85383-999-8 (pbk) – ISBN 1-85383-889-6 (hardback)
        1. Forest conservation. 2. Forest management. 3. Forests and forestry–
Environmental aspects. I. Pagiola, Stefano. II. Bishop, Joshua. III. Landell-Mills,
Natasha.

SD411 .S45 2002
333.75′16–dc21

                                                                            2002009275

List of Tables, Figures, and Boxes

TABLES

FIGURES

BOXES

Foreword

The many valuable ecosystem services provided by forests, including climate stabilization, carbon storage, protection of hydrological function, and biodiversity conservation, are finally gaining some attention. Just three decades ago the link between deforestation and global climate change had not yet been made. Just two decades ago, biodiversity was not a well-understood concept, and was even misspelled in the literature. Today governments, companies, and citizens are increasingly recognizing the value of the wide range of services our forest ecosystems provide.

Alongside this growing awareness are the growing numbers of startling natural calamities that burden society with great costs in terms of lives and money. Massive forest fires on Borneo close down Singapore's busy airport for weeks at a time. Unprecedented floods in China and El Salvador kill thousands. Fires burn in the cloud forests of southern Mexico for the first time in recorded history. The financial consequences of floods, fires, droughts, landslides, and extreme storms are bringing into focus the costs of forest destruction.

This awareness is drawing attention to the economic benefits of healthy ecosystems – benefits that until recently have been taken for granted. Indeed, as human demands grow and natural resources become more scarce, those who bear the costs of degradation – including downstream water utilities, local governments, private insurers, and society as a whole – are exploring opportunities to reduce risks and costs by financing forest conservation. At the same time, some forest owners, including low-income producers and indigenous communities, are seeking compensation for the costs of maintaining healthy forests. The interest in reducing costs, increasing incomes and expanding conservation is placing markets for ecosystem services at center stage.

This volume outlines a wide-ranging sample of the growing number of cases in which ecosystem services are finding real markets and real revenue flows. It covers experiences with emerging markets in carbon, water, and biodiversity from Brazil to India, and Australia to the United States. It touches on the diversity of mechanisms, from self-organized private deals and open trading schemes to public payment schemes. It also highlights the range of participants and beneficiaries, including national governments, municipalities, companies, environmental groups, and local communities.

These cases are stories from the first chapter of a dramatic shift in the way society manages its natural assets. It will take time to write the whole book. The sale of ecosystem services is a complex undertaking with a tremendous variety of market structures, payment schemes, and numbers and types of participants.

It has wide-ranging impacts from the local to the global. Issues of property rights, pricing, and interactions between services, not to mention services that have yet to be described, remain problematic. The innovations in this area are still limited in scale, scope, and impact, and trading in environmental services remains a nascent activity. The many players are just beginning to grasp the potential ways in which markets can help to protect forest services and improve livelihoods.

But the trend is clear. Many of the innovators described in this book participate in the Katoomba Group, a collection of experts in ecology, finance, markets, and environmental business from around the world. They have come together to catalyze these innovations. The Katoomba Group has spearheaded the work of learning about market approaches, building frameworks, and making deals. The three editors of this volume are lively and valued contributors to this group.

Many people are concerned about the profound implications of putting a price on nature. It poses real technical problems and raises serious cultural objections. Yet the reality today is that the world's largest ecosystems – forests – are valued mainly as sources of fuel, timber, and fiber. Across the globe these complex ecosystems are being replaced by other land uses: soya beans in Brazil, oil palms in Indonesia, maize in southern Mexico, or shopping malls in the northwest United States. The issue is clear: for forests to survive, they need to compete financially.

Given the tremendous social and environmental benefits of forest services, and the many stakeholders who stand to gain, including low-income people, it is vital to take maximum advantage of the potential of market approaches. Unless we are able to link commercial market activity to conservation objectives, the future of the global forest estate will be reduced to limited parks and protected areas.

The success stories laid out here, while modest, point to strategic directions that will carry us to a future that brings ecological, economic, and social approaches together and maintain forests in the landscape.

Michael Jenkins
Executive Director, Forest Trends
April 2002

Acknowledgements

A volume such as this owes much to the generous support, both intellectual and practical, of many people and institutions. Without their assistance, it would not have been possible to complete it. The greatest thanks, of course, go to the contributing authors. Their efforts have likewise been supported by many others, who are acknowledged in the individual chapters.

If this volume can be said to have a godparent, it would be Forest Trends, a young organization based in the United States. The idea for the book emerged during a conversation in a minibus, while returning from one of the excellent Katoomba Group meetings organized by Forest Trends. The Katoomba Group includes representatives of forestry and finance companies, environmental policy and research organizations, governmental agencies and influential private and non-profit groups who have been meeting regularly since early 2000 to explore innovative market-based approaches to conserving the world's forests. Several of the authors (and all three editors) are members of the group, which takes its name from the town of Katoomba, Australia, where its first meeting was held.

Financial support for the preparation of this book was provided by Danish International Assitance (Danida), Swiss Agency for Development and Cooperation (SDC), the UK arm of the Worldwide Fund For Nature (WWF-UK), and the Swedish International Development Cooperation Agency (Sida). The World Bank Institute (WBI), the World Bank's training arm, has also played an important role. WBI has long supported capacity-building in this area, including a series of training courses on new approaches to conservation financing. Some of the material included in this volume has its origins in teaching materials for these courses. WBI also generously provided funding for the preparation of many of the case studies included in this volume. It should be stressed that the above-mentioned organizations do not necessarily share or endorse the opinions expressed by the editors or by the individual authors.

The editors have also benefited from helpful discussions with numerous colleagues throughout the world, who have provided critical insights and guided our thinking on the issues addressed here. Without in any way implicating them in the views expressed in this volume, we would especially like to thank Arild Angelsen, Bruce Aylward, Steve Bass, Stuart Beil, Carl Binning, Ian Calder, David Cassells, Ken Chomitz, John Dixon, John Forgach, Maryanne Grieg-Gran, John Hudson, Saleemul Huq, Bill Hyde, Michael Jenkins, David Kaimowitz, John Kellenberg, Michael Linddal, Richard McNally, James Mayers, Patricia Moles, Pedro Moura Costa, Dan Nepstad, Ken Newcombe, Edgar Ortiz, John Palmer, David Pearce, Gunars Platais, Ina Porras, Manrique Rojas, Sara Scherr, Ronaldo

Seroa da Motta, Jerry Shively, Paul Steele, Tim Swanson, Paul Toyne, and Andy White.

Finally, we would like to thank Jonathan Sinclair Wilson and his team at Earthscan for their efforts to ensure that this volume is published in a timely fashion, and reaches the widest possible audience.

Stefano Pagiola, Joshua Bishop, and Natasha Landell-Mills
April 2002

List of Contributors

Joshua Bishop was director of the Environmental Economics Programme of the International Institute for Environment and Development (IIED) at the time of writing. He is currently senior adviser on economics and environment for The World Conservation Union (IUCN).

David Brand is director of the Hancock Natural Resource Group.

Gary Bull is an economist and policy analyst in the Faculty of Forestry at the University of British Columbia.

Elisa Corcuera Vliegenthart is an environmental planner and independent journalist.

Phil Cottle is a senior consultant with PartnerRe Agricultural Services, Partner Reinsurance Company Ltd.

Charles Crosthwaite-Eyre is a risk consultant with Aon Environmental Solutions.

Valdir F Denardin is a doctoral candidate in economics in the graduate program in development, agriculture, and society at the Federal Rural University of Rio de Janeiro, Brazil.

Marta Echavarria is founder and director of Ecodecisión.

Guillermo Geisse is the executive director of the Centre of Research and Planning of the Environment (CIPMA), Chile.

Zoe Harkin is a graduate student in forest economics in the Faculty of Forestry at the University of British Columbia.

Micheal Jenkins is executive director of Forest Trends.

Kerry ten Kate is a policy adviser at the Royal Botanic Gardens, Kew, United Kingdom.

John Kerr is assistant professor in the Department of Resource Development at Michigan State University.

Sarah A Laird is an independent consultant.

Natasha Landell-Mills is a research associate in the Environmental Economics Programme of IIED.

Wilson Loureiro is coordinator/chief and director for biodiversity of the Institute for Environmental Protection, Directorate of Parks and Protected Areas, Paraná, Brazil.

Peter H May is a resource economist in the Department of Development, Agriculture and Society of the Federal Rural University of Rio de Janeiro, Brazil.

Stefano Pagiola is a senior environmental economist in the Environment Department of the World Bank.

J B Ruhl is Professor at the College of Law of Florida State University, in Tallahassee, United States.

Ina-Marlene Ruthenberg is a senior economist in the Environmentally and Socially Sustainable Development Department of the Latin America and the Caribbean Regional Office of the World Bank.

James Salzman is professor at the Washington College of Law of the American University, in Washington, DC.

Claudia Sepúlveda is a sociologist in CIPMA, Chile.

Richard Tipper is director of Carbon Asset Management at the Edinburgh Centre for Carbon Management.

Fernando C Veiga Neto is a doctoral candidate in agronomy in the graduate program in development, agriculture, and society of the Federal Rural University of Rio de Janeiro, Brazil.

Ann Wong is a graduate student in ecosystem modeling in the Faculty of Forestry at the University of British Columbia.

Acronyms and Abbreviations

°C	degrees Celsius
A$	Australian dollars
ABS	access and benefit-sharing
AEPS	American Electric Power System
APA	área de proteção ambiental (environmental protection area) (Brazil)
AyA	Instituto Costarricense de Acueductos y Alcantarillados (Costa Rican Institute of Aqueducts and Drains)
BC	British Columbia (Canada)
BCCL	Promotion of Biodiversity Conservation within Coffee Landscapes (project, El Salvador)
BEC	Biogeoclimatic Ecosystem Classification (Canada)
CAF	Certificado de Abono Forestal (Forest Credit Certificate) (Costa Rica)
CALM	Department of Conservation and Land Management (Western Australia)
CBD	Convention on Biological Diversity
CBM-CFS	carbon budget model of the Canadian forest sector
CBM-FPS	Canadian budget model of the forest product sector
CC	conservation community (Chile)
CCB	Coeficiênte de Conservação da Biodiversidade (Biodiversity Conservation Coefficient) (Brazil)
CDM	Clean Development Mechanism
CEF	Conservation Enterprise Fund
CESMACH	Campesinos Ecológicos de la Sierra Madre de Chiapas (Ecological Small Farmers of the Sierra Madre of Chiapas) (Mexico)
CFS	Canadian forest service
CH_4	methane
CI	Conservation International
CIPMA	Centro de Investigación y Planificación del Medio Ambiente (Center for Environmental Research and Planning) (Chile)
CO	carbon monoxide
CO_2	carbon dioxide
CODEFF	Comité Pro Defensa de la Flora y Fauna (National Committee for the Protection of Flora and Fauna) (Chile)

COMCAM	Consortium of Municipalities in the Campo Mourão Region (Brazil)
CONAF	Corporación Nacional Forestal (National Forestry Agency) (Chile)
COP	Conference of the Parties (IPCC)
CORIPA	Consórcio Intermunicipal para Conservação do Remanescente do rio Paraná e Áreas de Influência (Intermunicipal Partnership for the Conservation of the Remainder of the River Paraná and Areas of Influence) (Brazil)
CPR	common pool resource
CREED	Programme on Collaborative Research in the Economics of Environment and Development
CRESEE	Regional Centre for Studies in Ecological Economics
CSWCRTI	Central Soil and Water Conservation Research and Training Institute (Chandigarh)
CU	conservation unit (Brazil)
CWA	Clean Water Act (United States)
Danida	Danish International Assistance
DFID	Department For International Development (United Kingdom)
ECCM	Edinburgh Centre for Carbon Management
EEQ	Empresa Eléctrica de Quito (Electrical Company of Quito) (Ecuador)
EMAAP-Q	Empresa Metropolitana de Alcantarillado y Agua Potable de Quito (Quito Metropolitan Area Sewage and Potable Water Company) (Ecuador)
ENSO	El Niño Southern Oscillation
EPA	Environmental Protection Agency (United States)
EU	European Union
FAN	Fundacion Amigos de la Naturaleza (Friends of Nature Foundation) (Bolivia)
FAO	Food and Agriculture Organization (United Nations)
FDA	Food and Drug Administration (United States)
FIA	International Automobile Federation
FLO	Fairtrade Labelling Organization
FONAFIFO	Fondo Nacional de Financiamiento Forestal (National Fund for Forest Financing) (Costa Rica)
FONAG	Fondo del Agua (Water Fund) (Ecuador)
FSOS	Forest Simulation Optimization System
FUNDECOR	Fundación para el Desarrollo de la Cordillera Volcánica Central (Foundation for the Development of the Central Volcanic Cordillera) (Costa Rica)
GDP	gross domestic product
GEF	Global Environment Facility
GEMCO	Greenhouse Emissions Management Consortium (Canada)
GERT	Greenhouse Emissions Reduction Trading project (Canada)

GHG	greenhouse gas
GTZ	Deutsche Gesellschaft für Technische Zusammenarbeit (German Corporation for Technical Collaboration)
ha	hectare(s)
HEPL	Habitat Enhancement in Productive Landscapes (project, Mexico)
HEP	hydroelectric power
HNFA	Hancock New Forests Australia
HNRG	Hancock Natural Resource Group
HRMS	Hill Resource Management Society (Sukhomajri)
IAP	Instituto Ambiental do Paraná (Paraná Environmental Institute) (Brazil)
ICBG	International Cooperative Biodiversity Group
ICDP	integrated conservation and biodiversity program
ICMS-E	Imposto sobre Circulação de Mercadorias e Serviços (ecological value-added tax with environmental revenue-sharing criteria) (Brazil)
IDESMAC	Instituto para el Desarrollo Sustenable en Mesoamérica (Institute for Sustainable Development in Mesoamerica) (Mexico)
IEF	Instituto Estadual de Florestas (State Forest Institute) (Brazil)
IFC	International Finance Corporation
IFOAM	International Federation of Organic Agriculture Movements
IHN	Instituto de Historia Natural (Natural History Institute) (Mexico)
IIED	International Institute for Environment and Development
INBio	Instituto Nacional de Biodiversidad (National Institute of Biodiversity) (Costa Rica)
INE	Instituto Nacional de Ecología (National Ecology Institute) (Mexico)
InTEC	integrated terrestrial ecosystem C-Budget model (Canada)
IPCC	Intergovernmental Panel on Climate Change
IUCN	World Conservation Union
JI	Joint Implementation
kg	kilogramme(s)
km	kilometer(s)
km²	square kilometers
lb	pound
m³	cubic meters
MARN	Ministry of the Environment (El Salvador)
MBC	Mesoamerican Biological Corridor
MINAE	Ministry of Environment and Energy (Costa Rica)
MST	Movimento dos Sem Terra (Movement of Landless Workers) (Brazil)
NCI	National Cancer Institute (NCI)

NFI	national forest inventory
NGO	non-governmental organization
NIH	National Institute of Health (United States)
NKMCAP	Noel Kempff Mercado Climate Action Project (Bolivia)
NOx	nitrogen oxide
NRC	National Research Council (United States)
NSF	National Science Foundation (United States)
NSW	New South Wales (Australia)
OCIC	Oficina Costarricense de Implementación Conjunta (Costa Rican Office of Joint Implementation) (Costa Rica)
PCF	Prototype Carbon Fund (World Bank)
PERRL	Pilot Emission Removals, Reductions and Learning program (Canada)
PERT	Pilot Emissions Reduction Trading program (Canada)
PPA	privately protected area
PROCAFÉ	Fundación Salvadoreña para Investigaciones del Café (Salvadoran Foundation for Coffee Research) (El Salvador)
PSA	Pago por Servicios Ambientales (Payments for Environmental Services) (Costa Rica)
R$	Brazilian Real (currency)
R&D	research and development
RAPP	Red de Areas Protegidas Privadas (Privately Protected Areas Network) (Chile)
RPPN	reserva particular do patrimônio natural (private natural patrimony reserve) (Brazil)
SDC	Swiss Agency for Development and Cooperation
SEMAD	Secretaria Estadual de Meio Ambiente e Desenvolvimento Sustentável (Environment and Sustainable Development Secretariat) (Brazil)
SENACSA	Servicio Nacional de Conservación de Suela y Agua (National Soil and Water Conservation Service) (Costa Rica)
Sida	Swedish International Development Cooperation Agency
SINAC	Sistema Nacional de Areas de Conservación (National System of Conservation Areas) (Costa Rica)
SMBC	Smithsonian Migratory Bird Center (United States)
SMP	Sarawak Medichem Pharmaceuticals
SNASPE	Sistema Nacional de Areas Silvestres Protegidas del Estado (National Protected Areas System) (Chile)
SO_2	sulfur dioxide
TAA	Trexler & Associates
tC	tonnes of carbon
tCO_2	tonnes of carbon dioxide
tC/yr	tonnes of carbon per year
TEV	total economic value
TFL	tree farm license

TNC	The Nature Conservancy
TSA	timber supply area
UIC	University of Illinois at Chicago
UNCED	United Nations Conference on Environment and Development
UNFCCC	United Nations Framework Convention on Climate Change
USAID	United States Agency for International Development
USDA	United States Department of Agriculture
VAT	value-added tax
VCR	Voluntary Challenge and Registry (Canada)
VRI	Vegetation Resources Inventory
WBI	World Bank Institute
WCEL	West Coast Environmental Law
WWF	Worldwide Fund For Nature

Chapter 1

Market-based Mechanisms for Forest Conservation and Development

Stefano Pagiola, Natasha Landell-Mills, and Joshua Bishop

Forests are under severe threat in many parts of the world. An average of almost 15 million hectares of forest were lost every year during the 1990s, mostly in the tropics (FAO, 2001a, 2001b). This loss of forests has been accompanied by a loss of the many valuable services that forests provide – such as regulation of hydrological flows and carbon sequestration – and of the biodiversity they contain (Myers, 1997).

Recent years have seen widespread experimentation with market-based mechanisms to address these problems. Many believe that market-based approaches can provide powerful incentives and efficient means of conserving forests and the public goods they provide, while at the same time offering new sources of income to support rural livelihoods. A recent review found almost 300 examples of such mechanisms worldwide (Landell-Mills and Porras, 2002) and the list is constantly growing.

While interest in market-based approaches to forest conservation is growing throughout the world, relatively little information is available on how these approaches have emerged and how they work in practice. This book brings together case studies of some of the most advanced experiments. Each case study discusses the challenges involved in creating markets for forest environmental services, including how to identify and quantify the different services that forests provide; establishing sustainable financing mechanisms; developing payments systems that provide adequate incentives to land managers; developing and adapting the institutional framework to suit local circumstances; and ensuring an equitable distribution of costs and benefits among different stakeholders.

BENEFITS PROVIDED BY FORESTS

We adopt here a very wide definition of 'forest', which includes any land use with substantial tree cover. Of course, not all forests are equally valuable. The structures, compositions, and locations of forests play important roles in determining the kinds of services they can provide, and to whom. Monoculture plantations clearly do not contain much biodiversity. They can, however, affect hydrological flows, and they can sequester carbon. Rather than restricting the discussion to a subset of forests, we find it more useful to ask which services any particular forest can provide. We would in any case have to ask this question, as even within natural forests there is considerable variation in the types and levels of services being provided to consumers.

Forests provide a wide variety of benefits (Baskin, 1997; Myers, 1997; Roper and Park, 1999; Schmidt and others, 1999; Sharma, 1992). In this book, we focus on three main categories of benefits, as follows:

- **Watershed protection.** Forests can play an important role in regulating hydrological flows and reducing sedimentation. Changes in forest cover can affect the quantity and quality of water flows downstream, as well as their timing.
- **Biodiversity conservation.** Forests harbor a significant proportion of the world's biodiversity. Loss of habitat, such as forests, is a leading cause of species loss.
- **Carbon sequestration.** Standing forests hold large carbon stocks, and growing forests sequester carbon from the atmosphere.

Chapter 2 reviews the role of forests in providing these services.

WHY ARE FOREST SERVICES LOST?

The causes of deforestation are many and complex (Angelsen and Kaimowitz, 2001; Brown and Pearce, 1994; Contreras-Hermosilla, 2000; Kaimowitz and Angelsen, 1998). This book focuses on situations in which market failure plays a key role. This is not to underestimate the importance of other factors, notably the prevalence of agricultural subsidies and timber trade policies that encourage forest conversion and unsustainable logging (Barbier and others, 1994; Binswanger, 1991; Browder, 1985; Mahar, 1988; Repetto and Gillis, 1988; Schneider, 1994). Nevertheless, the fact remains that even in the absence of perverse public policies, forest environmental services would still be under-supplied by the market, in most cases due to their nature as 'externalities' or 'public goods' (Baumol and Oates, 1988; Cornes and Sandler, 1996).[1]

Consider the case of farmers deciding whether to clear native forests in a frontier area for use as agricultural land. In making this decision, they will certainly consider the benefits they expect to derive from increased crop production, whether it be for sale or for their families' own consumption. They will also factor in the costs of tools needed to clear land, the fertilizers and other inputs needed to grow crops, and the labor needed to clear the forest and prepare the new cropland. But what about the other benefits that the forest provides, which will be lost or reduced if the forest is cleared? If the farmers collect fuelwood or other non-timber products, or graze their livestock in the forest area, they will factor the loss of these services into their decision.[2] They are unlikely to consider benefits such as watershed protection, on the other hand. Cutting down the forest might increase downstream flooding and sedimentation, for example, but these costs will not be borne by the farmers clearing the area; they will be borne by people living far downstream. Therefore, local land users will typically ignore these costs in their clearing decisions. The result is that, from the perspective of farmers deciding whether to clear a given stretch of land, the value of the forest appears to be far lower than it really is. Since the benefits of clearing are valued fully but the benefits of maintaining forest areas are not, it is likely that more forest will be cleared than is optimal. A full accounting of all the benefits would not necessarily lead to the preservation of all the forest, but it would almost certainly result in a lower rate of deforestation than that which currently takes place.

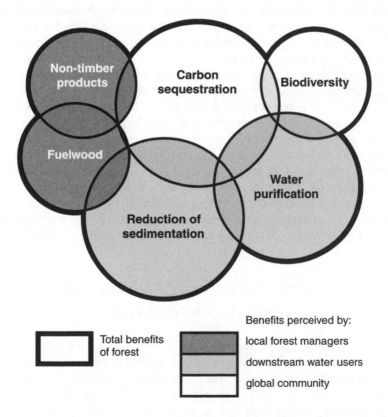

Figure 1.1 *Beneficiaries of forest services*

Figure 1.1 illustrates the problem in stylized form. Each circle represents one of the services provided by a particular forest. For the purposes of illustration, six such services are shown. Depending on the characteristics of the forest and of the users of each service, the circles may differ in magnitude: the forest illustrated here, for example, has large hydrological benefits and carbon sequestration benefits, but relatively minor biodiversity benefits. Other forests will have different benefits, in both absolute and relative terms. The figure also illustrates that some of these benefits overlap each other to varying degrees. The total benefits of the forest are given by the sum of its constituent benefits. Different stakeholder groups will tend to perceive a different mix of forest benefits, attributing more or less importance to each component according to their own priorities and preferences. In particular, local decision-makers may give priority to benefits arising from direct, usually extractive uses of the forest, such as the harvest of fuelwood and other non-timber forest products (illustrated by the dark shaded area). Hydrological benefits, for example, often do not accrue to local decision-makers in the forest itself, but instead to water users downstream (light shaded area). Likewise, carbon sequestration benefits accrue to global society as a whole (unshaded area), through their effect in mitigating climate change.[3] So long as local decision-makers receive no compensation for providing these benefits, they are unlikely to give them much consideration when making land use decisions.[4]

Responses to the problem of market failure in forests can take many forms. A common response has been for governments to assume responsibility for protecting and managing forest resources, either in protected areas or in forest management units. Yet governmental ambitions have rarely lived up to expectations. All too often governments lack sufficient information about which services are important and how to provide them, or they lack funds to pay for the necessary conservation. Governments are also not immune to political pressures, such as lobbying by agricultural or industrial interests that would profit from forest use.

Other approaches have included reforestation projects, a variety of initiatives that seek to educate local land users about the benefits of forests, and integrated conservation and development projects. The record of these projects has been mixed (Southgate, 1998). Often, they have failed to address the fundamental problem of market failure. They have also proved costly and difficult to implement.

MARKET-BASED MECHANISMS FOR FOREST CONSERVATION

The basic purpose of the market-based mechanisms examined in this book is to remedy market failure.[5] By selling the services provided by forests, either individually or in bundles, these mechanisms aim to generate funds that can then be used either: (i) to increase the private benefits of conservation to individual forest managers, and so change their incentives; or (ii) to generate resources that can be used to finance conservation efforts by public or private conservation groups.

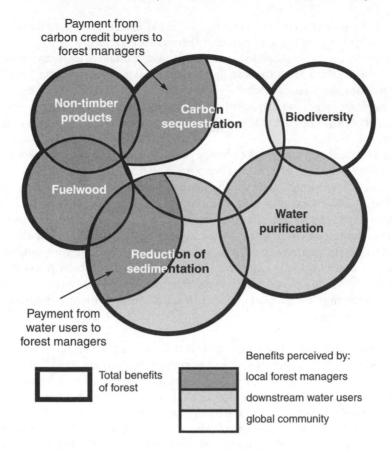

Figure 1.2 *Logic of market-based mechanisms for forest services*

The basic logic of market-based mechanisms is illustrated in Figure 1.2. Two hypothetical market-based mechanisms are shown: one that sells sedimentation reduction services to downstream water users, and one that sells carbon sequestration services to buyers needing credits to meet Kyoto emission reduction requirements.[6] These payments essentially transfer some of the benefits received by these groups to the local forest managers. As a result, the total benefits of forest conservation as perceived by forest managers increase, perhaps substantially. Assuming that the benefits of converting forests to other uses remain unchanged, it is now more likely that local forest managers will choose to preserve forests.

Several aspects of this diagram are worth noting:

• Even with payments for sedimentation-reduction and carbon sequestration, local forest managers still perceive only a subset of all forest benefits. This may not matter from a practical perspective. All that is needed from the perspective of changing forest management decisions is to increase the benefits of conservation that are perceived by local forest managers so that they outweigh the benefits they perceive from deforestation.

- A socially inefficient solution, in which forest managers choose to convert a forest even though its total social benefits are greater than the benefits of alternative uses, remains possible. Its likelihood is reduced, but not eliminated. Only when local land managers are compensated for supplying all non-local benefits can we be sure that forest management decisions are always socially optimal.

- For the same reason, market-based mechanisms fall short of providing a complete valuation of a forest's benefits. The flow of payments from various beneficiaries through such mechanisms is unlikely to exceed the perceived value of the benefits provided, because the beneficiaries would refuse to pay. These payments are quite likely to capture only part of the benefits provided, however, because of the difficulty of identifying all beneficiaries of all services and collecting appropriate payments. Such mechanisms, therefore, only provide a lower bound to the actual value of the services that forests provide.

- Merely collecting payments from the beneficiaries of forest services will not help to change forest management decisions unless these payments reach forest managers.

Compared to previous approaches to forest conservation, market-based mechanisms promise increased efficiency and increased effectiveness, as well as increased equity in the distribution of costs and benefits. Experience with market-based instruments in other sectors has shown that such policies, if carefully designed and implemented, can achieve environmental goals at significantly less cost than conventional 'command-and-control' approaches, while creating positive incentives for continual innovation and improvement (Ekins, 1999; Huber and others, 1998; OECD, 1993, 1994; Stavins, 1999). The reason for this is simple: the costs of achieving any given environmental objective are rarely constant across all situations. Market-based instruments take advantage of this difference by concentrating efforts where the costs are lower. Likewise, the benefits of conservation can differ substantially from case to case. Market-based instruments seek out and concentrate on the higher-benefit cases.

The claim for greater equity through the use of market-based based approaches is more controversial. Many are familiar with the so-called 'polluter pays principle', which states that those who impose environmental burdens on society, in the form of waste or pollution, should bear the costs (which will ultimately be passed on to consumers in the form of higher prices for goods and services). In the case of environmental services, the relevant corollary is the less well-known 'provider gets principle', which holds that those who provide an environmental benefit should be rewarded for doing so (or at least be compensated for their costs). Markets for environmental services are thus equitable, or at least 'fair' in a narrow sense, to the extent that real costs and benefits are recognized and remunerated.

Proponents of markets for forest environmental services go further, arguing that in most cases, those who provide such services – mainly rural land users –

are poorer than the beneficiaries or consumers of environmental services. To the extent that this claim holds true, and new financial mechanisms do in fact transfer resources from relatively rich consumers of forest environmental services to relatively poor suppliers, then markets for environmental services may be equitable in an even stronger sense. Whether the truly poor are able to take advantage of these new markets remains to be seen.

The mechanisms discussed here are market-based. Some are actual markets, others are only partially markets. For example, where governments introduce financial incentives to encourage the supply of environmental services, we cannot say that a market has truly been established. For this to be the case we would need to see evidence of buyers and sellers coming together, such that prices are set by the laws of supply and demand.

CASE STUDIES OF INNOVATIVE MARKET-BASED MECHANISMS

This book presents three sets of case studies, one for each of the following environmental services: watershed protection, biodiversity conservation, and carbon sequestration. Case studies in each section seek to tackle a number of key issues relating to market structures, the process of market development, and the resulting impacts on environmental, social, and economic indices. Each case study was written by market participants or individuals who are familiar with the evolution of the market mechanism.[7] Authors were selected for their expertise, their intimate knowledge of particular market mechanisms, and for the particular perspectives they offer.

Selling water services

Costa Rica's system of Payments for Environmental Services (PSA) is probably the most elaborate such system in place in the developing world. Stefano Pagiola discusses the role that sales of water services have played in this system (Chapter 3). Water services are one of four services that the PSA program seeks to provide. Since its creation, the PSA program has convinced several hydroelectric power generators and an industrial water user to pay for the system's forest conservation activities.

John Kerr examines one of the most celebrated examples of successful watershed management, that of Sukhomajri in India (Chapter 4). The experiment arose from the desire in the city of Chandigarh to protect the local lake from sedimentation. Doing so required it to find a way to convince upstream land users in the Sukhomajri watershed to change their land uses. In turn, that required them to find a mechanism to address differences in land use within the upstream community. Yet despite its success at finding a solution to this complex situation, the Sukhomajri model has not been widely adopted. Kerr examines the reasons for this.

Jim Salzman and J B Ruhl turn to a developed-country example, that of wetland banking in the United States (Chapter 5). This is an example of a market that emerged to help make a traditional command-and-control approach to conservation more efficient. United States law requires that there be no net loss of wetlands. Real estate developers can 'compensate' for any loss caused by their projects by restoring or enhancing wetlands elsewhere. A market has emerged that provides such services to developers, so that they do not have to undertake them themselves.

Large cities are some of the main beneficiaries of water services. New York City's decision to invest in conservation in the Catskills watershed rather than in building a much more expensive water purification plant has been widely publicized (Chichilnisky and Heal, 1998). Marta Echavarria examines an effort to establish a similar mechanism in a developing country, that of the FONAG water fund in Quito, Ecuador (Chapter 6).

Selling biodiversity services

The second set of chapters in this book examines emerging markets for biodiversity conservation. Stefano Pagiola and Ina-Marlene Ruthenberg discuss efforts to market shade-grown coffee in Mexico and El Salvador (Chapter 7). This scheme seeks to capitalize on consumers' willingness to pay for biodiversity conservation by inducing them to pay a premium for biodiversity-friendly shade-grown coffee. This premium would then encourage farmers to retain shade-grown coffee, thus maintaining its biodiversity benefits. This case study illustrates both the supply-side and the demand-side issues that can be encountered in creating market-based mechanisms. While challenges of making this mechanism work in the context of smallholder production have been successfully overcome, so far it has proved more difficult to persuade consumers to buy the product.

The creation of protected areas used to be almost exclusively a state function, but recent years have seen a proliferation of private reserves (Alderman, 1994; Langholz and others, 2000). This phenomenon has been particularly marked in Chile, filling the gap left by an indifferent government. Not only have individuals formed their own protected areas, but commercial enterprises have entered the market to assist them in doing so. Promising though this movement is, there is considerable scope to improve its contribution to conservation. Elisa Corcuera, Claudia Sepúlveda, and Guillermo Geisse examine the strengths and limitations of spontaneous markets for private land conservation in Chile (Chapter 8).

Sarah Laird and Kerry ten Kate examine the extent to which the commercial use of forest genetic resources can result in benefits for forest conservation and for local communities (Chapter 9). In the early-to-mid-1990s, biodiversity prospecting ('bioprospecting') was expected to provide an important new source of financing for forest conservation (Farnsworth and Soejarto, 1985; McAllister, 1991; Pearce and Puroshothaman, 1992; Principe, 1989; Reid and others, 1993). It has not turned out that way. While some pharmaceutical companies have proved willing to pay for access to samples of genetic material, the sums involved have been much smaller than anticipated. Moreover, only a small portion of these payments has actually been used for conservation. Laird and ten Kate examine why bioprospecting has fallen short of expectations, and propose ways to improve the situation.

Innovative fiscal instruments also have a role to play in encouraging forest conservation. Peter May, Fernando Veiga Neto, Valdir Denardin, and Wilson Loureiro examine the operation of one of the best-known efforts, Brazil's ecological value-added tax (Chapter 10). This mechanism channels a portion of the revenues from the tax to municipalities on the basis of their environmental performance. Initially seen as a way to compensate municipalities in which large areas of land are under conservation (and as such tended to be penalized under the traditional criteria for allocating value-added tax revenues), ecological value-added tax appears to have stimulated efforts to substantially increase conservation.

Ecotourism is another mechanism that seeks to generate financing for forest conservation, in this case by selling visitation rights to biodiversity. There is considerable interest in the use of ecotourism to generate income from biodiversity, and hence encourage its conservation (Brandon, 1996; Gössling, 1999). This mechanism has been substantially covered elsewhere, however, so no examples are included here.

Selling carbon services

Finally, several studies examine the potential for the sale of forest carbon sequestration services. Gary Bull, Zoe Harkin, and Ann Wong (Chapter 11) examine efforts to develop a market for forest carbon in the Canadian province of British Columbia (BC). Even in a relatively sophisticated forest industry, the creation of new markets for services such as carbon sequestration is far from simple. Substantial efforts are required on technical, legal, and commercial fronts.

Developing countries that wish to participate in international carbon markets face the same obstacles, plus additional challenges related to weak governmental capacity and other socioeconomic circumstances. Richard Tipper (Chapter 12) discusses a specific aspect of the problem: that of involving smallholders. Without such efforts, payments for carbon services might focus solely on large plantations or state-owned lands. This might help forest conservation, but it does little to encourage rural development. In the Scolel Té project in Mexico's southern state of Chiapas, efforts are being made to develop new models for financing land improvements, using carbon offsets as a source of investment capital.

David Brand (Chapter 13) describes efforts to develop markets for forest-based carbon sequestration services in Australia from the standpoint of the financial sector. The Hancock Natural Resource Group is attempting to develop innovative investment products that take advantage of the new opportunities created by emerging carbon markets. Investment funds such as the one described here could attract substantial new financing to the forest sector, and help protect the environmental services that Australian forests generate. What is required is an instrument that meets the complex (and shifting) demands of the Kyoto Protocol while remaining attractive to private investors – not an easy task.

Phil Cottle and Charles Crosthwaite-Eyre examine a related problem (Chapter 14). The long-term investments needed to make new forest-based carbon sequestration projects work face a variety of risks. Some of these risks are common to other forest projects, while others are peculiar to the carbon sequestration objective. The availability of insurance to help manage these risks would greatly increase the attractiveness of investments in this area. Cottle and Crosthwaite-Eyre outline some of the issues involved in managing and insuring risk in forest-based carbon projects, and illustrate them in the context of the Noel Kempff Mercado Climate Action Project in Bolivia.

Not all the case studies describe unambiguous successes. Some describe cases in which mechanisms have fallen short of early hopes. Other cases are in their early stages, and it is not yet possible to say whether they will be successes or failures. But all provide valuable illustrations of how the concept of market-based mechanisms can be turned into practice. Chapter 15 attempts to draw some initial lessons from the experience of these cases.

NOTES

1   An externality is any uncompensated cost or benefit. Public goods comprise a special class of externalities, distinguished by their non-excludability and non-rivalry (Cornes and Sandler, 1996). 'Non-excludability' means that consumers cannot be prevented from enjoying the good or service in question, even if they do not pay for the privilege. 'Non-rivalry' implies that the consumption of a good or service by one individual does not reduce the amount available to others. In general, the market will under-supply public goods due to the difficulty of making consumers pay for them. Collective action is normally required to ensure adequate provision. However, market mechanisms can still be used to keep costs down and to stimulate innovation.

2   In many cases even the loss of such tangible benefits may not be fully considered. Often, farmers do not have exclusive rights in tradition or law to products collected from forest areas, and sometimes it is simply impractical to prevent others from collecting these products. In contrast, most farmers enjoy stronger rights to products obtained from the land they cultivate (although tenant farmers are an important exception). Because of this difference in tenure security, a loss of extractive benefits from forests may well be given less weight than a gain in crops (see Bromley, 1989; Cousins, 2000; Ostrom, 1990). This kind of problem is widespread, but is not addressed by the mechanisms discussed here.

3   Although downstream beneficiaries are described here as a single group for ease of exposition, it is quite likely that those who benefit from reduced sedimentation differ from those who benefit from cleaner water. Likewise, those in the global community who are interested in biodiversity conservation are not always the same as those who are interested in carbon sequestration. Local forest managers are also often split into several subgroups.

4   From an analytical perspective, it is often useful to categorize different benefits according to those that bring benefits (such as harvest of timber and non-timber products) directly to local decision-makers, those that bring national-level benefits (such as regulation of hydrological services) and those that bring global-level benefits

(such as carbon sequestration). 'Local' benefits are perceived by decision-makers on the ground, and so would be included in a private (or 'financial') cost–benefit analysis from their perspective. 'Local' and 'national' benefits together would be included in a national-level social cost–benefit analysis of the kind usually undertaken by governments for project or policy evaluation. 'Global' benefits would not be included in a national-level cost–benefit analysis. They would be added to local and national benefits in order to conduct an international-level social cost–benefit analysis, although in this case it is less clear who should assume responsibility for securing global benefits.

5 This section is based in part on Pagiola and Platais (forthcoming).
6 The nature of watershed protection and carbon sequestration services, and the emission reduction requirements of the Kyoto Protocol, are described in more detail in Chapter 2.
7 In the interests of transparency, it should be pointed out that several of the contributing authors promote, or are important players in, the mechanisms they describe. Given our objective of highlighting the practical aspects of creating markets for environmental services, we felt that the risk of excessive enthusiasm is outweighed by the first-hand knowledge that these authors bring.

REFERENCES

Alderman, C.L. 1994. "The Economics and the Role of Privately-owned Lands used for Nature Tourism, Education, and Conservation." In M. Munasinghe and J. McNeely (eds.), *Protected Area Economics and Policy: Linking Conservation and Sustainable Development*. Washington: World Bank and World Conservation Union.

Angelsen, A., and D. Kaimowitz (eds.) 2001. *Agricultural Technologies and Tropical Deforestation*. Wallingford: CIFOR and CABI Publishing.

Barbier, E.B., J.C. Burgess, J. Bishop, and B. Aylward. 1994. *The Economics of the Tropical Timber Trade*. London: Earthscan.

Baskin, Y. 1997. *The Work Of Nature: How The Diversity Of Life Sustains Us*. Washington: Island Press.

Baumol, W.J., and W.E. Oates. 1988. *The Theory of Environmental Policy*. Second Edition. Cambridge: Cambridge University Press.

Binswanger, H. 1991. "Brazilian Policies that Encourage Deforestation in the Amazon." *World Development*, 19, pp.821–829.

Brandon, K. 1996. "Ecotourism and Conservation: A Review of Key Issues." Environment Department Working Paper No.33. Washington: World Bank.

Bromley, D.W. 1989. "Property Relations and Economic Development: The Other Land Reform." *World Development*, 17:6, pp.867–877.

Browder, J. 1985. *Subsidies, Deforestation, and the Forest Sector of the Brazilian Amazon*. Washington: World Resources Institute.

Brown, K., and D.W. Pearce. 1994. *The Causes of Tropical Deforestation*. London: University College London Press.

Chichilnisky, G., and G. Heal. 1998. "Economic Returns from the Biosphere." *Nature*, 391, pp.629–630.

Contreras-Hermosilla, A. 2000. "The Underlying Causes of Forest Decline." Occasional Paper No.30. Bogor: CIFOR.

Cornes, R., and T. Sandler. 1996. *The Theory of Externalities, Public Goods and Club Goods*. Second Edition. Cambridge: Cambridge University Press.

Cousins, B. 2000. "Tenure and Common Property Resources in Africa." In C. Toulmin and J. Quan (eds.), *Evolving Land Rights, Policy and Tenure in Africa*. London: DFID, IIED, and Natural Resources Institute.

Dixon, J.A., and S. Pagiola. 2001. "Local Costs, Global Benefits: Valuing Biodiversity in Developing Countries." In OECD, *Valuation of Biodiversity Benefits: Selected Studies*. Paris: OECD.

Dudley, N., J.P. Jeanrenaud, and F. Sullivan. 1995. *Bad Harvest? The Timber Trade and the Degradation of the World's Forests*. London: Earthscan.

Ekins, P. 1999. "European Environmental Taxes and Charges: Recent Experience, Issues and Trends." *Ecological Economics,* 31:1, pp.39–62.

Farnsworth, N., and D. Soejarto. 1985. "Potential Consequences of Plant Extinction in the United States on the Current and Future Availability of Prescription Drugs." *Economic Botany,* 39:3, pp.231–240.

Food and Agriculture Organization (FAO). 2001a. "Global Forest Resource Assessment." FAO Forestry Paper No.140. Rome: FAO.

Food and Agriculture Organization (FAO). 2001b. *State of the World's Forests 2001.* Rome: FAO.

Gössling, S. 1999. "Ecotourism: A Means to Safeguard Biodiversity and Ecosystem Functions?" *Ecological Economics,* 29, pp.303–320.

Huber, R.M., J. Ruitenbeek, and R. Seroa Da Motta. 1998. *Market Based Instruments for Environmental Policymaking in Latin America and the Caribbean: Lessons from Eleven Countries*. Discussion Paper No.381. Washington: World Bank.

Kaimowitz, D., and A. Angelsen. 1998. *Economic Models of Tropical Deforestation: A Review*. Bogor: CIFOR.

Landell-Mills, N., and I. Porras. 2002. *Silver Bullet or Fools' Gold? A Global Review of Markets for Forest Environmental Services and Their Impact on the Poor*. London: IIED.

Langholz, J.A., J.P. Lassoie, D. Lee, and D. Chapman. 2000. "Economic Considerations of Privately Owned Parks." *Ecological Economics,* 33, pp.173–183.

Mahar, D. 1988. "Government Policies and Deforestation in Brazil's Amazon Region." Environment Department Working Paper No.7. Washington: World Bank.

McAllister, D.E. 1991. "Estimating the Pharmaceutical Values of Forests, Canadian and Tropical." *Canadian Biodiversity,* 1:3, pp.16–26.

Myers, N. 1997. "The World's Forests and Their Ecosystem Services." In G. Daily (ed.), *Nature's Services: Societal Dependence on Natural Ecosystems*. Washington: Island Press.

Organisation for Economic Co-operation and Development (OECD). 1993. *Economic Instruments for Environmental Management in Developing Countries*. Proceedings of a Workshop held at OECD Headquarters in Paris on 8 October 1992. Paris: OECD.

Organisation for Economic Co-operation and Development (OECD). 1994. *Environment and Taxation: The Cases of the Netherlands, Sweden and the United States*. Paris: OECD.

Ostrom, E. 1990. *Governing the Commons: The Evolution of Institutions for Collective Action*. Cambridge: Cambridge University Press.

Pagiola, S., and G. Platais. Forthcoming. *Payments for Environmental Services*. Washington: World Bank.

Pearce, D., and S. Puroshothaman. 1992. *Protecting Biological Diversity: The Economic Value of Pharmaceutical Plants*. Global Environmental Change Working Paper No. 92–27. London: CSERGE, UEA, and UCL.

Powell, I., A. White, and N. Landell-Mills. 2002. "Developing Markets for Ecosystem Services of Forests." Washington: Forest Trends (processed).

Principe, P. 1989. *The Economic Value of Biodiversity Among Medicinal Plants*. Paris: OECD.

Reid, W.V., S.A. Laird, R. Gamez, A. Sittenfeld, D.H. Janzen, M.A. Gollin, and C. Juma. 1993. "A New Lease on Life." In W.V. Reid, S.A. Laird, C.A. Meyer, R. Gamez, A. Sittenfeld, D.H. Janzen, M.A. Gollin, and C. Juma, *Biodiversity Prospecting: Using Genetic Resources for Sustainable Development*. Washington: World Resources Institute.

Repetto, R., and M. Gillis (eds.). 1988. *Government Policies and the Misuse of Forest Resources*. Cambridge: Cambridge University Press.

Roper, C.S., and A. Park (eds.). 1999. *The Living Forest: Non-Market Benefits of Forestry*. Proceedings of an International Symposium, Edinburgh 24–28 June 1996, Forestry Commission. London: HMSO.

Schmidt, R., J.K. Berry, and J.C. Gordon (eds.) 1999. *Forests to Fight Poverty: Creating National Strategies*. New Haven: Yale University Press.

Schneider, R. 1994. "Government and the Economy on the Amazon Frontier." LAC Regional Studies Program Report No.34. Washington: World Bank.

Sharma, N.P. (ed.). 1992. *Managing the World's Forests: Looking For Balance Between Conservation and Development*. Ames: Kendall/Hunt Publishing Company.

Southgate, D. 1998. *Tropical Forest Conservation: An Economic Assessment of the Alternatives in Latin America*. Oxford: Oxford University Press.

Stavins, R.N. 2000. "Experience with Market-Based Environmental Policy Instruments." In K.-G. Mäler and J. Vincent (eds.), *The Handbook of Environmental Economics*. Amsterdam: North-Holland/Elsevier Science.

Chapter 2

Forest Environmental Services: An Overview

Joshua Bishop and Natasha Landell-Mills

Forest owners and users have long recognized that forests provide a range of environmental benefits, in addition to valuable commodities such as timber and fiber, fuelwood, edible and medicinal plants, and game. Well-known forest environmental services include watershed protection, recreation, and landscape beauty. More recently, scientists have demonstrated additional forest benefits, such as their role in stabilizing climate by sequestering carbon in biomass, or as storehouses of genetic information.

The loss of environmental services provided by forests is one of the main reasons for concern about deforestation. Many of these valuable services do not enter into markets, and thus are ignored when forest management decisions are made. The market-based mechanisms reviewed in this book seek to remedy this problem. Doing so requires, among other things, a good understanding of what environmental services a forest might provide, to whom, under what conditions, and how these services change when forests are lost or degraded. Only with such detailed knowledge will it be possible, and ultimately justifiable, to establish market-based mechanisms that attempt to preserve these benefits.

This Chapter provides a brief introduction to three major environmental services that forests are thought to provide, namely:

- watershed protection;
- biodiversity conservation; and
- carbon sequestration.

There are, of course, many other benefits provided by forests, including two important environmental services that are not discussed here: the recreational use of forests and their contribution to scenic beauty. These services, which are effectively and widely 'sold' through ecotourism enterprises, park entrance fees, and residential property markets, are well described elsewhere (see, for example,

Adamowicz and others, 1996; Garrod and Willis, 1992; Landell-Mills and Porras, 2002; Mantua and others, 2001; Roper and Park, 1999).

Recent attempts to develop markets for the three environmental services listed above are the focus of this volume. This Chapter focuses on the nature of the services themselves, and their relation to forest management. It also provides examples of empirical studies that attempt to measure forest environmental services in economic terms, using a range of different methods. We begin by placing forest environmental services within the broader context of the total economic value of forests, and briefly reviewing the methods that economists use to estimate these values.

FOREST VALUES AND VALUATION

There are many different ways to categorize the benefits that forests and other natural ecosystems provide. One of the most widely used frameworks distinguishes between different benefits in terms of whether they contribute directly or indirectly to human welfare, and whether they entail the consumptive or non-consumptive use of natural resources (Pearce and others, 1989; Munasinghe and Lutz, 1993). This framework typically includes four categories of value: direct use, indirect use, option, and non-use values. The total economic value (TEV) of any given land use is defined as the sum of its component values, provided they are mutually compatible (Barbier, 1991).

In this scheme, forest environmental services such as watershed protection and carbon sequestration are typically classified as indirect use values in view of their role in supporting and protecting economic activity and property. In addition to these values, biodiversity is sometimes considered to have option value, due to its potential but as-yet uncertain future role as a source of genetic information for the biochemical industry (Barbier and Aylward, 1996). Bio-diversity may also have non-use value, insofar as people value the knowledge that particular species or ecosystems are being conserved, even when they have no expectation of seeing or using them.

Another approach highlights the geographic or political dimension of forest values, distinguishing benefits that are enjoyed locally from those that accrue at a national or even global level. Alternatively, we may focus on the distinction between private and public values, or between 'instrumental' and 'intrinsic' values (Pearce and Pearce, 2001).

Whatever framework is used to classify forest benefits, most authors highlight environmental or 'ecological' services as one of the most important reasons for conserving forests or for managing them more carefully. Indeed, the extent to which forest environmental services are maintained is one of the main criteria used to distinguish more sustainable management regimes from less sustainable regimes (Higman and others, 1999).

Forest environmental services may appear to be free gifts from nature, requiring little to maintain them other than protection of the forests themselves.

However, conserving or enhancing environmental services often requires sacrificing other competing values and land uses, such as the extraction of valuable timber or the conversion of forest-land to agriculture (Barbier and Burgess, 1997; Lippke and Bishop, 1999). This raises the question of whether such sacrifice is justifiable. The answer depends on the relative importance of environmental services in particular situations, compared to competing forest uses and benefits, and on the extent to which multiple benefits can be obtained from a single site. Note also that different environmental services may not always be compatible, leading to difficult decisions about which services matter most.

Valuing forest environmental services

To help resource managers evaluate the trade-offs between competing uses of forest-land, economists have developed a range of methods for estimating the value of environmental services (and other forest benefits) in monetary terms. Because forest environmental services are not yet traded in most parts of the world, it is generally not possible to measure their value directly by looking at market prices. Hence efforts to assess their economic significance often require the use of indirect methods.

Economic valuation methods generally aim to measure consumer demand in monetary terms, that is, the willingness to pay of consumers for a particular non-marketed benefit in monetary terms, or their willingness to accept monetary compensation for the loss of the same. Valuation methods deliberately express the utility derived from non-market goods and services in the metric of the market, as this is considered to provide an accurate reflection of the relative preferences of producers and consumers for different goods and services.[1]

Techniques for estimating environmental values vary in their theoretical validity and degree of acceptance among economists, their data requirements and ease of use, and the extent to which they have been applied in (and perhaps their relevance to) different countries. Just as there are many different ways of classifying forest values, so also there are several ways of grouping economic valuation methods.

One simple distinction is between methods that derive estimates of value from the market behaviour of consumers ('revealed preferences'), and methods that rely on consumers' responses to direct questioning ('stated preferences'). The former group includes a range of indirect valuation methods such as travel cost models, hedonic pricing and substitute goods approaches, as well as methods that express environmental values in terms of their impacts on the costs of producing marketed goods, or the costs of replacing them (Pearce and others, 1999).[2] The most widely used stated preference methods are contingent valuation and choice experiments (Adamowicz and others, 1994, 1998; Mitchell and Carson, 1989; Carson, 1991; Carson and others, 1994). Methods for valuing environmental benefits are described in a number of recent publications.[3] Similarly, the empirical literature on valuing non-timber forest benefits and land use options is large and growing fast. Examples can be found for virtually all types of forest benefits and most valuation methods.

We now turn to a more detailed description of the three forest environmental services of particular interest in this book: watershed protection, biodiversity conservation, and carbon storage.

WATERSHED PROTECTION SERVICES

Forests are commonly associated with a range of environmental services delivered at a watershed scale, including:

- regulation of water-flow – that is, maintenance of dry season flows and flood control;
- maintenance of water quality – that is, minimization of sediment load, nutrient load (for example, of phosphorous and nitrogen), chemical load, and salinity;
- control of soil erosion and sedimentation;
- reduction of land salinization and/or regulation of groundwater levels; and
- maintenance of aquatic habitats (for example, reduction of water temperature through shading rivers or streams, ensuring adequate woody debris and habitat for aquatic species).

It is often argued that such services are sufficiently important to water users and residents downstream to justify conserving or planting forests, especially on steeply sloping and riparian land (Myers, 1997). Unfortunately, such claims are rarely based on detailed estimations or measurements of the off-site impacts of forest disturbance. The few detailed studies that are available reveal that the impacts of forests on water quantity, quality, erosion, sedimentation, groundwater levels, and aquatic productivity depend on many site-specific features, including terrain, soil composition, tree species, vegetation mix, climate, and management regimes (Calder, 1999).

Moreover, the nature and value of watershed services depend not only on the characteristics of the forest itself but also on the number and characteristics of the beneficiaries. Two identical forests will provide very different water services if one is located in a watershed inhabited by many people and the other in an uninhabited area. Arguably, the services provided in the former case are worth more because they are important to a greater number of people. Differences in income can also affect the relative value of different forest services, to the extent that value reflects people's ability to pay as well as their marginal willingness to pay.

Facts and myths about watershed protection

The complex linkages between land use and hydrology are not widely appreciated. On the contrary, several simple but mostly inaccurate myths persist about forest watershed protection services, often leading to inappropriate or inefficient watershed policies and management practices.

One widespread view is that forests act as 'sponges' by soaking up water and releasing it gradually, thereby enhancing water supply during the dry season. In practice, forests have two opposing impacts on base-level flows:

1   they tend to increase infiltration and soil retention, promoting groundwater recharge and reducing runoff; and
2   they use water in evapo-transpiration, thereby reducing groundwater recharge.

The net effect on flows varies according to the location. On balance, the evidence points to a strong link between deforestation, rising water tables, and increased dry season flows. However, in some instances deforestation reduces water supplies (Hamilton and King, 1983; Bosch and Hewlett, 1982). Factors that appear to influence the outcome include tree species, and the nature of the land use that replaces the forest and its associated management regime. In the specific case of so-called 'cloud forests', evidence suggests that increased water yields from cloud interception (fog deposition on vegetation) can offset higher rates of evapo-transpiration, resulting in increased dry season flows (Bruijnzeel, 2000). Where deforestation is associated with soil compaction (for example, due to road construction, use of heavy farm machinery, or conversion to pasture), runoff may increase at a greater rate than that at which evapo-transpiration reduces, leading to lower water tables.

Another common concern is the alleged link between deforestation and flooding. In theory, forests can mitigate the risk of floods by reducing the volume of water flowing overland during high-intensity storms. The evidence supporting these claims, however, suggests that such a relationship only holds true in relatively small catchments of less than 50,000ha. In larger catchments, flooding occurs sequentially in basins as storms pass over, allowing for the moderation of floodwaters. In prolonged and heavy storms large catchments can flood, but this is likely to occur even if such catchments are forested (Bruijnzeel and Bremmer, 1989, cited in Chomitz and Kumari, 1998). Moreover, in smaller catchments, the extent to which forests soak up excess water during rainy periods depends on the forest type and use.

Erosion control is another watershed benefit attributed to forests. It is argued that rainfall infiltration is higher in natural and mixed forests, thus reducing surface runoff and erosion. Moreover, by binding soils, tree roots are thought to reduce the susceptibility of soils to erosion, especially on steep slopes. The presence of trees may also help to reduce the impact of rain on soils, and thus the level of particle dislodgement. In practice, establishing clear relationships between forest cover and erosion is extremely difficult. The clearest evidence concerns the role of forests in reducing sheet erosion. Research on the determinants of erosion suggests that forests are less important than other factors, such as understory vegetation, soil composition, climate, raindrop size, terrain, and slope gradient. Forest use and management are also critical factors, with some studies showing that different logging regimes and road construction practices produce varying levels of sheet erosion. A review of case studies in Malaysia, for instance, suggests that selective logging may result in higher levels of erosion, compared to cocoa and oil palm production (Douglas and others, 1992). Less is known about gully erosion and landslides. In a study in Chiang Mai Province in Thailand, Forsyth (1996) suggests that gully erosion may be more important than sheet erosion in forested areas, due to the way that tree trunks and roots channel runoff. Landslides tend to be associated with steep slopes, saturated soils and tectonic movements, and are made more likely by human intervention, for example road building. While shallow landslides may be prevented by deep tree root systems, this is not the case with larger landslides (Bruijnzeel, 1990).

There is also the claim that forests help to prevent sedimentation of water bodies downstream, thereby preserving or prolonging the value of pieces of water infrastructure, such as irrigation channels, ports and shipping lanes, hydroelectric power reservoirs, and water treatment facilities. In fact, sediment delivery ratios depend on a range of site-specific factors, including the size of the catchment area, local geology and topology, the stability of riverbanks, and the state of land use and roads (Chomitz and Kumari, 1998). While changes in land use can affect sediment delivery, this must be compared to previous levels. Often the 'background' sedimentation rate is underestimated due to inadequate data. Few empirical studies account for all relevant variables.

Similar questions arise with respect to the impacts of forests on aquatic habitats. Several authors assert that forests help to maintain the health and productivity of aquatic ecosystems (see for example: Bennett and Reynolds, 1993; Hodgson and Dixon, 1988; Ruitenbeek, 1989, 1992). Forests are thought to be important in controlling silt and nutrient loading, water temperature, and turbidity, all of which have direct and indirect impacts on fish and other aquatic species. High sediment and nutrient loads are considered particularly damaging, causing eutrophication and algae blooms that starve aquatic life of oxygen and sunlight. In the case of rivers and estuaries, forests are thought to provide cover and shade to moderate water temperature and turbulence, as well as food and still pools for spawning and juvenile development. However, aside from some mangrove forests, the evidence provided is often superficial and there is a need for much more site-specific analysis to establish the nature and magnitude of the relationships involved.

Establishing precisely which services forests provide must be the point of departure for any form of watershed management, market-based or otherwise. It is equally important to be clear about which services are required, what level of service is required, and by whom. For instance, where downstream farmers suffer from soil salinization, they are likely to value upstream forests for their role in regulating groundwater levels. Where hydropower plant operators are downstream beneficiaries, they may value water quantity as much or more than water quality. Where there are a number of downstream beneficiaries with different needs, it may be necessary to trade off conflicting watershed services.

When researchers take the trouble to collect detailed information on the links between forests and watershed services, the results are often surprising. For example, in their study of the Arenal watershed in Costa Rica, Aylward and others (1998) conclude that the impacts of forest conversion on hydroelectric power production are broadly positive. Although increased sedimentation due to forest conversion slightly reduces the capacity of the Arenal reservoir to hold water for electric power generation (and for irrigated agriculture), the authors find that the benefits of increased water runoff, in terms of additional electric power generating capacity, are far more significant. Similarly, Niskanen (1998) concludes that reforestation imposes a significant cost through reduced water availability for irrigated agriculture. Such research highlights the need for careful measurement of hydrological functions before the introduction of watershed protection measures, market-based or otherwise.

BIODIVERSITY SERVICES

If current trends continue, an estimated 24 per cent of mammal species and 12 per cent of bird species face a 'high risk of extinction in the near future' (FAO, 2001). It is widely accepted that the primary cause of extinction is habitat loss, followed by overexploitation (in excess of natural regeneration), introduction of exotic species, and predator control. The loss of biological diversity ('bio-diversity') in tropical forests is of particular concern, accounting for the loss of an estimated 5 to 15 per cent of the world's species between 1990 and 2020. This rate of extinction is unparalleled in modern history, and was previously exceeded only at the end of the Cretaceous era, 65 million years ago (Reid and Miller, 1989).

Calls to stem the disappearance of forest habitat have intensified recently, as early warnings failed to generate sufficient protection. In 1997, protected areas covered 1.32 billion hectares, or 8.7 per cent of the world's surface (IUCN, 1998). However, roughly half of these permitted some form of utilization, while illicit intrusion, climate change, and other external factors pose a continuing threat to the health of natural ecosystems.

Measuring biological diversity

The diversity of life is generally defined at three levels: genetic, species, and ecosystem. However, measuring biodiversity is not straightforward. For example, can we measure species biodiversity simply by counting the number of species in a given area? Is the crude number of species what matters, or should we pay more attention to species endemism (uniqueness), taxonomic diversity (are ten species in one genus more diverse than five species in five separate genera?) or functional diversity (that is, species that perform a range of functional roles, from pollinator to predator to scavengers)? Such questions make it difficult to define a common unit of measure for species biodiversity. Similar uncertainties hamper efforts to measure the diversity of ecosystems (OECD, 1996), while genetic diversity is somewhat easier to handle.

The difficulty of measuring biodiversity has critical implications for the development of markets and incentive systems. In the absence of clearly defined 'units' of biological diversity, entrepreneurs and policy-makers must find alternative proxy measures to assess progress towards the desired goal. Thus we need to identify one or more tangible and easily measurable attributes, which accurately reflect the underlying diversity of species, ecosystems, and/or genes.

A fundamental risk is that the link between the proxy and biodiversity gets lost in the effort to develop a viable commercial enterprise. Thus we observe a widespread tendency to equate the marketing of biological resources with biodiversity conservation. Biological resources, it is argued, represent the manifestation of biological diversity, and without biodiversity such resources would cease to exist. Taking this logic a step further, it is argued that by marketing the full range of biological resources, we effectively market biodiversity (see for example: McNeely and others, 1990; Asquith, 2000; Reid and Miller, 1989). The danger of this approach is that if only a selection of resources or attributes are successfully marketed, buyers and sellers may neglect other aspects of biodiversity.

Valuing biodiversity

Like other environmental services, and indeed most natural resources, the extent and value of biodiversity is site-specific. Unlike watershed protection, however, the beneficiaries or 'consumers' of biodiversity are often very widely scattered. There is some evidence that demand for biodiversity is concentrated in relatively rich countries, where there is not only greater public awareness and concern for nature conservation, but also more ability to pay for it (Kramer and others, 1995; Pearce and others, 1999; Walsh and others, 1990).

In addition to pure existence value, one oft-cited justification for saving natural ecosystems is the potential or 'option value' of natural genetic material or naturally-occurring compounds (organic metabolites) for pharmaceutical research and development of new drugs (Pearce and Puroshothaman, 1992; Pearce and Moran, 1994; Ruitenbeek, 1989). Ultimately the entire biotechnology industry, still very much in its infancy, is predicated on the existence of a vast, unexplored natural 'library' of genetic and chemical information.

Early studies of the potential commercial value of a yet-to-be-discovered drug that might be lost due to the extinction of a single species produced estimates ranging from a few dollars to many millions. Adger and others (1995) and Kumari (1995a), for example, estimate the production value of plant-based drugs as a function of many variables, including the number of plant species in forests, the probability of a species providing a commercial drug (the 'hit rate'), the royalty paid to prospecting companies, the proportion of this paid to the country in which the plant is found, and the average value of drugs. Unfortunately, little information on these parameters is available for most countries, and so the resulting estimates of biodiversity values vary wildly. Depending on the assumptions made, reported annual values range from just US$0.20/ha (the minimum reported in Howard, 1995) up to $695/ha (the maximum reported in Kumari, 1995a).

Simpson and others (1996) and Barbier and Aylward (1996) reviewed the methodologies and results from several earlier studies and derived their own estimates of the pharmaceutical value of the marginal species (or biotic sample) and the maximum value of preserving land in identified biodiversity 'hot spots'. In these cases, detailed information on pharmaceutical research and development costs was used to estimate the net value of the wild product, rather than simply applying the market value of the final product as in some previous studies. The resulting modest estimates of pharmaceutical value reflect a better understanding of the difficulty of finding commercially useful genetic information or chemical compounds from wild organisms (that is, the low 'hit rate' of screening efforts), as well as the realization that only a small part of the market value of a new drug or product can be attributed to the natural environment. Most of the value is added further down the product pipeline, during the processes of testing, refining, seeking regulatory approval, production, and marketing. Both studies find values of only a few dollars per hectare, insufficient on their own to justify changing current land uses but perhaps significant when added to the other non-market values of conservation.

Other values of biodiversity include developing new chemicals for agricultural or industrial uses, as well as the wild genetic information that is a storehouse of information for crop breeding and selection. For example, Evenson (1990) uses data on varietal improvements in rice and changes in productivity over the period 1959–1984 to estimate the benefits of using genetic material from wild rice plants to improve the yields of cultivated rice. The resulting estimate of US$74 million, in present value terms, is relatively modest but realistic, with the additional merit of being based on historical rather than hypothetical data.

Attempts to estimate the future value of biodiversity remain speculative at best due to uncertainty about future incomes and preferences, as well as technological change. Recent experience suggests that technical innovation quickly reduces the value of material in the wild, once the genetic or chemical information it contains has been isolated (often at very low cost). Modern chemical, industrial, and agricultural processes allow firms and farmers to produce additional material (on the farm, the laboratory, or the factory) without recourse to the wild. This is good news, in the sense that there is less risk of overexploiting wild resources, but it also limits the value that can be attributed to biodiversity in its natural state.

The costs of biodiversity conservation

Conservation of biological diversity typically involves providing suitable habitats for a range of native plant and animal species. It may also include efforts to eradicate alien (exotic) species. Sometimes the most effective means of conserving forest biodiversity will involve strict protection – that is, the virtual absence of human use. However, reserves can be a costly way to conserve habitat, due to the loss of potentially valuable timber and other commodities.

The opportunity cost of maintaining biodiversity through forest reserves varies widely, reflecting differences in timber and land values (Perez-Garcia, 1994). We would expect the value of biodiversity to exceed commodity values in some regions but not in others. For example, where the net returns from harvesting timber are very low and there are large adverse effects on biodiversity from logging, strict protection seems an obvious choice (although some groups may be disadvantaged and may need to be compensated). Conversely, where the value of forestland for timber production or other uses is high, the argument for production rather than protection is strengthened.

Such trade-offs have stimulated widespread interest in how to combine biodiversity conservation with productive use of forest-land. One major strand of research has explored the impacts of industrial forestry (timber extraction) on non-timber species, and how to manage forests for both timber and biodiversity (Hunter, 1990, 1999; Lee and others, 1998). Efforts to conserve biodiversity can involve significant changes in forest management practices. These may include favoring particular tree species, less intensive logging or less frequent thinning, use of low-impact timber harvesting methods, restricting logging in certain areas (such as on steep slopes or alongside streams), and other measures intended to mimic the evolution and composition of natural (unmanaged) forests. Oliver (1992) argues that a diversity of forest structures can be maintained while still producing timber products. Natural disturbances such as fires and windstorms may be approximated by thinning, so that forest structures more quickly acquire the characteristics of older stands. Moreover, with such treatments the growth of wood is concentrated on fewer stems, producing larger-diameter trees and higher-quality wood, thereby earning higher prices and helping to defray the cost of more intensive management.

While it is not yet possible to define the habitat requirements of every forest species, a feasible alternative is to evaluate forests and management systems in terms of ecosystem characteristics and their suitability for broad classes of species. Hunter (1990) recommends a balance of forest structures as a 'coarse filter' approach to sustaining conditions for multiple species, as contrasted with a species-by-species approach. Carey and others (1996) correlate forest stand structure to several multi-species habitat indicators and develop alternative forest treatments that accelerate the development of diverse structures, compared to natural aging. Parviainen and others (1995) describe similar biodiversity inform-ation systems for Europe. The task is more difficult for tropical rainforests, where the number of species is greater and the nature of disturbances and recovery less well known. But if measurable indicators of biodiversity can be identified and management treatments are defined that produce corresponding forest structures, then the cost of producing them can also be determined (Lippke and Bishop, 1999).

FOREST CARBON SINKS

Widely dismissed as far-fetched only a few years ago, climate change ('global warming') is now increasingly recognized as real and dangerous. Climate change results partly from the greenhouse effect, which is caused by the build-up of greenhouse gases (GHGs) (including carbon dioxide (CO_2), methane (CH_4), and other compounds) in the atmosphere. The Intergovernmental Panel on Climate Change (IPCC), an international group of climate scientists set up to advise the United Nations Framework Convention on Climate Change (UNFCCC), estimates that a 30 per cent increase in atmospheric GHG levels over the course of the 20th century has caused world temperatures to rise by 0.6 degrees Celsius (°C), on average. The largest contributor has been fossil fuel burning, accounting for about 75 per cent of the increase in GHGs, followed by forest degradation and deforestation, accounting for a further 20 per cent. The IPCC has predicted that on present trends, temperatures will increase by a further 1.4 to 5.8°C over the next 100 years (IPCC, 2000).

The IPCC posits several potential impacts of higher global temperatures, including rising sea levels, more severe climatic events, coastal erosion, increased salinization, loss of protective coral reefs, increased desertification, damaged forest ecosystems, and increased prevalence of disease. The poor are particularly vulnerable to climate change. Not only are they more dependent on the weather for their livelihoods (for example, through agriculture) but they also tend to reside in tropical areas that are likely to suffer most from rising temperatures and sea levels. Moreover, the poor generally lack the financial and technical capacity to adjust to the impacts of global warming.

Forests and climate change

Forests are known to play an important role in regulating the global climate.[4] Green plants remove CO_2 from the atmosphere in the process of photosynthesis, using it to make sugars and other organic compounds used for growth and metabolism. Long-lived woody plants store carbon in wood and other tissues until they die and decompose. After this, the carbon in their wood may be released to the atmosphere as CO_2, carbon monoxide (CO), or CH_4, or it may be incorporated into the soil as organic matter.

Forestry-based carbon sequestration is based on two main approaches: active absorption in new vegetation, and avoided emissions from existing vegetation. The first approach includes any activity that involves planting new trees (such as afforestation, reforestation, or agroforestry) or increasing the growth rates of existing forest stands (such as improved silvicultural practices). It also includes the substitution of sustainably produced biomass for fossil fuels to reduce carbon emissions arising from energy production. The second approach involves the prevention or reduction of deforestation and land use change, or reduction in damage to existing forests. This may involve direct forest conservation, or indirect methods such as increasing the production efficiency of swidden agricultural systems, or improving the end-use efficiency of fuelwood resources, both of which reduce the pressure on standing forests. Improved logging practices and forest fire prevention are other examples of actions that protect existing carbon stocks.

In principle, it should be easier to develop markets for the carbon sequestration services of forests than for watershed protection or biodiversity conservation services. One reason is that the value of sequestered carbon is the same everywhere. A tonne of carbon sequestered in one place makes much the same contribution to reducing climate change as a tonne sequestered anywhere else. The measurement of carbon sequestration in plant biomass is also simpler than linking changes in land use to hydrological functions or to biological diversity. This means that it is easier to account for increases or decreases in carbon storage, and therefore easier to monitor and trade. Finally, estimates of the costs of carbon sequestration through forestry suggest that it is much cheaper than most other methods of tackling climate change, in particular the reduction of emissions from burning fossil fuels.

Estimating the benefits of forest carbon

In addition to being cheaper than alternative methods of reducing global warming, carbon sinks have the potential to add significant value to forest enterprises. The economic benefits of carbon storage are typically defined in terms of the damage-costs avoided. This approach builds on estimates of the marginal damages caused by releasing additional CO_2 into the atmosphere (Cline, 1992; Nordhaus, 1993). Fankhauser (1995) reviews previous research and conducts his own analysis in order to propose a 'central' or benchmark figure of US$20 per tonne. Fankhauser's analysis refines previous work by modeling the impacts of climate change on separate regions of the world (rather than simply extrapolating from the US economy).

Using these estimates, several case studies calculate the carbon storage value of forests in various settings. With the unit value of the benefit taken as given, the researcher simply needs to determine the amount of carbon stored or released under alternative land use scenarios for a particular region. For example, in a case study of a Malaysian peat swamp forest, Kumari (1995b) estimates the change in carbon stored per hectare under a range of management options. These changes are valued at US$14 per tonne, corresponding to the more conservative estimates available prior to the publication of Fankhauser's paper. Nevertheless, under a base case scenario involving unsustainable timber harvesting, carbon storage accounts for almost 70 per cent of the economic benefits measured, far more than timber or any other non-timber benefit estimated in the study. Other studies that estimate the carbon storage benefits of forests include: Adger and others (1995), Niskanen (1998), and Smith and others (1997). In general, because of the high carbon content of forests and the potentially significant effects of climate change, estimates of carbon storage values tend to swamp most other forest benefits, often including timber. Published estimates range from US$650 to $3500 per hectare, in net present value terms.

Climate change and the Kyoto Protocol

The creation of an international regulatory framework to counter climate change lies at the heart of the emerging market for forest carbon offsets. A major step was taken in 1997 with the signing of the Kyoto Protocol, which establishes mandatory limits on the emission of GHGs by industrialized and 'transitional' nations.[5] While each country is assigned a specific emission target, the average required reduction for industrialized ('Annex B' or 'Annex 1') countries is 5.2 per cent below 1990 levels, to be achieved by 2008–2012. This is equivalent to a total reduction of 456 million tonnes of carbon dioxide (tCO_2).

According to the Protocol, emission reductions may be achieved by reducing emissions and/or by increasing carbon sequestration and storage. The importance of forests as both sources of carbon (about one-quarter of global emissions come from burning forests, land clearance, and soil erosion) and stores of carbon (forests account for two-thirds of terrestrial carbon) means they can play a key role in generating carbon offsets, as described above.

In addition to setting national emission targets and defining which activities can be counted towards these targets, the Kyoto Protocol provides a framework for trading emission rights (Box 2.1). Recognizing that some countries will find it easier and cheaper to reduce emissions than others, the Protocol allows countries to trade emission rights to reduce the overall costs of meeting their targets. Countries wishing to emit more than their agreed limit may purchase additional rights from those countries that are able to reduce emissions beyond their target level.

However, as part of efforts to achieve a political settlement at the sixth Conference of the Parties (COP6) in July 2001, a number of limits were placed on emissions trading. In particular, forestry activities permitted under the Clean Development Mechanism (CDM, see Box 2.1) are restricted to afforestation and reforestation. Moreover, credits from forestry and other land-based sinks were capped at 1 per cent of a country's base-year emissions. Forest management may be used in Annex B countries and through Joint Implementation (JI, see Box 2.1), subject to country-specific caps. For example, Japan is limited to 4 per cent of its base-year emissions. More recently, at COP7 in Marrakech in November 2001, a decision was taken to restrict the banking of CDM- and JI-based carbon offsets (Box 2.1).

Unresolved issues in forest carbon sinks

The compromises and restrictions introduced at COP6 and COP7 reflect widespread doubts about whether and how forests should be treated in efforts to tackle climate change. The main areas of disagreement are about which types of sequestration, if any, should be counted towards a country's emissions-reduction target, and the extent to which national obligations may be fulfilled by financing

Box 2.1 THE KYOTO PROTOCOL, CARBON SINKS, AND EMISSIONS TRADING

The Kyoto Protocol sets out three 'flexibility mechanisms' to enable trade in emission rights:

1   International Emission Trading, allowing Annex B countries to trade emission permits known as 'assigned amount units' (Article 17);
2   Joint Implementation (JI), allowing countries to earn emission reduction units through projects in other Annex B countries (Article 6); and
3   the Clean Development Mechanism (CDM), allowing for the generation of certified emission reductions from projects in non-Annex B countries (that is, developing countries that are outside the capping regime) (Article 12).

The Protocol defines four potential carbon commodities, namely:

1   assigned amount units, achieved through emission reductions in Annex B countries that may be sold to other Annex B countries;
2   emission reduction units, achieved through emission reduction activities by one Annex B country in another Annex B country;
3   certified emission reductions, achieved through emission reduction activities by Annex B countries in non-Annex B countries; and
4   removal units, generated through investment in carbon sinks in Annex B countries for use in the existing compliance period.

All of these are sometimes referred to as carbon 'credits' or carbon 'offsets'. The first three may be achieved by reducing emissions at source, or by increasing the rate at which they are absorbed from the atmosphere into carbon sinks – for example, forests. Removal units – added at COP7 in November 2001 – are a special category of credits generated through carbon sequestration in Annex B countries. All credits represent carbon that is withdrawn from the atmosphere for at least 100 years, the minimum time (as defined by the IPCC) necessary to compensate for the radioactive forcing of a specified quantity of CO_2 or other GHG in the atmosphere.

However, not all carbon credits are equivalent. The Protocol places different restrictions on each, and these are particularly important with respect to the eligibility of forestry. For example, certified emission reductions cannot be earned from forest management, although assigned amount units, emission reduction units, and removal units can. Moreover, different credits are subject to varying restrictions on their 'bankability'. Whereas an unlimited amount of assigned amount units can be saved for use in later commitment periods (that is, after the first commitment period of 2008–2012), limits are placed on banking certified emission reductions and emission reduction units. A maximum of 2.5 per cent of each country's initial emission target may be banked using these credits. No banking of removal units is permitted.

For the Kyoto Protocol to come into force, at least 55 countries, representing at least 55 per cent of 1990 carbon emissions, must ratify it. Following COP6 in Bonn in July 2001, 178 countries had signed the Protocol. The recent decision of the United States – by itself responsible for about 25 per cent of global emissions – to reject the Protocol was a major blow to negotiators' efforts, but it is nevertheless expected that the necessary ratifications will be achieved by the end of 2002.

carbon sequestration (or emission abatement) in other countries. The role of forestry in mitigating climate change has been particularly contentious. Among other concerns, critics of carbon sequestration through forestry argue that:

- carbon sequestration projects are likely to favor plantation forestry at the expense of natural forests and thus biodiversity;
- projects that claim the avoidance of deforestation as a form of sequestration may never have been at risk (lack of 'additionality') or may simply displace deforestation to other regions ('leakage');
- reliable mechanisms to monitor and verify carbon sequestration and release on forest-land have not yet been perfected, making it difficult to confirm what is being sold; and
- smallholder farmers and small-scale forest users with insecure land tenure and poor access to capital may have trouble meeting the requirements of carbon buyers, or even find themselves pushed off the land in favor of large-scale forest carbon enterprise (Bass and others, 2000).

Such concerns have delayed the international negotiation of a framework for forest carbon sequestration, and likewise discouraged the emergence of a trade in carbon offsets. Avoided deforestation and forest management are often viewed as the least reliable forms of carbon sequestration, and have thus been subject to the greatest restrictions under the Protocol; neither is currently permitted under the CDM. Limits are also placed on the volume of reforestation- and afforestation-based offsets that can be purchased under CDM and JI. For forest activities undertaken in Annex B countries, a specific class of credits – the removal unit – has been created. As explained in Box 2.1, it is not bankable, in part due to concerns about permanence.

Despite such restrictions and continuing uncertainty about the ratification of the Kyoto Protocol and about how it will be implemented at a national level, there has been tremendous interest and innovation in preparation for an eventual carbon market. Private companies, non-governmental organizations (NGOs), international agencies, and national governments around the world have experimented with carbon measurement, mitigation, and trade. Many of these initiatives involve forms of carbon sequestration that would not be eligible under current Kyoto rules, but which may become acceptable in the future with improved methods of monitoring and verification.

CONCLUSION

Environmental services are thought to be among the most important benefits that forests provide. Watershed protection, biodiversity conservation, and carbon sequestration are routinely mentioned as justifications for forest conservation, or as key criteria and indicators of sustainable forest management. In many cases it is claimed that such environmental services are of greater value than timber and other commodities obtained from forests.

Scientific understanding of the role of forests in providing these environmental services has improved dramatically in recent years. It is increasingly clear that the nature and magnitude of environmental services are highly site-specific, and that their economic value varies with the number and activities of human populations both near and far. The costs and risks of securing environmental services through forestry are also much better understood, as are the conflicts and complementarities between different environmental services and other forest-land uses. The fact remains that in many parts of the world, valuable environmental services that could be obtained at a relatively low cost are wasted due to inappropriate or ineffective forest policies.

In general, public policy has lagged behind the scientific understanding of forest environmental services. Efforts to create more efficient and equitable mechanisms, notably for carbon sequestration, seem to proceed at a glacial pace. Fortunately there are many positive examples that show how forest environmental services can be brought into the marketplace in ways that protect the environment effectively, efficiently, and equitably. The following chapters in this book describe a number of these initiatives from all over the world.

NOTES

1   Some people reject the notion of comparing market costs and benefits with non-market social and environmental values (Anon, 1999). Others take issue with the assumptions and methods of estimating non-market values (Bennett and Byron, 1997). While monetary valuation methods are far from perfect, and are not the only way to assess forest benefits, they can be useful for illuminating trade-offs.

2   For those goods and services that are traded in markets, consumers reveal their preferences directly via the prices they pay. Economists almost always prefer to use market prices for valuation, where available.

3   See for example: Abelson, 1996; Cummings and others, 1986; Dixon and others, 1994; Freeman, 1993; Hanley and Spash, 1994; Hearne, 1996; Hufschmidt and others, 1983; Kopp and Smith, 1993; Mitchell and Carson, 1989; Munasinghe and Lutz, 1993; Vincent and others, 1991; Winpenny, 1991. Resources on the internet include the Environmental Valuation Reference Inventory (http://www.evri.ec.gc.ca) and the Environmental Valuation and Cost Benefit website (http://www.damagevaluation.com), among others.

4   Forests are also thought to affect local or regional climate conditions, for example through the role of vegetation in maintaining lower ambient temperatures or higher relative humidity (Nobre and others, 1991). This may be important for maintaining or enhancing the productivity of agricultural activities in adjacent areas (Lopez, 1997). Recent attempts to create markets for forest climate services have focused exclusively on carbon storage and climate change, although in principle local climate benefits could also be marketed.

5   Countries and their respective emission targets are listed in Annex B of the Kyoto Protocol and Annex 1 of the UNFCCC.

REFERENCES

Abelson, P. 1996. *Project Appraisal and Valuation Methods for the Environment with Special Reference to Developing Countries.* New York: Macmillan.

Adamowicz, W., J. Louviere, and M. Williams. 1994. "Combining Revealed and Stated Preference Methods for Valuing Environmental Amenities." *Journal of Environmental Economics and Management,* 26:3, pp.271–292.

Adamowicz, W.L., P.C. Boxall, M.K. Luckert, W.E. Phillips, and W.A. White (eds.). 1996. *Forestry, Economics and the Environment.* Wallingford: CAB International.

Adamowicz, W.L., P.C. Boxall, M. Williams, and J. Louviere. 1998. "Stated Preference Approaches for Measuring Passive Use Values: Choice Experiments and Contingent Valuation." *American Journal of Agricultural Economics,* 80:1, pp.64–75.

Adger, W.N., K. Brown, R. Cervigni, and D. Moran. 1995. "Total Economic Value of Forests in Mexico." *Ambio,* 24:5, pp.286–296.

Anon. 1999. *The Cost-Benefit Analysis Dilemma: Strategies and Alternatives.* New Haven: Yale University.

Asquith, N. 2000. *How Should the World Bank Encourage Private Sector Investment in Biodiversity Conservation?* Washington: World Bank.

Aylward, B., J. Echevarría, A. Fernández González, I. Porras, K. Allen, and R. Mejías. 1998. "Economic Incentives for Watershed Protection: A Case Study of Lake Arenal, Costa Rica." CREED Final Report. London: IIED.

Barbier, E.B. 1991. "The Economic Value of Ecosystems: 2 – Tropical Forests." London Environmental Economics Centre Gatekeeper Series No 91–01. London: IIED.

Barbier, E.B. and B.A. Aylward. 1996. "Capturing the Pharmaceutical Value of Biodiversity in a Developing Country." *Environmental and Resource Economics,* 8:2, pp.157–191

Barbier, E.B., and J.C. Burgess. 1997. "The Economics of Tropical Forest Land Use." *Land Economics,* 73:2, pp.174–195.

Bass, S., O. Dubois, P. Moura Costa, M. Pinard, R. Tipper, and C. Wilson. 2000. "Rural Livelihoods and Carbon Management." IIED Natural Resource Issues Paper No.1. London: IIED.

Bennett, C.P.A., and R.N. Byron. 1997. *Valuing Resource Valuation: Exploring the Role of Quantitative Valuation of Indonesia's Forest Resources.* Bogor: CIFOR.

Bennett, E.L., and C.J. Reynolds. 1993. "The Value of a Mangrove Area in Sarawak." *Biodiversity and Conservation,* 2:4, pp.359–375.

Bosch, J., and J. Hewlett. 1982. "A Review of Catchment Experiments to Determine the Effects of Vegetation Changes on Water Yield and Evapotranspiration." *Journal of Hydrology,* 55, pp.3–23.

Boyce, S.G., and W.H. McNab. 1994. "Management of Forested Landscapes: Simulations of Three Alternatives." *Journal of Forestry,* 92:1, pp.27–32.

Bruijnzeel, L.A. 1990. *Hydrology of Moist Tropical Forests and Effects of Conservation: A State of Knowledge Review.* Paris: UNESCO International Hydrological Programme.

Bruijnzeel, L.A. 2000. *Hydrology of Tropical Montane Cloud forests: A Reassessment.* Amsterdam: Tropical Environmental Hydrology Programme.

Calder, I. 1999. *The Blue Revolution: Land Use and Integrated Water Resource Management.* London: Earthscan.

Carey, A.B., B.R. Lippke, J. Sessions, C.J. Chambers, C.D. Oliver, J.F. Franklin, and M.J. Raphael. 1996. *Pragmatic, Ecological Approach to Small-Landscape Management: Final Report of the Biodiversity Pathways Working Group of the Washington Forest Landscape Management Project.* Olympia: Washington State Department of Natural Resources.

Carson, R.T. 1991. "Constructed Markets." In J.B. Braden and C.D Kolstad (eds.), *Measuring the Demand for Environmental Quality.* Amsterdam: North-Holland.

Carson, R.T., R.C. Mitchell, W.M. Hanemann, R.J. Kopp, S. Presser, and P.A. Ruud. 1994. "Contingent Valuation and Lost Passive Use: Damages from the Exxon Valdez." Discussion Paper No.94–18, Washington: Resources for the Future.

Chomitz, K.M., and K. Kumari. 1998. "The Domestic Benefits of Tropical Forest Preservation: A Critical Review Emphasizing Hydrological Functions." *World Bank Research Observer,* 13:1, pp.13–35.

Cline, W.R. 1992. *The Economics of Global Warming.* Washington: Institute for International Economics.

Cummings, R.G., D.S. Brookshire, and W.D. Schultze. 1986. *Valuing Environmental Goods: A State of the Art Assessment of the Contingent Valuation Method.* Totowa: Rowman & Allenheld.

Dixon, J.A., L.F. Scura, R.A. Carpenter, and P.B. Sherman. 1994. *Economic Analysis of Environmental Impacts.* London: Earthscan.

Douglas, I., T. Greer, K. Bidin, and M. Spilsbury. 1992. *Impacts of Rainforest Logging on River Systems and Communities in Malaysia and Kalimantan.* London: School of Oriental and African Studies.

Evenson, R.E. 1990. "Genetic Resources: Assessing Economic Values." In J.R. Vincent, E.W. Crawford, and J.P. Hoehn (eds.). *Valuing Environmental Benefits in Developing Economies.* Proceedings of a Seminar Series held February–May 1990. East Lansing: Michigan State University.

Fankhauser, S. 1995. *Valuing Climate Change: The Economics of the Greenhouse.* London: Earthscan.

Food and Agriculture Organisation (FAO). 2001. *State of the World's Forests.* Rome: FAO.

Freeman, A.M., III. 1993. *The Measurement of Environmental and Resource Values: Theory and Methods.* Washington: Resources for the Future.

Forsyth, T. 1996. "Science, Myth, And Knowledge: Testing Himalayan Environmental Degradation in Thailand." *Geoforum,* 27:3, pp.375–392.

Garrod, G., and K. Willis. 1992. "The Environmental Economic Impact of Woodland: A Two-Stage Hedonic Price Model of the Amenity Value Of Forestry in Britain." *Applied Economics,* 24: pp.715–728.

Hanley, N., and C. Spash. 1994. *Cost-Benefit Analysis and the Environment.* Cheltenham: Edward Elgar.

Hamilton, L.S., and P.N. King. 1983. *Tropical Forest Watersheds: Hydrologic and Soils Response to Major Uses and Conversions.* Boulder: Westview Press.

Hearne, R.R. 1996. "Economic Appraisal of Use and Non-Use Values of Environmental Goods and Services in Developing Countries." *Project Appraisal,* 11:4, pp.255–260.

Higman, S., S. Bass, N. Judd, J. Mayers, and R. Nussbaum. 1999. *The Sustainable Forestry Handbook.* London: Earthscan.

Hodgson, G., and J. A. Dixon. 1988. "Logging Versus Fisheries and Tourism in Palawan." Occasional Paper No.7. Honolulu: East West Environment and Policy Institute.

Howard, P. 1995. "The Economics of Protected Areas in Uganda: Costs, Benefits, and Policy Issues." In A. Bagri, J. Blockhus, F. Grey, and F. Vorhies (eds.), *Economic Values of Protected Areas: A Guide for Protected Area Managers*. Gland: IUCN.

Hufschmidt, M.M., D.E. James, A.D. Meister, B.F. Bower, and J.A. Dixon. 1983. *Environment, Natural Systems and Development: an Economic Valuation Guide*. London: Johns Hopkins.

Hunter, M. 1990. *Wildlife, Forests, and Forestry: Principles of Managing Forests for Biological Diversity*. Englewood Cliffs: Prentice Hall.

Hunter, M.L. (ed.) 1999. *Maintaining Biodiversity in Forest Ecosystems*. Cambridge: Cambridge University Press.

Intergovernmental Panel on Climate Change (IPCC). 2000. *Summary for Policy Makers: Land Use, Land-Use Change and Forestry*. Geneva: IPCC.

International Union for the Conservation of Nature (IUCN). 1998. *1997 United Nations List of Protected Areas*. Prepared by UNEP-WCMC and WCPA. Gland: IUCN.

Kopp, R., and V.K. Smith (eds.). 1993. *Valuing Natural Assets: The Economics of Natural Resource Damage Assessment*. Washinton: Resources for the Future.

Kramer, R.A., N. Sharma, and M. Munasinghe. 1995. "Valuing Tropical Forests: Methodology and Case Study of Madagascar." Environment Paper No.13, Washington: World Bank.

Kumari, K. 1995a. "Mainstreaming Biodiversity Conservation: a Peninsular Malaysian Case." *International Journal of Sustainable Development and World Ecology*, 2, pp.182–198.

Kumari, K. 1995b. "An Environmental and Economic Assessment of Forest Management Options: A Case Study in Malaysia." Environmental Department Working Paper No.26. Washington: World Bank.

Landell-Mills, N., and I. Porras. 2002. *Silver Bullet of Fools' Gold? A Global Review of Markets for Forest Environmental Services and Their Impact on the Poor*. London: IIED.

Lee, S.S., Y.M. Dan, I.D. Gauld, and J. Bishop (eds.) 1998. *The Conservation, Management and Development of Forest Resources in Malaysia*. Proceedings of a Workshop 21–24 October 1996. Kepong: Forest Research Institute.

Lippke, B., and J. Bishop. 1999. "The Economic Perspective." In M.L. Hunter (ed.), *Maintaining Biodiversity in Forest Ecosystems*. Cambridge: Cambridge University Press.

Lopez, R. 1997. "Environmental Externalities in Traditional Agriculture and the Impact of Trade Liberalization: The Case of Ghana." *Journal of Development Economics*, 53, pp.17–39.

Mantua, U., M. Merlo, W. Sekot, and B. Welcker. 2001. *Recreational and Environmental Markets for Forest Enterprises: A New Approach Towards Marketability of Public Goods*. Wallingford: CABI Publishing.

McNeely, J., K. Miller, W. Reid, R. Mittermeier, and T. Werner. 1990. *Conserving the World's Biological Diversity*. Gland: IUCN.

Mitchell, R., and R. Carson. 1989. *Using Surveys to Value Public Goods: The Contingent Valuation Method*. Washington: Resources for the Future.

Munasinghe, M., and E. Lutz. 1993. "Environmental Economics and Valuation in Development Decision Making." In M. Munasinghe (ed.), *Environmental Economics and Natural Resource Management in Developing Countries*. Washington: World Bank.

Myers, N. 1997. "The World's Forests and Their Ecosystem Services." In G. Daily (ed.), *Nature's Services: Societal Dependence on Natural Ecosystems*. Washington: Island Press.

Niskanen, A. 1998. "Value of External Environmental Impacts of Reforestation in Thailand." *Ecological Economics*, 26:3, pp.287–297.

Nobre, C.A., P.J. Sellers, and J. Shukla. 1991. "Amazonian Deforestation and Regional Climate Change." *Journal of Climate*, 4, pp.957–988.

Nordhaus, W.D. 1993. "Optimal Greenhouse Gas Reductions and Tax Policy in the DICE Model." *American Economic Review*, 83, pp.313–317.

Oliver, C.D. 1992. "A Landscape Approach: Achieving Biodiversity and Economic Productivity." *Journal of Forestry*, 90:9, pp.20–25.

Organisation for Economic Co-operation and Development (OECD). 1996. *Saving Biological Diversity: Economic Incentives*. Paris: OECD.

Parviainen, J., A. Schuck, and W. Bucking. 1995. "A Pan-European System for Measuring Biodiversity, Succession and Structure of Undisturbed Forests and for Improving Biodiversity-Oriented Silviculture." In C.R. Bamsey (ed.), *Innovative Silviculture Systems in Boreal Forests*. Proceedings of a symposium held in Edmonton, Alberta, Canada, October 2–8, 1994. Edmonton: Clear Lake Ltd.

Pearce, D.W., and D. Moran. 1994. *The Economic Value of Biodiversity*. London: Earthscan.

Pearce, D.W., and S. Puroshothaman. 1992. "Protecting Biological Diversity: The Economic Value of Pharmaceutical Plants." Global Environmental Change Working Paper No.92-27. London: CSERGE/UEA and UCL.

Pearce, D.W., A. Markandya, and E.B. Barbier. 1989. *Blueprint for a Green Economy*. London: Earthscan.

Pearce, D.W., D. Moran, and W. Krug. 1999. *The Global Value of Biological Diversity, A Report to the United Nations Environment Program*. London: CSERGE.

Pearce, D.W., and C.G. Pearce. 2001. *The Value of Forest Ecosystems*. Report to the Secretariat of the United Nations Convention on Biological Diversity, Montreal, Canada. London: CSERGE.

Perez-Garcia, J. 1994. "Global Forestry Impacts of Reducing Softwood Supplies from North America." CINTRAFOR Working Paper No.43. Seattle: College of Forest Resources, University of Washington.

Reid, W., and K. Miller. 1989. *Keeping Options Alive: The Scientific Basis for Conserving Biodiversity*. Washington: World Resources Institute.

Roper, C.S., and A. Park (eds.) 1999. *The Living Forest: Non-Market Benefits of Forestry*. Proceedings of an International Symposium, Edinburgh 24–28 June 1996. London: HMSO.

Ruitenbeek, H.J. 1989. "Social Cost–Benefit Analysis of the Korup Project, Cameroon." Godalming: WWF (processed).

Ruitenbeek, H.J. 1992. "Mangrove Management: An Economic Analysis of Management Options with a Focus on Bintuni Bay, Irian Jaya." EMDI Environmental Report No. 8. Jakarta: EMDI.

Smith, J., S. Mourato, E. Veneklaas, R. Labarta, K. Reategui, and G. Sanchez. 1997. "Willingness to Pay for Environmental Services Among Slash-and-burn Farmers in the Peruvian Amazon: Implications for Deforestation and Global Environmental Markets." CSERGE/CIAT/ICRAF Working Paper No.GEC97. London: CSERGE.

Vincent, J.R., E.W. Crawford, and J.P. Hoehn (eds.). 1991. *Valuing Environmental Benefits in Developing Economies*. Proceedings of a Seminar Series February–May 1990 at Michigan State University. East Lansing: Michigan State University.

Walsh, R.G., R.D. Bjonback, R.A. Aiken, and D.H. Rosenthal. 1990. "Estimating the Public Benefits of Protecting Forest Quality." *Journal of Environmental Management*, 30, pp.175–189.

Winpenny, J.T. 1991. *Values for the Environment: A Guide to Economic Appraisal*. London: HMSO.

Chapter 3

Paying for Water Services in Central America: Learning from Costa Rica

Stefano Pagiola[1]

The impact of deforestation on hydrological flows is a major concern throughout Central America. Sedimentation of reservoirs, dry season water shortages, flooding and the severity of the damage caused by Hurricane Mitch in 1998 have all been widely attributed, at least in part, to deforestation. This has resulted in strong political interest in addressing deforestation problems. The perceived failure of previous efforts to address these problems has led to new approaches (Pagiola and Platais, 2001). Perhaps the most promising is the development of systems of payments for environmental services, under which land users are compensated directly for the environmental services they generate (Pagiola and Platais, forthcoming). In this way, land users would have a direct incentive to include these services in their land use decisions, resulting in more socially-optimal land uses. Costa Rica pioneered this approach in 1997 by developing a formal, countrywide system of environmental service payments (Pago por Servicios Ambientales, PSA). Several other countries in the region have been watching this experience closely and are beginning to work on similar programs. This Chapter examines the experience of Costa Rica's PSA program in dealing with water services, and discusses how the lessons of this experience are beginning to be applied in other countries with similar problems.

WATER SERVICES PROVIDED BY CENTRAL AMERICAN FORESTS

Forest ecosystems are thought to play important roles in providing valuable hydrological services. This role has often been seen as significant in Central America, particularly in recent decades, as forest cover has declined and demand for water services has risen (Leonard, 1987; Kaimowitz, 2000). Although discussion of 'water services' in Central America has often tended to refer to them as an undifferentiated, generic service, various specific services can be distinguished, including the following:

- reducing sediment loads in waterways to reduce the sedimentation of reservoirs and the associated production and maintenance costs for irrigation systems, hydroelectric power (HEP) plants, water supply systems, and fisheries;
- regulating the timing of water-flows so as to reduce flood risk in the wet season and the likelihood of water shortages in the dry season;
- increasing the volume of available water, either year-round or specifically in the dry season; and
- improving the quality of available water for domestic use.

While forest cover is widely believed to provide all these services, the evidence is often far from clear (Hamilton and King, 1983; Bruijnzeel, 1990; Chomitz and Kumari, 1998; Calder, 1999).[2] In particular, specific data on the nature and magnitude of the links between forest cover and water services in Central America are extremely scarce (Kaimowitz, 2000). Notwithstanding these data constraints, it is clear that in a number of circumstances forests do play a role in the provision of water services, even if the precise nature and magnitude of this role is not always understood.

Whatever the specific nature of the link between forests and water services, the fundamental problem is that these services are generally used by people at some distance from the forests that help provide them. Land users in and near the forests themselves typically do not receive any compensation for providing environmental services. On the contrary, providing such services often imposes costs on these land users by restricting their land use choices. As a result, they usually ignore them in making their land use decisions, resulting in socially suboptimal land use decisions.

PREVIOUS RESPONSES

Costa Rica has experienced one of the world's highest rates of deforestation (Peuker, 1992; FONAFIFO, 2000; World Bank, 2000a). Between the late 1970s and the early 1990s, the country is estimated to have lost about 35–40 per cent of its forest cover, driven primarily by conversion to agriculture and pasture. This deforestation is widely thought to have adversely affected water services in the country (Leonard, 1987; Kaimowitz, 2000). According to the National Fund for Forest Financing (Fondo Nacional de Financiamiento Forestal, FONAFIFO), 'the preservation of forests has a high impact on the regularity of the hydrological cycle and the reduction of sedimentation in reservoirs' (2000, p31).

In Costa Rica and in the rest of Central America, responses to the deterioration of water services have usually taken several forms, including remedial measures (such as repairing the damage caused by flooding) and preventive measures (such as efforts to regulate land uses in sensitive areas), and conservation projects aimed at convincing land users to adopt land use practices perceived to be beneficial (including reforestation, agroforestry, physical conservation measures such as terraces, and vegetative conservation measures such as vetiver grass strips) (Lutz and others, 1994). In Costa Rica, a number of conservation projects have been implemented since the early 1980s, and they have adopted a variety of approaches. Some have depended on a hoped-for 'demonstration effect' – assuming that conservation practices were beneficial to farmers, who would adopt them of their own accord once their benefits had been demonstrated. Others have sought to entice land users to adopt the proposed practices in a variety of ways, including full or partial subsidies for the costs of adoption (paid either in cash or in kind), or by tying conservation adoption to other benefits, such as access to credit. For example, the Costa Rican National Soil and Water Conservation Service (Servicio Nacional de Conservación de Suela y Agua, SENACSA) subsidizes half the cost of building conservation works for small farmers (less than 5ha), and the full cost of conservation works on 'model farms' intended to demonstrate conservation techniques to other farmers (Cuesta, 1994).

None of these measures have proved effective (Enters, 1997; Pagiola, 1999, forthcoming). Remedial measures are often imperfect and expensive. Regulatory approaches are extremely difficult to enforce and may impose high costs on poor land users by forcing them to adopt land uses that generate lower returns. Conservation projects have often had temporary success, especially when they have paid subsidies. Once the projects end and the subsidies cease, however, land users have often reverted to their previous land uses, neglecting the conservation measures they had adopted or even actively destroying them (Lutz and others, 1994).

An important implication of this experience is that the common assumption that conservation measures are always in the land users' personal interest is often wrong.[3] A review of the profitability of conservation measures throughout Central America, for example, found that most were not profitable from the farmers' perspective (Lutz and others, 1994). Moreover, the cases in which conservation is profitable for land users are not necessarily those in which the external effects are most significant. Consequently, land users' interest in responding to degradation may not correlate with that of downstream water users. In Costa Rica, for example, Cuesta (1994) found that terraces were profitable in the Turrubares areas, but that even the much cheaper diversion ditches were not profitable in the Heredia area, despite erosion being more severe in the latter area. The reason for this difference is that soils at Turrubares are shallow, so that even low rates of erosion can have severe impacts on the area's profitable vegetable production. At Heredia, on the other hand, very deep soils with a favorable profile mean that even severe erosion has no effect on yields.

PAYMENTS FOR ENVIRONMENTAL SERVICES IN COSTA RICA

The principle of systems of payments for environmental services is simple. Compensating land users for the environmental services they provide creates a direct incentive for land users to include these services in their land use decisions (Pagiola and Platais, forthcoming).

Development

Beginning in 1997, Costa Rica developed an elaborate system of payments for environmental services based on this principle (Castro and others, 1997; Chomitz and others, 1999; FONAFIFO, 2000). Forestry Law No 7575, enacted in 1996, explicitly recognized four environmental services provided by forest ecosystems:

1   mitigation of greenhouse gas (GHG) emissions;
2   hydrological services, including provision of water for human consumption, irrigation, and energy production;
3   biodiversity conservation; and
4   provision of scenic beauty for recreation and ecotourism.

The law provides the regulatory basis for the government to contract landowners for the services provided by their lands, and has established a financing mechanism for this purpose in the form of FONAFIFO.

The PSA program did not start with a blank slate. Beginning in the 1970s, concern over dwindling timber supplies had led Costa Rica to provide incentives for reforestation. Initial efforts focused on tax rebates. They were superseded by the Forest Credit Certificate (Certificado de Abono Forestal, CAF), created under Forestry Law No 7032 of 1986. As a transferable instrument, the CAF broadened participation in reforestation, which had previously been limited to larger companies with significant tax liabilities. Participation was also broadened through the Forest Credit Certificate with Advance (Certificado de Abono Forestal por Adelantado, CAFA), which provided for front-loaded payments designed to allow credit-constrained farmers to invest in reforestation. The system was also gradually expanded beyond its initial focus on timber supplies to cover activities other than reforestation, including sustainable forest management and natural forest protection. Almost 116,000ha received financing through the old system.

By the time the PSA program was created, therefore, Costa Rica already had in place an elaborate system of payments for reforestation and forest management, and the institutions to manage it. The Forestry Law built on this base, with two major changes. First, it changed the justification for payments from support for the timber industry to the provision of environmental services. Second, it changed the source of financing from the government budget to an earmarked tax and payments from beneficiaries and created FONAFIFO to administer the program. In other respects, the PSA program was very similar to previous refor-estation incentives. Until 2000, the types of activities financed under the PSA program closely paralleled those financed by previous instruments: reforestation, sustainable forest management, and natural forest management. Many of the details of implementation, such as the payment amounts and the scheduling of payments, were also carried over from the earlier programs. Indeed, CAF certif-icates were used to pay participants in the first year of the PSA program. In 2000, the array of instruments was reduced to just two, reforestation and forest pro-tection, but other details remained unchanged.

Under the PSA program, participants must present a sustainable forest management plan certified by a licensed forester. In addition to the proposed land use, management plans include information on land tenure and physical access; a description of topography, soils, climate, drainage, actual land use, and carrying capacity with respect to land use; plans for preventing forest fires, illegal hunting, and illegal harvesting; and monitoring schedules. The task of contracting with farmers is generally undertaken by the National System of Conservation Areas (Sistema Nacional de Areas de Conservación, SINAC) or by non-governmental organizations (NGOs) such as the Foundation for the Development of the Central Volcanic Cordillera (Fundación para el Desarrollo de la Cordillera Volcánica Central, FUNDECOR). They handle applications, sign contracts, and monitor implementation. Once the plan has been approved, the land users begin adopting the specified practices, and receive payments over a five-year period. In some contracts, land users commit to maintaining the contracted land use for a further 10–15 years, a commitment that is registered with the deed to the property, so that contractual obligations transfer as a legal easement to subsequent owners for the life of the contract. Furthermore, landowners cede the rights to the GHG emissions reductions resulting from their activities to FONAFIFO.

Structure of the PSA program

The structure of Costa Rica's PSA program is shown in Figure 3.1. A system of payments for environmental services depends on three basic institutional functions (Pagiola and Platais, forthcoming). First, a mechanism is needed to collect and manage payments from service beneficiaries. FONAFIFO fulfils this role with the assistance of other institutions, such as the Costa Rican Office of Joint Imple-mentation (Oficina Costarricense de Implementación Conjunta, OCIC). Second, a mechanism is needed to contract service providers, pay them, and monitor their participation. These interactions are partly undertaken by SINAC and partly by private professional foresters ('*regentes*') who undertake them for a fee.[4] Third, a governing structure is required. Costa Rica's PSA program is overseen by a governing board composed of three representatives of the public sector (one from the Ministry of Environment and Energy, one from the Ministry of Agriculture, and one from the national banking system) and two representatives from the private sector (appointed by the board of directors of the National Forestry Office).

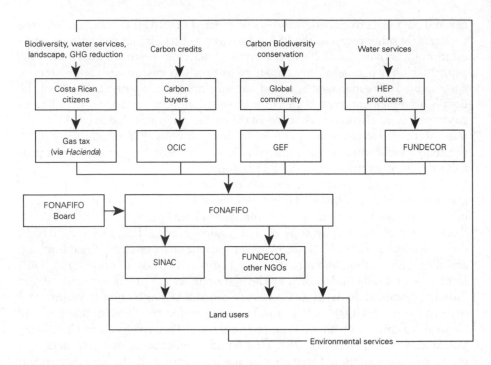

Figure 3.1 *The Costa Rican program of payments for environmental services*

The PSA program is financed in a variety of ways. To date, the bulk of financing has been obtained by allocating one-third of the revenues from a fossil fuel sales tax to FONAFIFO. Conflicts have developed over the use of these earmarked taxes, however, and only a small part of the earmarked funds have actually been received by FONAFIFO (FONAFIFO, 2000). At the beginning of the PSA program, great hopes were placed in the potential for sales of carbon emission reduction credits. A specialized organization, OCIC, was established to handle these transactions. However, results to date have been less promising than originally expected, generating only US$2 million in a single sale. Since 2000, the PSA program has also been supported by a loan from the World Bank and a grant from the Global Environment Facility (GEF) through the Ecomarkets project (World Bank, 2000b). This project includes a US$32.6 million loan from the World Bank to help the government ensure current levels of environmental service contracts, and US$8 million grant from GEF, which can be considered a payment from the global community for the biodiversity services provided by Costa Rica's biodiversity. Ultimately, it is envisaged that all beneficiaries of water services (including HEP plants, water supply entities, irrigators, domestic users, and manufacturers) would also pay for the water services they receive. At present, such payments have been received primarily from HEP producers.

Water service payments

The role of forests in providing hydrological services was explicitly recognized in Forestry Law No 7575, and payments from HEP generators and other water users were always envisaged to be one of the legs on which the PSA program would rest. Law No 7575 does not oblige beneficiaries to pay for services, however. Any payments must be negotiated with potential service buyers. Since its inception, FONAFIFO has dedicated substantial efforts to negotiating with water users for them to pay for the water services they receive.

A number of agreements have been reached with HEP producers (see Table 3.1). The first agreement, with private producer Energía Global, was reached in late 1997. Under this agreement, Energía Global reimburses FONAFIFO for part of the cost of payments made to participating land users in the watersheds above the two run-of-the-river hydroelectric plants operated by the company. This agreement was arranged with the assistance of FUNDECOR. A similar agreement was reached a year later with Platanar S A, also with the assistance of FUNDECOR. Perhaps more significantly, a framework agreement was reached with state power producer CNFL (see Table 3.1). The first application of this agreement covered reforestation and forest management activities on 5000ha in

Table 3.1 *Contracts for provision of water services to HEP providers in Costa Rica*

Company	Watershed	Area (ha)	Area covered by contract with service buyer (ha)	Area already contracted from land users, 2000 (ha)	Payment to participating land users[a] (US$/ha/year)
PSA program					
Energía Global	Río Volcán	3,466	2,493	765	10
	Río San Fernando	2,404	1,818	819	10
Platanar S A	Río Platanar	3,129	1,400	172	10 / 30[b]
CNFL	Río Aranjuez	9,515	5,000	688	42
	Río Balsa	18,926	6,000		42
	Lago Cote	1,259	900		42
Others					
La Manguera SA	La Esperanza		3,000		10

Notes: a Payment shown is the contribution made by the service buyers; participating land users receive the standard PSA contract payments (currently US$42/ha/year). In addition to the amounts shown, service buyers also reimburse FONAFIFO for its administrative costs.

   b Platanar pays US$10/ha/year for contracts with landowners with land titles, with FONAFIFO paying the rest; it pays US$30/ha/year for contracts with landowners without land titles, who are not otherwise eligible for PSA contracts.

Source: FONAFIFO data

the Aranjuez river basin; it has since been applied to the Río Balsa and Lago Cote watersheds as well. Additional agreements are being negotiated with other HEP producers. A memorandum of understanding has been signed with Hidroverde, in Pococí, but it has not yet resulted in a formal contract.

HEP producers are not, of course, the only water users. Efforts to arrive at similar agreements with other water users, and notably with domestic water users, have not yet borne fruit, however. The only non-HEP agreement signed so far is that reached with beer maker Cervecería Costa Rica in October 2001. Under this agreement, Cervecería Costa Rica will reimburse FONAFIFO for the entire cost of contracting PSA program participants (that is, payments to participants plus administrative costs) on 1000ha above the Barva aquifer. Cervecería Costa Rica is hoping to protect infiltration into the aquifer, which feeds the spring from which the company draws water to make beer and bottled water. FONAFIFO has been negotiating for some time with the country's main water utility, the Costa Rican Institute of Aqueducts and Drains (Instituto Costarricense de Acueductos y Alcantarillados, AyA), and hopes to arrive at an agreement soon. Negotiations are also underway with Rio Tropicales, a rafting company, for a contract that would target protection of the watersheds the company uses for its rafting trips (this would be partly a payment for water services, and partly a payment for preservation of scenic landscapes).

At present, HEP financing is still only a small part of total financing for the PSA program, amounting to a cumulative total of about US$100,000 since the program's inception, covering a little more than 2400ha. Once all current agreements are fully implemented, they should generate an annual payment stream of about US$0.5–0.6 million, covering an area of almost 18,000ha. Although not negligible, these figures are much smaller than the GEF payments for biodiversity conservation (US$1.8–1.9 million a year for five years), the fuel tax payments (US$6.4 million a year received to date), and even the limited financing obtained so far for carbon sequestration services (US$2 million since 1997).

Payments for water services outside the PSA

In addition to the agreements between HEP producers and FONAFIFO, there has also been a bilateral agreement between a private HEP producer, La Manguera SA, and the NGO that owns the watershed from which the La Esperanza HEP plant draws its water. In October 1998, La Manguera agreed to pay the Monteverde Conservation League US$10/ha/year to maintain the watershed under forest cover.

In 2000, Costa Rica approved a law to establish a trial 'environmentall-adjusted water tariff', the proceeds of which will be used to help maintain and reforest watershed areas near Heredia (Castro, 2001).[5] These payments will be distinct from the PSA program.

MAKING PAYMENTS FOR WATER SERVICES WORK

The process of designing and implementing a system of payments for water services requires several related but distinct issues to be addressed, including the following (Pagiola and Platais, forthcoming):

1 **Identifying and quantifying water services.** Which water services does a given land use in a given location generate? How much service is generated? How much is the service worth?
2 **Identifying key beneficiaries and charging them for water services.** Who should pay for water services? What level of charges should be imposed? How should the funds be managed?
3 **Developing payment systems that work.** How are payments actually to be made in order to efficiently achieve the desired change in land use sustainability?
4 **Addressing institutional and political economy issues.** What are the institutional preconditions that make the payments possible? Who are the winners and losers, and how can the resulting political economy implications be addressed?

Identifying and quantifying water services

Although it is commonly thought that forests help provide water services, our understanding of the links between forests and hydrological services is often poor, both qualitatively and – especially – quantitatively (Chomitz and Kumari, 1998; see also discussion in Chapter 2). This lack of specific knowledge exists throughout Central America, including Costa Rica (Kaimowitz, 2000).

When Costa Rica established the PSA program no specific information was available about the effects of forest cover on water-flows in Costa Rica. Rather, the program depended on a generalized view that forest cover provided beneficial water services – conventional wisdom that is widely shared in Central America (Kaimowitz, 2000). Since then, there has been some limited progress in this regard, and three studies have been conducted:

* A detailed analysis of the Lake Arenal watershed (which supplies water to Costa Rica's largest HEP dam, operated by CNFL, and to a large irrigated area) was conducted by a research team as part of the Program on Collaborative Research in the Economics of Environment and Development (CREED) (Aylward and others, 1998; Aylward and Echevarría, 2001). Because of the presence of the dam, more and better hydrological data exist for this watershed than for most others in Costa Rica. Their results indicate that deforestation increases sedimentation by 13–28 cubic meters (m^3)/ha/year, but also increases water yields.

- A study of the impact of forests on HEP production was commissioned by the Ecomarkets Project (CT Energía, 2000). This study conducted a cross-sectional analysis of six selected watersheds in an attempt to determine the relationship between land cover and dry season water flows, and found them to be positively correlated. The results are not very robust, however. Not only are they based on a very small number of data points (two observations for each of the six selected watersheds), without controlling for other factors, but in at least two of the watersheds the relationship appears to go in the opposite direction. CT Energía also found that sedimentation was likely to increase as forest cover declines.
- The Regional Centre for Studies in Ecological Economics (CRESEE) conducted a study of the effect of deforestation on water-flows and water quality in the province of Heredia (Castro, 2001). They concluded that forest cover increased both water-flows and water quality compared to grass cover. However, this study is problematic. It only compared differences in runoff between the two types of land use, without allowing for possible differences in evapotranspiration rates – a variable that the hydrological literature identifies as critical.

It is fair to say that these studies are not conclusive. All three suffered from data limitations, which in turn imposed methodological limitations. The CREED team's results are consistent with hydrological understanding, whereas the CRESEE results appear to run counter to it. The CT Energía results address an issue – the effects of forest cover on dry season flows – on which there is less consensus in the hydrological literature.

Despite their weaknesses, the CT Energía and CRESEE results play important roles in the development of payments for water services in Costa Rica. The CT Energía study was used to develop a formula to estimate the benefits of reforestation to HEP producers. Using this formula, the benefits of reforestation to HEP producers were estimated to be about US$20/ha/year on average – as low as US$6/ha/year and as high as $50/ha/year, depending on variables such as watershed size. These estimates are likely to become the basis for negotiations in any new agreement.

The CRESEE study was used to justify the introduction of Heredia's trial 'environmentally adjusted water tariff'. While it did not attempt to estimate the value of the water service benefits, it argued that they were substantially greater than the small additional sum requested of water users ($0.009/m^3, in addition to the basic rate of $0.23/m^3 for domestic water users) (Castro, 2001).

Clearly, there is still a significant need for better information on the exact nature and quantity of water services provided by forests. Unfortunately, this need is difficult to address, as it requires long-term data monitoring and time-consuming experiments.

Identifying key beneficiaries and charging them for water services

Different water users are usually interested in different types of water services. Water quality is usually more important for domestic use than for other uses. Municipal water supply systems need a constant supply, while irrigation systems only need water at certain times of year. In Costa Rica, as in other Central American countries, there are five main groups of water service beneficiaries:

1   HEP generators;
2   municipal water supply systems;
3   irrigation systems;
4   industrial users; and
5   populations in flood-prone areas.

Of these, the first four are the most promising candidates for participation in a program of payments for environmental services. They are easily identifiable and already organized, so it is relatively easy to negotiate with them. Should an agreement be reached for them to pay for the water services they receive, they already have the capability of collecting the required funds from their members. Populations in flood-prone areas, in contrast, are not organized (except to the extent that they are included in some of the other three groups) and there is no mechanism to collect payments from them.

Even within a group, there can be important differences in the nature of water services of interest. The Lake Arenal watershed studied by the CREED team, for example, has a large dam and storage reservoir (Aylward and others, 1998). Their presence means that any impact of deforestation on flooding is a minor concern, as the dam can regulate the flow reaching downstream areas. Seasonal variations in water-flow are also relatively minor considerations, as the reservoir can accumulate water-flows and release them as needed for electricity generation or irrigation. The most important consideration in this instance, then, is total water-flow. The greater this is, the more electricity can be produced, and the greater the capacity to smooth out seasonal variations. Under these conditions, reforestation could actually prove harmful if, as the CREED team's results show, pasture does indeed result in higher water-flows. On the other hand, lower forest cover would also result in higher sedimentation. The CREED team estimates that the resulting reduction in power generating capability would be much smaller than the benefit from increased water-flow.

In contrast, many of the new privately-operated HEP plants are run-of-the-river schemes, with minimal storage.[6] To the extent that they accumulate water, they do so only from day to day so as to generate power at times of peak demand. Such plants, therefore, are very dependent on stream-flow for their operation, a constraint that becomes particularly significant during the dry season. In addition, they are more vulnerable to sedimentation because of their limited storage capacity, and to damage to their tubing and turbines from sediment (as a smaller proportion of suspended sediment will precipitate out in their reservoirs). High peak-flows are harmful partly because they represent water that cannot be used for HEP generation, and partly because transported debris can clog intakes and damage turbines. Moreover, the limited storage capacity of these plants means they offer no defense against peak-flows to downstream areas. Under such conditions, reducing variations in stream-flows and ensuring the highest possible dry-season flow become very important. All of the HEP producers who have signed agreements with FONAFIFO to date operate run-of-the-river HEP plants.

Convincing these or other water users to pay for forest conservation in their watersheds requires demonstrating that conserving forests would be beneficial to them, either by improving water services or by preventing a deterioration. The case for the importance of watershed protection is perhaps easiest to make in watersheds that are providing satisfactory levels of water services and where forest cover is still substantially intact. Under these conditions, even if the precise link between forests and water services is unknown, a strong argument can be made from the basis of the precautionary principle to avoid changes that might threaten the situation (Kaimowitz, 2000). This argument was made in the case of the agreement between the Monteverde Conservation League and Manguera SA to protect the watershed above the La Esperanza HEP plant (Rojas and Aylward, forthcoming). However, when improvements in water services are being sought, more direct knowledge is needed of whether, and to what extent, particular land use changes can help generate these improvements.

According to FONAFIFO, many HEP producers and other water users share the prevalent view concerning the beneficial role of forests in protecting water services. In FONAFIFO's view, the lack of precise information about the effects of forest cover on water services has not been a significant constraint in the agreements that have been negotiated to date. But the relatively small number of agreements signed so far makes it difficult to determine how widely applicable this argument might be. Moreover, even when potential service buyers share the belief that forests are beneficial for water services, better information on the magnitude of forest–hydrology linkages would help them to justify the payments, particularly if the latter are substantial.

In the long term, accurate information on forest–hydrology linkages will be vital to retaining existing service buyers. If payments from beneficiaries are predicated on receiving water services, then those services need to be delivered. Without better information on how forest cover affects water services, it is hard to be confident that they will. In this respect, it is interesting to note that none of the agreements between FONAFIFO and HEP producers specify the level of water service that beneficiaries will receive; they only specify the area of forest to be protected. Monitoring efforts are likewise limited to ensuring that participating landowners adopt the specified land use practices; there is no monitoring of the water services themselves. This supports the view that HEP producers who have already reached agreements with FONAFIFO have strong beliefs about the beneficial impacts of forest cover. Whether others who have not yet joined the program share these beliefs, and whether they would find this arrangement acceptable, remains to be seen. That the number of agreements reached to date is so small might suggest that they do not. The single agreement with HEP producers outside the PSA program, at La Esperanza, implicitly guarantees water service delivery. The payment formula agreed between the water service buyer and the watershed owner provides for increasing or decreasing payments depending on water services actually received, as measured by the capability to produce electricity (Rojas and Aylward, forthcoming).

Understanding the hydrological impacts of land use change is also important in determining how much buyers should pay for water services. Buyers are clearly interested in paying the smallest possible amount, and certainly no more than the service is worth to them. The calculations are particularly difficult because water-service users are not being asked to pay for additional water services, but rather for the land use changes that are expected to generate those services. In the early days of the PSA program, the calculations where done in a very ad hoc way. The payments to participants were based on the amounts paid under the earlier subsidy programs. Since Law No 7575 listed four environmental services provided by forests, this payment was simply divided by four to arrive at the share that water services should pay for. Thus the agreement with Energía Global called for them to pay US$10/ha/year, or one-quarter of the then-standard PSA payment to participants of US$40/ha/year (FONAFIFO, 2000). A similar reasoning was used in the agreement with Platanar. The private agreement for the La Esperanza HEP plant followed the precedent set by these agreements. By the time the agreement with CNFL was signed, however, it had become clear that other sources of funding for the PSA program were not going to be as forthcoming as had been expected, and that even the revenue from the gas tax would be substantially less than anticipated. FONAFIFO was in a better position to negotiate higher payments by arguing that without them, conservation would simply not happen.

Securing payments from the beneficiaries of water services is particularly difficult when there are multiple water users in a watershed. In that case, each individual water user has an incentive to free-ride. It is noteworthy that every agreement reached by FONAFIFO with a water user covers interventions in watersheds in which there is a single dominant water user. The only exception is the agreement with Cervecería Costa Rica, which covers a watershed in which there are many other users. In this case, however, it appears that public relations was as important a motivation for Cervecería Costa Rica to join the program as actually receiving water services.

Once an agreement has been reached, implementation can occur rapidly because FONAFIFO already has the necessary institutional structure to receive and handle funds, and to enrol, monitor, and pay program participants. All the agreements signed to date include provisions for the water buyers to compensate FONAFIFO for its administrative costs. CNFL, for example, pays FONAFIFO an additional US$15/ha in the first year of every contract with a participant, to cover FONAFIFO's administrative and promotional costs.

Developing payment systems that work

Identifying the land uses that generate water services, and convincing water users to pay for these services, are only two elements of the problem. Once these tasks have been accomplished, a system of payments that induces land users to adopt the desired land uses must be developed. Doing so is far from easy. By definition, these uses will tend not to be in the land users' own interests.[7] The experience of previous watershed management efforts in Costa Rica and elsewhere has been marked by numerous failures. The approach adopted in systems of payments for environmental services is to provide an annual payment to participating land users. In moving from theory to practice, several concrete questions must be answered: How much should be paid? For how long? To whom?

Forestry Law No 7575 and subsequent decrees set the amount to be paid under each type of contract. In principle, the amount should be no less than the land users' opportunity cost (or they will not participate), and no more than the value of the benefit provided (or it would not be worthwhile to provide the service). In practice, the actual value of the benefit provided is extremely difficult to estimate, while the farmers' opportunity costs can usually be estimated relatively easily. For this reason, as well as to limit the budgetary requirements of the payment, payment levels are usually set at slightly more than the opportunity cost of relatively low-value land uses such as pasture. This is the approach that the PSA program adopted. Payments for forest conservation are about US$35–40/ha/year, while contracts for reforestation paid US$538/ha over five years.[8] The payment offered for forest management has proved to be quite attractive, and FONAFIFO has received far more applications for this contract than it has been able to finance. Reforestation has proven to be less popular; many landowners apparently consider the payment offered insufficient to justify investing in reforestation.[9] All PSA program participants undertaking the same activity receive the same payment, regardless of location or other characteristics.[10]

Article 69 of Forestry Law No 7575 authorizes conservation easements to be contracted for periods of five or 20 years. Until 2000, FONAFIFO only contracted five-year conservation easements, mainly because of the uncertainty of future funding. The contracts provide for payments spread over a five-year period. The specific schedule depends on the instrument. Forest conservation contracts – by far the most widely used – provided for equal annual payments over the five-year lifetime of the contract. In contrast, reforestation contracts front-loaded a large part of the payment into the early years of the contract, with much smaller payments in later years.[11] Forest conservation contracts are for five years, and are renewable by mutual agreement. Reforestation contracts provide a five-year payment but call for participants to continue with the agreed land use for 15 years, a restriction that is written into the land title so that it transfers to the new buyer if the land is sold.

Contracts undertaken under the Ecomarkets program and under the deals with the HEP producers have, from the start, tended to focus on longer duration contracts. The PSA contracts financed under the CNFL agreement, for example, are for ten-year periods rather than the PSA program's standard five-year period. All GEF co-financed contacts under the Ecomarkets project will have a contractual obligation of 20 years, in successive five-year periods that are automatically renewed when resources permit and landowners have met their contractual obligations.

The establishment of trustworthy contract monitoring and verification systems is an important part of any system of payments. Monitoring is undertaken primarily by the agencies responsible for contracting with farmers, including SINAC, FUNDECOR, and *regentes*, with regular audits to verify the accuracy of monitoring.

Institutional and political economy issues

By building on the basis of previous forest subsidy schemes, Costa Rica was able to develop an elaborate nationwide system of payments for environmental services relatively rapidly. As discussed below, this was not without its drawbacks. Many of the details of the previous schemes that were carried over into the PSA program were suboptimal from the perspective of generating water services, notably in the lack of targeting. With experience, many of these weaknesses are being gradually corrected. This is, of course, not a purely technical issue. The trend toward targeting has been pushed by the demands of service buyers, but it has been resisted by the country's reforestation lobby, which prefers untargeted – and, therefore, more easily accessible – payments. Had the dispute with the Ministry of Finance not limited the funding derived from the earmarked gas tax, however, service buyers interested in targeted interventions would most likely have had much less influence on the development of the PSA program.

Institutional limitations within potential water service buyers have at times impeded the development of the PSA program. They have played a major role, for example, in the failure to reach an agreement with domestic water supplier AyA despite four years of negotiations. As an organization long dominated by engineers, there was no natural interlocutor within AyA for FONAFIFO to negotiate with. Moreover, adding a fee to water bills to finance conservation activities would require regulatory approval, a particularly difficult hurdle to overcome in election years. Conversely, institutional characteristics among buyers have at times encouraged their participation. Energía Global, the first HEP producer to agree to pay for water services, is controlled by the family of the President of Costa Rica who created the PSA program. And as noted, Cervecería Costa Rica was keen to finance conservation activities for their public relations value.

On the service provider side, the main institutional barrier has been the requirement that participants should have title to their land. This is a limitation imposed by Costa Rican law, which forbids the use of public funds for contracts with landowners unless they have land titles. However, many Costa Rican landowners lack such titles. In the Río Volcan watershed, for example, this problem has limited participation in the PSA program to only 30 per cent of the area scheduled to be protected under the contract with Energía Global (see Table 3.1). Similarly, in the Río San Fernando watershed, only 45 per cent of the agreed area could be enrolled in the program. This constraint was even more severe in the Río Platanar watershed, where only 12 per cent of the agreed area could be enrolled. To overcome this problem, the agreement between FONAFIFO and Platanar S A was modified to allow for the participation of landowners without titles. When FONAFIFO is administering private funds the legal restrictions do not apply. The solution, therefore, was to create a parallel contract, similar in all respects to the PSA contract, but financed entirely with funds provided by Platanar. Whereas landowners with titles receive the standard PSA payment of US$42/ha/year, of which US$10 is contributed by Platanar, landowners without titles receive US$30/ha/year, which is contributed entirely by Platanar. FONAFIFO is negotiating similar modifications to existing contracts with other HEP producers.

Like any system, Costa Rica's PSA program faces substantial transaction costs. By law, the administrative costs of the PSA system are limited to 5 per cent of funds. In addition to its own administrative costs, the PSA program also imposes transaction costs on participants through the need to prepare management plans. The costs of preparing such programs are more onerous for smaller landowners. To avoid locking small landowners out, a mechanism was developed whereby groups of farmers can submit a joint management plan (Castro and others, 1997). Under this mechanism, NGOs such as FUNDECOR work to 'bundle' small land owners (with less than 20ha each, usually) together into one contract, and then FONAFIFO issues a single contract with the NGO. A study conducted between 1995 and 1997 found that 60 per cent of all PSA program participants, accounting for about 40 per cent of all land contracted, used such community-based contracts (World Bank, 2000b).

Negotiating individual agreements with each potential water-service buyer also imposes significant transaction costs. To reduce these costs, FONAFIFO is exploring the possibility of creating certificates that would certify that a given area has been protected. Rather than negotiating with FONAFIFO to establish a contract for the protection of a particular watershed, water-service buyers could then simply buy the required number of certificates. FONAFIFO would then use the proceeds to finance conservation in that watershed.[12]

RESULTS

The approach taken by the PSA program has been successful in the sense that requests to participate have far outstripped available resources. The following discussion focuses on five issues:

1   the effect of the PSA program on forest cover;
2   the efficiency of the PSA program in terms of generating the desired water services;

3   the cost effectiveness of water service generation;
4   its sustainability, in terms of ensuring the desired services are provided over
    the long term; and
5   its equity impacts.

Effect on forest cover

The PSA program has been very popular with landowners, with requests to participate far outstripping available financing. By mid-2000, over 200,000ha of forest had been incorporated into the program at a cost of about US$47 million.[13] FONAFIFO has pending applications covering an additional 800,000ha, which it has been unable to fulfil due to lack of funding.

Of the various contracts that PSA offers, forest conservation contracts have been by far the most popular, accounting for 82.5 per cent of all contracts. Sustainable forest management accounts for 10.2 per cent of contracts, and reforestation for 7 per cent of contracts (FONAFIFO, personal communication). The impact of the PSA program, therefore, is likely to have taken the form of preventing deforestation, rather than increasing current forest cover.

In assessing the impact the program has had on forest cover, a key question concerns how much of this gain is incremental – that is, how much deforestation or reforestation would have occurred on the same land in the absence of the PSA program? There is some evidence that pasture was in any case becoming less profitable, particularly in marginal areas, and that some reversion to forest might have occurred anyway (White and others, 2001). However, Aylward and others (1998) find that pasture can be quite profitable in some areas. Deforestation data are as unreliable in Costa Rica as they are in most countries, making this question difficult to answer. Estimates show that by 1997, annual deforestation rates had fallen from a high of perhaps 50,000ha to under 20,000ha; reforestation would have reduced the net loss of forests, and may in fact have led to a net gain in recent years (World Bank, 2000a).[14] The average of 40,000 ha protected by the PSA program every year thus may well be playing a significant role in protecting Costa Rica's forests, even if only a part of that area is truly incremental.

Efficiency in water service provision

The overall efficiency of the PSA program in terms of providing water services is probably not very high, though the paucity of data on forest–hydrology links makes this very difficult to evaluate. Water services depend on the nature of land use and its location. An undifferentiated payment system in which everyone can participate, and which pays everyone the same amounts, will be much more expensive than a targeted scheme, because it will include many participants who bring few or no benefits and may exclude, for lack of funds, many potential participants who would have brought great benefits. Until recently, the PSA program was largely untargeted: although some areas were identified as priority areas, in general any landowner, anywhere within Costa Rica, was eligible to participate. Criteria for participation were limited to the legal requirement of having a land title, and the preparation of a satisfactory management plan. There was some limited targeting in macro terms, aimed particularly at biodiversity conservation priorities, but no targeting in micro terms (for example, there was no effort to target particular areas within a watershed that are particularly valuable from the perspective of water services, such as riparian zones or steep slopes). An analysis of the efficiency of the PSA program in providing biodiversity protection services, for example, showed that the same degree of protection could be achieved more cost effectively by increasing the size of protected areas (World Bank, 2000b).[15] The ability to target a program of protected areas, thus maximizing the degree of protection gained per dollar spent, is a major reason for its greater efficiency over the PSA program in this regard.

Recent years have seen the PSA program evolve toward greater targeting. Service users such as HEP producers have insisted that conservation funded by their resources should be targeted in areas of interest to them. Thus, HEP producers only finance payments in the watersheds from which they draw their water. Similarly, GEF financing for biodiversity protection is targeted at land users in areas deemed to be of high biodiversity interest.[16] This weakness of the PSA program as originally implemented is thus rapidly being corrected. Subject to the uncertainties created by the limited hydrological data, cost effectiveness is probably also increasing.

Cost effectiveness of water service provision

Efficiency is not just a matter of generating high levels of services, but also of not doing so when the value of the service is low or the cost is excessive. In this sense, the cost that matters is the opportunity cost to society of the forgone land use, not the financial cost of the payment to land users. Given the relatively low payments to land users under the PSA program, the likelihood that this will happen is correspondingly low. Areas with high opportunity costs will simply not be enrolled in the program.[17]

A related problem is that of avoiding perverse incentives. For example, a United Nations Food and Agriculture Organization (FAO) study of Costa Rican reforestation incentives in the late 1980s and early 1990s (prior to the PSA program) found that companies were buying areas of natural forest, harvesting the timber, and then applying for reforestation credits (Morell, 1997). To address this problem, FONAFIFO requires applicants to certify that timber has not been harvested for at least two years prior to signature of the contract.

Sustainability

Sustainability has two dimensions: ensuring that beneficiaries continue to pay for the services they receive, and ensuring that service providers continue to provide the services.

Sustainability of payments means that service buyers must be satisfied that they are receiving the services they pay for. That there is practically no monitoring of this impact poses a potential threat, therefore, to the long-term sustainability of the program. Even if the linkage between forest cover and water services is exactly as expected, careful monitoring would still be useful as it would allow improved targeting of areas where forest cover is particularly useful, or refinement of the eligible land uses.

The sustainability of land use changes promoted by the PSA program is hard to assess at present because no contracts undertaken under the PSA have yet expired. In the case of forest conservation contracts – which form the vast majority of contracts agreed with landowners – there is no expectation of sustainability unless the contracts are renewed. Without continuing payments, landowners would clearly no longer have additional incentives to continue to conserve forests.[18] FONAFIFO does intend to renew these contracts, to the extent that resources allow.[19] In the case of reforestation contracts, the expectation is that landowners will continue with the agreed land use even after payments cease. Indeed, this is a legal requirement under the contract. The reasoning here is that the PSA payment help landowners to finance the initial investment of reforestation, converting what would have been an unprofitable investment into a profitable one. As PSA participants who signed such contracts are still receiving payments, it is impossible at this stage to assess what will happen once payments cease. The track record of other efforts to finance reforestation in similar ways does not give much basis for optimism, however.

Equity

About 60 per cent of PSA program participants are small and medium-sized farmers enrolled through community-based contracts (World Bank, 2000b). In general, landowners with high-productivity land are unlikely to participate in the PSA program, given the relatively low payments. Owners of low-productivity land are more likely to be poor than owners of high-productivity land. No socio-economic information is available about households in the watersheds targeted by water service payments. However, the low rate of titling in these watersheds suggests that they tend to be poor. Studies of the biological corridors targeted for GEF-financed payments under the Ecomarkets program – some of which overlap with watersheds targeted by water service payments – found them to be among the poorest areas in Costa Rica (World Bank, 2000b). The very high level of applications for participation in the PSA program provide a prima facie case that the payments provided are higher than the income that farmers might otherwise obtain from these lands. Thus, although neither the PSA program in general nor its water services activities in particular are specifically intended to alleviate poverty, it is likely that they provide valuable additional income to relatively poor farm households.

The restrictions on participation by landowners without titles is probably the most important limitation on poorer landowners benefiting from the PSA program. It is important to remember that this limitation originates in Costa Rican law, not in the PSA program itself. FONAFIFO has sought to overcome this hurdle, as in the case of the revised contract with Platanar.

Concern over the potential equity impact of the PSA program does not mean that the program should be allowed to become primarily a vehicle for the achievement of poverty alleviation or other social objectives, however. Targeting payments on a basis other than delivery of services would rapidly alienate service buyers, thus drying up funding. But to the extent that obstacles such as the need for land titles prevent poorer households from participating, efforts need to be made to overcome them.

CONCLUSIONS

Costa Rica's PSA program is an innovative approach to a problem that has hitherto defied solution. Pioneering also has its downside, however. As is inevitable with any innovative approach, there are some problems and weaknesses. Many of these are being addressed as the program develops.

Whatever the assessment of the overall PSA program, it is clear that so far only a very small part of the area treated under the program (2400ha out of the 200,000ha) has been specifically financed by payments for water services, although this proportion is set to increase rapidly in the next few years. The potential to finance forest conservation with payments for water services has barely been exploited. Looking at HEP producers, in addition to the four private plants that have agreed to pay for water services, there are five more plants that have not yet done so, and several others are at various stages of construction.

The main remaining weakness, which affects both the present effectiveness of the program and its future sustainability, is the lack of reliable and precise qualitative and quantitative information about the links between forest cover and water services.

The Costa Rican PSA program is nationwide in scope and seeks to provide a variety of services. In many cases, the system is too big. Many of the specific situations covered by the PSA program might have been handled by ad hoc mechanisms: this has been the case in La Esperanza, for example. But the Esperanza case is unusual in that the entire watershed is owned by a single entity, the Monteverde Conservation League. The service buyer was thus able to negotiate directly with the seller (Rojas and Aylward, forthcoming). In most cases, land in watersheds is owned by many landowners. Under these circumstances, creating ad hoc structures in each instance is likely to be difficult and expensive. As the PSA program already has in place the necessary institutional framework, it is able to take on new problems at very little additional cost.

Potential for replication

The problem addressed by the PSA program is a very common one: forests provide many services to people other than forest managers. In particular, forests play an important role in the provision of water services that are enjoyed by people downstream. This mismatch means that forest management decisions are often suboptimal. Costa Rica's efforts to pioneer a system of sustainable payments for environmental services has generated considerable interest. Its Central American neighbors have followed it particularly closely, and several are studying similar approaches.

Besides Costa Rica, El Salvador is the Central American country which has gone furthest toward creating a system of payments for environmental services (Pagiola and Platais, forthcoming; Herrador and Dimas, 2000).[20] Very high deforestation has reduced forest cover to less than 12 per cent of the country's area, the lowest level in Central America, and the second lowest in Latin America after Haiti. Deforestation is thought to have contributed to a multitude of problems, including increased vulnerability to flooding and landslides, both of which have become regular occurrences; reduced water availability during the dry season; and sedimentation of reservoirs and damage to irrigation and municipal water supply systems. As in the case of Costa Rica, however, the link between deforestation and these problems has not been established conclusively (Kaimowitz, 2000).

To address these problems, El Salvador is considering establishing a system of payments for environmental services similar to that developed in Costa Rica, with World Bank assistance.[21] This system would use payment mechanisms to obtain environmental services such as watershed protection and the creation of biodiversity corridors to link the country's protected areas (Pagiola and Platais, forthcoming). Initial thinking focused on efforts to reduce vulnerability to flooding and landslides, partly because of their urgency, and partly because of the availability of data allowing the identification of areas at risk. The same payment mechanism would also have been used to encourage the adoption of biodiversity-friendly land uses in corridors connecting the protected areas, with financing from GEF. Measures to secure other national benefits, including several water services, would have been introduced later, as data became available. The program has since evolved so that it would encompass a broader range of national benefits from the start, including not only risk reduction but also measures to reduce sedimentation of waterways and to improve water resource management. In every case, interventions would be tied directly to payments from beneficiaries from the start, rather than to generic funds like Costa Rica's gas tax. Initial efforts would be focused on four or five high priority sub-watersheds, rather than attempting to establish a national environmental services program.

El Salvador's high population density and the pressure on available land is likely to make reforestation impractical as the primary measure used to generate environmental services. Rather, land use practices that allow for the continued productive use of the land while generating positive externalities are being sought. For example, shade-grown coffee can harbor high levels of biodiversity (see Chapter 7), and may also provide water services.

Because of the planned reliance on beneficiary payments, and to maximize the efficiency of the program, it would be targeted from the start, both in macro (watershed) and micro (within the watershed) terms. To reduce transaction costs and simplify contracting, participants would not be required to produce management plans. Rather, the program would produce lists of eligible activities for target areas based on the services being sought (activities aimed at reducing sedimentation, for example, need not be the same as those aimed at creating biological corridors between protected areas). Contracts would be of relatively short durations, but renewable indefinitely. This would have two advantages: non-compliance could be punished simply by not renewing the contract, and the list of eligible activities could be revised frequently as better information becomes available on the links between particular land uses and environmental services.

The main challenges that El Salvador is facing in establishing such a system are two-fold. First, there is the need to identify areas that generate environmental services, and the specific activities within those areas that generate them. Second, the institutions that would manage the program need to be established, either by creating appropriate ones or by building the capacity of existing ones. A steering committee is being established to prepare the project, led by El Salvador's Ministry of the Environment (MARN) and including representatives from other government agencies, NGOs, potential services buyers such as the national electricity company, municipalities, and civil society groups.

NOTES

1   This Chapter has benefited from discussions with Edgar Ortiz of the Ecomarkets Project, Jorge Mario Rodríguez, Alexandra Sáenz Faerrón, Oscar Sánchez Chaves, Bayardo José Reyes Guerrero, and Luis Sage Mora at FONAFIFO, John Kellenberg, Jeff Muller, and Gunars Platais at the World Bank, and Bruce Aylward. Any remaining errors are the author's sole responsibility. All opinions expressed in this paper are the author's own and do not necessarily reflect those of the World Bank.
2   Many factors other than land use can also have significant impacts on water services. Pollution from domestic, industrial, and agricultural effluents is severely affecting water quality, for example, while settlement in low-lying areas has increased the number of people vulnerable to floods.
3   It is interesting to note that many projects provided subsidies for the adoption of particular land use practices even as they argued that it was in land users' interest to adopt them. Such subsidies have usually been justified as helping to overcome investment constraints or risk-aversion.
4   *Regentes* are licensed forest engineers. They are the forest equivalent of notaries public, qualified to certify whether activities meet forest management standards.
5   FONAFIFO is hoping to convince AyA to implement a similar water tariff supplement scheme in the municipalities that it supplies, with the resources being channelled through FONAFIFO to the PSA program.
6   Law No 7200 of 1990 partially privatized power generation in Costa Rica. Private power producers must use renewable energy sources, such as hydroelectricity, and are limited to plants of 20 megawatts of installed capacity. Their combined contribution cannot exceed 15 per cent of total installed capacity in the country.

7 Kishor and Constantino (1993), for example, found that clearing land for pasture was much more profitable for landowners than maintaining natural forest.

8 Payment levels have regularly been adjusted for inflation. Current payments for forest conservation are about US$42/ha/year.

9 FONAFIFO is studying the creation of a parallel program of reforestation incentives aimed at increasing timber production.

10 The only exception is in the case of the Platanar River watershed, as discussed below.

11 Under the reforestation contract, 50 per cent of the US$538 payment is paid in the first year, 20 per cent in the second year, 15 per cent in the third, 10 per cent in the fourth, and 5 per cent in the fifth.

12 FONAFIFO is also exploring the possibility of making these certificates transferable, and of selling them through an auction or other market mechanism rather than for a fixed price. Given that water services are very location-specific, however, it is unclear whether a meaningful secondary market for such certificates would exist.

13 Total forest cover in Costa Rica is about 2 million ha, of which a little over half is privately owned.

14 Note that this estimate includes the effect of the pre-PSA subsidies to reforestation and forest management.

15 However, increasing the size of protected areas would have been much more costly in financial terms, given the need to buy land for this purpose.

16 Under the Ecomarkets project, one-half of GEF's co-financed conservation easements is targeted to areas within Costa Rica's portion of the Mesoamerican Biological Corridor in Tortuguero, La Amistad Caribe, and Osa Peninsula. The other half is targeted on other priority areas as identified in a 1996 evaluation of conservation priorities (the GRUAS Report).

17 However, relatively low payments to land users have the disadvantage of making participation vulnerable to relatively small changes in the profitability of alternative land uses. The low level of payments under the PSA program was one of the reasons for Heredia's creation of a parallel system of payments for environmental services in its watershed. Opportunity costs of land are relatively high in that watershed, and payments under the PSA's program conservation contract would have been too low to attract participants.

18 It is important to stress that what matters is the duration of the payment, not the duration of the contract. A contract that last relatively few years before being renewed is in many ways attractive, as it permits a periodic adjustment of the terms of the contract and a reassessment of the usefulness of contracting in specific areas.

19 Since most financing sources now insist on targeting payments, contracts outside target areas may not be renewed. The process of contract renewal, therefore, will help to gradually increase the efficiency of service provision.

20 There have also been a number of local initiatives. For example, the municipality of San Francisco de Menéndez has agreed to pay for several guards at the El Imposible National Park, which will help to protect the watershed from which the community derives its water.

21 Since late 1999, the World Bank has been assisting El Salvador's Ministry of the Environment (MARN) to prepare a project that will establish a system of payments for environmental services in the country. Work was placed on hold following the devastating earthquakes that hit El Salvador in January 2001, but resumed in late 2001.

REFERENCES

Aylward, B., and J. Echevarría. 2001. "Synergies Between Livestock Production and Hydrological Function in Arenal, Costa Rica." *Environment and Development Economics*, 6, pp.359–381.

Aylward, B., J. Echevarría, A. Fernández González, I. Porras, K. Allen, and R. Mejías. 1998. "Economic Incentives for Watershed Protection: A Case Study of Lake Arenal, Costa Rica." CREED Final Report. London: IIED.

Bruijnzeel, L.A. 1990. *Hydrology of Moist Tropical Forests and Effects of Conservation: A State of Knowledge Review*. UNESCO International Hydrological Programme. Paris: UNESCO.

Calder, I. 1999. *The Blue Revolution: Land Use and Integrated Water Resource Management*. London: Earthscan.

Castro, E. 2001. "Costarrican Experience in the Charge for Hydro Environmental Services of the Biodiversity to Finance Conservation and Recuperation of Hillside Ecosystems." Paper presented at the International Workshop on Market Creation for Biodiversity Products and Services, OECD, Paris, 25–26 January 2001 (processed).

Castro, R., and F. Tattenbach, with N. Olson and L. Gamez. 1997. "The Costa Rican Experience with Market Instruments to Mitigate Climate Change and Conserve Biodiversity." Paper presented at the Global Conference on Knowledge for Development in the Information Age, Toronto, Canada, 24 June 1997 (processed).

Chomitz, K.M., E. Brenes, and L. Constantino. 1999. "Financing Environmental Services: The Costa Rican Experience and its Implications." *Science of the Total Environment*, 240, pp.157–169.

Chomitz, K.M., and K. Kumari. 1998. "The Domestic Benefits of Tropical Forest Preservation: A Critical Review Emphasizing Hydrological Functions." *World Bank Research Observer*, 13:1, pp.13–35.

Cuesta, M.D. 1994. "Economic Analysis of Soil Conservation Projects in Costa Rica." In E. Lutz, S. Pagiola, and C. Reiche (eds.), *Economic and Institutional Analyses of Soil Conservation Projects in Central America and the Caribbean*. Environment Paper No.8. Washington: World Bank.

Enters, T. 1997. "The Token Line: Adoption and Non-Adoption of Soil Conservation Practices in the Highlands of Northern Thailand." In S. Sombatpanit, M.A. Zöbisch, D.W. Sanders, and M.G. Cook (eds.), *Soil Conservation Extension: From Concepts to Adoption*. Enfield: Science Publishers Inc.

Fondo Nacional de Financiamiento Forestal (FONAFIFO). 2000. *El Desarollo del Sistema de Pago de Servicios Ambientales en Costa Rica*. San José: FONAFIFO.

Hamilton, L.S., and P.N. King. 1983. *Tropical Forest Watersheds: Hydrologic and Soils Response to Major Uses and Conversions*. Boulder: Westview Press.

Herrador, D., and L. Dimas. 2000. "Payment for Environmental Services in El Salvador." *Mountain Research and Development*, 20:4, pp.306–309.

Kaimowitz, D. 2000. "Useful Myths and Intractable Truths: The Politics of the Link Between Forests and Water in Central America." San José: CIFOR (processed).

Kishor, N.M., and L.F. Constantino. 1993. "Forest Management and Competing Land Uses: An Economic Analysis for Costa Rica." LATEN Dissemination Note No.7. Washington: World Bank.

Leonard, H.J. 1987. *Natural Resources and Economic Development in Central America: A Regional Environmental Profile*. New Brunswick: Transaction Books.

Lutz, E., S. Pagiola, and C. Reiche. 1994. "The Costs and Benefits of Soil Conservation: The Farmers' Viewpoint." *World Bank Research Observer*, 9:2, pp.273–295.

Morell, M. 1997. "Financing Community Forestry Activities." *Unasylva*, 188, pp.36–43.

Pagiola, S. 1999. "Economic Analysis of Incentives for Soil Conservation." In D.W. Sanders, P.C. Huszar, S. Sombatpanit, and T. Enters (eds.), *Using Incentives for Soil Conservation*. Science Publishers, Inc.

Pagiola, S. Forthcoming. "Farmer Responses to Land Degradation." In K. Wiebe (ed.), *Land Resources, Agricultural Productivity, and Food Security*. Cheltenham: Edward Elgar.

Pagiola, S., and G. Platais. 2001. "Selling Biodiversity in Central America." Paper presented at the International Workshop on Market Creation for Biodiversity Products and Services, OECD, Paris, January 25–26, 2001.

Pagiola, S., and G. Platais. Forthcoming. *Payments for Environmental Services*. Washington: World Bank.

Peuker, A. 1992. "Public Policies and Deforestation: A Case Study of Costa Rica." Latin America and Caribbean Regional Studies Program Report No.14. Washington: World Bank (processed).

Rojas, M., and B. Aylward. Forthcoming. "The Case of La Esperanza: A Small, Private, Hydropower Producer and a Conservation NGO in Costa Rica." In B. Kiersch (ed.), *Valuation of Land Use Impacts on Water Resources and Mechanisms for Upstream-downstream Cooperation in Rural Watersheds*. Rome: FAO.

White, D., F. Holmann, S. Fijusaka, K. Reategui, and C. Lascano. 2001. "Will Intensifying Pasture Management in Latin America Protect Forests – Or is it the Other Way Round?" In A. Angelsen and D. Kaimowitz (eds.), *Agricultural Technologies and Tropical Deforestation*. Wallingford: CABI Publishing.

World Bank. 2000a. *Costa Rica: Forest Strategy and the Evolution of Land Use*. OED Evaluation Country Case Study Series. Washington: World Bank.

World Bank. 2000b. "Ecomarkets Project: Project Appraisal Document." Report No. 20434-CR. Washington: World Bank (processed).

Chapter 4

Sharing the Benefits of Watershed Management in Sukhomajri, India

John Kerr[1]

A watershed or catchment is an area from which all water drains to a common point, making it an attractive unit for soil and water conservation. In seasonally dry areas, watershed management is seen as a way to raise rainfed agricultural production, conserve natural resources, and reduce poverty. These areas are common in South Asia and sub-Saharan Africa. They were little affected by the green revolution that transformed agriculture in more favorable areas. They suffer from low agricultural productivity, severe natural resource degradation, and high levels of poverty.

In much of India, watershed projects aim to capture water during rainy periods for subsequent use in dry periods (Farrington and others, 1999). This involves conserving soil moisture to support crop growth, capturing surface runoff water in small ponds or tanks, and encouraging water infiltration to recharge aquifers. In hilly areas the main project activity is the construction of water harvesting structures (for example, small dams) in the drainage lines of upper catchments to capture runoff water. To be sustainable, water harvesting requires the protection of the upper reaches of watersheds against erosion that would reduce water storage capacity in the lower reaches. What makes watershed development so attractive is that productivity and conservation objectives are highly complementary. Watershed projects exist in a broad range of sizes, but many of them operate at the level of small micro-watersheds that lie within a single village.

In densely populated areas, village-level watershed projects are often complicated by the fact that people use upper and lower reaches of watersheds for multiple, possibly incompatible purposes. Upper catchments often contain a large proportion of uncultivated common land that is typically denuded. In this case protecting against erosion requires revegetating the landscape, which in turn means placing limits on grazing and firewood collection (Farrington and others, 1999). This imposes costs on poor, often landless people who rely on these lands the most.[2] The benefits of water harvesting, meanwhile, accrue disproportionately downstream, where the wealthiest farmers typically own most of the irrigable land. In other words, upper catchments can provide an environmental service to lower catchments, but the people who use upper catchments would not receive any benefit from providing this service and so may not be willing to provide it without compensation (Johnson and others, 2001).

Under these conditions, watershed development raises the possibility of a trade-off between conservation and productivity objectives, on the one hand, and equity objectives on the other. When such trade-offs exist, successful watershed development requires either the development of institutional mechanisms to ensure that all parties benefit, or a plan to force upstream users to restrict resource use and provide the environmental service without compensation. Projects are unlikely to result in conservation and productivity benefits if agreements cannot be reached or downstream users cannot impose their will on upstream users.[3]

Most Indian watershed projects employ a variety of approaches to promote equity, but very few if any of them frame the issue as one of an environmental service that the upper catchment provides to the lower catchment. Instead, they undertake a variety of indirect measures, such as offering wage employment to the poor to compensate them for lost access to the commons, and implement various non-land-based activities such as credit and thrift groups (Kerr, 2002). These measures may provide real benefits to poor people, but they do nothing to give them an intrinsic interest in the watershed development effort. As such some people may still resent the loss of access to common lands, and they may have an incentive not to abide by project agreements.

Some projects aim to avoid working in areas that have large proportions of landless people or high dependence on common land. Fernandez (1994) explains that MYRADA, a non-governmental organization (NGO) in southern India, works only in areas in which less than 10 per cent of households are landless, since this makes it easier to generate sufficient benefits to support them while also closing access to common lands. A recent study in Maharashtra, meanwhile, found that two-thirds of NGO projects surveyed worked in villages with no common land, even though about three-quarters of villages do have common land (Kerr and others, 2002).

SUKHOMAJRI

Since the mid-1970s, the small village of Sukhomajri, in the northern Indian state of Haryana, has provided a model of watershed development in which productivity, conservation, and equity objectives are all in harmony. In the environmental literature it is one of the most often cited villages in India. It helped to inspire modern watershed development programs, which now command over US$450 million annually from all sources (Farrington and others, 1999).

This Chapter draws on the extensive literature about Sukhomajri in order to focus on the institutional mechanisms by which the village's inhabitants shared the costs and benefits of environmental restoration to ensure that everyone gained from the process. It describes the setting and the technical and institutional initiatives, summarizes the economic benefits and their distribution, and discusses lessons drawn from efforts to replicate the approach in other locations.

The Sukhomajri case actually involves two upstream–downstream environmental relationships with two separate institutional arrangements. The first involves the relationship between Sukhomajri and Chandigarh, a large city 15 kilometers (km) downstream, and the second involves the relationship between upstream and downstream land users within the village. In both cases, a form of market mechanism was utilized to secure the provision of environmental services in the form of soil conservation to prevent the siltation of downstream water bodies. These are discussed in turn.

SHARING BENEFITS BETWEEN SUKHOMAJRI AND CHANDIGARH

As related by Seckler (1986) and Sarin (1996), in 1974 officials and citizens in Chandigarh were concerned by the gradual siltation of Sukhna Lake, a popular recreation site. Attempts to dredge the lake proved to be not only expensive but futile. Sukhna Lake would eventually disappear completely unless the erosion in the lake's watershed was contained. P R Mishra, the director of the Chandigarh office of the Central Soil and Water Conservation Research and Training Institute (CSWCRTI), organized a project to install soil conservation structures in the lake's watershed. He traced the source of silt to a denuded, highly eroded hillside on the edge of Sukhomajri village, about 15km upstream. One side of the hill drained into the Sukhna lake watershed and the other side drained into Sukhomajri village, where runoff water flooded and destroyed agricultural lands. Mr Mishra's team revegetated both watersheds and installed conservation structures such as check dams and gully plugs to stop the flow of silt. When the rain came, the check dam in the Sukhomajri watershed filled with water, presenting the opportunity to irrigate the fields below. The team constructed three additional check dams to take advantage of the opportunity to provide irrigation. Meanwhile, the team requested that villagers refrain from allowing grazing animals into either the Sukhna Lake watershed or the Sukhomajri watershed.

The CSWCRTI's construction of runoff ponds in Sukhomajri compensated the village for providing Chandigarh with the environmental service of protecting the hillside in the Sukhna Lake watershed.[4] The city did not pay for the Sukhomajri project work; CSWCRTI carried out the work utilizing its own budget. This organization was best suited to conduct the work and, at the time, central government-funded agricultural research institutes had no mechanisms for accepting funds on a contractual basis. Also, in the 1970s there was little familiarity with the notion of markets for environmental services, so it is not likely that the project was conceived in this way. However, in effect it worked in the same way as an environmental services payment; it is unlikely that Sukhomajri's residents would have agreed to protect the Sukhna Lake watershed in the absence of the water harvesting opportunity.

SHARING BENEFITS WITHIN SUKHOMAJRI

In Sukhomajri, a problem quickly emerged: the runoff ponds provided irrigation water to only a minority of landowners with holdings below the pond. These people had every incentive to protect the watershed against erosion that would silt the pond; making it off-limits to grazing animals would be a small price for them to pay. However, others in the village, including the landless, had no such incentive and stood to lose if they were forced to abandon the hillside as a grazing resource. A stand-off between those who received irrigation and those who did not threatened to undermine the arrangement to protect the Sukhna Lake watershed and the smaller watershed of the catchment ponds.

Eventually, a simple but ingenious solution was reached that ensured that all households would benefit from eliminating grazing in the watershed. First, pipes were laid so that most fields in the village would receive water. More importantly, all households, both landed and landless, would share equally in the ownership of the water in the catchment ponds. Moreover, water rights would be tradable so that the landless could sell their share to landowning households, which could use it for irrigation. Alternatively, landless households could hire cropland and utilize their water share directly (Seckler, 1986). Villagers insisted that this arrangement, which was unique in the region, would be necessary to ensure that everyone had an incentive to protect the watershed (Sarin, 1996).

Village-level management in Sukhomajri revolves around the Hill Resource Management Society (HRMS), which has one representative from each household. The HRMS provides a forum for all households to discuss their problems, manage the local environment and maintain discipline among their members. It sets the rules of access to resources, and particularly those concerning equal access to water and biomass. When the water sharing system was first devised, each household received a tradable coupon good for its share of water, which was not tied to the right to land. This system was cumbersome and raised complications as water levels fluctuated from year to year, so the villagers came up with the idea that anyone who withdrew water from the pond would have to buy it from the HRMS, which in turn would distribute the proceeds equally among the members (Sarin, 1996).

In addition to receiving equal access to water, villagers also shared the rights to collect *bhabber* grass growing in the watershed. *Bhabber* is a strong, fibrous grass used as pulp for paper when it is mature; it provides good fodder when it is young (when it is known as *mungri*). Before the project, the Forest Department would lease *bhabber* grass to paper mill contractors at low prices. Sometimes the contractors would sell fodder back to the villagers at a higher price. Eventually the Forest Department agreed to give the lease directly to the villagers, on the condition that the Forest Department would receive no less revenue than it had in the past. The idea was that grass production would increase if villagers had a greater incentive to protect and nurture it. This system was so successful that Sukhomajri eventually became the first village in India to be charged income tax on the value of biomass grown on common lands in the village (Mahapatra, 1998). The villagers (through the HRMS) receive about 45 per cent of the proceeds. A similar arrangement will be made for timber when it is cut. Forest trees technically belong to the Forest Department, which plans to keep 75 per cent of the net revenue from harvesting the lumber and give the rest to the villagers (Agarwal, 1999).

OUTCOMES

Watershed development in Sukhomajri resulted in benefits in both the Sukhna Lake and Sukhomajri watersheds. It led to a major transformation in the village, with spectacular success in regenerating vegetation on the hillsides, increasing agricultural production, and raising incomes throughout the village.

Soil conservation

Siltation into Sukhna Lake declined by about 95 per cent, saving the city of Chandigarh about US$200,000 annually in dredging and related costs (Chopra and others, 1990). In effect, the project saved the lake, because it is not clear that the city would have been willing to invest so much to maintain the lake's recreation benefits. Siltation and flooding in the Sukhomajri watershed also came to a halt.

Revegetation

At the time the project began in 1976, barely 5 per cent of the hillside above Sukhomajri contained vegetative cover. By 1992, the production of various useful grasses rose from 40 kilogrammes (kg) per hectare to three tons on average, and tree density rose from 13 per hectare to 1292 per hectare. Agarwal (1999) estimated the value of the 400ha Sukhomajri forest at over US$20 million, capable of generating at least US$700,000 annually through sustainable yield harvesting. The Forest Department has not harvested any trees; it has yet to make a decision on when to do so. Forest grass is also a valuable resource. *Mungri* provides fodder and *bhabber* is sold to paper mills. Its price fluctuates, but in the 1990s the forest yielded nearly US$3000-worth of *bhabber* annually. From this sum, the Forest Department levies a series of taxes worth about 55 per cent of the net profit while the HRMS keeps the rest. Villagers also harvest the young *mungri* grass to feed to their livestock; the value of the amount collected is not known but it contributes to a highly profitable milk economy. Anyone who collects *mungri* must pay the HRMS. The HRMS distributes all of its revenues (from sales of water, *bhabber*, and *mungri*) equally among all households.

Livestock

At the time the project began in 1976, most of Sukhomajri's inhabitants depended on livestock for their income. Most of the herd consisted of goats that could forage in the degraded watershed, plus a number of half-starved grazing cows. With the increase in production of *mungri* grass and the ability to grow irrigated fodder in the dry season, people were able to transform the herd into one consisting mainly of stall-fed buffaloes and improved dairy cows. The number of goats fell from 246 in 1975 to 10 in 1986, while the number of buffaloes rose from 79 in 1975 to 291 in 1986 (Agarwal, 1999). This led to an increase in milk production from 334 litres per day in 1977 to over 2000 in the late 1990s (Mahapatra, 1998). This transformation enabled the village to become a major producer of milk, with annual sales of about US$8000.

Crops

The increase in the irrigated area enabled a major increase in crop production, with maize and wheat yields more than doubling within ten years (Agarwal, 1999). Cropping patterns diversified.

Incomes and housing

Higher dairy and crop production and employment and wages, all made possible by the protection of the Sukhomajri watershed, led to greatly improved living standards. Household incomes rose by an average of 50 per cent between 1979 and 1984, with all households gaining (Agarwal, 1999). Before the project most people lived in mud-and-thatch houses, but by 1998 almost 90 per cent of people lived in modern brick-and-mortar houses, with the remainder living in semi-modern houses (Agarwal and Narain, 1999). A survey in 1998 showed that Sukhomajri contained a smaller proportion of people living below the poverty line than the state of Haryana as a whole (Agarwal, 1999, citing Gulati and Sharma, 1998). This is impressive because Haryana is one of the richest states in India, while Sukhomajri lies in one of its poorest regions.

In summary, the project led to strong improvements in natural resource conditions in both Chandigarh and Sukhomajri, and it caused equitable increases in household income in Sukhomajri. An economic analysis of the project estimated a rate of return of around 10 to 19 per cent depending on the assumptions made (Chopra and others, 1990).

Experience with replication efforts

The highly successful experience in Sukhomajri led to efforts to replicate the technical model of village-level watershed management elsewhere. The first experiments came in a small number of neighboring villages with funding from the Ford Foundation and the CSWCRTI. Today, watershed projects throughout the country follow essentially the same technical approach.

The initial replication efforts succeeded in a few neighboring villages that adopted the same institutional arrangement to share net benefits. Efforts to spread the approach more widely in the area, however, faced difficulties. CSWCRTI and the Ford Foundation had to play important roles not only in providing funding and technical assistance, but also in helping to enforce benefit-sharing mechanisms. In Sukhomajri the water distribution system was largely self-governing, but outside organizations had to play a bigger role when the project was replicated elsewhere. In many locations, people were unable to abide by water sharing mechanisms, and the CSWCRTI had to play the role of external arbitrator to force everyone to comply.

Certain other aspects of the institutional model have been replicated as well. In particular, in 1990 the Indian government initiated the Joint Forest Management program, whereby the Forest Department shares the value of biomass with villagers. A few watershed projects grant rights to biomass or fishing to landless people under informal arrangements. Sharing irrigation water, on the other hand, is a rarity that has worked in very few projects.

Almost all projects publicize their commitment to poverty alleviation, and many stress the need to help poor and landless people, but only a small minority of NGO projects have tried to develop institutional mechanisms by which landless people would share in the direct benefits of watershed development (Kerr and others, 2002). More specifically, very few of them seek mechanisms to share the enhanced irrigation water resources made possible by the project. As irrigation water is by far the most valuable resource generated by watershed management, this omission represents a failure to use watershed development as an equity-enhancing tool that gives all parties a stake in watershed development.

Instead, virtually all projects focus on generating temporary employment for landless people. Watershed development involves digging trenches, building small dams and barriers, and planting vegetation. This employment provides an important benefit to landless people, particularly because it is available during the slack season and because it is paid at the government-sanctioned minimum wage, which often exceeds the market wage. Project planners envision that successful watershed development will eventually lead to permanently increased employment by expanding the irrigated area and stimulating the local economy (Kerr and others, 2002).

It is difficult to estimate the efficiency of Sukhomajri's mechanism for watershed protection relative to approaches used in other watershed projects. In Sukhomajri the system has clearly succeeded in enhancing the natural resource base and increasing incomes, yet it has failed to spread. At the same time, despite the huge investment in watershed development throughout India, similar success stories are scarce, regardless of the mechanism used to encourage watershed protection (Kerr and others, 2002). In other words, the alternative systems that other projects use – mainly providing employment and non-land-based income-generating activities – do not appear to have been effective on a widespread basis either.

LESSONS: WHY DID THE SYSTEM WORK IN SUKHOMAJRI AND WHY DID IT FAIL TO SPREAD?

The experience of Sukhomajri and efforts to replicate its success offer several lessons. Three key factors were instrumental to the success of the Sukhomajri project. First, a watershed externality between Sukhomajri and the city of Chandigarh led to the initial interest in developing the Sukhna Lake and Sukhomajri watersheds. Construction of the Sukhomajri water harvesting structures effectively acted as a payment by downstream interests to compensate land users in Sukhomajri for refraining from using the upper watershed. Second, water harvesting initially benefited only farmers with land immediately below the water harvesting structure, so it provided no incentive for other people to protect the upper watershed. The initiative to share water rights among all residents, including the landless, can be seen as a type of environmental service payment. In fact the system was not a payment per se, but rather an agreement to share the benefits that would accrue from providing the service. Third, the remaining challenge was to encourage collective action to protect the common property forest. The usual possibility of free-riding exists in Sukhomajri as some people could be tempted to try to procure more than their share of forest products.

With this background in mind, this section presents some explanations of why the institutional mechanism of sharing water resources among all inhabitants worked in Sukhomajri but has not been widely replicated elsewhere.

Benefits must be substantial and attributable to watershed protection

Potential benefits, in terms of enhanced soil, water, and biomass resources, vary between villages depending on agroclimatic conditions, including whether the topography, soil types and climate are conducive to water harvesting.[5] If benefits are substantial, sharing them among all the affected people is much more feasible than if they are low. If benefits are not substantial enough to share, environmental services payments may not be economically viable, and collective action may not be forthcoming.

Both the Sukhna Lake and Sukhomajri watersheds offered substantial, traceable benefits. The unusually direct link between erosion in Sukhomajri and siltation of Sukhna Lake led to the initial investment by the CSWCRTI. In many cases, upstream–downstream relationships are harder to define, thus hampering the opportunity to offer payment for an environmental service.

Within the village, Sukhomajri benefited from water harvesting and reforestation, both of which offered considerable economic benefits. In fact, as mentioned earlier, water harvesting would not have been sustainable without afforestation, which prevented the rapid siltation of water harvesting structures. In this sense, water harvesting and afforestation are complementary. Afforestation without the added benefit of water harvesting would be much less attractive.

In Sukhomajri – as in some of India's other famous water harvesting success stories, such as Ralegaon Siddhi (Agarwal, 1999) – the terrain is well suited to water harvesting, with steep hills and drainage lines that can easily be dammed to capture water. The benefits of water harvesting are obvious to all. In contrast, in some places conditions for water harvesting are poor and the amount of additional water generated is relatively small. Similarly, in many cases it may be very difficult to attribute the availability of water in an aquifer to watershed project activities or to land use patterns upstream.

Benefits from grass and tree growth are also substantial in Sukhomajri. In much of India, degraded lands are characterized by the potential for rapid regeneration of biomass as long as they are protected against overgrazing and overharvesting (Bentley, 1984). In some drier areas in western India, growth potential is much lower and so afforestation is less attractive economically.

Transaction costs must be manageable

Collective action for watershed management involves transaction costs, most significantly around sharing benefits and 'social fencing' (self-policing without the use of fences). Sharing benefits requires establishing and maintaining arrangements to monitor and charge for the use of water and biomass, and to distribute the proceeds. Social fencing requires either that villagers trust each other to refrain from allowing their livestock to graze in the watershed, and/or that they devote resources to supervision. They must be willing to work collectively with their fellow villagers, and they must invest their time and goodwill to develop and sustain mechanisms for resolving conflicts.

In Sukhomajri, evidently these transaction costs have been bearable as the system appears to work. One reason for this may be that the village is unusually homogeneous and cohesive. With a small population who all belong to the same caste, the costs of cooperation may be lower than in most other villages. (The population was less than 500 at the beginning of the project and is about 1500 now.) With less than 10 per cent of the households having no land, benefits could be shared among all of them with relatively little dilution of landed households' shares. Also, the relatively even distribution of land holdings made it easy to agree to share water rights equally among households rather than on a per hectare basis.

In other villages, the costs of collective action may be too high relative to the benefits gained for people to bear. Costs of collective action vary across villages, often in nebulous ways that may be difficult for outsiders to perceive. In particular, villages vary in their social heterogeneity and in the extent to which people from different castes, religions, or socioeconomic groups trust each other. In some villages, working together to solve problems may be relatively easy, whereas in others it might go against hundreds of years of mistrust. In the latter case, not only does working together impose psychological costs in its own right, but the perceived risk that others will not honor agreements creates the expectation of monetary costs.

The notion of social capital is helpful in describing this situation (Woolcock, 1998; Uphoff and Wijayaratna, 2000). Sukhomajri has a relatively high degree of social capital owing to its unusual degree of homogeneity and cohesiveness. Other villages may have social capital in the form of pre-existing social institutions for acting collectively and managing conflicts.[6] Those villages with less social capital will face higher costs in coordinating their actions, making benefit-sharing arrangements less attractive. Many watershed projects implicitly or explicitly aim to build social capital through social institutions that facilitate collective action.

External assistance and supervision may be needed

CSWCRTI and the Ford Foundation played a strong role in the success of Sukhomajri and some of its neighbors. In addition to providing technical and financial assistance, they also played the role of arbitrator to help resolve conflicts and initiate and enforce water-sharing agreements. Seckler (1983) noted that in a village near Sukhomajri where the project was replicated, water sharing worked fine for a few years but then, when the project representative pulled out, a powerful landowner attempted to monopolize the irrigation water. In India's hierarchical, caste-divided society, in some villages it may be possible for irrigated landowners (who are typically wealthier and more powerful) to force others to go along with the program to ban grazing in the watershed. However, in addition to being inequitable, this system is likely to be unsustainable, because it eliminates the incentive for people to protect the upper watershed. In fact, project success in the village cited by Seckler did prove to be short-lived. Seckler (1983) speculated that some kind of external organization would have to play the role of impartial arbitrator in perpetuity.

Along similar lines, the Forest Department played an important role in creating enabling conditions in Sukhomajri by agreeing to change its claim to biomass in the upper watershed. Officially, the Forest Department owned the forest and the right to all proceeds from selling its products. By sharing the rights and revenues with Sukhomajri's HRMS, residents had a greater incentive to protect the watershed. In Sukhomajri this concession was offered as a special case. Eventually, however, the approach was formally adopted all over India under the Joint Forest Management program (Sarin, 1996).

Weak people need leverage to protect their interests

Fourth and perhaps most important, politically weak people need either legal rights or some other form of leverage if they are to insist on receiving an equitable share of benefits. In Sukhomajri, initially most households had no access to irrigation, but as livestock owners they all had leverage over those who did receive irrigation. If they allowed their livestock to overgraze the watershed, irrigation ponds would fill with silt and no landowners would benefit from them. This helped to pave the way for an equitable agreement.

In many other watersheds, potential losers from watershed development may have less leverage over their more powerful neighbors. In this case they might benefit from legal reform to grant them equitable access to natural resources. Unfortunately, legal provisions governing rights to water are not helpful in this regard. In most watersheds the most efficient way to harvest water is through percolation into groundwater aquifers, to be lifted through wells using electric pumps. This contrasts with Sukhomajri, where water was drawn from a pond by gravity. Indian water law states that whoever owns a piece of land has the right to pump whatever groundwater lies beneath it, so long as they do not interfere with drinking water supplies (Singh, 1991). Landowners who refuse to share water with others have the backing of the law, so watershed project authorities have no leverage over them. This presents a major constraint to efforts to develop innovative mechanisms to share water resources (personal communication from S P Tucker, former development commissioner, Andhra Pradesh).

Redesignating groundwater as a common property resource, owned by some well-defined group around village or aquifer boundaries, could help to give everyone an incentive to protect groundwater resources. For example, if landowners had to pay the communal owners a fee for the water they extracted from the ground (as they do in Sukhomajri), everyone – including the landless – would have an incentive to protect natural vegetation and maintain water harvesting structures to encourage water infiltration. The strength of this incentive would vary with location-specific water harvesting potential, but in any case it would create stronger incentives than those that currently exist.

As mentioned above, most watershed projects are very conservative when it comes to promoting equity through usufruct sharing mechanisms. Recently the central government proposed innovative new guidelines that explicitly call for arrangements to share the benefits of water and biomass (Government of India, 2000). These new guidelines are very progressive, but so far they offer no suggestions about how to accomplish this. A change in water law would be an important prerequisite to putting their vision into practice.

In summary, replicating watershed development requires it to generate a substantial number of benefits. People must be willing to live with the associated transaction costs, an external organization should play a facilitating role, and mechanisms to share net benefits must be generalized so that they can be easily implemented in any setting. None of these conditions can be guaranteed, so it is important to screen villages before starting work. The Indo-German Watershed Development Project in Maharashtra, one of the country's more successful watershed efforts, explicitly takes such an approach by working only where, among other things, water harvesting potential is high, people have already demonstrated the capacity to work collectively, and farmers agree not to grow water-intensive crops (Farrington and Lobo, 1997). Such screening mechanisms will continue to be important for success in watershed development, but a change in groundwater law would probably increase the prospects of favorable outcomes.

NOTES

1 The author thanks Stefano Pagiola, Natasha Landell-Mills, and Benjamin Kiersch for helpful comments on the paper, and Madhu Sarin for an explanation of benefit-sharing arrangements in Sukhomajri.
2 In the long run they would benefit from revegetation, but the loss of access for several years represents a very high cost.
3 Of course, in a third situation the upstream–downstream conflicts may be less important, such as when there is little or no grazing land in the upper catchment, or few people who depend on it, or when the topography does not present opportunities for water harvesting. However, watershed management offers the greatest potential benefits where water harvesting opportunities are the most promising, and this primarily means hilly areas with uncultivable land in the upper catchment. These are the cases with the greatest likelihood of upstream–downstream conflicts.
4 For details about the technical work conducted in Sukhomajri, see Grewal and others, 1989.
5 Benefits also depend on the value of the water delivered. Other things being equal, water harvesting is more valuable where water is scarce.
6 Without using the term 'social capital', Jodha (1986) demonstrated the importance of existing social institutions in facilitating the introduction of collective action to manage common property resources.

REFERENCES

Agarwal, A. 1999. "Population and Sustainable Development: Some Exploratory Relationships." Paper presented at the BMZ opening event at Expo 2000, Hanover, Germany, November 22, 1999.
* Agarwal, A., and S. Narain. 1999. "Community and Household Water Management: The Key to Environmental Regeneration and Poverty Alleviation." Paper presented to EU-UNDP Conference, Brussels, February 1999.
Bentley, W. 1984. "The Uncultivated Half of India: Problems and Possible Solutions." Discussion Paper No.12. New Delhi: Ford Foundation.
Chopra, K., G. Kadekodi, and M.N. Murthy. 1990. *Participatory Development: People and Common Property Resources.*. New Delhi: Sage Publications.
Farrington, J., C. Turton, and A.J. James (eds). 1999. *Participatory Watershed Development: Challenges for the Twenty-First Century*. New Delhi: Oxford University Press.
Farrington, J. and C. Lobo. 1997. "Scaling up Participatory Watershed Development in India: Lessons from the Indo-German Watershed Development Program." Natural Resource Perspectives No.17. London: Overseas Development Institute.
Fernandez, A. 1994. "The MYRADA Experience: the Interventions of a Voluntary Agency in the Emergence and Growth of Peoples' Institutions for Sustained and Equitable Management of Microwatersheds." Bangalore: MYRADA.

Government of India. 2000. "Common Approach for Watershed Development." New Delhi: Ministry of Agriculture and Cooperation.

Grewal, S.S., S.P. Mittal, Y. Agnihotri, and L.N. Dubey. 1989. "Rainwater Harvesting for the Management of Agricultural Droughts in the Foothills of Northern India." *Agricultural Water Management,* **16**, pp.309–322.

Gulati, S.C., and S. Sharma. 1998. "Population-Poverty-Environment Interface: Case Study of Sukhomajri, Jattamajri, Ralegan Siddhi and Panoli villages." New Delhi: Centre for Science and Environment.

Jodha, N.S. 1986. "Common Property Resources and the Rural Poor in Dry Regions of India." *Economic and Political Weekly,* 21:27.

Johnson, N., A. White, and D. Perrot-Maître. 2001. "Financial Incentives for Watershed Management: Issues and Lessons for Innovators." Washington: Forest Trends.

Kerr, J. 2002. "Watershed Development, Environmental Services, and Poverty Alleviation in India." *World Development,* 30:8.

Kerr, J., with G. Pangare and V. Pangare. 2002. "Watershed Development Projects in India: An Evaluation." Research Report. Washington: IFPRI.

Mahapatra, R.. 1998. "Sukhomajri at the Crossroads." *Down to Earth*, 7:14, pp.29–36.

Sarin, M. 1996. *Joint Forest Management: The Haryana Experience.* Ahmedabad: Centre for Environment Education.

Seckler, D. 1983. "Sukhomajri 1983: Retrospect and Prospect." Internal memo. New Delhi: Ford Foundation (processed).

Seckler, D. 1986. "Institutionalism and Agricultural Development in India." *Journal of Economic Issues,* 22:4, pp.1011–1027.

Uphoff, N., and C.M. Wijayaratna. 2000. "Demonstrated Benefits from Social Capital: the Productivity of Farmer Organizations in Gal Oya, Sri Lanka." *World Development,* 28:11, pp.1875–1890.

Woolcock, M. 1998. "Social Capital and Economic Development: Toward a Theoretical Synthesis and Policy Framework." *Theory and Society,* 27:2, pp.151–208.

Chapter 5

Paying to Protect Watershed Services: Wetland Banking in the United States

J Salzman and J B Ruhl

Over the last 15 years, approximately 0.5 million hectares of wetlands have been destroyed in the continental United States – roughly 1 per cent of the total.[1] Beyond the aesthetic loss, this has resulted in real economic loss. Wetlands provide a range of ecosystem services, from trapping nutrients and sediments, water purification, and groundwater recharge to flood control and support of bird, fish, and mammal populations. While not sold in markets, all of these services have real value. Often, however, their value is only realized after the wetlands have been destroyed, when property owners survey their flooded homes or face a large tax increase to pay for a new water plant to treat polluted drinking water. Opinions may differ over the value of a wetland's scenic vista, but they are in universal accord over the contributions of clean water and flood control to social welfare (Ewel, 1997).

While not a high priority issue, the public does recognize the general value of wetlands. During President George Bush Sr's election campaign in 1988, he pledged to ensure there would be 'no net loss' of wetlands. President Clinton reiterated this commitment in his campaign four years later. Thus far in his administration (early 2002), President George W Bush has allowed a Clinton-era rulemaking to move forward, closing a legal loophole that has resulted in the destruction of at least 8000ha of wetlands in the past few years.

Throughout the 1990s, more and more people moved to coastal and waterside properties, increasing pressure to develop wetlands. Pressures for development come up against strong laws that aim to protect wetlands. To defuse this conflict and threats to wetlands protection, the government has developed a market mechanism that seeks to ensure wetland conservation at minimum cost (both economically and politically). This mechanism, known as wetlands mitigation banking, is a habitat trading program that has been field-tested for over a decade.[2] In wetlands mitigation banking, a 'bank' of wetlands habitat is created, restored, or preserved and then made available to developers of wetlands habitat who must 'buy' habitat mitigation as a condition of government approval for development. This mechanism has also provided a model for endangered species protection and could easily be extended to other settings, including watershed protection.

This Chapter describes the legal and institutional background to wetlands mitigation banking, identifies the expected advantages, and highlights emerging difficulties. The discussion focuses on two main limitations: currency adequacy and exchange adequacy. The Chapter ends by drawing out key lessons for market-based approaches to watershed protection.

SECTION 404 PERMITS

The primary law conserving wetlands in the United States is the Clean Water Act (CWA), passed in 1972. Section 311 of the CWA broadly prohibits 'the discharge of any pollutant by any person' into navigable waters, where a pollutant is defined as a discrete unit of pollution (for example, an emission of sulfur dioxide or discharge of toxic waste). At face value, this would seem to prevent the filling of most wetlands.[3] The CWA provides a limited exception to this prohibition in Section 404, which authorizes the Secretary of the Army to 'issue permits, after notice and opportunity for public hearings for the discharge of dredged or fill material into navigable waters at specified disposal sites'.[4] These permits, administered principally through the Army Corps of Engineers (Corps) and known as '404 permits', 'wetland permits', or 'Corps permits', are the cornerstone of federal efforts to encourage protection of wetland resources through market-based means. The permitting program, however, suffers many exceptions and nuances. For the purposes of this discussion, we note that many routine land development activities require and receive 404 permits before they can proceed. Our focus is on how market mechanisms have been developed within this framework to promote the conservation of wetlands.

In granting 404 permits, the Corps guidelines (Federal Register, 1990) call for a 'sequencing' approach, which essentially lists wetland protection actions in the following order of desirability:

1   avoid filling wetland resources;
2   minimize adverse impacts on those wetlands that cannot reasonably be avoided; and
3   provide compensatory mitigation for those unavoidable adverse impacts that remain after all minimization measures have been exercised.

Thus, when applying for a 404 permit, a developer must convince the Corps that no reasonable alternatives exist in the development of the wetlands, that the design of the development minimizes harm to the wetlands, and, if these two conditions have been satisfied, that other wetlands have been restored to compensate for the wetlands destroyed (known as 'compensatory mitigation').[5]

The Environmental Protection Agency (EPA) and the Corps have traditionally preferred on-site to off-site locations for compensatory mitigation activities, and have preferred in-kind mitigation to mitigation that uses a substantially different type of wetland.[6] As an example, if a shopping mall is built on a salt marsh, on-site mitigation would require restoring a wetland on immediately adjacent land (as opposed to a distant site), and in-kind mitigation would require restoring a salt marsh (as opposed to a fresh water cattail marsh). Finally, regardless of location, the EPA and the Corps favor measures that restore prior wetland areas, followed by enhancement of low-quality wetlands and creation of new wetlands. Least favored of all is the preservation of existing wetlands.

Despite the restrictions imposed by the 404 program, the economic boom of the 1990s and growth in real estate values have increased pressure to develop wetlands. Notwithstanding its official status as the least-favored alternative in the agencies' sequence of preferences, compensatory mitigation has been popular. Compensatory mitigation frees highly valued wetlands for development. Building a shopping center around an avoided wetlands site, on choice commercial development land, can present costly design constraints. The option of transferring the wetlands to some less valuable site is financially attractive to property developers.

While attractive to property developers, the project-by-project compensatory mitigation approach has failed in terms of environmental protection (Veltman, 1995; Liebesman and Plott, 1998). For instance, many developers went through the motions of so-called 'landscape mitigation' – planting what was required or regrading where required to meet the minimum letter of the permit – then moved on, leaving the 'restored wetland' to revert back to its original habitat (Bowers, 1993). Whether on-site or near-site, the piecemeal site-by-site approach complicates the Corps' ability to articulate mitigation performance standards, monitor success, and enforce conditions.

ENTER A MARKET MECHANISM

In the light of these problems, in the early 1990s the Corps and the EPA started to shift compensatory activities from on-site to off-site mitigation, thus opening the door to the wetlands mitigation banking approach. This approach allows a developer who has mitigated somewhere else in advance of development to draw from the resulting bank of mitigation 'credits' to offset damage to wetlands as the development is implemented. The concept has progressed beyond this personal bank model to large commercial and public wetlands banks that are not tied to a particular development and that sell mitigation credits to third-party developers (Gardner, 1996; Silverstein, 1994). Proponents of wetland mitigation banking argue that, by aggregating small wetlands threatened by development into larger restored wetlands in a different location, it offers both efficiency and ecological benefits (Veltman, 1995; Rolband, 1994). The Corps describes commercial wetlands banks as:

> *an implicit move away from a rigid, on-site, in-kind preference for piecemeal compensatory mitigation toward a broader-based trading system that takes advantage of qualitative differences among wetlands and that can use the potential economic profits from the development of some low-valued wetlands (that may be doomed in any event). (Brumbaugh, 1995)*

To help describe how wetland banking works in practice, a pictorial representation is given in Figure 5.1. The development project depicted obtains a permit from the Corps to fill 25ha of wetlands, and negotiates the permit conditions – in this case, to restore 50ha elsewhere. Rather than undertaking this restoration work itself, the developer negotiates to acquire the required 50ha from a wetland mitigation bank that has been approved by the Corps. In simple terms, wetlands mitigation banking can be described as a transaction in which the wetlands mitigation banker informs the regulatory agency that the permits should be released to the developer with mitigation requirements (Gardner, 1996). Wetland mitigation banking resembles a commodity market, with entrepreneurial wetlands banks offering for sale (and profit) off-site wetlands as 'credits' to anyone who is in need of mitigation for their 404 permits (Liebesman and Plott, 1998).

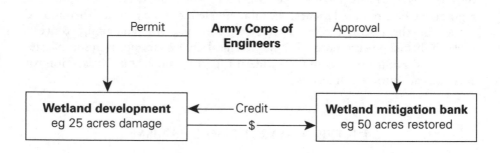

Figure 5.1 *Wetland mitigation banking in practice*

The establishment of wetlands mitigation banks must follow clear federal (and, increasingly, state) guidelines. According to Federal Guidance for the Establishment, Use and Operation of Mitigation Banks (Federal Register, 1995), a prospective bank must submit a prospectus to the Corps. This prospectus is reviewed by a mitigation bank review team that takes account of its compliance with the sequencing approach and other preferences applicable to compensatory wetlands mitigation. The review team and the bank then negotiate all the details of bank objectives, ownership, operation, and enforcement before the proposed bank is submitted for public notice and comment. In addition to these federal guidelines, a number of states have provided statutory or regulatory frameworks for using wetlands mitigation banks to ensure compliance with state wetlands protection laws (ELI, 1993; Gardner, 1996; Rolband, 1994).

While there is no uniform bank model, most banks fit either a 'single client' or 'entrepreneur' approach (ELI, 1993; Gardner, 1996). Under single client models, one developer, whether public (for example, a state roads department) or private (for example, a utility company), establishes a bank for personal use. The entrepreneur model involves a bank developer who intends to sell 'credits' to a number of land developers from those building a mall or a housing complex to state highway departments building roads. In both cases, the banking entity must gain the approval of federal and state regulators.

With the support of federal agencies, as well as many environmental advocacy groups, land development interests, and academics, the wetlands mitigation banking program has blossomed since the late 1980s, and there are over 70 such commercial mitigation banks operating in the United States today (ELI, 1993; Liebesman and Plott, 1998; Gardner, 1996; Brumbaugh, 1995).[7] According to the Corps of Engineers, 9500ha of wetlands were filled in exchange for 16,500ha restored or created in mitigation from 1993 to 2000 (NRC, 2001). Nationally, the cost of credits can run from as low as US$7500 in rural areas to US$100,000 per acre in urban or suburban regions. In theory, the price covers the costs of maintaining and monitoring the site to ensure it maintains conditions conducive to wetland plant and animal life (Jenkins, 2001; Myers, 2001). In Illinois, for example, the town of Libertyville hired a private company to convert 80 acres of corn fields into a wetland bank for US$1.2 million. For every acre sold to developers as a mitigation credit, developers pay about US$65,000 and the town gets US$6000 (Krishnamurthy, 2001).

While a number of case studies in the literature provide trade-specific information on the size of mitigated areas, there is surprisingly little aggregate data available on deals negotiated to date (NRC, 2001). Indeed, we have come across no studies that track trends in regional or local volume of trading over time (either number of trades or land area), the prices of mitigation credits or the costs of establishing and operating banks. Reflecting this dearth of data, the most comprehensive study on mitigation banking to date, a 2001 report by the Natural Research Council (NRC), recommended the creation of a national database to track the loss and restoration of wetlands function over time (NRC, 2001).

Notwithstanding this lack of information, the Corps and EPA are positive about the benefits of wetland banking. They identify a number of advantages of wetland mitigation banking over individual mitigation projects (Federal Register, 1990):

- It may be more advantageous for maintaining the integrity of the aquatic ecosystem to consolidate compensatory mitigation into a single large parcel of contiguous parcels when ecologically appropriate.

- Establishment of a mitigation bank can bring together financial resources and planning and scientific expertise not practicable to many project-specific compensatory mitigation proposals. This consolidation of resources can increase the potential for the establishment and long-term management of successful mitigation that maximizes opportunities for contributing to bio-diversity and/or watershed function.
- Use of mitigation banks may reduce the time spent on permit processing and provide more cost-effective compensatory mitigation opportunities for projects that qualify.
- Compensatory mitigation is typically implemented and functioning in advance of project impacts, thereby reducing temporal losses of aquatic functions and uncertainty over whether the mitigation will be successful in offsetting project impacts.
- Consolidation of compensatory mitigation within a mitigation bank increases the efficiency of limited agency resources in the review and compliance monitoring of mitigation projects, and thus improves the reliability of efforts to restore, create, or enhance wetlands for mitigation purposes.
- The existence of mitigation banks can contribute toward attainment of the goal of no overall net loss of the nation's wetlands by providing opportunities to compensate for authorized impacts when mitigation might not otherwise be appropriate or practicable.

These potential benefits of wetlands mitigation banking certainly seem attractive, particularly when compared to the miserable performance of past one-off compensatory mitigation. However, these benefits are not universally accepted. Research indicates, for instance, that some systems of small isolated wetlands can provide more biodiversity than a large contiguous wetland. In sufficient abundance and proximity, small isolated wetlands provide greater variability of conditions, insurance against natural perturbations and source–sink population dynamics than can a contiguous wetland of equal total size. A policy favoring large contiguous wetlands necessarily disadvantages species that depend on systems of small isolated wetlands (Semlitsch, 2000).

Clearly a number of questions remain. In particular, we need to ask whether performance has matched expectations. Has wetlands mitigation banking led to the conservation of wetlands and no net loss of wetlands? Below, we disentangle the experience of wetlands mitigation banking by focusing on whether the trades have exchanged equivalent value (the currency adequacy) and how the exchanges have been restricted to ensure equivalent value (the exchange adequacy).

CURRENCY ADEQUACY

In any environmental trading market, whether exchanging sulfur dioxide, halibut, chlorofluorocarbons, or wetlands, a fundamental issue is determining the trading metric – the 'currency'. It is the currency that establishes what is being traded and therefore protected. Currencies drive the structure of environmental trading markets, directly influencing their construction, rules of exchange and provision for public participation. Whether we can confidently trade x for y depends on what we are trying to maximize and our standard of measurement, both of which turn on the currency of exchange. Put simply, unless the currency captures what we care about, we can end up trading the wrong things.

To ensure equivalent trades of wetlands, the currency must incorporate important values provided by both the wetlands to be lost and the wetlands used for mitigation. Of course, this begs the questions of what the relevant values are, how we measure them, and how we reflect them in a conveniently traded currency (ELI, 1993). If all that concerns us about wetlands protection is hectares of wetlands, then the job is simple – identify wetlands and count up the hectares. However, if the delivery of the functional value of wetlands to the environment and society is our concern, hectares leave much to be desired as a currency for trading. Not all wetland hectares are created equal. Wetlands differ by type, location, time frames, and in terms of the services they deliver, for example, habitat protection, flood control, and water filtration. In other words, wetlands are non-fungible when their ecosystem values are considered (King and Herbert, 1997). But if the currency does not capture service values, then they are absent from the transaction. Thus, developing and using a wetland assessment methodology that measures these and other relevant values, or some reliable indicator thereof, is a critical first step in developing a framework for wetland mitigation banking (ELI, 1993).

The Corps has given its local field offices wide discretion in selecting the method of wetland accounting (Veltman, 1995). Roughly 40 different wetlands assessment methods have been developed for use in different contexts, many of which could be used in mitigation banking decisions. These methods vary in terms of the type of habitats in which the method is used, the basic targets of assessment, and the functional and social values encompassed in the assessment (Bartoldus, 1999). Reviews of wetland assessment methodology[8] conducted since wetland banking sprang onto the scene in 1985 have categorized assessment methods into three major types:

1 Simple indices are derived from quickly and easily observed characteristics of a wetland, and usually serve as surrogate indicators of one or more ecological functions (for example, percentage cover of aquatic vegetation).
2 Narrowly tailored systems attempt to measure directly a limited range of wetland services, such as wildlife habitat, through a detailed procedure focusing on that particular wetland service (for example, percentage duck habitat).
3 Broadly tailored systems examine a range of wetland functions covering a number of observable characteristics.

To be useful, methodologies must incorporate service valuation measurements for both the wetlands to be lost and the wetlands used for mitigation. Where values differ due to service population differences, service delivery type, and/or efficiency differences, simple trading ratios may be used. Ratios may also be used to cater for margins of error, for instance where the Corps is uncertain over the true range of functions. To the extent that reliable measurements of function value can be made, wetlands mitigation banking offers a flexible mechanism for achieving wetland protection goals at minimum cost. In practice, however, reviews of assessment methodologies suggest that explicit measures of service values remain beyond the reach of virtually all assessment methods in use. This conclusion is backed up by our own survey of 41 banks established after the Institute for Water Resources' First Phase Report in 1994.

Wetlands assessment methods used by wetlands mitigation banks have advanced very little from the beginning of the banking program. The broader assessment methods tend to be expensive and produce reams of qualitative results. For ease of comparison, wetlands managers tend to reduce these results to quantitative value scores that often mask the ecological rationales. Wetlands mitigation banking entities seem focused on using the simplest and most expedient assessment method that the relevant regulatory bodies will approve, and the regulatory bodies do not appear to require, or even encourage, a more sophist-icated approach (Kusler and Niering, 1998). A comprehensive currency is too expensive to mint and too arduous to use (Rolband, 1994; Kusler and Niering, 1998). Instead of developing and refining valuation approaches for assessment and trades, wetlands mitigation banking assessment methods have stagnated in the acre-based and narrow function-based approaches, resulting in the use of relatively crude currencies for wetlands habitat trading purposes.

EXCHANGE ADEQUACY

A critical implication of the fact that crude currencies have tended to prevail in wetlands banking programs is that they have been accompanied by tightly constrained trading schemes as authorities have attempted to control for environmental externalities. By contrast, were wetland assessment methods to fully reflect wetland function values, they could limit externalities sufficiently to allow the authorities to loosen their grip and allow trading regardless of type, space, and time differences. Below, key trading constraints imposed on wetland mitigation banking to deal with the use of crude currencies are highlighted.

Nonfungibility of type

Because crude currencies such as hectares and habitat function fail to capture complex differences in wetlands, wetlands mitigation banking programs are reluctant to stray far from strict in-kind policies. For example, federal guidance issued in 1995 allows out-of-kind mitigation in banking only 'if it is determined to be practicable and environmentally preferable'. Even when out-of-kind trading is allowed, the Corps typically imposes fixed trading ratios between hectares of the wetland types as a surrogate for more precise measurements of comparative function value. Trading ratios also are often imposed to adjust for different mitigation forms (for example, restoration versus preservation) and for the general uncertainty that the bank wetlands will exhibit as much acre-for-acre integrity as the filled wetlands (ELI, 1993). The consequence of this in-kind requirement is a thinning of the wetlands trading market from all wetlands to the defined in-kind type.

Nonfungibility of space

The value of wetlands' services depends fundamentally on their landscape context (Salzman and Ruhl, 2001). Even controlling for type, a bog wetland in Maine may not provide the same function values as one in Oregon, or even one in the next county. Further, even if it does, it certainly will not deliver the services of nutrient trapping, flood control, or nursery habitat to the same parties. To overcome this problem, the Corps and EPA impose the concept of a geographically defined service area on wetlands banks to define the area 'wherein a bank can reasonably be expected to provide appropriate compensation for impacts to wetlands and/or other aquatic resources' (Federal Register, 1995). In general, service areas should be no larger than the watershed within which the bank is located, unless reaching beyond that market is 'practicable and environmentally desirable' (Federal Register, 1995). Coupled with an in-kind constraint, this service area constraint significantly narrows the potential supply of wetlands in the trading market.

Nonfungibility of time

One of the purported advantages of wetland banking programs is that the bank has created the wetlands before the credits are drawn, so that the mitigation is secured before the wetlands are filled. In accordance with this principle, the Federal Guidance (1995) provides that '[t]he number of credits available for withdrawal (that is, debiting) should generally be commensurate with the level of aquatic functions attained at a bank at the time of debiting'.[9] With large commercial banks, however, the expense and time involved with establishing functional wetlands, particularly those of types that require long maturation periods, could make the banking cost prohibitive if credits could not be drawn before the bank's wetland values are fully in place. The Federal Guidance thus allows some leeway in the timing requirement, allowing credit withdrawal before equal wetland values are established, if the bank possesses adequate financial assurance and has exhibited a high probability of success (Federal Guidance, 1995; Brumbaugh, 1995). In some cases this policy results in lags of up to six years between the times of wetland destruction and wetland replacement (Desma, 1994).

FAT AND SLOPPY VERSUS THIN AND BLAND

Practical constraints on the implementation of sophisticated assessment methods – in terms of costs, time demands, and complexity – have prevented wetland mitigation banking from ensuring currency adequacy. Developers have an incentive to use the least expensive currency the government will allow. The government has an incentive not to make the currency too expensive to mint, or no one will use it and the trading program will expire of its own accord. Thus, wetland banking has been forced into the next best alternative: designing market constraints to plug up the holes that the crude currency otherwise leaves open to externalities. Assessment methodology has become the proverbial tail that wags the dog, keeping the wetlands program from tapping the full benefit of market trading efficiency as the market makers (the EPA and the Corps) attempt to shore up the weak currency with market constraints. There is good reason to believe this problem will be endemic to habitat trading programs in general, including forested watersheds, until ecologists can deliver a cheaply calculated, refined currency for habitat values.

In addition to environmental concerns associated with currency inadequacy, it is also worth pointing to equity concerns. A recent study of wetland banking in Florida found that trades, even in the same watershed, have produced 'a transfer of wetlands from highly urbanized, high-population density areas to more rural low-population density areas' (King and Herbert, 1997). The same problem has plagued mitigation banking in Virginia, where a recent study found that most mitigation banks are located in rural areas while most wetland losses take place in urban and suburban areas (Jennings and others, 1999). As can be expected from a market efficiency perspective, developers want to develop wetlands where land is dear (urban areas) and wetland banks want to invest in offsets where land is cheap (rural areas). The existing wetlands mitigation banking framework lets them do so. This results in trades that move wetlands out of areas where they may provide services to urban populations and into sparsely populated areas.

Should we be concerned about the 'market-driven "migration" of wetlands across the urban–rural landscape' (King and Herbert, 1997), even though it is a reflection of the efficiency of trading? If we care about the equity of who receives wetland services and their value, then the answer is yes.[10] But if we care primarily about keeping the wetland banking market 'fat' (in other words, involving high levels of participation), then the answer is no, since adding another restriction would surely thin the market down.

Given this state of affairs, the aggressive integration of open trading models into wetlands and other habitat contexts poses concerns for environmental protection as well as equity. Even the most developed habitat assessment methods presently in use are ill-prepared to produce reliable, inexpensive, and ready measurements of a habitat's environmental and service values. Such measurements require far more money and time to produce on a site-specific basis than developers, habitat bankers, and the government seem prepared to allocate. In the absence of such measurements, the government and environmental groups have generally demanded, at a minimum, constraints on habitat trading markets. The risk is that at some point the constraints imposed on wetlands mitigation banking threaten to swallow the market – with its own serious costs.

In asking whether mitigation banking is a good thing, it is critical to investigate what type of, and how much, banking is optimal. To answer this requires the analysis of what the costs and benefits would be from applying more sophisticated assessment procedures. What is the trade-off between improved environmental outcomes and increased transaction costs? Broadening our frame of reference, are gains from the mitigation areas sufficient to offset the losses in the conversion area? From a distributional perspective, are there identifiable groups that would be harmed by conversion in one area and not compensated by mitigation in another? And if so, how severe is that damage, and what mechanisms might be put in place to compensate these losers? Answers to these questions are, however, elusive. New data are urgently needed and a clear understanding of wetland currencies must be attained.

LESSONS FOR WATERSHED MARKETS

Despite concerns over the exchange mechanism, and in particular whether equivalent values are being exchanged, environmental trading markets remain popular and are growing. Mature environmental trading markets are active in reducing air pollution and regulating land development, and are under serious consideration for endangered species habitat. It is easy to imagine the use of such a mechanism in forestry, where a particular land use is valued for its watershed protection services.

Yet creating an environmental market by no means ensures environmental protection. Beyond implementation issues such as the creation of stable property rights and effective compliance monitoring, the currency must be able to accurately capture the value to be measured, the ecosystem service values. Otherwise, confidence in the procedural and substantive adequacy of the trading system will be eroded. Developing an assessment methodology that measures the ecosystem service value or some reliable indicator for watershed protection will be the critical first step in developing a framework for any trading-based mechanism.

The actual shape of the trading mechanism for forest and watershed protection will, of course, depend upon the particular setting and management goals. If the currency can be easily set, measures of value determined cost effectively, and trading restrictions established that still provide a market with high levels of participation, then trading mechanisms will work well. If any of these are lacking (as most are in the case of wetlands), then one will have less confidence that the trading ensures and promotes environmental protection. It is also worth noting, as a final caution, that while compensatory wetland mitigation policies relying primarily on wetland creation can result in no net loss of wetlands, they are likely to result in overall loss of habitat since the land being converted to wetlands is usually open space already. That is, the net result is less undeveloped land than before.

NOTES

1 Information on the current status of US wetlands can be found at http://www.epa. gov/owow/wetlands.
2 For comprehensive analyses of the wetlands mitigation banking see ELI, 1993; Gardner, 1996; IWR/US Army Corps of Engineers, 1994a and b; Salzman and Ruhl, 2001; and Ruhl and Gregg, 2001.
3 Although the CWA makes no reference to wetlands with respect to the 404 program, early in the program's history judicial interpretation required the Corps to extend its reach to tidal wetland areas.
4 The EPA has the power to veto Corps permits if it finds that the discharge would have an unacceptably adverse effect on environmental resources, but it has exercised this power infrequently (Burkhalter, 1999).
5 Section 404 does not mention a mitigation requirement for permit issuance. Rather, this provision of the statute directs EPA, in conjunction with the Corps, to develop guidelines that the Corps must apply in deciding whether to authorize the fill disposal at a wetlands site.
6 Ecologists generally divide wetlands into seven major types, within which there is tremendous variation from region to region in terms of physical characteristics and functions. (ELI, 1993).
7 While these figures provide a ball-park figure, it should be noted that estimates vary considerably. For example, Brumbaugh (1995) reports that there were more than 100 in 1995 with hundreds more in development at that time, and Jenkins (2001) finds 250 banks across the country.
8 The four most comprehensive studies are: ELI, 1993; IWR/US Army Corps of Engineers, 1994a and b; and Bartoldus, 1999.
9 Studies of wetland restorations have found a remarkably low rate of success. The Florida Department of Environmental Regulation found a success rate of 45 per cent for tidal wetlands creation and 12 per cent for freshwater wetlands creation (Veltman, 1995).
10 This is not to suggest that the shift from urban to rural wetlands is necessarily an unwise policy. In some settings, the urban wetlands to be developed may be comprised of many small, isolated wetlands of poor quality, whereas the rural mitigation bank may produce a large, contiguous, high-quality habitat. We are suggesting, however, that the shift between the human populations serviced may be significant and thus should be considered in any evaluation.

REFERENCES

Bartoldus, C. 1999. *A Comprehensive Review of Wetland Assessment Procedures: A Guide for Wetland Practitioners.* St. Michaels: Environmental Concern Inc.

Bowers, K. 1993. "What is Wetlands Mitigation?" *Land Development,* Winter issue.

Brumbaugh, R. 1995. "Wetland Mitigation Banking: Entering a New Era." *Wetlands Research Program Bulletin,* 5:3/4, pp.1–8.

Burkhalter, S. 1999. "Oversimplification: Value and Function: Wetland Mitigation Banking." *Chapman Law Review,* 2:1, pp.261, 267.

Desma, M.G. Le. 1994. "A Sound of Thunder: Problems and Prospects in Wetland Mitigation Banking." *Columbia Journal of Environmental Law,* 19, pp.497–506.

Environmental Law Institute (ELI). 1993. *Wetland Mitigation Banking.* ELI Research Study. Washington: ELI.

Ewel, K. 1997. "Water Quality Improvement by Wetlands." In G.C. Daily (ed.) *Nature's Services.* Washington: Island Press.

Federal Register. 1990. "Memorandum of Agreement Between Department of the Army and the Environmental Protection Agency Concerning the Clean Water Act Section 404(b)(1) Guidelines, 55 FED. REG. 9210, 9211-12 (March 12)." Washington: US Government.

Federal Register. 1995. "Federal Guidance for the Establishment, Use, and Operation of Mitigation Banks, 60 FED. REG. 58,605 (November 28)." Washington: US Government.

Flournoy, A.C. 1996. "Preserving Dynamic Systems: Wetlands, Ecology, and Law." *Duke Environmental Law & Policy Forum,* VII:1, pp.105–132.

Gardner, R.C. 1996. "Banking on Entrepreneurs: Wetlands, Mitigation Banking, and Takings." *Iowa Law Review,* 81:527, pp.527–587.

Institute for Water Resources (IWR), U.S. Army Corps of Engineers. 1994a. *National Wetlands Mitigation Banking Study: Wetland Mitigation Banking.* Alexandria: IWR and U.S. Army Corps of Engineers.

Institute for Water Resources (IWR), U.S. Army Corps of Engineers. 1994b. *National Wetlands Mitigation Banking Study: First Phase Report.* Alexandria: IWR and U.S. Army Corps of Engineers.

Jenkins, C. 2001. "Repaying a Debt to Nature; New Wetlands Offset Filled Ones." *Washington Post,* July 15, p.T01.

Jennings, A., R. Hoagland, and E. Rudolph. 1999. "Down Sides to Virginia Mitigation Banking." *National Wetlands Newsletter,* 21:1, p.9.

King, D., and L.W. Herbert. 1997. "The Fungibility of Wetlands." *National Wetlands Newsletter,* 19:5, pp.10–13.

Krishnamurthy, M. 2001. "Wetlands Restoration Pays Off for Libertyville." *Chicago Daily Herald,* August 14, p.4.

Kusler, J., and W. Niering. 1998. "Wetland Assessment: Have We Lost Our Way?" *National Wetlands Newsletter,* 20:2, pp.1–3.

Liebesman, L., and D.M. Plott. 1998. "The Emergence of Private Wetlands Mitigation Banking." *Natural Resources and Environment,* 13, pp.341–344, 370–371.

Myers, A. 2001. "Progress Report: As Wetlandsbank Enters Ninth Year, Jury of Environmentalists Still Out on Mitigation Efforts." *Broward Daily Business Review,* April 19, p.A1

Myers, N., R. Mittermeier, C. Mittermeier, G. da Fonseca, and J. Kent. 2000. "Biodiversity Hotspots for Conservation Priorities." *Nature*, 403:6772, pp.853–858.

National Research Council (NRC). 2001. *Compensating for Wetland Losses under the Clean Water Act*. Washington: National Academy Press.

Office of Program Policy Analysis and Governmental Accountability (OPPAGA). 2000. *Wetland Mitigation*. Report No.99-40. Tallahassee: OPPAGA, Florida Legislature.

Rolband, M. 1994. "The Systemic Assumptions of Wetland Mitigation: A Look at Louisiana's Proposed Wetland Mitigation and Mitigation Banking Regulations." *Tulane Environmental Law Journal*, 7:497, pp.510–11.

Ruhl, J.B., and J. Gregg. 2001. "Integrating Ecosystem Services into Environmental Law: A Case Study of Wetlands Mitigation Banking." *Stanford Environmental Law Journal*, 20, pp.365–392.

Salzman, J., and J.B. Ruhl. 2001. "Currencies and the Commodification of Environmental Law." *Stanford Law Review*, 53, pp.607–694.

Semlitsch, R.D. 2000. "Size Does Matter: The Value of Small Isolated Wetlands." *National Wetlands Newsletter*, 22:1, pp.5–8.

Silverstein, J. 1994. "Taking Wetlands to the Bank: The Role of Wetland Mitigation Banking in a Comprehensive Approach to Wetlands Protection." *Boston College Environmental Affairs Law Review*, 22:129, pp.145–161.

Veltman, V. 1995. "Banking on the Future of Wetlands Using Federal Law." *Northwestern University Law Review*, 89, pp.655–689.

Chapter 6

Financing Watershed Conservation: The FONAG Water Fund in Quito, Ecuador

Marta Echavarria[1]

Do you know where your drinking water comes from? It is very likely that the water that comes out of your tap is brought through miles of pipeline from a protected area. This is particularly true in Latin America, where many national parks and protected forests were originally established to protect water sources. Over time, however, the link between biodiversity conservation and hydrological maintenance has often been lost. National park authorities often lack clear management objectives and resources to insure the regeneration of hydrological resources. Water users, whether they are city dwellers, farmers, or electricity consumers, are frequently not even aware of the source of their water. As a result water resources are being depleted and quality is deteriorating in many countries. In Quito, the capital of Ecuador, threats to water resources are spurring action. In early 2000 the city established a water fund (Fondo del Agua, FONAG) to finance the management and conservation of surrounding watersheds. Early experiences are encouraging. This paper describes FONAG, outlines its early experience, and highlights emerging risks and opportunities.

QUITO'S WATER NEEDS AND SUPPLY

Quito has a population of over 1.5 million people. It is located in an Andean valley at about 2800 meters above sea level. In total the city consumes around 7 cubic meters (m^3) of water per second. Drinking water is provided by a municipal public company, the Quito Metropolitan Area Sewage and Potable Water Agency (Empresa Metropolitana de Alcantarillado y Agua Potable de Quito, EMAAP-Q), supplying over 260,000 homes. Consumption is expected to increase by about 50 per cent by the year 2025 (Southgate, 2001), increasing pressure on water resources. At the same time, financing for increasing supplies is tight. An estimated 30 per cent of consumption is not being charged for, and those water fees that are collected fail to cover the costs of maintaining the distribution network, let alone broader efforts at watershed protection. Currently, drinking water needs to be subsidized by the city and the central government.

About 80 per cent of Quito's drinking water comes from two protected areas, the Cayambe Coca Ecological Reserve and the Antisana Ecological Reserve (Echavarria, 1997). Water is collected through two main systems. The Papallacta Optimization water project diverts water from Cayambe Coca and distributes it to the northern part of the city, while the Mica water project in Antisana provides water for the neighborhoods in the southern part of the city. Both are operated by EMAAP-Q.

The Cayambe Coca and Antisana Ecological Reserves cover over 520,000ha and are parts of the country's national park system, managed by the Ministry of the Environment. Their natural ecosystems are characterized by *páramos*, high-altitude Andean grasslands, and cloud forests recognized for their capacity to retain humidity and regulate water-flows (Hofstede, 1995; Stadtmuller, 1983). As the snows from local glaciers in Cayambe, Antisana, and Cotopaxi melt and precipitation occurs, the liquid is retained in the soils and vegetation and is slowly released, depending on the geology of the area, forming different water bodies. Due to the high altitude, temperatures are low and limit evaporation. The high soil organic matter insures long-term water retention. In addition, the water vapor that is carried by the wind currents, and the evapotranspiration generated by the vegetation in the lower elevation cloud forests is an important source of moisture. The Cayambe Coca glaciers alone store 1.4 cubic kilometers (km^3) of water. The reserve is the source of 11 important rivers, and houses numerous lagoons and wetlands.

In addition to EMAAP-Q, important water users in and around Quito include farmers who depend on water for irrigation, rural households that rely on water for drinking and sanitary purposes, flower plantations in the Central Valley, and hydropower stations. The electricity supplier for Quito (Empresa Eléctrica de Quito, EEQ) generates around 22 per cent of its hydropower in the watersheds surrounding Quito. HCJB, a Christian radio station, generates its own hydropower and is currently building another plant within Cayambe Coca. There are plans to build a hydroelectric plant in the Quijos River, one of the most important watersheds in the area. Several important irrigation projects also draw water from Cayambe Coca.

THREATS TO QUITO'S WATER RESOURCES

Although the Cayambe Coca and Antisana Ecological Reserves are formally protected for conservation, they face a number of threats. More than 7000 people live within Cayambe Coca. They require water for their crops and have ancestral rights to use the grasslands for extensive cattle raising. Over 20,000 people live in communities and agricultural cooperatives surrounding the reserves. Their principal activities are dairy production and the sale of timber. Unsustainable agricultural practices, such as overgrazing and burning of grasslands, affect the viability of the *páramos*. In addition to EMAAP-Q's water diversion projects described above, there are other development initiatives – such as an oil pipeline and irrigation and hydroelectricity plants – that put further pressure on the area, affecting land cover and natural vegetation.

Although no hydrological studies have been undertaken, it is widely believed that these productive activities risk undermining the local watershed functions, in particular the maintenance of water flow and quality. Not only do water diversion projects reduce supplies downstream, but the associated network of paved roads is thought to reduce groundwater replenishment. Likewise, the drainage of wetlands has negative impacts for water retention, and the combination of grazing and burning of the *páramo* reduces soil moisture content. The loss of vegetative cover can lead to erosion processes, and the subsequent sediment load could affect water quality, particularly for drinking purposes.

POTENTIAL SOLUTIONS TO ADDRESS THESE THREATS

To control these threats, the Ministry of Environment hired a local environmental non-governmental organization (NGO), Fundación Antisana, to design management plans for the two reserves. Fundación Antisana's analysis singled out a number of actions for improving information and protecting the local hydrology. Five stand out, and these are outlined below.

Watershed valuation

There are critical information gaps concerning the hydrological system, how it works, what benefits it offers to local populations, and how these are affected by human intervention. In order to effectively value the watershed services provided by these natural ecosystems, further research has to be undertaken. There is also a need to improve monitoring, both to assess trends in water supply and to evaluate the impact of any interventions.

Land purchase or compensation measures

Although the land within the reserves is technically patrimony of the government, the original landowners were never compensated for their loss of land title. Continuing land conflicts have meant that land may need to be bought or compensation paid (for example, conservation easements or payments for environmental services designed to encourage more appropriate land uses) to ensure the protection of water sources.

Enforcing protection

To prevent damage to the upper watersheds, it is important to have an effective system for controlling illegal logging, hunting, fishing, burning, overgrazing, and trash disposal.

Targeted land management

To improve or protect hydrological functions, special measures may be needed to protect waterholes, prevent erosion, and stabilize stream banks and slopes.

Sustainable production systems

To reduce the human pressures in critical watershed areas, it is necessary to promote sustainable resource use by local communities. Sustainable agricultural practices, for instance, can prevent further damage and generate income for local inhabitants.

To implement these measures, funding is necessary. However, as in most developing countries, the Ecuadorian park service (Sistema Nacional de Areas Protegidas) lacks sufficient resources to fulfil its mandate. To overcome this problem, Fundación Antisana, with support from the United States Agency for International Development (USAID) and the Nature Conservancy, developed the idea of a new independent water fund – FONAG – dedicated to financing watershed protection around Quito to complement other conservation efforts that were already underway.

THE EMERGENCE OF FONAG

The central idea behind FONAG is simple: watersheds surrounding Quito provide critical water services to local inhabitants, and beneficiaries should pay for the continued provision of these services. Different institutional mechanisms that implement this idea exist in Latin America and can provide interesting lessons. For example, in Paraná State in Brazil, 5 per cent of the sales tax collected is distributed to the municipalities, based on their commitment to conserve areas surrounding watersheds that provide drinking water to urban centers (see Chapter 10). In Costa Rica, reforestation projects receive an economic incentive that recognizes the water service provided by the trees that are planted (see Chapter 3). In the Cauca Valley of Colombia, agricultural water users pay an additional voluntary user fee to invest in hydrological protection measures and other initiatives in the upper part of the watersheds (Echavarria, 1999).

After reviewing various options, in 1997 Fundación Antisana proposed the creation of a mutual fund with the voluntary participation of water users, most notably EMAAP-Q. EMAAP-Q had no permanent watershed protection effort in its jurisdiction, nor the capacity to implement such a program. Considering that its business was the sale of water, it was accepted that efforts needed to be undertaken to protect water sources. Similar arguments were used to persuade other organizations that depended on water for their production process, such as the electrical utility EEQ, to contribute to watershed protection efforts. In order to protect the resources, water users need to work together.

A proposal for FONAG was presented by Fundación Antisana and the Nature Conservancy to different decision-makers, including the Mayor of Quito, the leading municipal authority. The proposal highlighted the emerging hydro-logical problems facing Quito and potential mechanisms for financing watershed protection. The decision-makers involved at the time, particularly the Mayor of Quito (during the period concerned there was a change of administration when the Mayor of Quito decided to run for the presidency), were willing to consider the proposal seriously, realizing the critical role played by water resources in urban development. Another important driver for the acceptance of the FONAG proposal was the change in the law governing public financing in 1999. Pre-viously, government organizations were not allowed to invest funds in private financial mechanisms. The change in regulation permitted public organizations like EMAAP-Q and EEQ to assign resources to a private and autonomous financial mechanism such as FONAG.

Following an intense process of promotion, negotiation, and fine-tuning, FONAG was launched in 2000. Its main features are depicted in Figure 6.1 and briefly described below.

FONAG is a non-declining endowment fund that can receive money from government and from private organizations and NGOs. An independent financial manager invests funds, and returns to these investments are used for watershed protection. The endowment is not spent. The rationale behind using only the

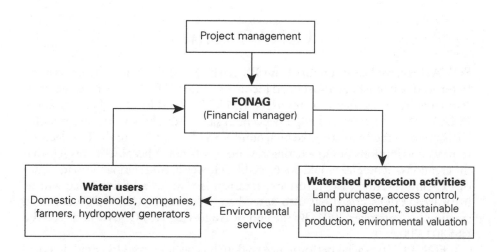

Figure 6.1 *Flows of funds and benefits in FONAG*

financial returns is to ensure the future availability of resources. FONAG is governed by a contract that establishes the terms for the fund, its institutional structure, and what resources can be used for.

The aim of the fund is to collect payments from water users and channel these funds to watershed protection activities. To achieve its aim, FONAG is managed by a board of directors and supervised by a technical secretariat that reviews its financial performance and ensures project implementation. Following open competition, Enlace Fondos – which is part of a socially-responsible private bank – was selected as FONAG's financial manager. The technical secretariat reviews how the financial manager distributes the investments and periodically informs the board of directors. Currently, project management regulations are being developed in order to set procedures and project areas to be funded.

Critically, FONAG has an open governance structure that seeks to encourage broad stakeholder participation. This is particularly important since payments by water users are voluntary, and success depends on generating willingness to pay. To encourage participation, all those who put money into the fund can become members of the board, either individually or by electing a representative, as in the case of a small irrigation water user group. In order to insure commitment, donors must sign the fund's contract. Voting power is dependent on the amount of resources provided to the fund.

Although this is a voluntary mechanism, there has been an effort to establish common criteria for determining the amount users should contribute. Ideally, the amount paid to the fund should be a reflection of the value of water for its particular use. However, because information on water values is lacking, it has been suggested that a more practical option is to encourage water users who are heavily dependent on water resources for their business to pay a percentage of their monthly sales.

FONAG TODAY

FONAG received seed funding from EMAAP-Q and the Nature Conservancy. In terms of establishing a sustained income stream, FONAG has received commitments from two major water users: EMAAP-Q and EEQ. In January 2000, EMAAP-Q committed to paying 1 per cent of sales of drinking water on a monthly basis, amounting to an average of around US$14,000 per month. The decision to pay contributions out of existing revenues was made because it was felt that the creation of a user fee would not be viable. However, considering the inadequacy of existing revenues, the future expectation is that an additional fee will be instituted. EEQ's board has also agreed to a flat fee of US$45,000 per year, starting in September 2001. By the end of August 2001, FONAG had received US$301,700.

FONAG's financial performance to date has been marred by rapid deterioration in the global economic outlook. Since 1998, Ecuador has undergone one of its worst economic and financial crises. Consequently, returns on FONAG's investments, which are all domestic, have averaged 7.6 per cent, significantly below expectations (FONAG, 2001).

Implementation of watershed protection activities will begin in the second half of 2002, when it is expected that sufficient resources will have been accumulated. According to the FONAG's rules, resources can be implemented in project areas identified in Fundación Antisana's original study (see discussion above). FONAG expects to channel resources through independent implementation organizations (private and public) that comply with a clear set of criteria, such as a positive track record in the area where the project is proposed (three to five years); good community relations; institutional credibility; and the linking of a proposal to the management plans of the reserves.

In sum, significant progress has been made in setting up the institutional arrangements for FONAG to function. The board of directors meets regularly, and payments to the financial management are made on time. EMAAP-Q is covering salaries for the technical secretariat for the first and second year of operation. The Nature Conservancy continues to provide in-kind support for FONAG, notably through its Parks-in-Peril Program and Freshwater Initiative, which is supporting research to improve understanding of the hydrological relationships in the reserves, the impacts that human activities have on these relationships, and the actions necessary for their protection. Fundación Antisana is providing similar technical support. In upcoming years, FONAG aims to focus on generating broader support and willingness to pay from other users, private and public, such as the flower producers and other private organizations.

EXPECTED BENEFITS

Although no economic cost–benefit analysis was undertaken, FONAG expects to provide wide-ranging benefits. First, FONAG aims to protect the quantity and quality of water on which the citizens of Quito depend for drinking, domestic use, and electricity. In particular, investment in maintaining the hydrological balance of the reserves is likely to reduce the current and future maintenance costs of the existing water supply and electricity infrastructure as well as future investment costs (Southgate, 2001). Although there are no estimates of how far maintenance and investment costs would be reduced, EMAAP-Q feels confident enough to consider a water development project of US$600 million dollars to increase supply for 2016–2050.

Second, the projects should benefit the communities in the upper watersheds, where the environmental service is being provided. These communities, which encompass almost 30,000 people, lack access to basic amenities and social services and have extremely low standards of living. By directing resources toward these neglected rural sectors, FONAG can play an important role in poverty alleviation.

A number of indirect benefits are also likely. Improved scientific understanding of hydrological relationships will result from planned research. Inter-institutional cooperation will also result from the development of the fund and project implementation. FONAG will mobilize additional resources through local and national organizations, which will improve watershed management capacity and experience.

POTENTIAL PITFALLS

A number of emerging problems with FONAG should also be identified. FONAG's voluntary nature leaves it open to unexpected funding shortfalls and free-riding, despite the legal commitment entered into by those who sign the fund's contract. FONAG is particularly vulnerable to unexpected reductions in payments, since its revenue depends on just two water users. If either EMAAP-Q or EEQ decide to halt or cut back payments, this will have severe implications for FONAG. With respect to free-riding, this is already evident as smaller users look to larger users to foot the bill for watershed protection. While long-term contracts that are legally binding go some way toward minimizing the risks of sudden reductions in payments, overcoming incentives to piggy-back on others' payments is perhaps the most significant challenge facing FONAG.

Given the importance of domestic water consumption in total consumption, it is reasonable for EMAAP-Q to be dominant. Yet the fact that two water users control FONAG's revenue stream is not just worrying because it raises FONAG's exposure to shifts in willingness to pay by these organizations; it also gives these institutions a dominant role in FONAG's governance. EMAAP-Q, as the leading water user, has significant power to impose its will, and its interests may differ from those of other water users. For example, EMAAP-Q needs large amounts of high quality water, which could prevent access by other users or limit their activities. It is critical that a broader set of beneficiaries should participate to ensure that FONAG operates to the advantage of a wider cross-section of watershed inhabitants.

EMERGING LESSONS

Although FONAG is still very new, a few lessons are beginning to emerge.

Political leadership

Local political support is a critical prerequisite for implementing new and innovative mechanisms for conservation, such as this fund. Without the commitment of the Mayor of Quito and a group of enthusiasts, FONAG would not be a reality. As the environment gains prominence in the public agenda and city dwellers increasingly demand solutions to their environmental problems, such support will be increasingly likely.

Water users' support

Ensuring the support of the two leading water users, EMAAP-Q and EEQ, was paramount. The open governance structure of FONAG means that it offers a space for discussion and consensus-building around the protection of watersheds, as well as a financing mechanism. Users can leverage their resources by pooling them. The board can be an interesting forum in which to coordinate activities and exchange opinions, furthering understanding of the hydrological system. Gaining broad-based support is critical to FONAG's future viability.

Concentration of power

The difficulty of gaining water users' support for FONAG has meant that efforts have concentrated on ensuring that the largest users contribute. However, this has also resulted in the concentration of decision-making power and voting rights in EMAAP-Q and EEQ. While it is important that those who pay have a say over how FONAG spends its funding (since this provides a key incentive for contributions), there are risks that the interests of poorer groups are overlooked.

Water pricing

Ecuador has been implementing policies to make water pricing more transparent and to phase out subsidies, particularly for irrigation and drinking water. In 1998, EMAAP-Q's earnings only covered 54 per cent of its costs (Southgate, 2001). While the company is gradually increasing its tariffs to reflect its operation and maintenance costs, to date no account has been taken of watershed management costs. This should change, however, as EMAAP-Q increases its payments for watershed protection and these costs are passed on to its customers. A recent survey of water users in Quito suggests that there is a willingness to pay higher fees (Corporación OIKOS, 2000).[2]

Scientific understanding

FONAG's success in delivering watershed benefits is dependent on its understanding of local hydrological relationships. Yet information is scarce, making it difficult to set investment priorities. The Nature Conservancy's Freshwater Initiative should eventually help, but results will take time to feed through. It is essential that FONAG strengthens its scientific understanding of local hydrology and monitors the impacts of its efforts to improve water flows.

POTENTIAL FOR REPLICATION

While FONAG's progress in realizing a sustainable financial mechanism for watershed protection is unusual, its goals are not. Rather, they fit well with efforts in many cities around the world to raise the profile of watershed protection in the provision of regular and high quality water services. Kingston in Jamaica, Tegucigalpa in Honduras, and Caracas in Venezuela are just a few examples of capital cities that depend on water resources that flow from surrounding protected areas. The Nature Conservancy is working with a number of local NGOs in Latin America to apply similar mechanisms in Bogóta, Colombia and Tarija, Bolivia. FONAG may thus provide a valuable model for others.

Despite the model's potential, any attempt at replication must take account of local conditions and political, physical, and legal constraints. Critically, for this model to work, a number of prerequisites need to exist. It is important to have a scientific understanding of the hydrological relationships and broad-based participation to develop the mechanism. Participation, in turn, depends on a willingness to pay among beneficiaries – particularly among the largest water users. The feasibility of an endowment fund also depends on available funding to establish a large enough endowment to generate adequate annual returns that finance watershed protection activities. Supporting legislation is also critical. For instance, in Ecuador, legislation allowing public entities to participate in private funds and rules governing the new financial mechanism were essential.

Clearly, not all these prerequisites exist everywhere, and in many cases a FONAG-type fund would be inappropriate. In Cuenca, another Ecuadorian city, for instance, a different approach is emerging. In this case a system of contributions by water users has also been introduced, but a specific fund has not been set up. Rather, the city's water company, ETAPA, assigns the resources for watershed protection, buys land to protect, and implements hydrological protection projects. In other instances, sinking funds – where the initial endowment is gradually drawn down – may be preferable.

Finally, there are clear potential risks associated with scaling up the FONAG model. Efforts to implement a water fund at the national level are likely to be bureaucratic, involve higher transaction costs and be far removed from local realities. A critical prerequisite for FONAG has been the generation of willingness to pay among specific beneficiaries. However, where payments are not destined for the protection of a particular watershed, but go to a regional or national fund, water users are less likely to be willing to contribute.

NOTES

1   FONAG is the result of many individual and institutional efforts, which a short publication may not reflect. The author would like to highlight that this mechanism is a group effort of many years' standing, and recognize that it has taken actions, efforts, and unmitigated support from public and private institutions, including Fundación Antisana, the Nature Conservancy, present and past mayors of Quito, EMAAP-Q, EEQ, the Ministry of Environment, and many others.

2   This may not seem credible considering the adverse reactions to increased prices. However, in Quito water prices are still low ($1.04/m^3), and 5 per cent of the city's population still do not have a reliable service. This causes them to rely on water

deliveries by truck, which are expensive (around $4/m^3$) and of poor or uncontrolled quality.

REFERENCES

Corporación OIKOS. 2002. "Programa de Comunicacion y Educacion sobre la Problematica del Agua de Quito." Quito: Corporación OIKOS (processed).

Echavarria, M. 1997. "Agua: !Juntos Podremos Cuidarla! Estudio de Caso Para un Fondo Para la Conservación de las Cuencas Hidrográficas Para Quito, Ecuador." Quito: The Nature Conservancy/USAID.

Echavarria, M. 1999. "Agua: Valoración del Servicio Ambiental que Prestan las Áreas Protegidas." Manual de Capacitación América Verde No.1, Vol.1. Quito: The Nature Conservancy.

FONAG. 2001. "Technical Secretariat Report." Quito: FONAG.

Hofstede, R. 1995. "Effects of Burning and Grazing on a Colombian Páramo Ecosystem." Ph.D. dissertation. Amsterdam: University of Amsterdam.

Southgate, D. 2001. "Los Valores Ambientales y su Internalización." Paper presented at the Tenth Anniversary Celebration of Fundación Antisana. Quito, July 26, 2001.

Stadtmuller, T. 1983. *Los Bosques Nublados en el Trópico Húmedo*. San José: Universidad de las Naciones Unidas.

Chapter 7

Selling Biodiversity in a Coffee Cup: Shade-grown Coffee and Conservation in Mesoamerica

Stefano Pagiola and Ina-Marlene Ruthenberg[1]

There is an important need to find ways to preserve biodiversity outside protected areas, in agricultural landscapes (Pagiola and others, 1997; Ricketts and others, 2001). Shade-grown coffee provides a very promising means of doing so, as it is very biodiversity-friendly, particularly in its more traditional, 'rustic' form. Recent decades have seen coffee production shifting either to shadeless 'sun' coffee or to annual crops or pasture, both of which provide substantially lower biodiversity benefits. The mechanism described here seeks to harness consumers' willingness to pay for conservation by inducing them to pay a premium for biodiversity-friendly shade-grown coffee. This premium would then encourage farmers to retain shade-grown coffee, thus maintaining its biodiversity benefits.

The chapter examines efforts to apply this approach to help protect Meso-america's rich biological diversity, which is severely threatened by land use change and other pressures.[2] Mesoamerica is a particularly promising area in which to use shade-grown coffee as a conservation tool, as coffee is an important crop throughout the region. Two projects that are seeking to apply this approach will be examined in detail: the Promotion of Biodiversity Conservation within Coffee Landscapes project (BCCL) in El Salvador, and the El Triunfo Biosphere Reserve: Habitat Enhancement in Productive Landscapes project (HEPL) in Chiapas, Mexico. Both of these projects are being implemented by the World Bank with financing from the Global Environment Facility (GEF). They have very similar objectives but use different approaches and are being implemented in different contexts, providing a valuable opportunity to see the mechanism at work.

BIODIVERSITY IN MESOAMERICA

Mesoamerica has extremely high levels of biodiversity, as a result of its unique location as a land bridge between two continental landmasses. Moreover, mountain ranges running through the length of the region have created distinct ecosystems on the Atlantic and Pacific sides, as well as a multitude of micro-ecosystems. Mesoamerica has both a great variety of species and a high level of endemism. It is also an important habitat for migratory species. The region has been named one of the world's biodiversity hot spots – areas of very high biodiversity that are under severe threat (Mittermeier and others, 1999).

As indicated by this designation, biodiversity in Mesoamerica is severely threatened. Central America experienced very high rates of deforestation during the 1960s and 1970s, with forest cover falling from about two-thirds to about one-third of the total area (UNRISD, 1995). An assessment of Mesoamerica's 33 eco-regions found that 11 were critically threatened, 11 endangered, and five vulnerable; five were relatively stable and only one was relatively intact (Dinerstein and others, 1995).

As in other parts of the world, the primary approach taken to conserving biodiversity in Mesoamerica has been the creation of a network of protected areas, which currently covers about 12 per cent of the region. This network has grown rapidly in recent decades (Boza, 1993). Many of the region's protected areas are only 'paper parks', however. Budgetary resources to manage existing parks are often inadequate, despite substantial efforts to develop additional sources of funding (Pagiola and Platais, 2001). Moreover, many protected areas are under substantial pressure for conversion to alternative uses. Even in Costa Rica, where almost 14 per cent of the country's area is protected, the isolation and fragmentation of protected areas threatens their viability (Boza, 1993). This problem is even more severe in densely populated countries such as El Salvador, where less than 1 per cent of the total area is protected. Expanding the protected areas is not a realistic option in most cases, however, due in part to a lack of funds for acquiring land and managing the enlarged parks, and in part to high rural population densities.

SHADE-GROWN COFFEE IN MESOAMERICA

In Mesoamerica, shade-grown coffee provides the greatest opportunity for biodiversity-friendly agricultural production. Because of the presence of trees, shade-grown coffee fields provide an environment that tends to be quite attractive to birds, particularly in the more traditional (so-called 'rustic') style of coffee production, with canopies from diverse native tree species (Perfecto and others, 1996; Moguel and Toledo, 1999). Shade-grown coffee areas have particularly high avian biodiversity (Greenberg, 1996; Moguel and Toledo, 1999). In contrast, coffee grown without shade ('sun' or 'technified' coffee) has very low biodiversity levels. A significant proportion of Mesoamerica's coffee production is shade-grown. Large areas also meet the basic criteria for organic production – essentially by default, due to farmers' inability to afford modern inputs.[3]

Extensive areas of coffee exist in Mesoamerica (Table 7.1). On average, coffee areas are about 13 per cent as extensive as protected areas. In El Salvador, the coffee area is more than ten times as large as the entire system of protected areas. Thus biodiversity-friendly coffee could extend protected areas by a significant proportion. The potential role of biodiversity-friendly coffee becomes all the more important when location is taken into account. Many coffee areas are located close to protected areas, thus expanding their area and connecting them to each other. This role is particularly important in countries such as El Salvador, where protected areas are small and isolated.

Throughout the region, shade-grown coffee production has been under pressure (Perfecto and others, 1996; Avalos-Sartorio and Becerra-Ortiz, 1999). Conversion to higher-yielding sun coffee varieties was heavily promoted from the 1970s onwards to increase farmer returns and reduce the risk of coffee rust, a fungal disease.[4] In Mesoamerica, conversion to technified coffee was most extensive in Costa Rica (Pratt and Harner, 1997), and least extensive in El Salvador, mainly because of the political turmoil in the country during the late 1970s and 1980s (Harner, 1997). More recently, low coffee prices are encouraging a shift from coffee production to other crops.[5]

Table 7.1 *Coffee and protected areas in Mesoamerica (square kilometers)*

	Total area	Forest area	Protected area	Coffee	Cocoa
Belize	22,960	n/a	4,834	n/a	2
Costa Rica	51,100	12,480	7,006	1,000	200
El Salvador	21,040	1,050	102	1,650	4
Guatemala	108,890	38,410	18,277	2,600	45
Honduras	112,090	41,150	11,120	2,490	58
Mexico[a]	1,958,200	553,870	72,842	7,568	814
Nicaragua	130,000	55,600	9,638	941	13
Panama	75,520	28,000	14,408	350	40

Note: a Data for Mexico are for the entire country, not just the part in Mesoamerica.
Source: World Bank, 2001

Decisions on whether to maintain land under shade-grown coffee are made by the farmers involved, in light of their own preferences and constraints. They do not generally consciously decide to damage biodiversity. But in making their decisions, they do not usually consider the benefits provided by biodiversity, because most of these benefits do not accrue to them. Farmers who are deciding whether to maintain shade-grown coffee or convert it to sun coffee or to other crops will consider the benefits from increased crop production resulting from the switch, and the cost of making the switch, but they will not consider the loss of biodiversity benefits nor the loss of other benefits such as watershed protection. The reason is simple: whereas farmers receive payment for (or consume directly) the crops they grow, they receive no compensation for the ecological services that biodiversity provides. These benefits, therefore, simply do not enter into their decision-making.

SELLING BIODIVERSITY IN A COFFEE CUP

The potential role of shade-grown coffee in protecting biodiversity in Mesoamerica, coupled with growing world consumption of specialty and gourmet coffees, have led several groups to launch efforts to certify shade-grown coffee in the hope that it will attract a price premium from environmentally-conscious consumers (Bingham Hull, 1999). Sales of specialty coffees reached over US$5 billion in 2000 in the United States alone, and are expected to continue to grow at rates of 5–10 per cent annually (Giovannucci, 2001).

The shade-coffee movement was sparked by the Smithsonian Migratory Bird Center (SMBC) in the mid-1990s. In addition to undertaking and financing research on the relationship between shade-grown coffee and biodiversity, the SMBC organized a workshop in 1996, which brought together environment-alists, farmers, and gourmet coffee companies to discuss using shade-grown coffee as a strategy to save Latin American forest areas. The idea was also picked up by other conservation groups eager to use shade-grown coffee as a means of conserving biodiversity. These groups acted to educate consumers about the merits of shade-grown coffee, distributors about its market potential, and producers about its potential for higher returns.

The World Bank and the GEF have both become interested in shade-grown coffee because of its potential to simultaneously address local development issues and broader environmental issues. These projects also fit into the broad program of work that both institutions are undertaking to help support the Mesoamerican Biological Corridor (MBC).

The principle of the approach is to capture consumer willingness to pay for biodiversity conservation by charging a premium for biodiversity-friendly coffee. This premium would increase the relative attractiveness to farmers of producing shade-grown coffee rather than sun coffee or other crops. As a result, it is hoped that farmers will retain their shade-grown coffee rather than switching to another, less biodiversity-friendly land use. This approach is at the core of both the BCCL project in El Salvador and the HEPL project in Chiapas, Mexico.

CASE STUDY AREAS

The two case study areas illustrate the range of conditions encountered in coffee-producing areas in Mesoamerica.

El Salvador[6]

Although El Salvador is a relatively small and highly populated country (6 million people in an area of 21,000 square kilometers (km^2)), it is endowed with rich ecosystems that result from its tropical location and a combination of unique ecological factors, including the presence of volcanic soils and its isolation from the Atlantic Central American moist forests. The central volcanic chain forms a series of 'islands' that has led to the development of endemic forms. This phenomenon is especially pronounced in the northern mountain range, which is contiguous with Guatemala and Honduras. El Salvador also includes vital stop-over sites for hundreds of thousands of migratory birds.

El Salvador is the most densely populated country in Latin America. Almost 40 per cent of its land area is under crops (including tree crops), more than twice the Central American average. Its rural population density of almost 400 people per km^2 of cropland is also almost twice the regional average. Extensive deforestation has left El Salvador with only 2 per cent of its land area still under natural forest; this is the lowest proportion in Central America and the second-lowest proportion in the western hemisphere, after Haiti. Only about 12 per cent of the territory has any forest cover at all, and most of it has been heavily disturbed. This deforestation has been driven by conversion to cattle ranching, agriculture, and human settlements. The remaining natural ecosystems of El Salvador are also subject to the same pressures.

Despite the heavy pressure it has come under, biodiversity remains abundant in El Salvador. With careful protection, management, and restoration, the remaining natural areas can play an important role in the conservation of biodiversity in Mesoamerica. Any significant expansion of protected areas is impossible, however, because of the high population density.

El Salvador has about 196,000ha under coffee cultivation, accounting for about 9 per cent of the country's area, and about 20,000 coffee producers (GEF, 1998; Harner, 1997). About 5 per cent of El Salvador's coffee area is farmed using rustic practices, in which the coffee is grown under an essentially intact native forest canopy; about 20 per cent is under commercial polyculture systems, with a mostly planted shade-tree canopy; about 30 per cent is under 'simplified' commercial polyculture systems, with a planted canopy consisting of only a few species; and about 40 per cent is under virtual monoculture, with one (or very few) species of canopy tree. Although the trend toward technification has been slow, it is ongoing. Informal estimates suggest that about 30 per cent of the area cultivated with coffee would be eligible for certification as shade-grown coffee, based on a criterion of having at least 40 per cent shade cover.

As an example of the conservation potential of shade-grown coffee in El Salvador, a survey of shade-grown coffee plantation in the Sierra del Bálsamo (a coffee region about 20km southeast of the Los Andes National Park) found 97 bird species, of which 30 per cent are threatened forest specialists or endemic to northern Central America. Several endangered mammals (cacomistle, ocelot, and Mexican porcupine) were also encountered.

Although some of the project's activities are national in focus, targeted research and other activities are focused on the Apaneca mountain range, a 75,000ha corridor linking the El Imposible and Los Volcanes protected areas. This area has been identified as one of the most important national biodiversity corridors, as well as being a strategic link to the MBC.

Chiapas, Mexico[7]

Coffee is Mexico's second-largest agricultural export. Mexico is the fifth-largest coffee producer in the world by volume and by area of land in coffee production; it leads the world in organic coffee exports. The El Triunfo Biosphere Reserve is located in the southern Mexican state of Chiapas, which is the principal coffee-producing state in Mexico and the second most important state for organic coffee. The reserve covers 120,000ha, comprising an internal buffer zone of about 93,500ha and a core zone of about 25,700ha. The core zone is pristine forest and is owned by the federal government. The internal buffer zone is private land owned by communities, *ejidos*, and individual farms of differing sizes, with a total population of about 14,000 people. About 60 per cent of the buffer zone (56,000ha) is densely forested, with the remaining 40 per cent of these lands (about 37,400ha) under agricultural production (mainly coffee, cattle, and maize). The reserve has remarkable biodiversity conservation value, with relatively large tracts of still-intact cloud forest and a high diversity of native animal and plant species, including many that occur only in the Sierra Madre of Chiapas and Guatemala. The reserve is the major stronghold of the highly threatened horned guan (*Oreophasis derbianus*) and azure-rumped tanager (*Tangara cabanisi*); it also harbors substantial populations of the resplendent quetzal (*Pharomachrus mocinno*) and many North American migratory bird species of conservation interest. The reserve is an integral part of the MBC.

The reserve has lost 17,000ha of forest in the past 20 years. Forest clearing for the establishment of new coffee plantations is one of the most important threats to the reserve; coffee growers are attracted by the excellent conditions created by the area's elevation and climate. Furthermore, for the many small and very poor producers living in the area it is the only cash crop that they can grow and market.

Coffee is the dominant crop in the reserve's buffer and influence zones. Most coffee is planted by small producers on farms of less than 5ha. The production system includes natural shade-trees in high densities. Around 70 per cent of coffee production in and around the reserve is produced in a rustic fashion under diverse shade, without agrochemicals, and therefore could be eligible for certification as organic and as 'biodiversity-friendly'. Some big coffee plantations have tech-nified their production system, reducing the diversity and quantity of shade and introducing the use of agrochemicals. A trend had begun among smallholders to replicate this system.[8]

The El Triunfo Region is characterized by its remoteness and by the dispersion of its population, resulting in a very low level of public service provision, little public infrastructure and weak institutions, many of which struggle with a legacy of being instruments of political interest groups. The area's coffee farmers, who manage farms smaller than 5ha, belong to one of the poorest social sectors in the poorest state in Mexico – Chiapas – and are thus highly marginalized.

MAKING IT WORK

The Rainforest Alliance began discussions with SalvaNATURA early in 1997 about creating a certification program in El Salvador, to improve the management of the buffer zones around and between two major national parks. SalvaNATURA had been managing the El Imposible national park in western El Salvador since 1991, and was looking for ways to promote biodiversity-friendly activities in the areas surrounding the park. Promoting shade-grown coffee offered a natural approach to doing so.

In Chiapas, interest in shade-grown coffee emerged from the initiative of a resourceful reserve director who was looking for ways to integrate biodiversity conservation mechanisms into the reserve's economic activities. The concrete idea was triggered by a study that showed the high variety of birds present in small coffee-producing farms in El Triunfo, and was the foundation of a project application to the GEF. The HEPL project is being implemented by the Institute for Sustainable Development in Mesoamerica (Instituto para el Desarrollo Sustentable en Mesoamérica, IDESMAC), a Chiapas-based non-governmental organization (NGO), jointly with the National Ecology Institute (Instituto Nacional de Ecología, INE), which is responsible for administering the biosphere reserve, and the Natural History Institute (Instituto de Historia Natural, IHN), a decentralized institution of the Chiapas state government.

In parallel, environmental NGO Conservation International (CI) has also been working with coffee producers in the El Triunfo area. CI has received financing from a GEF program administered by the World Bank's private-sector financing arm, the International Finance Corporation (IFC), to create the Conservation Enterprise Fund (CEF) to provide debt and equity financing to small- and medium-sized enterprises undertaking conservation activities. One of the groups financed by this program is a coffee cooperative in the El Triunfo area, Campesinos Ecológicos de la Sierra Madre de Chiapas (CESMACH), which is also benefiting substantially from the HEPL project. A US$93,000 loan from the CEF helped CESMACH to promote organic and shade-grown coffee for export. These two GEF projects are highly complementary: with the help of CI and the CEF, a successful business deal was reached with a major US coffee retailer (Starbucks), while the HEPL project provided the necessary underpinning of technical assistance.

The BCCL project in El Salvador was approved in 1998 (GEF, 1998). The HEPL Project in Chiapas, Mexico, was approved in 1999 (GEF, 1999). Both projects took advantage of the GEF's new medium-sized grants window, which provides streamlined procedures for small grants (less than US$1 million) that are available to NGOs. They are among the first medium-size grants approved by the GEF, and the first GEF projects related to sustainable agricultural systems.

The BCCL and the HEPL had similar objectives but different approaches (Table 7.2). Broadly, the BCCL project consisted of parallel efforts to aid coffee producers to certify their farms and to stimulate the market for the resulting certified coffee. The existence of relatively strong institutions in El Salvador's coffee sector allowed the BCCL project to directly develop substantive activities. The HEPL project focused on strengthening community-based organizations for coffee production as well as conservation efforts in the context of a very poor, remote, and highly marginalized rural area. Its coffee production, shade-grown certification, and marketing activities were part of a broader program of building capacity for sustainable rural development and of native species conservation through participatory mechanisms.

Table 7.2 *Project activities and budget* (US$ 000)

Activity	Total	GEF contribution
El Salvador		
Promotion of Biodiversity Conservation within Coffee Landscapes Project (BCCL)		
Development of extension services	384	186
Development of a shade-grown coffee certification program	947	309
Test-marketing and market development for certified coffee[a]	2,015	111
Monitoring of biological and socioeconomic impacts	454	119
Total	**3,800**	**725**
Chiapas, Mexico		
El Triunfo Biosphere Reserve: Habitat Enhancement in Productive Landscapes Project (HEPL)		
Strengthening of community participation and capacity-building of local institutions	437	251
Development and extension of sustainable agricultural production systems, including shade-grown coffee certification and commercialization	991	313
Conservation of native species population of flora and fauna, monitoring of project impacts, and environmental education	693	161
Total	**2,121**	**725**

Notes: Amounts shown are those budgeted at project approval stage; actual expenditures varied slightly.

   a   Includes US$1.9 million from the World Bank-financed Enhancing Competitiveness Technical Assistance Project.

Sources: GEF, 1998, 1999

In both projects, developing the capabilities of local organizations to deliver key inputs and manage the work program was a key theme (Giovannucci and others, 2000). This proved easier in El Salvador, where a core of organizations working with coffee producers already existed. In contrast, Chiapas had few credible organizations due to its remoteness and overall marginalized situation. Several existing community organizations were discredited by having been used by the governing party as vehicles for top–down policies. Both projects adopted decentralized approaches, with different agencies performing different functions, rather than attempting to create a single agency to undertake all project-related activities.

Consumer willingness to pay

The belief that consumers would be willing to pay a premium for biodiversity-friendly coffee is based on the rapid growth of the specialty and gourmet coffee market and on the success of other 'cause-related' or 'story' coffees, including organic and fair trade coffee (Rice and McLean, 1999).[9]

The first step in convincing consumers to pay a premium for shade-grown coffee is to educate them about its biodiversity benefits. Various efforts have been made on this front by a variety of organizations: some target consumers in general, some target coffee drinkers, and some target environmentally-conscious people. On the latter front, it is noteworthy that practically all the websites of US birding associations includes encouragement to select shade-grown coffee over its alternatives, in some cases with extensive documentation of its benefits for avian biodiversity and often with direct links to on-line retailers of shade-grown coffee. Although the BCCL financed the preparation of various marketing materials for Salvadoran shade-grown coffee, neither the BCCL nor the HEPL projects made extensive efforts on this front, which is far outside the area of expertise of their funding agencies. The HEPL bank project team joined forces with other interested organizations to commission the largest-ever survey of sustainable coffees in North American markets (Giovannucci, 2001).[10]

Certification

If consumers are to pay a premium for biodiversity-friendly coffee, they need assurance that this premium is in fact having the desired result. Some form of certification of shade-grown coffee is necessary, therefore. The certification problem can be divided into two parts. First, that of creating a certification process that consumers recognize and trust, and which certifies something they care about. Second, that of certifying farms to the appropriate standards so they can sell their coffee as shade-grown and benefit from the premium.

Gaining consumer recognition

At present, shade-grown coffee is just starting to be recognized in the market. Two main certification schemes have been proposed: the 'bird-friendly' label sponsored by the SMBC, and the 'Eco-OK' label sponsored by the Rainforest Alliance. In addition, numerous importers and dealers have their own labels. When the projects began, none of the labels had achieved widespread recognition, however. Nor was there widespread agreement on the specific criteria that would qualify coffee for certification as shade-grown. In contrast, organic coffee had already achieved extensive recognition, and could draw on the International Federation of Organic Agriculture Movements (IFOAM) for agreed criteria that would qualify a coffee as organic. Similarly, actors in the fair-trade market had developed an international alliance, the Fairtrade Labelling Organization (FLO).

Certifying producers

As indicated in Table 7.2, both projects devoted substantial efforts and resources to the issue of producer certification. The different approaches taken illustrate some of the dilemmas encountered in developing a standard certification program. In both locations, expert workshops were held to define criteria for certification that would be compatible with market demands and practical for local producers. In both cases, a key element of the debate was whether shade-grown coffee should also meet organic certification criteria. In El Salvador, growers opposed the inclusion of organic criteria in the certification requirements. For many of them, meeting organic production criteria would have required changes in production practices. Moreover, organic certification requires considerable periods of time: it can only be awarded three years after the last application of agrochemicals. In contrast, the strategy agreed in Chiapas was to work toward a comprehensive seal that embraced the concepts of 'organic', 'fair trade', and 'biodiversity friendly'. This difference was partly based on organic production being well established in Chiapas. A local coffee cooperative supported by the Catholic Church was already successfully exporting organic coffee to Europe. Furthermore, most coffee growers in the El Triunfo area were already 'default organic' producers; meeting organic standards did not require radical changes in production practices.[11] Moreover, HEPL project participants were nervous about staking their success entirely on shade-grown certification, as that market was still largely hypothetical at the time. Including organic criteria meant that certified coffee could take advantage of the existing premium for organic coffee, providing a fallback in case the premiums for shade-grown coffee did not materialize as expected. It is important to bear in mind that for certification to work, the entire marketing chain needs to be certified, not just the farm. Even if a farm is certified, its coffee can only be sold as certified if the processor is also certified.[12]

No certification program existed for either organic or biodiversity-friendly coffee in El Salvador prior to the BCCL. About 2000ha of coffee were certified as organic and another 2000ha were undergoing certification, but this depended on bringing in inspectors from outside the country at the producers' expense. A certification mechanism was established with the help of the Rainforest Alliance's

Eco-OK program, which trained El Salvador's most prominent environmental NGO, SalvaNATURA, to be the country's first coffee-certifying agency.

In Chiapas, about 2 per cent of coffee production was certified as organic before the HEPL project; none was certified as shade-grown. The National Association for Sustainable Coffee Production (Consejo Civil de la Cafeticultura Sustentable de Mexico), which brings together all the larger coffee producer organizations in Mexico, was created under the HEPL project. This association promotes the jointly developed shade-grown coffee certification criteria nation-wide; it trains and disseminates information; works on mechanisms for quality assurance; and aims to become the accrediting agency for certifiers of shade-grown coffee in Mexico. One private certification company is now certifying coffee in five of the seven producer organizations under the HEPL project in the El Triunfo Biosphere Reserve.

Ensuring that the cost of complying with certification criteria would be within the reach of coffee producers was a major consideration for both projects. They both addressed the problem by supporting, using GEF funds, the creation and operation of the certificating agencies, and also by subsidizing the cert-ification fees paid by some producers. For example, in El Salvador the cost of certification includes a one-time fee (currently US$940) to inspect farms to determine whether they comply, and then an annual fee of US$7.5/ha for use of the seal. The large flat fee for the inspection would clearly pose a very substantial obstacle for smaller farms, and so the BCCL project subsidized this cost on a sliding scale depending on farm size: farms of less than 7ha were fully subsidized, while farms of more than 70ha received a 32 per cent subsidy. In Chiapas, where small producers predominate, a mechanism for collective certification was developed, allowing groups of farmers to be certified jointly and pay a single certification fee. This was similar to the group certification used in Costa Rica's PSA program (see Chapter 3). This reduced the US$2900 certification fee to about US$30 per farm, depending on the number of farms in a group. Making collective certification work, however, required considerable efforts to develop organizations that could work with farmers. Five of the seven producer groups under the HEPL project are now in the process of receiving both organic and shade-grown certification. Shade certification adds about 15 per cent to the cost of organic certification.

Certification can also impose costs on participating farmers who need to adapt their production systems and their farms to meet the criteria.[13] There are no data on the magnitude of these costs, which are borne entirely by the farmers themselves, but anecdotal evidence shows that they can at times be quite sub-stantial. Several farms in El Salvador, for example, expended over US$1000 to adapt their farms to meet certification criteria (in their case, primarily to meet the social requirements of the criteria) – about as much as the certification fee itself. In the case of El Triunfo, the adaptation costs are minor due to the subsistence production systems that had been applied by small farmers in the area.

Extension

As with many agricultural activities, an extension system is necessary. In this case, it not only helps farmers to improve their agricultural practices, but it also helps them to publicize and explain criteria for certification and to provide technical assistance in meeting them. Such a system is particularly important if meeting certification criteria requires changing the production system. Although calculations show that certification can be profitable even at current yields, it would clearly be advantageous to have an extension system that can help to increase yields while remaining within the certification criteria, as that would magnify the impact of any price premium. Perhaps even more important, as noted earlier, is assistance in improving product quality. In both countries, however, extension efforts were hampered by the paucity of information on shade-grown coffee systems. In recent decades, most research on coffee had been focused on technified coffee. As a result, there is very little to extend (GEF, 1998). With renewed interest in shade-grown coffee, research is now resuming, but it will be some time before useful information is available.

In El Salvador, PROCAFÉ,[14] a private extension agency, provides extension services through its existing national network and helped to develop a technical manual, the *Guide to Producing Biodiversity Friendly Coffee* (PROCAFÉ, 2001). In Mexico agricultural extension services are generally very weak. They are particularly weak in the El Triunfo area. The HEPL project invested in building in-house extension service capacity for organic and shade-grown coffee in the producer organizations. As the project ends, sustaining these extension services is one of the key areas that need to be addressed.[15]

Other requirements

As certification requires farmers to make an investment, reasonably secure property rights are an important prerequisite if the mechanism is to work. It is reasonable to assume that coffee farmers do feel reasonably confident of their property rights, since in fact all have already made long-term investments in coffee production.

The availability of credit can also play an important role in allowing coffee producers to invest in certification, as well as in helping to finance annual production costs. Rural credit availability is typically scarce, and what credit is available is often biased against shade-grown coffee (CEC, 2000). In El Salvador, SalvaNATURA offered a subsidized line of credit to participating farms. In Chiapas, the HEPL project does not include a credit component because of the overall poor experience with credit in rural development projects. Instead, the HEPL project helped producer organizations to identify sources of credit from financial institutions. By guaranteeing the creditworthiness of producer groups, the HEPL helped them to secure loans for pre-harvest operations on softer conditions than the overall market rate. While this was the overall strategy of the project, it also proved necessary for the project to help farmers to secure short-term credit for certification and post-harvest activities.

RESULTS

Certification of shade-grown coffee so as to capture a premium from environmentally-conscious consumers is still a very new mechanism, and so its results are still difficult to assess. Although the producer side of the mechanism seems to have been implemented effectively, the consumer side remains weak.

Certification

In El Salvador, the first two farms were certified in April 1999. As of September 2001 seven had been certified, with a combined area of 920ha.[16] Another 40 farms, covering 289ha, have been approved by SalvaNATURA and are awaiting formal issuance of the Eco-OK seal. An additional 177 farms, covering almost 7500ha, are in the process of certification. In Chiapas, 859ha were certified in 1999–2000, 72ha in 2000–2001, and an expected 915ha in 2001–2002, bringing the total area certified to 1846ha, covering 797 farms grouped in seven associations – well beyond the project's target of 1500ha certified.

Other parts of the marketing chain have also been certified. The work has not always kept pace with farm certification, however. In El Salvador, certified farms produced about 700,000kg of coffee in 2001. Of this quantity, however, about 124,000kg were not processed by certified processors and so could not be sold as certified. In the event, however, low sales of certified coffee (see below) meant that this was not a constraint.

These results show that producer certification can be achieved even under relatively difficult situations such as those encountered in Chiapas. This success clearly requires keeping the cost of certification low, including the cost of certification itself and the cost of any changes in production practices required to achieve certification. The cost of certification can be particularly high when production is very fragmented and access is difficult, as in the case of Chiapas. As this case shows, however, this obstacle can be overcome with approaches such as collective certification. Keeping the cost of production changes low can potentially create a tension with the requirements of inducing consumers to accept the product. Many consumers who care about the environment are also likely to care about organic production and social equity. The temptation, then, is to impose relatively stringent and demanding requirements for certification, dealing not just with production practices but with a broad array of environmental and social objectives. Doing so, however, risks making certification too onerous for many producers, thus undermining the financial logic of the mechanism. It also risks placing poor producers at a particular disadvantage. This is a situation in which the best can be the enemy of the good, and can – perversely – have an adverse equity impact.

Achieving this level of success in certifying producers did require fairly substantial external resources. In Chiapas in particular, substantial efforts were required to establish and strengthen institutions to undertake certification and extension services (Giovannucci and others, 2000). The question thus becomes whether such a mechanism could operate without subsidies on a purely commercial basis. If the mechanism proves successful and certification services become more widely available, it is likely that average costs would fall. Even so, in some situations external support may be necessary, particularly to ensure that poorer producers have access to the mechanism. This is similar to the problem encountered in ensuring that smallholders in Chiapas can participate in markets for carbon sequestration (see Chapter 12).

Marketing

Beyond the problem of adopting appropriate, recognized certification criteria, other marketing constraints must also be taken into account. Many wholesalers and retailers need minimum volumes, assured quality, and reliable flows if they are to carry a product. Many shade-grown coffee producers are very small – indeed, entire producing areas in Mesoamerica are very small from this perspective. However, there are many small specialty roasters and importers that can handle small volumes, so this problem is less important than it might seem. Quality considerations are harder to address. Market studies show that without acceptable quality, other characteristics do not matter (CEC, 1999; Giovannucci, 2001). Yet achieving high and consistent levels of quality in smallholder environments is difficult. One analyst has called this 'perhaps the biggest stumbling block for further development on the production end' (Giovannucci, personal communication).

Premium for certified shade-grown coffee

The bottom line for the mechanism resides in its ability to deliver a price premium to producers. On this score, it must be said that results to date have been disappointing. Unlike organic coffee, which typically receives a premium of 10–15 per cent over comparable non-organic coffee (ICO, 2000), shade-grown coffee only occasionally earns a premium. To date, premiums for shade-grown coffee have resulted solely from ad hoc transactions with individual purchasers. In 1999, Salvadoran farms certified under the BCCL program sold 100 bags[17] of shade-grown coffee with a US$25 premium over the standard 'C' contract price, and 7000 bags with a US$6 premium. However, no certified coffee was sold in 2000, and only 500 bags were sold in 2001, half with a US$13 premium and half with a US$8 premium. Of these premiums, the amount received by producers varied depending on whether the sale was arranged by the producers themselves (in which case they kept the entire premium) or by El Salvador's coffee brokering organization, ONEX (in which case the broker kept 25 per cent of the premium).[18] In Chiapas, there have been two high-profile sales of coffee to Starbucks, which were arranged with the assistance of CI, resulting in a premium of US$100 per bag in 2001. In 2002 the premium is likely to be higher, given the very low coffee prices. Sales of shade-grown coffee as such have been limited, however. Because shade-grown coffee from Chiapas is also certified as organic, however, participating farmers have at least received the organic premium. Data from three producer groups show that premiums as high as 100 per cent have occasionally been received, though about 40 per cent has been more typical. To further diversify its marketing strategy, the producer organization has also received fair-trade certification.

The main constraint to shade-grown coffee sales has been the lack of recognition of the category in the market. Awareness of shade-grown coffee has grown rapidly in the industry. A survey of North American retailers, roasters, wholesalers, distributors, and importers found that over 76 per cent were aware of the product category, and about one-third sold it (Giovannucci, 2001).[19] This awareness does not necessarily extend to consumers, however. Research by the Commission for Environmental Cooperation shows that coffee consumers do not generally recognize the shade-grown coffee concept (CEC, 2000). Until such time as the shade-grown label becomes widely recognized and accepted by the coffee market, any benefits will depend on brokering individual deals with interested buyers.

At first, neither project had a substantial commercialization component except for a stand-alone marketing study. As the problems in obtaining the hoped-for premiums became evident, first the HEPL project and subsequently the BCCL project realized the need to strengthen marketing efforts and retrofitted commercialization components. The projects increased their marketing efforts, including participation in specialty coffee trade fairs. It is as yet too early for these efforts to have borne fruit, however. In El Salvador, some sales of certified coffee were made with the assistance of Sustainable Harvest, a US coffee importer that specializes in sustainable coffees and had been retained by the BCCL to assist in marketing efforts.

Farmer incentives

Growers in El Salvador have understandably considered results to date to be disappointing. Sales of certified coffee have accounted for a very small proportion of available certified coffee: just 34,500kg of the 565,800kg of certified coffee available in the 2001 season were actually sold as shade-grown coffee, with the rest being sold as standard coffee. Some are regretting that they did not also seek organic certification for their coffee, and are working to achieve it under a project financed by the German aid agency Deutsche Gesellschaft für Technische Zusammenarbeit (GTZ). With premiums for shade-grown coffee still so limited in El Salvador, the corresponding incentives for coffee farmers to participate have obviously been equally limited (PROCAFÉ, 2000). Indeed, it appears that many certified farms decided to participate at least as much out of personal environmental conviction as out of expectations of improved profitability. That's fine as far as it goes, but it is unlikely that shade-grown coffee will be widely attractive to most producers without a monetary incentive.

In Chiapas, more substantial premiums have been received and the corresponding incentives to farmers have obviously been higher. That these premiums are derived from their coffee being organic rather than shade-grown per se is a technicality of little consequence to the producers. Predictably, IDESMAC reports considerable interest from non-participating farmers in becoming certified.

Even in past years with higher coffee prices, many analyses showed that shade-grown coffee, with its lower production costs, could be more profitable than technified coffee despite its lower yields (Gobbi, 2000). Today, with coffee prices at historic lows, the balance has probably shifted substantially in favor of shade-grown coffee even in the absence of a price premium. Technified coffee is particularly penalized by low prices, because the extra yield cannot compensate for the higher costs of production. Shade-grown coffee, with its lower costs, suffers relatively less from low coffee prices. Moreover, the income derived from other products – such as timber, fuelwood, fruit, and under-story crops – helps to cushion the impact of low revenues from coffee sales.

A premium for shade-grown coffee would obviously tilt the balance even further toward shade-grown coffee. With prices so low, however, the relevant comparison is no longer with technified coffee. Given the cost of switching from technified coffee to shade-grown coffee (for example, the cost and time needed to establish the minimum 40 per cent cover required for certification as shade-grown) it is very unlikely that anyone would undertake such an investment given current coffee prices, even if shade-grown coffee carried a substantial premium. Rather, the comparison must be with alternative non-coffee uses of the same land. Most coffee-producing areas in Mesoamerica have a rather limited range of alternatives. Particularly in areas such as Chiapas, the only realistic alternative to coffee production is likely to be subsistence food production. If coffee prices remain as low as they are, even this might appear attractive, however. A premium for shade-grown coffee would obviously be of great assistance in reducing incentives for farmers to abandon coffee entirely and turn to other, much less biodiversity-friendly land uses.

In addition to receiving a premium for the coffee itself, there is also some potential for producers to capture some of the benefits of the biodiversity in their coffee farms through ecotourism, and particularly by catering to the bird-watching market. Some larger coffee estates already offer bird-watching tours of their farms. In areas where shade-grown coffee is planted on small farms, as in the El Triunfo area, efforts to capture benefits through ecotourism will obviously require the creation of mechanisms to share the benefits of such activities. The problem is similar to that encountered with collective certification, however, so there is no reason to expect that it cannot be solved if ecotourism proves to be a realistic option.

Finally, it is worth noting that coffee producers also receive non-monetary benefits. Local communities in the El Triunfo area, for example, take pride in living in a 'paradise'. They have told project staff that they value the forest and the birds – so long as they can also make a living.

Conservation impact

Initial monitoring by SalvaNATURA confirms that shade-grown coffee provides high levels of biodiversity benefits. Although the two projects have resulted in the certification of significant areas of shade-grown coffee, available data are insufficient to allow an evaluation of the extent to which they helped to either reduce the trend of converting shade-grown coffee to other uses, or preferably to increase it. The next few years may well provide a natural experiment, however. Very low coffee prices are likely to result in many coffee farmers switching to other land uses. Will certified shade-grown coffee farms switch at a lower rate than other areas? Already there seems to be some indications that this may be the case. In El Salvador, anecdotal information points to a trend for technified coffee producers to diversify their production by planting fruit and timber trees in their properties. This obviously will make their coffee more akin to shade-grown. While this is probably primarily a reaction to very low coffee prices rather than a deliberate effort to switch to shade-grown coffee production, the effect is the same. Should marketing efforts succeed in generating a premium for shade-grown coffee, this incipient trend can only accelerate.

A universal concern that arises from efforts to improve returns in forest frontier areas is that they will encourage further clearing of primary forest (Angelsen and Kaimowitz, 2001). Shade-grown coffee may be biodiversity-friendly, but it remains less desirable than primary forest. If providing a premium for shade-grown coffee causes small farms to expand at the expense of primary forest, the mechanism might well prove counterproductive from a conservation perspective. Both projects attempted to guard against this danger by making certification contingent on preservation of remaining forest areas. Whether this precaution is sufficient is difficult to determine under current circumstances: with coffee prices as low as they are, it is very unlikely that any Mesoamerican farmer would consider investing in clearing and planting new coffee areas.

Other environmental benefits

In addition to helping to protect biodiversity, shade-grown coffee also has the potential to provide other benefits. With its substantial ground cover, shade-grown coffee probably provides similar hydrological benefits to forest. The nature and magnitude of such benefits are not completely understood, however, and may not be as large as is commonly supposed (Hamilton and King, 1983; Bruijnzeel, 1990; Chomitz and Kumari, 1998; Calder, 1999). The value of these benefits varies, moreover, with location. Regulating hydrological flows is likely to be much more valuable in densely populated El Salvador, for example, than in sparsely populated Chiapas. This also might create opportunities to generate additional benefits for shade-grown coffee producers. El Salvador is planning to develop a system of payments for environmental services, for example (see Chapter 3). To the extent that coffee areas can be demonstrated to provide valuable services such as regulating hydrological flows, they might be eligible for payments under this system. In Chiapas, the El Triunfo Reserve is actively pursuing the idea of creating a hydrological market (Burstein, 2000). Considerable work remains to be done before this can become a reality. In particular, the extent to which coffee areas provide hydrological benefits has been very poorly documented to date. With its high tree component, shade-grown coffee also contributes to carbon sequestration. A study in Guatemala is measuring the carbon sequestered in shade-grown coffee fields (Cuéllar and others, 1999).

Development impact

The main beneficiaries of the project are the coffee producers. For coffee producers, selling shade-grown coffee provides the possibility of increasing their income. This would be particularly important under current circumstances, with prices for uncertified coffee being so low. To the extent that prices for certified coffee fluctuate less than regular coffee prices, the mechanism could also alleviate one of the major sources of uncertainty in their livelihood. In El Salvador, this potential has yet to be realized. An evaluation of the socioeconomic impact of the BCCL found little discernible impact to date, primarily because of the low or non-existent premiums obtained to date for shade-grown coffee (Cabezas, 2001). Any significant impact is clearly dependent on obtaining such a premium. No formal evaluation has yet been conducted in Chiapas, but the impact there is likely to be greater thanks to the organic premium obtained by participating producers; early indications suggest that the project will reach its objective of increasing the average net income of small producers by about 25 per cent.

The poverty impact is likely to be greater in Chiapas, where shade-grown coffee is produced mainly by small farmers, than in El Salvador, where coffee is typically produced by better-off farmers. IDESMAC reports anecdotal evidence that out-migration levels are lower among program participants than in the region as a whole.

Beyond any impact arising from higher incomes, other positive impacts can be foreseen. Civil society participation was an integral part of the planning and implementation of both projects. The participatory organizations that have either been strengthened or been established as a result of the projects are also likely to confer their own benefits. Social capital has increasingly been recognized as playing an important role in the development process.

Sustainability

The sustainability of the mechanism depends on two main factors. First is the sustainability of market demand for shade-grown coffee. As the ability to capture consumer willingness to pay for biodiversity-friendly coffee has been demonstrated to only a very limited extent to date, it is premature to try to judge how sustainable that demand might be. The second factor is the sustainability of the certification mechanisms and the social structures that make them work. This is related to the first problem in many ways. If a sufficient premium for shade-grown coffee cannot be obtained regularly, certification mechanisms are unlikely to keep working, particularly once external support from the GEF-financed projects ends.

CONCLUSIONS

As a means of capturing and channeling consumer willingness to pay for conservation, shade-grown coffee is still a very new mechanism. The experience of the BCCL project in El Salvador and the HEPL project in Chiapas shows that making this mechanism work in the field can require substantial efforts, but that no problems are insurmountable. Even in what would appear at first to be a relatively unpromising environment such as Chiapas – with small, scattered, and dispersed production and little extant social capital – certification can be made to work and to reach even small producers. Such efforts may require some degree of external assistance, however, particularly to ensure that small producers do in fact have access to the mechanism.

The experience of both projects also shows, however, that the operation of such mechanisms cannot rely solely on efforts at the supply end. No matter how effective these efforts may be, they will ultimately have little impact unless there is effective demand for the service or product. In the case of shade-grown coffee, there is substantial evidence of consumer interest in conservation and of their willingness to pay. However, efforts to capture this willingness to pay have had only limited success to date. Unlike the market for organic products, which is now much more mature, the market for shade-grown coffee is still relatively undeveloped. Although certification schemes exist, they are still little recognized by consumers.[20] Prices are still based on individually negotiated deals and thus tend to vary substantially. To the extent that shade-grown coffee is also certified as organic, as in Chiapas, it can piggy-back on the premium already available from the more mature market.

Potential for expansion/replication

If premiums for shade-grown coffee are obtained regularly, the potential for the expansion of the mechanism becomes quite significant. The most important potential clearly applies to other coffee-producing areas. There are also other production systems that contain relatively high levels of forest cover and biodiversity, and which might benefit from similar approaches. Shade-grown cocoa has very similar characteristics to shade-grown coffee, for example (Parrish and others, 1998, 1999; Greenberg, 1998). As can be seen from Table 7.1, the potential for shade cocoa to contribute to biodiversity conservation is smaller, as it covers a much smaller area. Another GEF-financed medium-size project, Biodiversity Conservation through Promotion of Organic Cacao Production in Forest Landscapes project (GEF, 2001), is applying the same approach to shade cocoa in Costa Rica. This project became effective in mid-2001, too late for inclusion in this Chapter. The Nature Conservancy has also used this approach to promote shade cocoa in the Talamanca region of Costa Rica (Parrish and others, 1998).

NOTES

1 The opinions expressed in this Chapter are the authors' own and do not necessarily reflect those of the World Bank. The authors would like to thank Enoc Altunar López of IDESMAC, Ines Maria Ortiz of PROCAFÉ, and Paola Agostini and Gonzalo Castro of the World Bank for their assistance, and Beatriz Avalos-Sartorio for helpful comments. The authors are particularly grateful for the assistance of Daniele Giovannucci, who worked in both project teams, making very important contributions to commercialization efforts and to understanding markets for biodiversity-friendly coffee.

2 As used here, the term Mesoamerica includes all of Central America (Guatemala, Belize, Honduras, El Salvador, Nicaragua, Costa Rica, and Panama) and parts of southern Mexico. This definition follows that of the Central America biodiversity hot spot as defined by Mittermeier and others (1999).

3 Demand for organic coffee, although driven primarily by consumer perceptions of health risks associated with agrochemical residues, also tends to have environmentally benign effects. There is considerable overlap between shade-grown and organic coffee production, in that sun coffee is almost never organic, while shade-grown coffee usually is. As discussed below, however, the formal requirements for organic certification go well beyond the absence of agrichemical use, often making it difficult for producers to qualify.

4 Unfortunately, available data rarely distinguish shade coffee production from sun coffee production, making it difficult to trace changes in relative areas.

5 Evidence from the Mexican state of Oaxaca indicates that low coffee prices have also encouraged increased deforestation of adjacent forests, as coffee farmers seek additional income sources (Avalos-Sartorio and Becerra-Ortiz, 1999).

6 Unless otherwise indicated, all data in this section are drawn from the BCCL project brief (GEF, 1998).

7 Unless otherwise indicated, all data in this section are drawn from the HEPL project brief (GEF, 1999).

8 In Mexico as a whole, about 11 per cent of the coffee area is estimated to be under technified coffee, 42 per cent under shaded monoculture, 10 per cent under commercial polyculture, and 39 per cent under traditional polyculture (Moguel and Toledo, 1999).

9 Broadly, organic certification requires limited use or no use at all of agrochemicals, and measures to preserve soil fertility. Fair-trade certification requires buyers to develop long-term relationships with producers, guarantee them minimum prices, and provide them with credit. Together, organic, fair-trade, and shade-grown coffees are sometimes referred to as 'sustainable' coffees (Giovannucci, 2001).

10 Consumer surveys carried out by the Commission for Environmental Cooperation (CEC, 1999) showed that about 20 per cent of US coffee consumers and about 40 per cent of Canadian coffee consumers would be willing to pay a US$1 per pound (lb) premium for such coffee. A survey by the SMBC found that consumers were willing to pay a premium of about US$0.25–0.50/lb for environmentally and socially

sustainable coffee, while a survey undertaken by Duke University students found that 36 per cent of consumers were willing to pay a premium of US$1/lb for shade-grown coffee (cited in Rice and McLean, 1999). However, methodological problems and small sample sizes place these and other existing surveys' results in doubt.

11 The term 'default organic' is widely used to describe farmers who use little or no agrochemicals in their production. However, it should be noted that organic standards are not simply a matter of not using agrochemicals, but are also about retaining soil fertility using manure and other natural means. Meeting some of these additional criteria has caused problems for many producers.

12 In 1996, coffee sold as premium Hawaiian Kona coffee was found to include a significant proportion of lower-quality coffee. The resulting scandal emphasized the need for reliable verification of origins and quality claims (Rice and McLean, 1999).

13 Both the SMBC and the Eco-OK certification standards go beyond production criteria. For example, Eco-OK also includes conservation criteria (for example, farmers must reforest and/or conserve nearby non-coffee forests) and social criteria (for example, farmers must provide adequate housing for workers, as well as an occupational health program, including access to periodical health examinations). The various criteria are allotted point values, with 800 points out of a possible 1000 being necessary for certification.

14 The Fundación Salvadoreña para Investigaciones del Café (PROCAFÉ) is a private, non-profit organization that provides extension services to Salvadoran coffee producers. It is financed by an export fee. PROCAFÉ provides free technical advice to coffee producers, but resources are insufficient to serve all producers.

15 The HEPL project has also promoted the integration and mainstreaming of bio-diversity conservation values into government programs, particularly those of the Ministry of Agriculture. The Federal Ministry of Agriculture and the Mexican Coffee Council have expressed their intention to use the results of the HEPL project and to disseminate and promote them broadly.

16 Several of these farms are cooperatives in which coffee is farmed either collectively or individually, so the small number of certified farms masks a much larger number of certified producers.

17 A bag of coffee contains 69kg.

18 Several of the certified coffee farms in El Salvador operate their own processing plants.

19 Note, however, that this is based on a very inclusive definition of 'shade-grown'. Only 12 per cent of firms surveyed sold certified shade-grown coffee (Giovannucci, 2001).

20 For some time, there has been debate about the desirability of consolidating certification schemes, or of establishing a 'super-seal' that would encompass the others (Rice and McLean, 1999). Little progress has been made in this direction, however. According to Giovannucci's (2001) survey of the coffee marketing industry, demand for such a super-seal has increased substantially in recent years.

REFERENCES

Angelsen, A., and D. Kaimowitz. 2001. "Introduction: The Role of Agricultural Technologies in Tropical Deforestation." In A. Angelsen and D. Kaimowitz (eds.), *Agricultural Technologies in Tropical Deforestation*. Wallingford: CABI Publishing in association with CIFOR.

Avalos-Sartorio, B., and M.R. Becerra-Ortiz. 1999 "La Economía de la Producción y Comercialización del Café en la Sierra Sur, Costa e Istmo del Estado de Oaxaca: Resultados Preliminares." *Ciencia y Mar*, III:8, pp.29–39.

Bingham Hull, J. 1999. "Can Coffee Drinkers Save the Rain Forest?" *The Atlantic Monthly*, 284:2, August, pp.19–21.

Boza, M.A. 1993. "Conservation in Action: Past, Present, and Future of the National Park System of Costa Rica." *Conservation Biology*, 7:2, pp.239–247.

Bruijnzeel, L.A. 1990. *Hydrology of Moist Tropical Forests and Effects of Conservation: A State of Knowledge Review*. UNESCO International Hydrological Programme. Paris: UNESCO.

Burstein, J. 2000. "Pago por Servicios Ambientales en México." Paper presented at the Foro para el Desarollo Sustentable, San Cristóbal de las Casas, Chiapas, Mexico.

Cabezas, J.R. 2001. "Impacto Socioeconómico y Ambiental de la Caficultura Amigable con la Biodiversidad." Nueva San Salvador: PROCAFE.

Calder, I. 1999. *The Blue Revolution: Land Use and Integrated Water Resource Management*. London: Earthscan.

Chomitz, K.M., and K. Kumari. 1998. "The Domestic Benefits of Tropical Forest Preservation: A Critical Review Emphasizing Hydrological Functions." *World Bank Research Observer*, 13:1, pp.13–35.

Commission for Environmental Cooperation (CEC). 1999. "Measuring Consumer Interest in Mexican Shade-grown Coffee: An Assessment of the Canadian, Mexican and US Markets." Montréal: CEC (processed).

Commission for Environmental Cooperation (CEC). 2000. "Background Note for Participating Experts." Paper presented at the Experts Workshop on Shade-Grown Coffee, Oaxaca, Mexico, March 29–30, 2000 (processed).

Cuellár, N., H. Rosa, and M.E. Gonzalez. 1999. "Los Servicios Ambientales del Agro: El Caso del Café de Sombra en El Salvador." Boletin No.34. San Salvador: PRISMA.

Dinerstein, E., D.M. Olson, D.J. Graham, A.L. Webster, S.A. Primm, M.P. Bookbinder, and G. Ledec. 1995. *A Conservation Assessment of the Terrestrial Ecoregions of the Latin America and the Caribbean*. Washington: World Bank in association with the World Wildlife Fund.

Giovannucci, D. 2001. "Sustainable Coffee Survey of the North American Specialty Coffee Industry." Philadelphia: Global Consulting (processed).

Giovannucci, D., P. Brandriss, E. Brenes, I.-M.Ruthenberg, and P. Agostini. 2000. "Engaging Civil Society to Create Sustainable Agricultural Systems: Environmentally-Friendly Coffee in El Salvador and Mexico." Washington: World Bank (processed).

Global Environment Facility (GEF). 1998. "El Salvador: Promotion of Biodiversity Conservation Within Coffee Landscapes." Medium Size Grant Project Brief. Washington: GEF.

Global Environment Facility (GEF). 1999. "El Triunfo Biosphere Reserve: Habitat Enhancement in Productive Landscapes." Medium Size Grant Project Brief. Washington: GEF.

Global Environment Facility (GEF). 2001. "Costa Rica: Biodiversity Conservation Through Promotion of Organic Cacao Production in Forest Landscapes." Medium Size Grant Project Brief. Washington: GEF.

Gobbi, J.A. 2000. "Is Biodiversity-Friendly Coffee Financially Viable? An Analysis of Five Different Coffee Production Systems in Western El Salvador." *Ecological Economics, 33*, pp.267–281.

Greenberg, R. 1996. "Birds in the Tropics: The Coffee Connection." *Birding*, December, pp.472–481.

Greenberg, R. 1998. "Biodiversity in the Cacao Agroecosystem: Shade Management and Landscape Considerations." Paper presented at the Cacao Workshop, Panamá, March 30–April 2, 1998.

Hamilton, L.S., and P.N. King. 1983. *Tropical Forest Watersheds: Hydrologic and Soils Response to Major Uses and Conversions*. Boulder: Westview Press.

Harner, C.N. 1997. "Sustainability Analysis of the Coffee Industry in El Salvador." Paper CEN 706. Alajuela: Centro Latinoamericano para la Competitividad y Desarrollo Sostenible (CLACDS).

International Coffee Organisation (ICO). 2000. "Organic Coffee." Summary of Round Table Discussion on Coffee Produced by 'Organic' Farming Methods and the Position in the Year 2000. London: ICO (processed).

Mittermeier, R.A., N. Myers, P. Robles Gil, and C.G. Mittermeier. 1999. *Hotspots: Earth's Biologically Richest and Most Endangered Terrestrial Ecoregions*. Mexico City: CEMEX.

Moguel, P., and V.M. Toledo. 1999. "Biodiversity Conservation in Traditional Coffee Systems of Mexico." *Conservation Biology, 13*:1, pp.11–21.

Pagiola, S., J. Kellenberg, L. Vidaeus, and J. Srivastava. 1997. *Mainstreaming Biodiversity in Agricultural Development: Toward Good Practice*. Environment Paper Number 15. Washington: World Bank.

Pagiola, S., and G. Platais. 2001. "Selling Biodiversity in Central America." Paper presented at the International Workshop on Market Creation for Biodiversity Products and Services, OECD, Paris, January 25–26, 2001.

Parrish, J.D., R. Reitsma, and R. Greenberg. 1998. "Cacao as Crop and Conservation Tool: Lessons from the Talamanca Region of Costa Rica." Paper presented at the First International Workshop on Sustainable Cocoa Growing, Panamá, March 30–April 2, 1998.

Parrish, J.D., R. Reitsma, R. Greenberg, K. Skerl, W. McLarney, R. Mack, and J. Lynch. 1999. "Cacao as Crop and Conservation Tool in Central America: Addressing the Needs of Farmers and Forest Conservation." America Verde Working Paper No.3. Arlington: The Nature Conservancy.

Perfecto, I., R.A. Rice, R. Greenberg, and M.E. van der Voort. 1996. "Shade Coffee: A Disappearing Refuge for Biodiversity." *BioScience, 46*:8, pp.598–608.

Pratt, L., and Harner, C.N. 1997. "Sustainability Analysis of the Coffe Industry in Costa Rica." Paper CEN 761. Alajuela: Centro Latinoamericano para la Competitividad y Desarrollo Sostenible (CLACDS).

PROCAFÉ. 2000. "Evaluación Financiera de los Diferentes Sistemas de Producción de Café en El Salvador." Nueva San Salvador: PROCAFÉ.

PROCAFÉ. 2001. "Guía Para la Producción de Café Bajo Sombra Amigable con la Biodiversidad." Nueva San Salvador: PROCAFÉ.

Rice, P.D., and J. McLean. 1999. *Sustainable Coffee at the Crossroads*. Washington: Consumer's Choice Council.

Ricketts, T.H., G.C. Daily, P.R. Ehrlich, and J.P. Fay. 2001. "Countryside Biogeography of Moths in a Fragmented Landscape: Biodiversity in Native and Agricultural Habitats." *Conservation Biology*, 15:2, pp.378–388.

United Nations Research Institute for Social Development (UNRISD). 1995. "Deforestation in Central America: Historical and Contemporary Dynamics." Geneva: UNRISD (processed).

World Bank. 2001. *World Development Indicators 2001*. Washington: World Bank.

Chapter 8

Conserving Land Privately: Spontaneous Markets for Land Conservation in Chile

Elisa Corcuera, Claudia Sepúlveda, and Guillermo Geisse[1]

The creation and administration of national parks has traditionally been the sole responsibility of the government. It entails substantial costs and is seldom fully manageable. However, the free market may provide unexpected help. In Chile, for example, private landowners are buying land for conservation purposes, at their own cost. This article explores this spontaneous market phenomenon, its roots, characteristics, benefits, and shortcomings.

Privately protected areas (PPAs) could fulfill an important complementary role in public land conservation. Understanding who is investing money in land conservation, and why, is the basis for proposing mechanisms to adequately tap into the existing land conservation market, promoting further investment, enhancing its benefits while minimizing its shortcomings and ensuring that social benefit is maximized at a minimum cost.

ENVIRONMENTAL THREATS WITHIN THE CURRENT MACROECONOMIC STAGE

Chile's hardline free market economic policies are frequently cited as an example of efficiency and stability in Latin America. Over the last decade, Chile's gross domestic product has increased from approximately US$30.3 to $70.5 billion – more than doubling – and exports reached US$31.8 billion in 2000 (World Bank, 2001; CAPP, 2000).

However, not all statistics and realities are as encouraging. In 1998, according to Chilean Central Bank's statistics, less than 15 per cent of total exports were manufactured products, the rest being primary natural resources with little or no added value such as minerals, wood chips, cellulose, and salmon (CAPP, 2000). Environmental impact mitigation measures for these growing industries don't always exist, and when they do they are often not up to international standards. While economic growth is no doubt positive, we cannot ignore the fact that environmental threats have flourished alongside macroeconomic indicators.

Chile encompasses equatorial to Antarctic regions, providing an extraordinary diversity of ecosystems and habitats. Environmental impacts in the deserts of the north originate mostly from mining. The central Mediterranean regions suffer from urban expansion, overpopulation, and agrochemical and industrial pollution. All Chilean marine and terrestrial aquatic ecosystems are considered to be overexploited and most of their native species are endangered.

Central and southern Chile is considered a conservation hot spot on a global scale. It has gained this dubious honor due to its unusually high levels of endemism and threat (Dinerstein and others, 1995). The Valdivian forest eco-region (from 37°S to 42°S), classified as a temperate rainforest, is included among the 25 highest priorities in the Worldwide Fund For Nature (WWF)'s 'Global 200' conservation strategy (Olson and Dinerstein, 1998) because of its high levels of endemism and threat, and the window of opportunity to protect extensive forest remnants. The Valdivian rainforest is one of only five temperate rainforest ecosystems worldwide. It is highly threatened, but is still classified as a 'frontier forest' by Bryant and others (1997) due to the persistence of large non-intervened expanses. Large-scale logging, small-scale firewood extraction, forest fires, clearing, salmon production, and penetration highways threaten the sparsely populated temperate rainforests of the south.

PUBLIC APPROACH TO FOREST CONSERVATION

Due to the evident pressure the temperate rainforest is under, the environmental non-governmental organization (NGO) community, and even some large forestry companies, have started to demand a government policy with respect to native forests. However, government reaction has been slow. A native forest law has been trapped in Congress for nine years.

Slow advances in the legal arena are a reflection of government policies that consider environmental concerns to be impediments to economic growth. The government is only interested in protecting the environment as long as it does not affect Chile's perceived macroeconomic potential. Dissenting voices have not been able to publicize environmentally-based development, or the negative externalities of natural resource exploitation, on the national stage (CIPMA, 2002).

In this context, public and private land conservation have been assigned low priorities. The budget for the national park system's administering agency has not grown for years, even in the face of increasing demands and needs. Regarding private lands conservation, Chile's first General Environmental Law, enacted in 1994, included a promising article (No 35) which recognized the potential importance of PPAs, and mandated the government to create an administration and tax deduction system for them. In spite of three attempts by government agencies to implement Article 35, it has not prospered due to its low political priority (CONAF, 1994; CONAF, 1996; Tacón and others, 2001). New impetus for legislation may come from the Environmental Agenda issued by the government in March 2002, which includes the preservation of natural heritage as one of its four priorities, and stresses the role of private protected areas. A commission to implement article 35 has been formed, but it remains to be seen if this new impulse will prosper.

CIVIL SOCIETY'S RESPONSE: A SPONTANEOUS MARKET FOR LAND CONSERVATION

For decades, Chilean travelers have chosen the southern lakes region, with its scenic volcanoes, rainforests, waterfalls, glaciers, and fiords as a summer holiday destination (Tacón and others, 2001). To many middle and upper class Chileans, the rainforests of the south are a connection to sweet childhood memories of relaxing moments, and a symbol of escape from stressful city lives. While the Chilean government inches toward the creation of environmental policies, the decline of native forests and the spread of pine and eucalyptus plantations and clearcut forests have become evident eyesores for travelers.

During the 1990s, a trend began to emerge. Perhaps worried by the rapid decrease in forest coverage, and convinced that the government was not likely to do anything significant soon, people started to buy land with the objective of protecting its natural and scenic resources. Acquisitions seem to have been independently initiated by different groups. While only two or three private parks are known to have existed during the late 1980s, an increasing number of conservation purchases occurred between 1990 and 1995, attracting the attention of research institutions and the environmental community (Sepúlveda and others, 1998).

Convinced that PPAs could be a valuable complement to the public parks and reserve system, the Center for Environmental Research and Planning (Centro de Investigación y Planificación del Medio Ambiente, CIPMA), an independent non-profit research institution, compiled the first PPA cadastre in 1996. CIPMA's first cadastre identified 39 PPAs of 40ha or more, covering almost 363,000ha. Pumalín Park, located in Region X, was by far the largest, covering about 250,000ha. Of the other PPAs, 14 (44 per cent) were also located in Region X, accounting for about 40,000ha (36 per cent of the non-Pumalín PPA area). CIPMA's cadastre also proposed a categorization of PPAs, generating the first analysis of the type of actors involved and their motivations (Sepúlveda and others, 1998).

In parallel, the National Committee for the Defense of Flora and Fauna (Comité Pro Defensa de la Flora y Fauna, CODEFF), an environmental non-profit organization, initiated a PPA network called the Privately Protected Areas

Network (Red de Areas Protegidas Privadas, RAPP). RAPP's main activity is the maintenance of a relatively up-to-date database of affiliated PPAs, which include areas that vary from 1ha to 300,000ha (although not all PPAs belong to RAPP). RAPP membership has grown from 63 areas covering almost 300,000ha in 1998 to 118 areas covering 386,570ha in 2001. Although RAPP data show that PPAs continue to be concentrated in Region X, growth in PPAs has been faster in other areas. In 2000, Region X PPAs accounted for 21 per cent of all PPAs and 80 per cent of the entire area (17 per cent, if Pumalín is omitted).

Since October 2000, CIPMA has been implementing a Valdivian eco-region project financed by the Global Environment Facility (GEF). One of the components of this project is a promotion program to support private conservation areas in Region X. As part of this work, a detailed database of privately protected areas in Region X is being developed (CIPMA, 2000a; CIPMA, 2000b).

Table 8.1 *Public and private protected areas in Chile*

Region	Area (ha)	Public protected areas Number	Area (ha)	RAPP-affiliated privately protected areas (1999) Number	Area (ha)	Area in PPAs as % of total protected area
I Tarapacá	5,878,560	5	633,706	0	0	0
II Antofagasta	12,525,330	4	345,272	0	0	0
III Atacama	7,470,470	3	148,544	0	0	0
IV Coquimbo	4,065,630	4	15,175	0	0	0
V Valparaíso	1,639,613	7	44,494	8	2,690	9
Metropolitana	1,554,940	2	13,194	5	9,654	34
VI O'Higgins	1,645,630	3	46,460	8	23,698	36
VII Maule	3,066,150	7	18,669	17	7,258	28
VIII Bio bio	3,693,930	5	84,359	5	11,141	12
IX Araucanía	3,194,640	13	296,732	12	1,227	0
X Los Lagos	6,824,670	13	606,557	21	264,243	31
XI Aisén	10,899,717	17	4,288,656	16	5,149	0
XII Magallanes	13,203,350	11	7,581,753	1	120	0
Chile	**71,972,394**	**94**	**14,123,571**	**93**	**325,180**	**2**

Source: Elaborated from data in Moreira and others, 1998; and CODEFF, 1999

These sources provide a picture of the importance of Chile's budding private conservation movement (Table 8.1). Initiatives are of a varied nature, but they show that the private sector is devoting considerable amounts of money to purchasing and managing private lands for conservation purposes. Without any government action or incentive, a market for land protection has emerged. However, there are two caveats: first, the available information only covers some of the existing initiatives, because their voluntary nature means that less visible PPAs are not included in case-by-case cadastres or voluntary membership networks. Second, there is no accepted definition of 'protected'. PPA status in Chile is a verbal statement of good intentions by the landowners involved, and therefore conservation practices vary greatly in efficiency and results. PPAs include strict conservation projects, but also plots of lands with productive uses such as logging or ranching, and a wide range of environmental practices. In addition, with a few exceptions, PPAs lack baseline studies, management plans, and dedicated personnel.

CLASSIFICATION AND DESCRIPTION OF CURRENT PRIVATE LAND CONSERVATION INITIATIVES

CIPMA's 1996 research and cadastre proposed a categorization for Chilean PPAs containing five main types of projects, each of which is described in further detail below (Sepúlveda and others, 1998). These are:

1 private parks (38 per cent of initiatives);
2 land donations to the national park system (7.5 per cent of initiatives);
3 conservation communities (CCs) (25 per cent of initiatives);
4 eco-real estate and ecotourism projects (22 per cent of initiatives).

In addition, a public–private form of lands protection was included:

5 private administration of government conservation lands (7.5 per cent of initiatives).

Private parks

Private parks and reserves are the most common type of private conservation initiative, but they vary greatly in their characteristics. Their sizes range between 45ha and 300,000ha. Although many are open to the public, in some access is restricted to authorized researchers. There are exceptions, but many PPAs seek some degree of formal recognition by becoming nature sanctuaries or hunting-free zones.

The biggest and best-known private park is Pumalín, which covers approximately 300,000ha in Patagonia. Pumalín was purchased by US millionaire Douglas Tompkins specifically as a conservation reserve. Tompkins has invested over US$5 million in land purchases alone. As a person with connections to the deep ecology movement, his main motivation is assumed to be conservation per se. Established in 1991, and still in its consolidation stages, Pumalín received 12,700 visitors in 2000. Of these, 1000 stayed in cabins, 3200 camped, and 8500 were day visitors. Its tourism and management infrastructure clearly surpasses those of most national parks.

Another interesting case is that of Oncol Park, owned and managed by the Valdivia Lumber Company. Oncol is located 29km from the city of Valdivia, and covers 754ha in the heart of the Valdivian eco-region. Of extraordinary ecological and scenic value, this park was a pioneer of the private conservation movement, as it was created in 1989. In spite of being managed with little publicity, its numbers of annual visitors have ballooned from less than 200 in 1990 to almost 12,000 during the 2000–2001 summer season (Ibáñez, personal communication). Oncol has first-class recreational and interpretive trails, camping areas, guest houses, lookouts, and other forms of infrastructure. The Valdivia Lumber company has invested a total of around US$190,000 in the park (Muñoz, 2001). Unlike many other PPAs, Oncol has a management plan. Although it needs to be updated, this plan allows for adequate land stewardship policies.

Land donations to the national park system

Land donations to the national park system are a modest emerging phenomenon. During the 1990s four relatively small plots of land, varying from 147 to 417ha, were donated to Chile's National Forestry Agency (Corporación Nacional Forestal, CONAF) with the objective of expanding current protected areas or creating new ones (Sepúlveda and others, 1998). In Region XI, CODEFF purchased two plots of land totaling 400ha with funds from the Frankfurt Zoological Society, and ceded them to CONAF under the legal instrument of the *comodato*, through which the landowner reserves the right to revoke the donation if CONAF ever uses the land for purposes other than conservation. In addition, a private land-owner donated 417ha in Region VII to create the Bellotos del Mellado National Reserve (Sepúlveda and others, 1998).

Finally, a donation was made in 1995 by the Millalemu Logging Company, a subsidiary of Shell. It is located in a transitional area between temperate rain-forests and Mediterranean vegetation, and is rich in rare species such as the Pitao, Red Micha, Roble maulino, Huillipatagua, and Queule. On these 147ha, CONAF created the Los Queules National Reserve (Sepúlveda and others, 1998).[2] It is common for portions of landholdings purchased by forestry companies to have legal restrictions on logging due to slope or soil characteristics, or because they contain endangered species. Although legal restrictions are seldom enforced, a certain degree of protection remains. Land with restricted characteristics can be a burden to lumber companies that are respectful of the law. Donating them for conservation not only contributes to a better public image; it can also have a financial benefit, relieving them of the cost of maintaining and guarding 'unproductive' areas.

Conservation communities

CIPMA's 1997 cadastre showed that nearly 25 per cent of all land conservation initiatives at that time took the form of conservation communities (CCs). This type of PPA produces a considerable degree of internal homogeneity, hinting at the great potential for replicable institutional formulas. Although they sometimes differ in their details and legal structure, the core concept of a CC is the purchase of a plot of land in equal shares by a group of people, mainly for conservation and recreational purposes. Most CCs give their members the right to build a cabin or home within a reduced area earmarked for development, while the rest of the land is viewed as a communal park. The areas of CCs vary from 90ha to 35,000ha, and their number of members or shareholders range from 4 to 62 (Sepúlveda and others, 1998). Several CCs have hired temporary consultants, both scientists and administrators, to assist them in managing their properties with conservation criteria. However, because of their recent creation, most communities' medium- and long-term plans are not consolidated. It is possible to differentiate between those that have a clear public use vocation – these could eventually become private parks – and those that are oriented primarily toward recreational uses for their members. It is especially interesting to note that none of these initiatives have for-profit objectives, and that only a couple have decided to undertake income-generating schemes (such as ecotourism) as a way to relieve the burden of management costs.

CCs are usually initiated by groups of friends or acquaintances. One example is Ahuenco, created by a group of scientists who bought a 290ha plot of land on Chiloé island. While doing research into the establishment of a marine park, they saw an evident need to protect the area's safest bay, its sole penguin nesting and breeding area, remnants of old-growth forests, and spectacular scenery. The potential sale of the area to a resort developer made protection urgent. Although no single researcher was able to meet the seller's price by him- or herself, an expanded group closed the deal and set itself the mid-term objective of purchasing two more plots and thus connecting Ahuenco to a nearby national park (total purchase objective: 1210ha). As of 2002, one plot remains unprotected.

Eco-real estate projects and ecotourism-based land protection projects

Eco-real estate projects are similar to CCs in that they divide a large piece of land into a reduced development area and a broader communal park, but they differ in that they are usually initiated by real estate firms and have profit rather than conservation as their main purpose. Current projects vary from 2500 to 20,000ha. Advertisements for eco-real estate projects have appeared with increasing frequency in national newspapers during the last decade, confirming the importance of this type of project in the local market. Most have been developed in the southern part of the country. There is also a significant market for second homes in rural areas around Santiago. Both schemes are aimed at middle to upper class people, who are offered an exclusive holiday or weekend spot with access to a private park of relatively significant extent and ecological value. Apparently, the demand for conservation, as expressed in the creation of private parks and conservation communities, has triggered a market response: developers are supplying conservation parcels in communal parks and ready-made protection projects, saving buyers the inconvenience of organizing their own individual or group grassroots project.

One of the first, largest, and most publicized eco-real estate projects has been the 20,000ha Tepuhueico Lake Development and Park on Chiloé Island (Region X). During its initial stages, the project successfully sold 100 plots and used the rest as a communal park. The original project included internal bylaws and design standards that regulated the size of constructions, types of materials, and boat motor capacity, and excluded domestic animals (among other restrictions). Encouraged by people's obvious willingness to pay for plots of land in a beautiful setting, with their 'own' vast forest and unpolluted lake, the Tepuhueico Lake real estate company decided to develop a second phase, thus violating the spirit of the original agreement. Unfortunately, the limits of the communal park were not clearly established in the first phase buyers' contract, making legal action difficult. To date, 1000 parcels have been sold, reducing the original conservation park to 15,000ha. The company plans to sell another 4000 parcels. More critically, large areas that were meant to form a park, and which could originally be accessed only by water, have now been divided up by 40km of roads. However, protection areas within other eco-developments can be better safeguarded. For example, the Oasis La Campana development in Chile's Mediterranean eco-region transferred the title of its 1000ha communal park to a foundation created specifically for that purpose (Moreno, 2001).

Some ecotourism developers have also discovered the financial benefits of being able to offer clients their own PPA as an attraction. The purchase of areas to serve as centerpoints or base camps for nature/adventure experiences has become increasingly common. Such is the case with CampoAventura, an 80ha protected parcel in Cochamó at the northern limit of Patagonia with charming and intentionally rustic dwellings. It serves as the headquarters for three-to-ten-day horseback riding treks into the exuberant surroundings of adjacent valleys (which are under no protection status other than that offered by their inaccessibility).

The largest ecotourism-based land protection project is Alerce Mountain Lodge, set in a 2000ha PPA adjoining a national park in Region X. Purchased in 1995 with the original intention of harvesting valuable old-growth Alerce wood, timber activity has now been reduced to a minimum, and activities have centered around its exclusive lodge. Clients pay hefty sums to enjoy its luxurious accommodation and natural surroundings. Once again, due to the lack of research, it is not clear how important profit or conservation motives were in the decision to change the project's focus.

Private administration of public conservation areas

Although not a completely private form of land conservation, the administration of public lands by non-profit private foundations in Chile was a temporary phenomenon which is interesting to explore. During the 1990s the Chilean government, lacking the resources to protect and administer its vast network of conservation areas, decided to experiment with the administration of national lands by private foundations. The first experiences involved concession contracts for a set number of years. These were awarded by the Ministry of Public Property

(Ministerio de Bienes Nacionales) to environmental organizations, which were to administer the areas according to clear conservation purposes. Three foundations – Melimoyu, Lahuén, and EDUCEC – received administrative rights for government 'paper parks' (public lands on which protection went no further than a printed decree) or unoccupied public lands that ranged in size from 17,000ha to 35,000ha. Unfortunately, these early experiences met with limited success, and contracts were not renewed when they expired in 1997, apparently by mutual consent. The reasons for this have not been properly explored, but are related to the private foundations' inability to generate sufficient resources to finance maintenance costs, as well as the absence of a clear public–private cooperation policy (Sepúlveda and others, 1998).

In 2001, the Ministry of Public Property had initiated a second round of concession contracts for the private administration of public lands. This time, concessions tend to be focused on ecotourism business ventures, especially through the Austral Plan, a project that provides significant tax incentives for this type of private investment in the portion of Patagonia contained within Region XI.

Motivation of market participants

Whether for idealistic reasons, recreational purposes, profit, or a mixture of these, people are demonstrating their willingness to pay to own private parks and/or spend considerable sums to enjoy a holiday in such areas. This willingness to pay for land conservation competes with extremely strong lumber interests (as already described) and traditional uses of the land: rural landholders are used to extensive, unproductive cattle operations, the use of forest fires to clear pastures, and firewood extraction. The power of land conservation market forces and the characteristics and motivations of the actors involved have not been quantified or scientifically described, but even anecdotal references can be quite enlightening.

For example, in addition to the approximate figure of US$5 million that has been invested in direct land purchase, Pumalín Park faces annual expenses estimated at US$700,000, while annual earnings are estimated at only US$50,000 (*Qué Pasa*, February 3 2001). Although the park has received over 12,000 visitors in one season, many of these are tourists who travel the Austral Highway through Pumalín Park, stopping just for the day and thus paying no entrance fee or lodging costs. The Conservation Land Trust, created by owner Douglas Tompkins specifically for this purpose, provides 98 per cent of maintenance funds. This foundation has also financed most of the infrastructure projects, which include a cafeteria, trails, camping areas, a schoolhouse for local inhabitants, and demonstrative productive units. These have cost approximately US$20 million (*Qué Pasa*, 3 February 2001). The park provides approximately 250 permanent jobs.

Although an extremely interesting case study, Pumalín Park lies in a category of its own and does not reflect the characteristics of the national market. It is

Table 8.2 *Examples of the conservation community market*

Conservation community	Area protected (ha)	Number of shares	Cost per share (US$)	Monthly per-share maintenance fee (US$)
Altos del Huemul	35,000	90	n/a	none
Ahuenco A	290	25	5,500	25
Ahuenco B	450	34	5,500	25
Factoria	2,000	43	10,000	25
Namuncay	400	20	27,000	50
Quirra-Quirra	207	25	7,250	25
Lago las Rocas	600	3	n/a	none

Note: n/a: information not available.
Source: Author's calculations based on information provided by Corcuera, 2001; Calcagni, 2001; Durston, 2001; Gómez, 2001.

interesting to examine data on conservation communities and eco-development projects, which are more representative in their origin and nature (see Tables 8.2 and 8.3).

Tables 8.2 and 8.3 show that there are Chileans willing to spend substantial sums on land conservation, without necessarily expecting a financial return. In fact, people are willing to make regular payments in order to cover the costs of stewardship. This is surprising in the local context, because philanthropy toward environmental non-profit organizations for land conservation is practically non-existent. In Chilean society as a whole there is little tradition of donation to non-profit organizations others than those that are church-related or aimed at poverty reduction, which are viewed by many as more urgent concerns. Nevertheless, large sums are made available when conservation is linked to personal enjoyment and ownership. The spread of CCs and eco-real estate projects is a sign of market success and indicates the potential for initiatives that combine conservation objectives with individual enjoyment and ownership. In a country with strong constitutional protection and deep respect for private property rights, it is noteworthy that CCs and eco-real estate projects are institutionalizing formulas that confirm the pre-eminence of private property, while making it compatible with conservation objectives.

SOCIAL BENEFITS OF PRIVATELY PROTECTED AREAS

The most notable characteristics of the private lands conservation movement in Chile are its complete spontaneity and positive social effects. Non-systematic qualitative interviews with PPA project originators (Villarroel and others, 1998; Villarroel, 2001; Sepúlveda, 2001) show that PPAs have been created by individuals whose motives include pure conservation and profit in differing combinations.

Table 8.3 *Examples of the eco-real estate market*

Real estate project	Area protected (ha)	Total project area (ha)	Number of lots	Cost per lot (US$)	Monthly costs (US$)
Oasis La Campana	1,000	2,500	484	20,000	25
Lago Tepuhueico	15,000	20,000	5,000[a]	6,500–14,000	none
San Francisco de Los Andes	1,800	8,100	400	11,500–30,000	60
Parque Los Volcanes	1,150	1,600	330	14,000	22
Parque Kawelluco	800	1,200	400[b]	n/a	25
La Invernada	660	530	94	11,500	25

Note: a 1,000 sold to date.
           b 60 sold to date.

Source: Elaborated from information provided by Moreno, 2001; Sepúlveda and others, 1998; Tapia, 2001; Larraín, 2001; De Pablo, 2001; Fierro, 2001;
           Correa, 2001; Ziller, 2001; Donoso, 2001.

It is possible to hypothesize that the main motivations for purchasers include the desire to protect an untouched scenic and recreational landscape, and the desire for the personal right to enjoy these places and later leave them to their children – what we might call 'personal-benefit idealism'. Social benefit is probably only a secondary motivation, nothing more than a desirable side-effect. Luckily for the country, the private purchase and conservation of land do have important positive externalities. Perhaps the most important are:

- scenic protection and its resulting benefits for tourism, recreation, and quality of life;
- biodiversity conservation; and
- providing environmental services such as carbon sequestration, water supply protection, flood regulation, and erosion protection, among others.

PPAs are helping to provide these benefits to society at no cost to the government. However, in many ways the benefits provided by PPAs fall significantly short of what they could.

Un-met biodiversity conservation priorities

The National Protected Areas System (Sistema Nacional de Areas Silvestres Protegidas del Estado, SNASPE) covers almost 20 per cent of Chile's territory (CONAF, 2001), which is a large proportion by international standards. However, 84 per cent of all protected areas are found in the rainforests and icecaps of Patagonia, leaving 19 out of 85 vegetational formations completely unprotected and many more under-represented (Gajardo, 1995; Moreira and others, 1998).

A conservation strategy aimed at optimizing biodiversity protection would privilege the conservation of rare and unprotected ecosystems (Simonnetti, 2000). However, the opposite is true in the case of private land conservation markets. Region X, where the highest density of PPAs is found, already has 9.2 per cent of its area under public protection. Although this might be considered sufficient, there are significant gaps in the representation of several Valdivian forest sub-types: most of the 600,000ha are concentrated in the Andes. In the central valley and coastal range, where diversity is higher and subject to a greater development pressure, protection is almost nonexistent. There are other regions where the situation is much more pressing: in regions IV through VII, for example, SNASPE covers less than 1 per cent of the territory (Calcagni and others, 1999). In spite of the need for PPAs in central Chile, private protection projects tend to concentrate in the south, perhaps because of lower land prices and the fact that the scenery is more universally appealing.

Size and connectivity

Most Chilean public parks are not big enough to sustain long-term, genetically viable populations of most large mammals (Mella, 1994). Furthermore, there is a low level of connectivity between the park system's units (Tacón and others,

2001). CIPMA's cadastre and RAPP membership show that, with notable exceptions, most PPAs in Chile cover less than 400ha, and few are adjacent or close to national parks (Sepúlveda and others, 1998). 400ha is a much smaller area than most umbrella species require in order to maintain viable populations; adequate ranges have been estimated at between 10,000ha and 25,000ha (WWF, forthcoming).

There is a clear role in stand-alone conservation for those few initiatives that cover thousands of hectares or include site-specific values, such as the previously mentioned penguin nesting/breeding area at Ahuenco. However, due to their small average size, the most useful role for a PPA in biodiversity conservation is probably as a buffer zone around an existing park, or as a connecting biological corridor between other protected areas (Tacón and others, 2001). Although some of the current initiatives have taken on buffer and connectivity roles, this is far from common and follows no plan. Where it occurs, it results from scenic coincidences.

Management standards and quality

Knowledge of ecosystems and species within PPAs is highly variable and informal. Well-meaning landowners sometimes cannot recognize valuable species or systems on their lands, and therefore do not adopt the best conservation measures. Activities such as grazing or logging frequently continue within unilaterally declared 'protected' areas, without any evaluation of the areas best suited to these activities, a zoning proposal, or measures to help mitigate their environmentally harmful effects.

Although some PPAs are well managed, this is unusual. And even though private landowners should not be loaded down with scientific or management requirements, information and incentives should be offered in order to promote their voluntary adoption. Some of the most important indicators of a well-managed park include the existence of a baseline study and scientific inventory, and the creation of a management plan that clearly establishes areas appropriate for different uses. This management plan should then be applied, and the effectiveness of resulting conservation should be monitored on a continuous basis. Constant vigilance is desirable, and landowners must be willing to take legal action to ensure conservation objectives. In Chile, such standards and practices are seldom applied. They require a high degree of professional knowledge, time, and resources, and bring the individual landowner low returns.

Access and recreation opportunities for the urban poor

Access and recreation opportunities for the urban poor are important equity issues that are not addressed by public and private land conservation initiatives. 78 per cent of the country's inhabitants are in Regions IV to VII, but these regions encompass only 1.4 per cent of protected areas. The most extreme case is that of the Metropolitan Region, which has 40 per cent of the country's population but only 0.13 per cent of publicly protected areas (Calcagni and others, 1999). Public and private parks tend to be located in the southern lakes district and

Patagonia, both of which are far from the country's most important cities, partly because of the decrease in land prices as population densities fall. Thus the urban poor, who do not have the money to travel thousands of kilometers, have little access to parks and the recreational opportunities in natural surroundings that they offer.

Links to rural development

As is clearly expressed in speeches by government officials, Chile has unfortunately adopted a government policy of 'development first, conservation later'. Pumalín Park, as the largest project, has suffered considerable criticism in certain quarters. Many politicians have emphatically argued that the park prevents an entire region from implementing much-needed development, and that it marginalizes rural inhabitants. But such statements tend to be based on the erroneous premise that development and conservation are mutually exclusive. Land conservation can encourage rural development by bringing in tourist dollars, and is compatible with the production of non-timber forest products (such as bamboo, mushrooms, seeds, honey, and handicrafts) and with a great variety of services like water production, fisheries, and ecotourism. Land conservation should and can include local communities, and contribute to the improvement of traditional extractive uses such as silviculture, cattle operations, and agriculture. The opportunity cost of conservation has also been greatly exaggerated: Pumalín's lands have very few alternative uses, as most of the area has very steep slopes.

Working with local farmers and communities to develop new models of conservation-based development is a long-term task, however, which requires continuous presence in the field and funds for community projects. Investments must be made in intangible assets such as education and relationship-building, and the benefits take years to become apparent. For private landowners who are generally motivated by recreation and conservation, the complicated politics of community conservation and its high costs prove quite discouraging, and few examples of community-based parks exist. One exception is Mapu Lahual, a network of locally administered community parks being implemented by six Huilliche indigenous groups in Region X's coastal range. With initial encouragement from CONAF, and now backed by the Temperate Rainforest Fund (a fund created with financial contributions from WWF and the Council of the Americas-Chile), these communities consider ecotourism an attractive alternative to current timber extraction activities (Comunidad Indígena Maicolpi, 2000).

Unfortunately, to date few other private conservation initiatives in Chile have incorporated rural and indigenous communities into the management of parks, are producing non-timber forest products, or have significantly been dedicated to 'sustainable productivity'. Farmers and communities rarely have ecological mindsets, while private landowners with better economic situations see that they will get better returns for their investments from simple recreation. If rural development linked to conservation is to become a reality, the effort should be led by the public sector, for private actors will need significant education and/or incentives.

Continuity

One of the greatest drawbacks of PPAs as they are currently structured is that they depend entirely on their owners' goodwill and resources. The Chilean public parks system enjoys a certain degree of security due to their creation through legal decrees that can be burdensome to change. In comparison, PPAs are many times more vulnerable, for they can be dismantled on a landowner's whim. With a few exceptions, there are no assurances that these areas will not be sold to (or inherited by) people with different objectives, or that the current owners themselves will not modify or eliminate their conservation objectives, as has already happened in some areas. Existing legal protection and continuity alternatives for PPAs are inadequate and need to be improved:

- **Purchase by a CC.** 'Communities', as defined by law, are groups of people who freely associate for a purpose. If any member wishes to leave the community and requests individual title to his or her corresponding amount of land, the other community members must allow it. In order to avoid this possibility, existing CCs have adopted complex statutes, and in some cases have even separated the ownership of the land (held by an anonymous society that issues shares) from the community itself. However, as these are recent improvisations it is unclear how well they will work.
- **Purchase by an NGO or foundation.** NGOs, as non-profit institutions, have limitations on changing their objectives, and a social responsibility that is usually taken very seriously. Ownership of PPAs by NGOs would thus provide greater continuity. However, land purchases have a very high capital cost, and then become a perpetual monitoring and stewardship burden. For this reason, most non-profits understand that land acquisitions can only be done with a corresponding endowment fund that ensures continuity. Since most Chilean NGOs are strapped for cash, the total percentage of private initiatives that correspond to direct purchase by foundations is quite small so far. Although it is a valuable alternative for specific and highly fragile environments, purchase by NGOs is probably not the right solution. It is also not an option for landowners who wish to retain ownership of their land.
- **Nature sanctuary.** Private landowners can ask the government to declare their land a nature sanctuary. This status obliges owners to request permission from a special committee before any significant changes are made. In addition, this status mandates an environmental impact assessment for any roads, pipelines, or other large public infrastructure projects, thus offering a limited degree of protection. However, very few sanctuaries exist, mainly because there are no incentives for the landowner, only restrictions. This category could be improved, and standards and incentives for landowners encouraged, thus making it a more effective mechanism (García and others, 1998).
- **Donation and *Comodato*.** The donation of a plot of land to a public or private agency, specifically for environmental protection purposes, offers a certain degree of legal security and continuity. However, it has only been

applied to four plots of land so far. It is a very limited legal mechanism in its ability to attract donors for, as we have seen, private landowners seem to enjoy the ownership of natural surroundings for personal recreation purposes. Giving away land, even with restrictions, is not an attractive option for most (Villarroel and others, 1998; García and Villarroel, 1998; García, 2000b).

• **Conservation easements.** A recent idea in the context of Latin American legislation, conservation easements have been used for decades in the United States and other common law countries. They consist of partial restrictions on the owners' rights to use their land in order to maintain its conservation values. Restrictions are agreed on a flexible and voluntary basis by negotiations between specialized non-profit organizations called 'land trusts' and the landowner, and then become obligatory (Chacón and Castro, 1998). Although theoretically possible within Latin American civil law, this mechanism has so far scarcely been tested and there are many legal questions as to its recognition and enforceability. Questions arise mainly from the fact that legislation recognizes easements in general and for specific purposes such as transit, but nowhere in Chilean legislation is there a specific reference to conservation easements. Clear and unquestionable legislation recognizing conservation easements, and eliminating certain burdensome requisites such as the existence of dominant and servant parcels, would make this continuity tool available (Corcuera, 2000; Bañados, 2000).

PUBLIC ROLE IN THE OPTIMIZATION OF A LAND CONSERVATION MARKET

So far in Chile, the government has protected public areas, and the private market has protected others. Public–private cooperation has been scarce, and there are no strategic, legal, or economic policies related to private land conservation that motivate and improve the social and biodiversity results of initiatives. The fact that people are moving significant resources into land conservation proves that there is a market force that could be tapped by a proactive government, enhancing the positive externalities of private conservation.

Strategically, it would be useful to have a national-level policy that identifies and maps areas according to their biodiversity conservation priority. It should privilege under-represented ecosystems, connectivity between existing public and private parks, the creation of buffer areas, and social access. Although scientific research that prioritizes areas for conservation has traditionally been considered a governmental responsibility, recent efforts demonstrate that the private and non-profit sectors are starting to assume partial responsibility. For example, the most comprehensive assessment of the Valdivian rainforest eco-region to date was created by WWF (forthcoming). Smaller efforts, such as subregional and watershed conservation priority-setting, have also been conducted by the private sector. This was the case, for example, in the Cochamó watershed in Region X, studied by Fundación Lahuén (Frank and others, 2001). However, no scientifically credible NGO with plentiful economic resources and a wide public audience has made it a priority to lead a national-level strategic private conservation priority-setting exercise. Few, if any, local private organizations have the power to successfully lead such an effort. Assuming that the government will create incentives for PPAs (monetary or not) in the future, a strategic framework would be a basic tool necessary to prioritize support for private conservation projects according to their social benefit.

Another required strategic measure is to define quality standards for the management of PPAs. These standards would be the yardstick against which private conservation initiatives could be measured, and support could be offered only to those that comply with minimum standards. CIPMA and CONAF have currently agreed a standards proposal that will begin to be tested in the three demonstration units of CIPMA's Valdivian eco-region GEF project, and which would achieve its true potential if adopted on a national scale (Proyecto CIPMA-FMAM, 2001).

Legal alternatives

Currently, the only available legal protection options are the improvable mechanisms of nature sanctuaries, CCs, land donations, and direct purchase, and the relatively untested option of conservation easements. Better and clearer long-term legal conservation options are needed, along with the appropriate incentives for private landowners to adopt them.

The most attractive legal options would provide significant conservation improvement without costing the government anything. Examples include the explicit legislative recognition of conservation easements, or a specific statute for CCs that responds to their environmental and continuity needs but avoids the limitations of the current community regulation framework. The choice of instruments needs to be based on an understanding of landowners' motivations, something that unfortunately has not been present to date. The most significant effect of these clarification and simplification measures would be to provide a legal basis for the permanence of current projects for which conservation is a primary objective. However, if one also wants to excourage and guide the privately-owned land conservation market, no doubt there must be incentives for landowners to adopt legal protection even if their primary objectives are recreation and/or profit.

Incentives

A range of market, tax, and social recognition incentives are needed. In Latin America, the most effective policies have combined the elimination or reduction of property taxes – which are normally too low for this to be an effective incentive in itself – with weightier economic 'carrots' such as direct subsidies or lower income taxes, access to competitive funds, and training and technical assistance for the creation of conservation-associated businesses (Tacón and others, 2001).

Although the cost of a comprehensive package of incentives has not been estimated, interviews with current PPA owners indicate that their preferred methods would be relatively cheap: for example, such measures as technical assistance, training, and formal recognition (Villarroel and others, 1998).

A proactive government policy would both increase the area protected under PPAs and re-direct existing ones toward greater social benefit. However, this requires the determined involvement (which has so far been absent) of the government in improving the market from strategic, legal, and economic points of view. Article 35 of the Environmental Law stated that the government would seek to promote PPAs: there is much to be gained if the government makes that theoretical policy spring to life.

PRIVATE ROLES IN THE OPTIMIZATION OF A LAND CONSERVATION MARKET

In the absence of government action to structure and improve the private conservation market, the local environmental NGO community is leading a series of projects aimed at improving the overall effects of private land conservation. Potentially the most valuable projects, in terms of generating replicable policy mechanisms and market regulations, are as follows.

1 **The creation of management standards.** As mentioned above, the creation of a set of common definitions for PPAs and compatible uses is of the utmost importance. CIPMA's Valdivian eco-region project is working on this in partnership with CONAF. It is generating and describing PPA categories and their corresponding management standards, using a protocol that recognizes different degrees of conservation intensity. Proposed PPA categories vary from strict conservation to mixed productive uses. Landowners could voluntarily apply for certification under the appropriate category; if accepted into the scheme, they would gain access to various incentives. This protocol is being applied and tested in three demonstration areas before being adjusted and applied to PPAs at large.
2 **Green real-estate brokerage.** A small-scale approach to this issue has been initiated by CODEFF. It intends to implement a green real estate brokerage program that attempts to link conservation buyers and sellers. Unfortunately, to date the program has provoked more interest among sellers than among buyers.
3 **Non-monetary incentives.** CIPMA's Valdivian eco-region project is implementing a PPA promotion program in Region X, which includes a set of non-monetary incentives (training, technical assistance, information, and social recognition). The project hopes to gather information about the effectiveness of the different incentives. This experience will contribute to a new set of non-monetary incentives that could be applied in other regions.

4 **Voluntary legal agreements.** Many currently-unsecured initiatives are supported by environmentally conscious landowners who would probably like their land to be protected in perpetuity. Such people tend not to know very much about legal methods to ensure long-term conservation, and of course they also don't want to lose money. The US experience shows that non-profit organizations can play a very important role in reaching agreements with private landowners that legally ensures the permanence of their protected areas. Some NGOs have taken the lead in researching legal options, informing landowners, and negotiating agreements, and have often assumed stewardship and responsibility for monitoring costs in perpetuity. Because of the shortage of knowledge and finance in the Chilean NGO community, there is still a long way to go, but such an approach has great potential.

5 **Eco-regional and subregional priority-setting studies.** As previously mentioned, in recent years the non-profit sector has begun to lead strategic ecological planning exercises. However, the frequency and range of assessments must improve enormously if this is to be significant. It is also unclear how far these private products will be accepted and used within the public sector.

6 **Information exchange.** The private sector in Chile has started to develop a wealth of practical and theoretical knowledge as to what works and what does not in terms of private conservation. For the most part, this knowledge exists only in each project landowner's head, and within a few non-profit organizations. Independently of the level of governmental involvement over the next few years, it is crucially important for the private sector to create opportunities for mutual learning such as conferences and seminars, field visits, publications, and training materials.

CONCLUSION

As an analysis of the Chilean experience shows, the spontaneous emergence of a land conservation market is a positive phenomenon that helps to achieve desirable social objectives at a minimal public cost. Nevertheless, private action does not by any means ensure that conservation takes place at the desired scale, or in locations where biodiversity threats are most pressing. Nor does it occur with any degree of connectivity, to appropriate standards, close to those who need it most, or in a way that promotes sustainable rural development. Conservation, when left to the free market, tends to occur in limited areas of scenic beauty, under inappropriate management standards, without any legal assurance of long-term continuity, with minimal contributions to local sustainable businesses, and at great distance from urban cores and the people who would most benefit from access to natural recreational opportunities.

Public policy should be encouraged, and market and social incentives could be used to promote and support private conservation initiatives, expand their coverage, and improve their management and effectiveness. In-depth knowledge of investor behavior and motivations will be critical in the development of appropriate incentives. Available qualitative data allow us to hypothesize that private landowners might not need much incentive to adopt appropriate management practices, or to commit to the long-term continuity of conservation, but that it might be considerably more difficult to attract investors to areas of limited scenic beauty, or persuade landowners to open their parks to the poor. After all, many conservation communities and eco-real estate projects are formed primarily for the enjoyment of their members or shareholders. PPAs are probably better suited to some objectives than others.

In addition, no individual PPA can fulfill all the objectives. Recreational opportunities for the urban poor might not be compatible with the conservation of hot spots, or with landowners' personal recreation and environmental protection objectives. These things vary greatly from project to project, and incentives should reflect the differences that exist between various private conservation initiatives. The formal regulation of PPAs must recognize this heterogeneity and should include different degrees of productive use compatible with conservation, so that incentives can be directed toward a diverse range of objectives. The practical testing of non-monetary incentives, such as those included in CIPMA's Valdivian eco-region project, will generate valuable lessons for the design of replicable appropriate measures.

Even considering the relative importance of Pumalín Park in the universe of Chilean PPAs, and private initiatives' shortcomings overall, it is no less than astounding that, in the absence of public policy and incentives, in little more than ten years the private market has protected an area estimated at well over 450,000ha. We can only guess at what the private land conservation market could achieve with proactive government policies and a mature and specialized non-profit sector. Among the free-market opportunities to promote biodiversity protection and sustainability, few are as ripe and promising as the private land protection market.

NOTES

1 The authors would like to thank the many private landowners who contributed valuable information about their conservation projects for their assistance, innovation, and commitment to conservation. CONAF and CODEFF also helpfully provided data on PPAs and RAPP membership, respectively. This Chapter would not have been possible without the support of the GEF and the World Bank, who provide finance and technical support respectively to CIPMA's Valdivian eco-region project. Finally, the authors wish to thank the editors for their helpful comments and suggestions.

2 Lumber companies are the biggest landholders throughout most of southern Chile. They bought enormous tracts of land at very low prices a few decades ago, when the government was offering attractive incentives packages to promote the creation of a logging industry. Forest companies have continued to acquire land throughout the 1990s, mostly by purchasing private plots from small farmers in economic trouble, indigenous communities, and absentee landowners.

REFERENCES

Bañados, F. 2000. "¿Cómo Acceder a la Montaña? Derecho de Propiedad u Bien Común." *Ambiente y Desarrollo*, XVI:4, pp.44–50.

Bryant, D., D. Nielsen, and L. Tangley. 1997. "The Last Frontier Forests: Ecosystems and Economies on the Edge." Washington: WRI.

Calcagni, R., D. García, P. Villarroel, and K. Yunis. 1999. "Lugares Naturales y Calidad De Vida". Keynote address at the Sixth Scientific Meeting for the Environment. Santiago, 6–8 January 1999.

Calcagni, R. 2000 "Iniciativas Comunitarias de Conservación: Construcción de una Comunidad Público-Privada Para el Cuidado de la Vida". *Ambiente y Desarrollo*, XVI:3, pp.19–20.

Centro de Análisis de Políticas Públicas (CAPP). 2000. "Informe País: Estado del Medio Ambiente en Chile 1999." Santiago: CAPP – Universidad de Chile.

Chacón, C., and R. Castro (eds.). 1998. *Conservación de Tierras Privadas en América Central.* San José: CEDARENA.

Centro de Investigación y Planificación del Medio Ambiente (CIPMA). 2000a. "Valdivian Forest Zone: Public-Private Mechanisms for Biodiversity Conservation." Santiago: CIPMA.

Centro de Investigación y Planificación del Medio Ambiente (CIPMA). 2000b. "Lanzamiento de Proyecto CIPMA-FMAM, Región de Los Lagos: Áreas Protegidas Privadas." *Ambiente y Desarrollo*, XVI:4, pp.61–72.

Centro de Investigación y Planificación del Medio Ambiente (CIPMA). 2002. "El Círculo Virtuoso del Desarrollo Sustentable." Paper presented at the Séptimo Encuentro Científico Sobre el Medio Ambiente, Antofagasta, May 28–30, 2002.

Comité Pro Defensa de la Flora y Fauna (CODEFF). 1998. "Tabla Resumen de Crecimiento de la RAPP." RAPP Bulletin No.2. Santiago: CODEFF.

Comité Pro Defensa de la Flora y Fauna (CODEFF). 1999. *Las Áreas Silvestres Protegidas Privadas de Chile. Una Herramienta para la Conservación.* Santiago: CODEFF.

Comunidad Indígena Maicolpi. 2000. "Red de Parques Comunitarios Mapu Lahual." Project proposal presented to the Fondo de Bosque Templado (processed).

Corporación Nacional Forestal (CONAF). 1994. "Reglamento Áreas Silvestres Protegidas Privadas." Draft. Santiago: CONAF (processed).

Corporación Nacional Forestal (CONAF). 1996. "Anteproyecto de Ley que Establece Incentivos para la Creación y Manejo de Áreas Silvestres Protegidas Privadas." Draft. Santiago: CONAF (processed).

Corporación Nacional Forestal (CONAF). 2001. "Estadísticas." CONAF website: http://www.conaf.cl/html/estadisticas/estadisticas.html. Accessed September 23, 2001.

Corcuera, E., F. Steiner, and S. Guhathakurta. 2000. "Potential Use of Land Trust Mechanisms for Conservation on the Mexican–U.S. Border. " *Journal of Borderlands Studies*, XV:2, pp.1–23.

Corcuera, E. 2000. "Conservación de Tierras Privadas en Chile y el Mundo: ¿Coincidencia o Tendencia?" *Ambiente y Desarrollo*, XVI:4, pp.36–43.

Dinerstein, E., D.M. Olson, D.J. Graham, A.L. Webster, S.A. Primm, M.P. Bookbinder, and G. Ledec. 1995. *A Conservation Assessment of the Terrestrial Ecoregions of the Latin America and the Caribbean.* Washington: World Bank in association with the World Wildlife Fund.

Frank, D., E. Corcuera Vliegenthart, and C. Castillo. 2001. "Estudio de Ordenamiento de la Cuenca del Río Cochamó." Puerto Montt: Fundación Lahuén.

Gajardo, R. 1995. *La Vegetación Natural de Chile: Clasificación y Distribución Geográfica.* Second edition. Santiago: Editora Universitaria.

García, D., A. Moreira, C. Sepúlveda, and P. Villarroel. 1998. "Áreas Protegidas Privadas en la Legislación Chilena." Documento de Trabajo No.51. Santiago: CIPMA.

García, D. 2000a. "Áreas Silvestres de Propiedad Privada: Oportunidad de *Aggiornamento* para el SNASPE." *Ambiente y Desarrollo,* XVI:3, pp.14–15.

García, D. 2000b. "Protección de Áreas Silvestres Privadas: Desde la Casualidad a la Deliberación." *Ambiente y Desarrollo,* XVI:4, pp.31–35.

García, D., and P. Villarroel. 1998. "Las Áreas Silvestres Protegidas de Propiedad Privada en la Legislación Chilena." *Ambiente y Desarrollo,* XIV:4, pp.21–32.

Geisse, G., and C. Sepúlveda. 2000. "Iniciativas Privadas y Política Pública de Conservación Ambiental." *Ambiente y Desarrollo,* XVI:3, pp.6–13.

Mella, J.E. 1994. "Áreas Silvestres Protegidas y la Conservación de los Mamíferos Terrestres Chilenos." Unpublished Masters Thesis. Santiago: Universidad de Chile.

Moreira, A., P. Villaroel, C. Sepúlveda, and D. García. 1998. "Evaluación y Diseño Biogeográfico y Gestión Operacional del SNASPE en Chile." Working Paper No.53. Santiago: CIPMA.

Olson, D.M., and E. Dinerstein, 1998. "The Global 200: A Representation Approach to Conserving the Earth's Distinctive Ecoregions." Washington: World Wildlife Fund-USA.

Proyecto CIPMA-FMAM. 2001. "Primer Informe de Avance Anual." Valdivia: CIPMA (processed).

Sepúlveda, C. 2001. "Las Motivaciones Detrás de la Filantropía Ambiental: Reflexiones Sobre el Contexto Cultural." *Ambiente y Desarrollo,* XVII:1, pp.86–89.

Sepúlveda, C., P. Villaroel, A. Moreira, and D. García. 1998. "Catastro de Iniciativas Privadas en Conservación de la Biodiversidad Implementadas en Chile." Working Paper No.49. Santiago: CIPMA.

Simonnetti, J. 2000. "Diversidad Biológica." In Centro de Análisis de Políticas Públicas (ed.), *Informe País. Estado del Medio Ambiente en Chile 1999.* Santiago: Lom Ediciones.

Tacón, A., C. Sepúlveda, and V. Hugo Valenzuela. 2001. "Primer Documento de Apoyo al Grupo de Trabajo Público-Privado para la Conservación de la Biodiversidad en la Décima Región." Proyecto CIPMA-FMAM. Valdivia: CIPMA (processed).

Villarroel, P. 2001. "Las Áreas Silvestres Protegidas Privadas Como Experiencia de Filantropía Ambiental: El Caso de la Región de Los Lagos." *Ambiente y Desarrollo,* XVII:1, pp.90–93.

Villarroel, P., D. García, A. Moreira, and C. Sepúlveda. 1998. "Tipología de Modalidades de Cooperación Público-Privadas para la Conservación Viables en Chile." Documento de Trabajo No.52. Santiago: CIPMA.

World Bank. 2001. *World Development Indicators 2001.* Washington: World Bank.

World Wildlife Fund (WWF). Forthcoming. "Evaluación Ecológica de la Ecorregión Valdiviana: Amenazas y Prioridades para la Conservación de la Biodiversidad." Valdivia: WWF.

PEOPLE INTERVIEWED

(All were interviewed during September–November 2001)

Calcagni, R. – Founder, Namuncai Park.
Correa, F. – Administrator, San Francisco de Los Andes Reserve.
De Pablo, F.J. – Founder, Alto Huemul Natural Sanctuary.
Donoso, J.P. – Manager, La Invernada Reserve.
Durston, J. – Manager, Quirra-Quirra Reserve.
Fierro, M. – Founder, Lago Las Rocas Private Reserve.
Gómez, R. – Founder, Lago Las Rocas Private Reserve.
Ibáñez, E. – Forest Keeper, Oncol Park.
Larraín, R. – Administrator, Parque Kawelluco.
Moreno, M. – Manager, Oasis La Campana Ecological Reserve.
Muñoz, A. – Forest Consultant.
Tapia, M. – Bookkeeper, Tepuhueico Park.
Ziller, A. – Inmobiliaria Ayko Ltd., Los Volcanes Park.

Chapter 9

Linking Biodiversity Prospecting and Forest Conservation

Sarah A Laird and Kerry ten Kate

In the last 15 years, biodiversity prospecting has attracted a great deal of attention as, variously, a source of wonder drugs, an activity undertaken by rugged adventurers involving remote indigenous peoples, a potential funding mechanism for biodiversity conservation, and more recently an ethically dubious activity undertaken by 'biopirates'. It is in fact usually a far humbler activity than generally believed, in terms of its ethical, economic, and conservation footprint as well as its prevalence.

In the 1980s and 1990s, the convergence of a new wave of natural-product-collecting by industry and a growing interest in the links between business, development, and conservation made biodiversity prospecting seem a natural vehicle for funding conservation of forests and other biologically diverse environments. Indeed, access to genetic resources and benefit-sharing (ABS) played a central role in the objectives and articles of the Convention on Biological Diversity (CBD), which entered into force in 1993.

The reality, however, was more complicated. In the early 1990s, there existed few legal or economic links between biodiversity prospecting, conservation, and sustainable development, except a hopeful leap of faith from the fact that many drugs have natural origins, and that many sell very well. The 1990s produced few returns to forest conservation, forest inhabitants, and sustainable development from biodiversity prospecting. But the potential to make the link was and remains real, and has been bolstered by developments in national law and policy, contractual agreements, and innovative partnerships, and by a shift in the way genetic resources and traditional knowledge are exchanged and perceived. These have all made possible greater returns from biodiversity prospecting to conservation and source countries in the future.

In this Chapter, we focus on some of the ways biodiversity prospecting has or can contribute to forest conservation. These benefits can be divided into two categories: a broad benefit in terms of raising the profile of forest ecosystems, and more direct benefits that may result from partnerships, including a range of monetary and non-monetary benefits. We also examine the potential negative impacts of biodiversity prospecting on forest and species conservation. We then discuss existing legal and institutional constraints to achieving more benefits for conservation from these activities, and make recommendations on steps that might be taken to overcome some of these constraints. Throughout, we focus on pharmaceutical biodiversity prospecting, although it is important to note that this is just one industry sector involved in biodiversity prospecting. Others include the seed, crop protection, horticulture, botanical medicine, personal and cosmetic care, and biotechnology sectors.

VALUE OF PHARMACEUTICAL GENETIC RESOURCES FOUND IN FORESTS

Genetic resources found in biologically diverse forest and other ecosystems hold great potential for the development of a wide variety of useful products, including pharmaceuticals. In part as an argument for conservation, the value of potential and actual drugs derived from the forest has been highlighted by many analysts and organizations.

Estimates of the value of pharmaceutical products derived from biodiversity

The value of natural products in medicine

The most common approach to valuing natural product pharmaceuticals is an anecdotal one, occasionally including speculative or non-representative figures, which highlights a few well-known cases of commercially valuable drugs derived from forests, and by inference argues that biologically diverse forest ecosystems have high option values. For example, *Catharanthus roseus*, the rosy periwinkle, yielded compounds of great value in treating childhood leukemia and Hodgkins disease. One product – Navelbine (Vinorelbine tartrate), marketed by Glaxo-SmithKline – had sales worth US$115.4 million in 2000 (MedAd News, 2001). While this case certainly illustrates the potential for nature to yield valuable medicines, the rosy periwinkle is a pan-tropical weed, and is therefore not a strong indication of the option values held in biologically diverse forest ecosystems.[1]

Quantifying the role of natural products in prescriptions issued

Some studies have moved beyond the anecdotal to quantify the role of natural products in medicine. In the first study of its kind, Farnsworth and others (1985) reported that at least 119 compounds derived from 90 plant species can be considered as important drugs, and 77 per cent of these are derived from plants used in traditional medicine. Between 1959 and 1980, 25 per cent of all prescriptions dispensed from community pharmacies in the United States contained at least one compound now or once derived from, or patterned after, compounds derived from higher plants. More recently, Grifo and Rosenthal (1997) undertook a study of the top 150 proprietary drugs from the United Sates' National Prescription Audit for the period January–September 1993, which is a compilation of virtually all prescriptions filled during this time. They found that 57 per cent of prescriptions contained at least one major active compound now or once derived from, or patterned after, compounds derived from biological diversity. They also found that the commercial use for the base compound in most of the top 150 plant-derived prescription drugs correlates with the reported traditional medical uses (see Box 9.1).

BOX 9.1 *USING TRADITIONAL KNOWLEDGE TO AID BIODIVERSITY PROSPECTING*

Traditional knowledge and cultural diversity are closely linked to biological diversity (Posey, 1999). Historically, traditional knowledge has led researchers to most of the existing drugs and some new ones, crops, ornamental varieties, and other commercial products. Traditional knowledge, predominantly gleaned from public-domain publications, continues to be used as a general indicator of non-specific bioactivity suitable for a panel of broad screens; as an indicator of specific bioactivity suitable for particular high-resolution bioassays; and as an indicator of pharmacological activity for which mechanisms-based bioassays have yet to be developed (Cox, 1994). Most companies do not actively collect ethnobotanical data in the field, but many consult the literature once some activity has been demonstrated. Although traditional knowledge is of less importance today in industry research programs, the close links between cultural and biological diversity in forest ecosystems suggest that it will continue to prove valuable to outside researchers. Such knowledge is under similar threat as forests, however.

The economic value of top-selling natural-product drugs

A different approach was taken by Newman and Laird (1999) to estimate the role of natural products in the top-selling 'blockbuster' division of pharmaceuticals, and their contribution to the bottom line of pharmaceutical companies today. They found that natural products continue to be a major player in the sales of pharmaceutical agents: 11 of the 25 best-selling drugs in 1997, representing 42 per cent of industry-wide sales, are either biologicals, natural products, or entities derived from natural products, with a total 1997 value of US$17.5 billion. The study also found that a significant portion – between 10 and 50 per cent – of the ten top-selling drugs of each of the top 14 pharmaceutical companies are either natural products or entities derived from natural products.[2]

The most striking example of a forest species yielding a commercial drug in recent years is that of the compound paclitaxel, from the forest tree *Taxus baccata*. Paclitaxel is used in the treatment of ovarian cancer, non-small-cell lung cancer, Kaposi's sarcoma, and breast cancer. Marketed by Bristol-Myers Squibb under the brand name Taxol, it was the 24th best-selling drug in 2000, with worldwide sales of US$1.6 billion. Taxotere (docetaxel) is marketed by Aventis for breast cancer and non-small-cell lung cancer, and had sales in 2000 of US$687 million (Med Ad News, 2001). Thus the combined sales value of drugs based on *Taxus baccata* in 2000 was US$2.3 billion.

Estimates of the value of forest ecosystems as a source of pharmaceutical genetic resources

The value of drugs and other products generated from forest genetic resources is potentially very large. For the purpose of conservation decisions, however, some have attempted to move from consideration of the value of drugs to consideration of the value of the species and habitats as a source of useful genetic information. In some cases (for example, Principe, 1989; Pearce and Puroshothamon, 1992), this meant estimating the probability of discovering a commercially valuable chemical entity, and then multiplying this by the value of such a discovery. Simpson and others (1994) tried to value marginal species on the basis of their incremental contribution to the probability of making a commercial discovery and extended this to the marginal hectare of habitat by combining their results with a common model of the species–area relationship. They found that the incentives for habitat conservation generated by pharmaceutical research would probably prove negligible.

Aylward and others (1993) examined the economic value of species information and its role in biodiversity conservation, particularly through the experiences of Costa Rica's National Institute of Biodiversity (Instituto Nacional de Biodiversidad, INBio), but also more broadly looking at the potential for 'pharmaceutical prospecting' to contribute to conservation. They calculated the net return to producers of biotic samples, working backwards from gross drug sales, and used a second model based on returns from royalties and fees paid per sample. Like Simpson and others (1994) they found the sums involved to be negligible, and argued that as long as demand for biotic samples remains low, the returns from pharmaceutical prospecting 'cannot be expected to generate a market solution to the biodiversity crisis' (Aylward, 1993, p.64).

Throughout their study, Aylward and others make a critical distinction between biodiversity and species information, and emphasize the important role of partnerships and investment in research and development (R&D) in improving the return from biodiversity prospecting. At the time, partnerships between companies and source countries were limited to INBio, but over the last ten years the most significant benefits from biodiversity prospecting have resulted from the research process and partnerships, as we will discuss below. While in most cases biodiversity prospecting payments per hectare of forest would prove negligible in such scenarios, the direct and indirect benefits for conservation can be significant. Successful commercialization of a drug, while obviously still

Table 9.1 *Selected cases of forest species*

Forest species	Compounds of primary interest, and main use	Source country	Date first collected	Collecting organization and its home country	Date commercialized
Pilocarpus jaborandi	Pilocarpine (ophthalmology)	Brazil	1870s	Various	1870s
Camptothecen acuminata	Topotecan (anti-cancer)	China	1950s	USDA, US	1996
Taxus baccata	Taxol (anti-cancer)	US	1962	USDA, US	1991
Ancistrocladus korupensis	Michellamine A and B (anti-HIV)	Cameroon	1987	Missouri Botanical Garden, US	Still in research
Calophyllum spp	Calanolide (anti-HIV)	Sarawak, Malaysia	1987	PCRPS/Arnold Arboretum, US	Still in research

desirable, is not the only or even the best measure of potential benefits derived from biodiversity prospecting for development or conservation.

Current industry interest in natural products

While all of the above provide us with an indication of the historical and current value of natural products in medicine and pharmaceutical company sales, in order for biodiversity prospecting to contribute to forest conservation today, it must also be the case that pharmaceutical companies retain a strong interest in natural products R&D, and that new drugs coming on the market reflect the figures cited above.

Cragg and others (1997) analyzed data on new drugs approved by either the US Food and Drug Administration (FDA) or comparable entities in other countries. Their analysis focused on the areas of cancer and infectious diseases, and their results demonstrate that natural products continue to play an important role in drug discovery. Of the 87 approved cancer drugs they examined, 62 per cent are of natural origin or are modeled on natural product parents. Results varied by disease indication, with drugs of natural origin dominant in the area of anti-bacterials (78 per cent) and anti-infectives (63 per cent), and synthetics dominating in categories like analgesics, antidepressants, antihistamines, and cardiotonics.

In recent decades, interest in accessing biodiversity for pharmaceutical development has been cyclical: high in the 1960s when successful antibiotics and anti-tumor agents were found in nature; falling off in the 1970s with the advent of recombinant DNA technology and molecular pharmacology; and rising again in the 1980s, as technologies such as robotic high-throughput screens and improved separation techniques made it cost effective to explore many hundreds of thousands of samples a year.

Scientific developments in the fields of biochemistry, molecular biology, cell biology, immunology, and information technology continue to transform the process of drug discovery and development. Advances in molecular biology and genomics produce a previously inaccessible range of disease targets for the development of new drugs. New technologies – such as combinatorial chemistry, high-throughput screens, and laboratories-on-a-chip – provide unprecedented numbers of compounds, and better and faster ways to test them. In this environment, natural products are often viewed as too slow, costly, and problematic. In many sectors, research dollars are flowing out of natural products and into synthetic chemistry for rational drug design, combinatorial approaches, and genetics that focus largely on human material.

However, natural products continue to hold key advantages: diversity and novelty resulting from millennia of evolution. In addition, improvements in the technology associated with purifying and analyzing compounds in complex mixtures have decreased the time involved in separating and analyzing natural products. Although they may compete for research dollars, combinatorial chemistry and natural products are increasingly seen as complementary sources of new compounds for screening.

Natural products R&D tends to form a relatively small portion of most companies' programs – between 1 and 5 per cent on average, as reported in a survey undertaken in 1998–1999 (ten Kate and Laird, 1999). Even so, natural products research remains a significant economic activity. Spending by research-based pharmaceutical companies on R&D in 2001 exceeded US$30.5 billion (with 36 per cent of this spent on pre-clinical functions). More than US$500 million is spent to develop each new chemical entity, factoring in failures and interest costs over the entire period of the investment (PhRMA, 2001).

The material acquisition strategy of natural products research programs further supports economic arguments for the conservation of biologically diverse habitats. One effect of the CBD and national ABS legislation has been a restriction in the geographic range and number of countries that companies work in. However, most companies continue to highly value chemical diversity and novelty in the collections made for their high-throughput screening programs – the very qualities biologically diverse ecosystems can deliver. As one industry representative said: '. . .biological diversity promotes chemical diversity, and specific niches where organisms grow and compete would foster greater generation of secondary metabolites, so we can look for specific niches as a way of generating chemical diversity' (quoted in ten Kate and Laird, 1999, p.62). Others reported a desire for '...ever-increasing taxonomic, ecological and geographical diversity' in their collections (pp.62–63). In addition to Taxol, other recent cases support this approach, including the rare endemic vine *Ancistrocladus korupensis* from Cameroon, which yielded the promising anti-HIV compound michellamine-B (Laird and others, 2000).

POLICY AND PUBLIC AWARENESS-RAISING ABOUT THE IMPORTANCE OF FOREST CONSERVATION

Over the last decade, biodiversity prospecting has regularly been used to argue for the economic value of biodiversity and forests. The argument is generally directed at policy-makers and the general public, rather than local resource users, who are unlikely to change management practices based on this kind of argument. It is intended to highlight a largely hidden but potentially significant financial gain from retaining biological diversity and sustainably managing forests. This has helped to attract support for forest conservation and the work of conservation organizations, albeit often in ways that are indirect and difficult to quantify.

The public awareness-raising role of biodiversity prospecting has been particularly compelling. Few other conservation messages have sparked popular interest to quite such an extent, and a large majority of conservation groups – including many that did limited or no work on biodiversity prospecting issues – drew upon 'medicinal riches' arguments to raise money from the public. Although the claims were often overly optimistic and speculative, the public information campaigns in the late 1980s and 1990s touting the 'medicinal riches of the rainforest' helped to galvanize public support for forest conservation.

An important aspect of these messages is that they supported conservation not just of forest cover (as global warming campaigns effectively do), but of biologically diverse and intact forest ecosystems, and of rare and endemic species. They also made an argument for the potential or option values held in forests, complementing use values like recreation, timber, watershed protection, and landscapes, and the intrinsic or existence values of nature (WRI, 1992; Pearce and Puroshothaman, 1992; Balick and others, 1996; Bowles and others, 1996). A number of studies undertaken in the 1980s and 1990s also produced results demonstrating the greater value over time of minimally destructive uses of the forest relative to more destructive practices such as clearing for agriculture, ranching, and intensive logging. These less destructive uses include biodiversity prospecting, as well as ecotourism and marketing of forest products (for example, Schwartzman, 1992; Peters and others, 1989; Balick and Mendelssohn, 1992; Godoy and Lubowski, 1992; Principe, 1989).

Although the odds of developing a drug from any given natural product collection remain small, a few cases in the last ten years alone bolster these arguments for the pharmaceutical potential of forests. For example, *Taxus brevifolia* was collected in a forest under heavy pressure from logging. Previously discarded as a junk species, it has proved far more valuable than the timber that grows around it. National forest areas in the United States are often expected to 'pay their own way', but this is generally interpreted narrowly to mean logging, mining, ranching, and other entrenched interests. These industries are heavily subsidized by the federal government and rarely cover their own costs or return significant benefits beyond limited jobs to the local economy. Taxol, on the other hand, has yielded massive commercial revenues as well as important drugs. For a time there was concern relating to over-collection of the species in the wild, but for the most part the impact of this activity has been far less damaging than logging or other uses of the forest in this area. In other cases, the degradation or destruction of forests has actually endangered the potential for species or individuals to yield compounds of interest as potential drugs. *Calophyllum lanigerum* was collected in 1987 from forests in Sarawak, and showed promise against HIV, but when a team went back to re-collect from the same tree it had been logged, and other individuals did not show the same activity. A massive collecting program was undertaken around Southeast Asia to identify individuals containing the same compounds of interest.

It is clear that the public and governmental awareness of the potential value of forests was raised by biodiversity prospecting arguments. It is less clear to what extent this translated into concrete benefits for conservation and development. The arguments helped fuel a boom in funding and support for rainforest and other forest conservation in the 1980s and 1990s, both from governmental donors and the general public. Indirectly, they helped to change attitudes about the value of forests. However, policy formulations resulting from the high profile of biodiversity prospecting in the 1980s and 1990s do not primarily emphasize direct benefits for conservation. Forest and environment laws tend to include little about equity and biodiversity prospecting issues, which are addressed in separate ABS measures, and in some cases draft laws to protect indigenous knowledge, as in Peru (Tobin, 2002). These, in turn, tend to include little on forest and biodiversity conservation. Ten years after the United Nations Conference on Environment and Development (UNCED) and entry into force of the CBD, few countries integrate the CBD objectives of conservation, sustainable use, and equity into one body of law. These issues will be discussed at greater length below.

CAPTURING THE BENEFITS OF BIODIVERSITY PROSPECTING FOR CONSERVATION AND DEVELOPMENT

The bulk of benefits for conservation and development resulting from biodiversity prospecting in the last decade have resulted from the research process, and an increasing use of partnerships between companies and source countries. For products already on the market, they have also involved raw material sourcing partnerships. The types of benefits that result from these partnerships include reciprocal access to other genetic resources, opportunities for in situ and ex situ conservation, access to information and research results, participation in research, technology transfer, and training and capacity-building. Where partnerships result in commercial products, financial benefits can include fees, milestone payments, and royalties.[3]

More involved benefit-sharing arrangements have resulted from cases where commercialization occurred after the entry into force of the CBD, and the parties involved held on-going discussions on the nature of their partnership. For example, a joint venture between Medichem Pharmaceutical and the state government of Sarawak for the development of *Calophyllum* is perhaps the most advanced agreement to promote collaborative research on drug development that enables the provider country to build capacity and become more competitive in drug development (see Box 9.2).

These examples of benefit-sharing show that direct benefits for conservation do not necessarily result from these types of supply agreements or partnerships. Partnerships can have significant impacts for a country's capacity to undertake research and develop its own biodiversity, and incorporate numerous spin-off benefits for research institutions, universities, local businesses, and others, but their impact on conservation is at best indirect. Although not the most significant or common result, concrete and direct benefits can also accrue to conservation from biodiversity prospecting, including capacity-building and support for biodiversity science; sustainable economic activities based on the supply of raw materials; and direct financial contributions to conservation programs and objectives.

Capacity-building and support for biodiversity science

Biodiversity prospecting can help to build skills and capacity in areas critical for sustainable management and conservation, but which are typically under-funded

BOX 9.2 *JOINT VENTURE BETWEEN MEDICHEM PHARMACEUTICAL AND THE STATE GOVERNMENT OF SARAWAK*

In 1994, following the discovery of promising anti-cancer activity in *Calophyllum lanigerum*, the US National Cancer Institute (NCI) signed a 'Letter of Collection' with the State Secretary of the government of Sarawak. NCI worked on two Calanolide compounds with Medichem Research, a pharmaceutical company based in Illinois. In 1995, NCI granted the company exclusive rights to all further developments under a license which specified that Medichem Research was obliged to negotiate an agreement with the Sarawak government. This fulfilled the NCI's obligations under the 1994 Letter of Collection. In 1996, Medichem Research entered into a joint venture with the Sarawak government called Sarawak Medichem Pharmaceuticals (SMP). SMP has the right to file patents (to be owned jointly by Medichem Research and the Sarawak government) on all subsequent innovations arising out of this work. The Sarawak government is sharing in the risks as well as the rewards of the joint venture by providing funding up to the completion of Phase I clinical development of one of the compounds. Additional funds needed for further stages of development will be raised by the two parties to the joint venture. Clinical trials started in 1997.

Another facet of the partnership is its flexibility. The benefit-sharing arrangements can be shaped over time to reflect the partners' respective contributions. Currently, the agreement is that royalties arising once the drug is marketed will be split 50:50, based on the contribution of chemical knowledge and expertise by Medichem Research and the contribution of investment by Sarawak. The agreement on how benefits will be shared may change, depending on how current investment patterns develop over time. In addition to the joint venture, a number of other benefits have been shared between the parties. The University of Illinois at Chicago (UIC) and the Sarawak Forest Department have conducted collaborative survey and conservation work. UIC received funding for its work from the NCI. UIC, as well as Medichem Research and the Sarawak government, will share in any royalties from SMP patents. Through its collaboration with other organizations and the funding from Medichem and Sarawak, the NCI has been able to promote the development of calanolides. The Sarawak government has the exclusive right to supply latex from *Calophyllum teysmannii* for the extraction of one of the compounds. Sarawak scientists have been trained in screening and isolation at the NCI and Medichem Research. A Malaysian PhD chemist is treasurer of the joint venture and is based in the SMP offices in Illinois, where he is observing clinical trials and conducting pre-clinical studies and toxicological work on two back-up compounds. Two other Sarawak physicians are assigned to participate in the clinical work.

Source: ten Kate and Wells, 1998; ten Kate and Laird, 1999 and in short supply in biologically-diverse regions. These include training communities, field staff, and researchers in inventory and collection methods, taxonomy, ecology, and natural products chemistry. For example, as part of its biodiversity prospecting work the International Cooperative Biodiversity Group (ICBG) in Suriname employed and trained ten Surinamese botanists in collecting, vouchering, and drying plant samples (Guerin-McManus and others, 1998). Biodiversity prospecting can also support capacity-building in information management, such as databases, software, herbaria, and other ex situ facilities.

In some cases, such as INBio in Costa Rica, biodiversity prospecting is explicitly linked to basic biodiversity science and management needs, like national inventories. The ICBG, which is funded by the US National Institute of Health (NIH), the National Science Foundation (NSF), and the US Agency for International Development (USAID), also explicitly links drug discovery, sustainable development, and conservation. Examples of project components that directly address conservation management and information needs include forest dynamics and inventory plots in Cameroon; ecological studies of butterflies and other insects in Peru; and training and equipment for data management and specimen preservation at the National Herbarium in Suriname (Rosenthal and others, 1999).

Sustainable economic activities based on biodiversity

Biodiversity prospecting can support the growth of domestic institutions and industries based on biodiversity, including the supply of samples to industry for screening, higher-level research partnerships, and the supply of raw or processed materials for advanced research and manufacturing purposes. In turn, this can encourage the retention of biodiversity to protect future earnings.

INBio in Costa Rica has developed a series of partnerships with companies over the last ten years to supply samples and associated services, which in turn support INBio's inventory and other activities. These companies include early and on-going partnerships like those with Merck, Diversa, BTG, Indena, and Givaudane and Roure, as well as more recent partnerships with Phytera, Eli Lilly, and the Akkadik corporation (INBio, 2002b).

The re-supply of bulk raw materials for research and development, and subsequent industrial-scale collection or cultivation of plants for the manufacture of commercial products, can also yield significant benefits for local communities and source countries, and in some cases conservation. Following supply problems encountered with Taxol in the United States a few years earlier (see Box 9.3), the NCI invested heavily in Cameroon to develop cultivation options for *Ancistrocladus korupensis*, providing local employment and some capacity-building. Shaman Pharmaceuticals similarly invested for a number of years in sustainable harvesting regimes in Latin America for their main species of interest, Sangre de Drago (*Croton lechleri*).

These cases illustrate the potential for raw material sourcing to provide local income and benefits based on the realization of option values held in forest. But they also highlight the unreliability of this type of activity. *Ancistrocladus korup-ensis* is presently considered too toxic and has been dropped by the NCI research program, along with local agroforestry trials and other investments in sourcing in Cameroon. Shaman Pharmaceuticals has folded, and it is not clear if another company will pick up its product (although in this case, Sangre de Drago has significant local markets to fall back on).

In other cases, companies may change their sourcing strategy in response to scientific discoveries (which may enable synthesis), concerns about the relia-bility of supply (in terms of quality and volume), and cost-efficiency. Taxol was first sourced in the United States from *Taxus brevifolia*, but concerns associated with sustainability and sufficient volume shifted some sourcing to India and then Europe. It is now produced through semi-synthesis from 10 desacetylbaccatin III isolated from a different species, *Taxus baccata*, by the Italian company Idena working with Bristol-Myers Squibb (see Box 9.3). For many years *Pilocarpus jaborandi* was sourced from the wild in northeast Brazil, but the employment conditions were harsh and the work unreliable and poorly paid (Davis, 1993). Working conditions have reportedly improved on the plantations in which it is now grown, but it is unclear how this will impact on the 25,000 individuals who wild-harvested *Pilocarpus jaborandi* (Pinheiro, 1997). It is clear that the supply of raw materials involves a complex web of economic, political, and social factors which can combine to create significant benefits for local groups and conserv-ation, but may easily not do so, and must be monitored carefully.

Financial benefits for conservation programs and areas

Biodiversity prospecting's prominence on the conservation agenda, at UNCED and elsewhere, was partly based on the idea that it would serve as a funding mechanism for conservation. However, few biodiversity prospecting agreements or access laws explicitly require financial and other benefits to be shared with conservation programs and areas. In fact, as with other natural resources, benefits are often channeled away from rather than toward biologically-diverse areas, ending up in the hands of the central government, urban-based companies, or institutions with little interest in conservation or local communities (for example, see Laird and others, 2000).

Tithing a portion of all financial earnings from biodiversity prospecting for conservation is a relatively easy and potentially valuable way to directly link these activities, and has been tried in a minority of cases. In Costa Rica, INBio donates 10 per cent of all biodiversity prospecting budgets, and 50 per cent of all royalties, to the Ministry of Environment and Energy (MINAE). As of early 2000, INBio's contributions had come to US$400,000 for conservation activities, directed through MINAE; US$790,000 to conservation areas; US$713,000 to public universities; and US$750,000 to internal support for activities at INBio, partic-ularly the National Inventory Program (INBio, 2002a).

In 1993, Western Australia's Department of Conservation and Land Manage-ment (CALM) entered into an agreement with the pharmaceutical company

AMRAD. Under the agreement, CALM ensures sustainable collection of all raw materials, and commits a portion of the funds received from AMRAD to directly benefit conservation in the following ways: US$380,000 into conservation projects in Western Australia; US$190,000 for the conservation of rare and endangered flora and fauna; and US$190,000 into other conservation activities, including information technology such as geographical information systems, data capture and population dynamics studies. This matched the discretionary budget of CALM's science division for that year.

The ICBG describes its work as being similar to integrated conservation and development programs (ICDPs), in which conservation is an expected outcome of development efforts that 'create an opportunity, means and incentive to change patterns of resource use. . . [and create] a shift in attitude and behavior by land-owners, policy-makers and others who affect natural resource use' (Rosenthal and others, 1999, p.14). In addition to direct development benefits resulting from their programs, many ICBGs financially support activities such as traditional woodcraft enterprises in Suriname, propagation of ornamental plants in Mexico, and propagation of medicinal plants for markets in West Africa, Vietnam, Mexico, and Peru (Rosenthal and others, 1999).

POTENTIAL NEGATIVE IMPACTS OF BIODIVERSITY PROSPECTING

The negative impacts of biodiversity prospecting on conservation tend to cluster into three areas: poor collection of samples for research purposes, unsustainable bulk collection of raw material, and potential inequitable relationships with forest dwellers. None necessarily characterize biodiversity prospecting, nor are they the norm. However, there have been sufficient reported cases of each to warrant mention here.

Poor collection of samples for research purposes

As with any collecting effort, collections for biodiversity prospecting, if under-taken by irresponsible collectors, can be destructive. Small amounts are generally required of each initial sample (on average 0.5kg for plants), but once a species shows promise, larger quantities are needed. Companies repeatedly emphasize the value of high quality and reputable intermediary collectors, but there remain exceptional cases in which individuals have overharvested rare or threatened species during sample collections.

Unsustainable bulk collections of raw material for manufacture

As we have seen above, and in Box 9.3, vast quantities of raw material are required for the manufacture of drugs. Roughly half of new products can be wholly synthesized, but many are still produced by isolation from raw materials (for example, *Catharanthus roseus*), and others are semi-synthetically produced from natural precursors (for example, *Podophyllum emodi*). For a number of years the demand for Taxol from the wild exceeded available sustainable supplies and gave rise to significant concern about the species' survival. A great deal was invested to develop alternative supplies of raw material.

Companies are loath to depend upon unreliable – which includes unsustainable – supplies of raw material, and will go to great lengths to develop reliable supplies. However, in some cases there is a lag of many years before this is possible. In others, particularly in the botanical medicine industry, companies do not consider the investment in sustainable supplies to be worthwhile, wild-harvest material as long as possible, and then move on to alternative sites or species when populations are exhausted (Laird and Pierce, forthcoming).

BOX 9.3 *TAXOL: DEVELOPING A SUSTAINABLE SUPPLY*

Taxol was developed from the Pacific Yew tree, *Taxus brevifolia*. Originally collected in 1962 in the Pacific northwest of the United States by the United States Department of Agriculture (USDA), Taxol was not commercialized until the early 1990s. Increasing amounts of raw material were required as the compound moved through discovery and development, giving rise to significant concern about the sustainability of wild harvests of the tree.

By 1985, almost 7000kg of the bark of *T brevifolia* had been collected in Oregon to supply pre-clinical and early clinical studies. This volume of bark yielded approximately 1.3kg of the drug in total. For Phase I clinical trials demand for raw material rocketed again, and 27,000kg of bark was collected in 1989. This raised concerns about the environmental impact of the harvest. Hauser Northwest, a company under contract to Bristol-Myers Squibb, collected 723,000kg of bark in 1991 and 1992, under supervision of the Forest Service. Part of the agreement between the NCI and Hauser involved Hauser's commitment to fund an environmental impact assessment in conjunction with the Forest Service, Bureau of Land Management and USDA. However, it was clear that alternative sources of Taxol must be developed, and the NCI funded surveys of *Taxus* species in Canada, Mexico, Russia, the Ukraine, Georgia, and the Philippines. Needles, more sustainable to harvest than bark, showed promise as a source of the baccatin precursors to the active compound paclitaxel. Research in France and an agreement with the Italian company Indena led to the supply of baccatins from a European yew species, *Taxus baccata*, for conversion to the active compound using methods developed in Florida. For a period, Indena sourced yew needles from India under a 'renewable resource' agreement, but discovered that suppliers felled trees, so the company transferred its sourcing to Europe.

Inequitable relationships with forest dwellers

Biodiversity prospecting generally involves a wide range of groups that might not normally interact with each other. For example, pharmaceutical companies and their intermediaries collecting material from remote forest areas will usually work in collaboration with local communities. In order for biodiversity prospecting to most effectively benefit conservation and forest communities, the priorities and objectives of local groups must be served, and they must be involved in consultations and the research process. In some cases, local communities have not been properly informed of the nature and implications of collections. While national laws on access to genetic resources, associated knowledge, and benefit-sharing are now under development in some 50 countries, in the majority of cases the legal framework as yet does not protect a range of communities' rights, including rights to prior informed consent and benefit-sharing (Posey, 1999). As the policy and ethical environment in which biodiversity prospecting takes place has evolved over the last ten years, these and other relationships have become more equitable, but there is still a long way to go in most countries.

LIMITATIONS TO REALIZING THE LINKS BETWEEN BIODIVERSITY PROSPECTING AND CONSERVATION

As we have seen, biodiversity prospecting for pharmaceuticals has the potential to generate large monetary and non-monetary benefits for conservation and development. Biodiversity prospecting is not generally a destructive use of biological diversity, but its benefits for conservation have proven to be few and far between. This is due to a variety of factors, which are discussed below.

The lack of an adequate legal and policy framework

The CBD entered into force in 1993, reflecting the convergence of conservation and development agendas, and coinciding with a period of growth in biodiversity prospecting. While the CBD provided an international framework for the exchange of genetic resources, the development of strategies, national measures, and appropriate structures to implement new access and benefit-sharing regimes was left to national governments. Many governments have struggled to develop appropriate measures and institutions. As a new area of law and policy, the process has necessarily proven slow and difficult. Many new lessons have been learned through trial and error in the last ten years (Barber and others, 2002; Glowka, 1998; ten Kate and Wells, 2001).

In the last decade researchers and indigenous peoples' groups have also explored the parameters of what constitutes equitable research relationships, and have begun to articulate appropriate terms for biodiversity research and prospecting collaborations. This has resulted in a range of indigenous peoples' statements and declarations, researchers' codes of ethics, and institutional policies that support and have sometimes guided the development and implementation of national measures (Laird, 2002).

Although significant advances have been made on a range of fronts, this remains an area in flux. As a result, the legal and policy framework necessary to ensure that biodiversity prospecting acts more effectively to promote conservation and development objectives in source countries is not yet available in most regions, although the last decade has witnessed significant progress in this direction.

The most significant benefits from biodiversity prospecting are linked to science and technology, not conservation

Biodiversity prospecting takes place within the most technologically and scientifically advanced industries and research programs in the world. Only a very small portion of the time and resources spent on developing a pharmaceutical compound from natural products is spent anywhere near a forest. As a result, the most significant benefits to result from biodiversity prospecting partnerships grow from post-collection stages of the research process, and most effectively accrue to research institutions, universities, companies, and others in source countries who work in laboratories, generally far from forests.

Biodiversity prospecting partnerships can be an extremely effective way to transfer technology, build capacity, and promote development based on indigenous biodiversity. However, because research and development are quite quickly disconnected from the original source of material – the forest or other habitat of collection – making links with conservation has proven difficult. Explicit provisions built into contracts and national laws for financial contributions to conservation areas and programs, as well as building biodiversity science to help study, manage, and conserve threatened species and habitats, can act to strengthen this link, but they have been the exceptions to date.

The biodiversity prospecting dialogue and policy emphasis has been on equity and development, not conservation and development

Discussions and policy formulation relating to biodiversity prospecting over the last ten years have increasingly focused on the equity of these relationships, rather than on conservation. Although biodiversity prospecting is seen by some as a potential funding mechanism for conservation, many high biodiversity developing countries have emphasized the need to correct historical inequities built into the genetic resources trade, known today as 'biopiracy'. High biodiversity countries feel under no obligation to transfer benefits from their national patrimony primarily to conservation, and requirements for them to do so run contrary to the spirit of fairness that is being promoted.

At the same time, the rights of indigenous peoples' groups to control commercial and other research on their resources or knowledge have become a central feature of access and benefit-sharing discussions within the CBD policy process. Despite the fact that these groups feature in only a handful of current biodiversity prospecting cases, issues relating to prior informed consent and benefit-sharing with local groups have received a great deal of attention. In this way, biodiversity prospecting has served a useful role in bringing intergovernmental attention to indigenous peoples' rights and equity issues in ways that have not been common to any great extent previously.

REALIZING THE CONSERVATION POTENTIAL OF BIODIVERSITY PROSPECTING

Biodiversity prospecting is not a solution to the problem of forest destruction. However, it can play an important role in regions with the requisite scientific, technological, and legal foundations, and as part of a package of economic activities that minimally impact on forest ecosystems and allow countries and local groups to benefit from their biological diversity. In order to maximize benefits for conservation from these activities, a number of basic steps and strategies are required, including effective national consultations, strategies, and legislation; policies for research institutions and protected areas; and funds for conservation.

National access and benefit-sharing legislation

The legal and policy framework must be in place to set terms for collectors and partnerships, and must require a portion of the benefits to be shared with conservation areas and programs. Several countries, such as the Philippines, the five countries of the Andean Commission, and Costa Rica, have introduced access and benefit-sharing laws, and over 40 other countries are currently developing access and benefit-sharing legislation.

Effective national consultation process

An inclusive and effective national ABS consultation process, conducted separately or in conjunction with other environmental law consultations, will help to ensure that the objectives set, including those for conservation, reflect the priorities of a wide range of stakeholders. This is not only a fair way to proceed, but a far more effective way to achieve these objectives.[4]

Effective national strategy

National ABS strategies can help to ensure that a portion of the benefits from biodiversity prospecting is channeled to conservation. Developing a strategy requires the articulation of underlying objectives, and allows discussions to move beyond rhetorical commitments to 'conservation' into realistic plans for implementation.[5]

Policies for research institutions and protected areas

Most biodiversity prospecting collections today are undertaken in collaboration with local research institutions or companies. As representatives of their countries' interests, it is critical that these institutions have clear and transparent institutional policies. For example, a consortium of botanic gardens recently developed a publication entitled 'principles on access to genetic resources and benefit-sharing, Common Policy Guidelines to assist with their implementation and Explanatory Text' (Latorre García and others, 2001) and the Limbe Botanic Garden in Cameroon has developed its own package of access and benefit-sharing policy documents and agreements.[6]

At the same time, a great deal of collecting is done in or around national parks and other conservation areas, or with the support of park staff (Laird and Lisinge, 2002). For example, *Ancistrocladus korupensis* was collected around the Korup National Park in Cameroon; the thermophile *Thermus aquaticus* was collected in Yellowstone National Park in the United States, yielding the enzyme taq polymerase, which is used in a range of biotechnology applications with annual sales in excess of US$200 million (ten Kate and others, 2002); and the pharmaceutical Sandimmune, with worldwide sales in 2001 of US$1.2 billion, was developed from a soil sample collected in Hardangervidda National Park in Norway (Svarstad and others, 2002; MedAd News, 2001). It is important, therefore, for protected areas to develop their own institutional policies to guide biodiversity research and prospecting activities.

In order to capture benefits from biodiversity prospecting, multiple layers of access and benefit-sharing controls are necessary, and formalizing institutional and protected area policy and the nature of partnerships, in line with national and international law, is an important layer in this framework.

Fund for conservation

In some countries it may prove useful to establish a trust or other fund to distribute biodiversity prospecting financial benefits (Guerin-McManus and others, 2002). A fund can channel benefits to a range of activities and serve a number of objectives, including conservation. INBio has developed its own model of allocating a portion of financial revenues to conservation agencies and areas in Costa Rica, but in many countries a dedicated biodiversity prospecting fund might be required.

CONCLUSION

Biodiversity prospecting has the potential to generate significant monetary and non-monetary benefits for conservation. However, its primary contribution to high biodiversity countries has been and will remain in scientific and technological capacity-building. These types of benefits are the backbone of biodiversity prospecting partnerships, and result whether or not a product is commercialized.

Although the bulk of benefits from biodiversity prospecting may go toward science and technology development, it is still possible and necessary for conservation areas and programs to benefit indirectly and directly. Given historical relationships and trends in global law and economies, it is understandable that the starting point in the debate on biodiversity prospecting policy would be fairness and equity. However, advances have been made on these issues over the last ten years, and it is possible now to realize more effective links between biodiversity prospecting and conservation, while continuing to address the important equity concerns associated with the commercial use of genetic resources.

NOTES

1   Common and widespread weeds are often an invaluable source of medicine for local communities (for example, see Stepp and Moerman, 2001), and many have found their way into pharmaceutical drugs. However, forests have also historically yielded numerous invaluable compounds from quite rare or endemic species. These include quinine (*Chincona ledgeriana*), pilocarpine (*Pilocarpus jaborandi*), physostigmine (*Physostigma venenosum*), and tubocuranine (*Chondodendron tomentosum*).

2   Examples of natural product blockbusters in worldwide sales in 2000 include: Zocor (simivastatin) marketed by Merck & Co with sales of US$5.3 billion; Augementin (amoxicillin and clavulanate potassium) marketed by GlaxoSmithKline with sales of US$1.9 billion; and Pravachol (pravastatin sodium) marketed by Bristol-Myers Squibb, with sales of US$1.8 billion. Zocor and Augementin are naturally-derived, meaning they begin with a natural product that is then chemically modified to produce the drug. Pravachol is a natural product, meaning that it is chemically identical to the pure natural compound. Biologicals – entities that are proteins or polypeptides either isolated directly from the natural source or more usually made by recombinant DNA techniques followed by production using fermentation – also feature prominently in the best-selling drugs of 2000. They include: Procrit (US$2.7 billion in sales in 2000) marketed by Johnson & Johnson, and Epogen (US$2 billion) and Neupogen (US$1.2 billion) marketed by Amgen (Med Ad News, 2001).

3   See ten Kate and Laird (1999) for a more detailed discussion of benefit-sharing in the pharmaceutical and other industries.

4   See Swiderska (2001) for a review of recent ABS consultation processes, and recommendations for improved effectiveness.

5   See ten Kate and Wells (2001) for a review and recommendations for national ABS strategies.

6   Available at www.rbgkew.org.uk/conservation and www.rbgkew.org.uk/peopleplants/manuals, respectively.

REFERENCES

Anderson, A. (ed). 1990. *Alternatives to Deforestation: Steps Toward Sustainable Use of the Amazon Rain Forest*. New York: Columbia University Press.

Aylward, B.A. 1993. "The Economic Value of Pharmaceutical Prospecting and its Role in Biodiversity Conservation." LEEC Discussion Paper No.93-05. London: IIED.

Aylward, B.A., J. Echeverria, L. Fendt, and E.B. Barbier. 1993. "The Economic Value of Species Information and its Role in Biodiversity Conservation: Case Studies of Costa Rica's National Biodiversity Institute and Pharmaceutical Prospecting." A report to the Swedish International Development Authority, prepared by the London Environmental Economics Centre and the Tropical Science Center in collaboration with INBio.

Balick, M.J., E. Elisabetsky, and S.A. Laird. 1996. *Medicinal Resources of the Tropical Forest: Biodiversity and its Importance for Human Health*. New York: Columbia University Press.

Balick, M.J., and R Mendelsohn. 1992. "Assessing the Economic Value of Traditional Medicines From Tropical Rain Forests." *Conservation Biology*, 6:1, pp.128–130.

Barber, C., L. Glowka, and A.G. LaVina. 2002. "Developing and Implementing National Measures for Genetic Resources Access Regulation and Benefit-Sharing." In S.A. Laird (ed.), *Biodiversity and Traditional Knowledge: Equitable Partnerships in Practice*. London: Earthscan.

Bowles, I., D. Clark, D. Downes, and M. Guerin-McManus. 1996. *Encouraging Private Sector Support for Biodiversity Conservation: The Use of Economic Incentives and Legal Tools*. Conservation International Policy Papers, Volume 1. Washington: Conservation International.

Cox, P.A. 1994. "The Ethnobotanical Approach to Drug Discovery: Strengths and Limitations." In, *Ethnobotany and the Search for New Drugs*. Ciba Foundation Symposium 185. New York: Wiley.

Cragg, G.M., D.J. Newman, and K.M. Snader. 1997. "Natural Products in Drug Discovery and Development." *Journal of Natural Products*, 60:1, pp.52–60.

Davis, S. 1993. *Pathways to Economic Development Through Intellectual Property Rights*. Environment Department. Washington: World Bank.

Farnsworth, N.R., O. Akerele, A.S. Bingel, D.D. Soejarto, and Z. Guo. 1985. "Medicinal Plants in Therapy." *World Health Organization*, 63, pp.965–81.

Farnsworth, N.R., and D.D. Soejarto. 1985. "Potential Consequences of Plant Extinction in the United States on the Current and Future Availability of Prescription Drugs." *Economic Botany*, 39, pp.231–240.

Glowka, L. 1998. "A Guide to Designing Legal Frameworks to Determine Access to Genetic Resources." Environmental Policy and Law Paper No.34, Bonn: IUCN Environmental Law Centre.

Godoy, R., and R. Lubowski. 1992. "Guidelines for the Economic Valuation of Nontimber Tropical Forest Products." *Current Anthropology*, 33:4, pp.423–430.

Grifo, F., and J. Rosenthal (eds.). 1997. *Biodiversity and Human Health*. Washington: Island Press.

Guerin-McManus, M., K. Nnadozie, and S.A. Laird. 2002. "Sharing Financial Benefits: Trust Funds for Biodiversity Prospecting." In S.A. Laird (ed.), *Biodiversity and Traditional Knowledge: Equitable Partnerships in Practice*. London: Earthscan.

Guerin-McManus, M., L. Famolare, I. Bowles, A.J. Stanley, R.A. Mittermeir, and A.B. Rosenfeld. 1998. "Bioprospecting in Practice: A Case Study of the Suriname ICBG Project and Benefit-Sharing under the Convention on Biological Diversity." In, *Case Studies on Benefit-Sharing Arrangements*. Conference of the Parties to the Convention on Biological Diversity, 4th meeting, Bratislava.

Instituto Nacional de Biodiversidad (INBio). 2002a. "Bioprospecting: An Essential Component in the Conservation Strategy." San José: INBio.

Instituto Nacional de Biodiversidad (INBio). 2002b. "Biodiversity Prospecting Program."
San José: INBio.

ten Kate, K., L. Touche, A. Collis, and A. Wells. 2002. "Access to Genetic Resources and
Benefit-Sharing in a Protected Area: An Agreement Between Yellowstone National
Park and the Diversa Corporation." In S.A. Laird (ed.), *Biodiversity and Traditional
Knowledge: Equitable Partnerships in Practice*. London: Earthscan.

ten Kate, K., and A. Wells. 2001. "Preparing a National Strategy on Access to Genetic
Resources and Benefit-Sharing: A Pilot Study." Royal Botanic Gardens, Kew and
UNDP/UNEP Biodiversity Planning Support Programme.

ten Kate, K., and S.A. Laird. 1999. *The Commercial Use of Biodiversity: Access to
Genetic Resources and Benefit-Sharing*. London: Commission of the European Communities and Earthscan Publications Ltd.

ten Kate, K., and A. Wells. 1998. "Benefit-Sharing Case Study: The Access and Benefit-
sharing Policies of the United States National Cancer Institute: A Comparative Account
of the Discovery and Development of the Drugs Calanolide and Topotecan." Sub-
mission to the Executive Secretary of the Convention on Biological Diversity by the
Royal Botanic Gardens, Kew (processed).

Laird, S.A., (ed.). 2002. *Biodiversity and Traditional Knowledge: Equitable Partnerships
in Practice*. London: Earthscan.

Laird, S.A., and E.E. Lisinge. 2002. "Biodiversity Research and Prospecting in Protected
Areas." In S.A. Laird (ed.), *Biodiversity and Traditional Knowledge: Equitable
Partnerships in Practice*. London: Earthscan.

Laird, S.A., A.B. Cunningham, and E.E. Lisinge. 2000. "One in Ten Thousand? The
Cameroon Case of *Ancistrocladus Korupensis*." In C. Zerner (ed.), *People, Plants and
Justice: Case Studies of Resource Extraction in Tropical Countries*. New York: Columbia
University Press.

Laird, S.A., and A.R. Pierce. Forthcoming. *Sustainable Sourcing of Raw Materials in the
Botanical Medicine Industry*.

Latorre García, F., C. Williams, K. ten Kate, and P. Cheyne. 2001. "Results of the Pilot
Project for Botanic Gardens: Principles on Access to Genetic Resources and Benefit-
Sharing, Common Policy Guidelines to assist with their implementation and Explan-
atory Text". Kew: Royal Botanic Gardens.

Med Ad News. 2001. "Top 500 Prescription Drugs by Worldwide Sales." *Med Ad News*,
May, pp.70–85.

Newman, D.J., and S.A. Laird. 1999. "The Influence of Natural Products on 1997
Pharmaceutical Sales Figures." In K. ten Kate, and S.A. Laird (eds.), *The Commercial
Use of Biodiversity: Access to Genetic Resources and Benefit-Sharing*. London:
Commission of the European Communities and Earthscan Publications Ltd.

Pearce, D., and A. Puroshothamon. 1992. "Preserving Biological Diversity: The Economic
Value of Pharmaceutical Plants." CSERGE Discussion Paper No.92–97. London:
CSERGE.

Peters, C.M., A.H. Gentry, and R.O. Mendelssohn. 1989. "Valuation of an Amazonian
Rainforest." *Nature*, 339, pp.655–656.

Pharmaceutical Research and Manufacturers Association (PhRMA). 2001. *Pharmaceutical Industry Profile 2001*. www.phrma.org.

Pinheiro, C. 1997. "Jaborandi (*Pilocarpus sp., Rutaceae*): A Wild Species and its Rapid
Transformation into a Crop." *Economic Botany*, 52:1, pp.49–58.

Posey, D.A. 1999. *The Cultural and Spiritual Values of Biodiversity*. Nairobi: UNEP.

Principe, P. 1989. *The Economic Value of Biodiversity Among Medicinal Plants*. Paris:
OECD.

Rosenthal, J.P., D. Beck, A. Bhat, J. Biswas, L. Brady, K. Bridbord, S. Collins, G. Cragg, J. Edwards, A. Fairfield, M. Gottlieb, L.A. Gschwind, Y. Hallock, R. Hawks, R. Hegyeli, G. Johnson, G.T. Keusch, E.E. Lyons, R. Miller, J. Rodman, J. Roskoski, and D. Siegel-Causey. 1999. "Combining High Risk Science With Ambitious Social and Economic Goals." In J.P. Rosenthal (ed.), *Drug Discovery, Economic Development and Conservation: The International Cooperative Biodiversity Groups.* Special Issue of *Pharmaceutical Biology*, 37, pp.6–21.

Schwartzman, S. 1992. "Land Distribution and the Social Costs of Frontier Development in Brazil: Social and Historical Context of Extractive Reserves." In D.C. Nepstad and S. Schwartzmann (eds.), *Non-timber Forest Products from Tropical Forests: Evaluation of a Conservation and Development Strategy.* Advances in Economic Botany No.9. New York: New York Botanical Garden.

Simpson, D.R., R.A. Sedjo, and J.W. Reid. 1994. *Valuing Biodiversity for Use in Pharmaceutical Research.* Washington: Resources for the Future.

Stepp, J.R., and D.E. Moerman. 2001. "The Importance of Weeds in Ethnopharmacology." *Journal of Ethnopharmacology*, 75, pp.19–23

Svarstad, H., S. Dhillion, and H. Bugge. 2002. "Novartis' Golden Egg from a Norwegian Goose." In S.A. Laird (ed.), *Biodiversity and Traditional Knowledge: Equitable Partnerships in Practice.* London: Earthscan.

Swiderska, K. 2001. "Stakeholder Participation in Policy on Access to Genetic Resources, Traditional Knowledge, and Benefit-Sharing: Case Studies and Recommendations." *Biodiversity and Livelihoods Issues*, No.4. London: Earthprint Ltd.

Tobin, B. 2002. "Biodiversity Prospecting Contracts: The Search for Equitable Agreements". In S.A. Laird (ed.), *Biodiversity and Traditional Knowledge: Equitable Partnerships in Practice.* London: Earthscan.

World Resources Institute (WRI). 1992. *Global Biodiversity Strategy: Guidelines for Action to Save, Study and Use Earth's Biotic Wealth Sustainably and Equitably.* Washington: WRI.

Chapter 10

Using Fiscal Instruments to Encourage Conservation: Municipal Responses to the 'Ecological' Value-added Tax in Paraná and Minas Gerais, Brazil

Peter H May, Fernando Veiga Neto, Valdir Denardin, and Wilson Loureiro[1]

The 'ecological' value-added tax (Imposto sobre Circulação de Mercadorias e Serviços, ICMS-E), which is now being adopted by most Brazilian states, has been widely lauded as an instrument of fiscal reform that rewards local governments for their commitment to protecting forest and biological resources. The ICMS-E is the first economic instrument to pay for services provided by standing forests in Brazil. This Chapter analyzes the consequences and effectiveness of the ICMS-E as currently applied in the states of Paraná and Minas Gerais. Similar mechanisms are in the process of being implemented and/or discussed in a number of other Brazilian states (Bernardes, 1999).

The ICMS-E is a mechanism that allocates part of the revenues derived from the ICMS to municipalities on the basis of their performance on various environmental criteria. The ICMS-E originated as a means of compensating municipalities that have conservation areas – whether totally protected or restricted sustainable use areas, hereafter referred to as conservation units (CUs) – within their territories for the resulting loss of revenue. As a positive externality, the instrument also seeks to stimulate both improvement of these areas and the creation of new conservation units.[2]

The ICMS-E appears to have had a significant impact. Grieg-Gran (2000) shows that, in Minas Gerais and in Rondônia, the compensatory impacts have been considerable for some municipalities, especially those with large areas under protection. She also shows that the ICMS-E provides incentives for conservation that are sufficiently attractive to motivate municipalities with low-productivity agriculture to increase the area under conservation.

In Paraná and Minas Gerais, the area under protection increased markedly following implementation of the ICMS-E. In this Chapter, we examine the mechanisms through which this effect occurred. Municipalities receive ICMS-E revenues, but state law neither earmarks nor offers guidance on how they are to be used. Bernardes (1999) has noted that much of the apparent impact of the ICMS-E appears to have been reflected in actions by state governments (creation of state CUs) and by private landholders (designation of private reserves and inclusion in environmental zoning areas). Did the ICMS-E really induce these actions? If so, how? How were the municipal incentives transmitted to states and to private individuals?

This Chapter seeks to better understand how and under what conditions the ICMS-E works. It relies on a combination of quantitative and qualitative analysis. We selected relevant municipalities or regional groupings, according to pre-defined criteria such as the total values allocated and the observed increment in the number of conservation units, in particular those that involve private properties. Fieldwork in case study areas was undertaken from November 2000 to April 2001, with at least two researchers of the team always present. We carried out interviews with a broad range of local stakeholders – including mayors, environmental and administrative officials, CU managers, and representatives of local civil organizations and producer groups – to identify the instrument's importance at the local level, difficulties in its implementation, and the potential for greater effectiveness. In this Chapter, we focus on a sample of the municipal case studies, describing some of the more significant responses.

HISTORY OF THE ICMS-E AND CRITERIA FOR IMPLEMENTATION

The ICMS is a state levy on the circulation of goods, services, energy, and communications, specified by Article 155 of the Federal Constitution (Section I, Item B). It is the largest source of state revenues in Brazil. Under the Federal Constitution (Article 158), 25 per cent of ICMS revenues are allocated to the municipalities. Of the latter share, 75 per cent are distributed according to an index of municipal economic output, while the remaining 25 per cent are distributed according to criteria defined by each state. It is through these complementary state laws that the ICMS-E is introduced into state tributary legislation.

Paraná

Paraná was the first state to adopt the ICMS-E. The impetus toward creation of the ICMS-E arose in municipalities where significant land use restrictions for conservation purposes limited revenues from value-added taxation (Loureiro,

1998). Piraquara is a classic example of this situation: 90 per cent of municipal territory protects a major watershed for the Curitiba metropolitan region, and CUs occupy the remaining 10 per cent. A number of municipalities organized themselves to obtain technical and political support from the state legislature and government agencies. The latter were convinced that the municipalities' concerns were fair, and that traditional police power was insufficient to guarantee environmental conservation. The ICMS-E was developed as a means to compensate municipalities with large conservation areas for the restrictions they faced, while improving incentives for conservation. In 1989 the State Constitution was amended to enable adoption of the ICMS-E (State Law No 59/1991). Complementary state laws and regulations refined the criterion, establishing the specific conditions for its operation and for the resulting revenue-sharing reallocations.

After introduction of the environmental criterion, ICMS pass-throughs to municipalities were amended so that the proportion allocated according to value-added was reduced from 80 per cent to 75 per cent, with 5 per cent now allocated based on environmental criteria (other criteria, such as area and population, remained unchanged). Of the 5 per cent now dedicated to the ICMS-E, half is allocated based on the proportion of municipal area under CUs and half on the proportion in watershed areas. We focus here on the portion based on biodiversity conservation.

Allocation criteria

The ICMS-E program is administered by the Paraná Environmental Institute (Instituto Ambiental do Paraná, IAP). Pass-throughs to municipalities whose territories harbor CUs or special protected areas are based on an environmental index, the Biodiversity Conservation Coefficient (Coeficiênte de Conservação da Biodiversidade, CCB). The CCB is defined as the relation between the surface area of the CU (or other protected area), characterized as satisfactory in physical quality (or in process of being recuperated), and the surface area of the municipality, corrected by a conservation factor associated with different management categories (Loureiro, 1998). This framework has been echoed by ICMS-E criteria adopted in other states. A key feature of the criteria is that besides the quantitative dimension of the area in CUs, they also include a quality index.[3] This allows the CCB to reflect improvements over time in qualitative features of CUs and their relationship with the surrounding community.

To determine the additional funds allocated to each municipality, the sum of conservation coefficients for each municipality is divided by the sum for the entire state, producing a municipal conservation coefficient. These weights are then applied to the share of the ICMS-E allocated toward biodiversity conservation (50 per cent), apportioned as a share of each year's ICMS tax revenues. Municipal entitlements under ICMS-E are aggregated with their regular revenue shares from value-added taxation, and are transferred to municipal governments on a weekly basis.

Minas Gerais

As in Paraná, the ICMS-E in the state of Minas Gerais originated in municipalities that considered themselves at a comparative disadvantage due to the proportionally large protected areas within their territories. In 1992–1993, municipalities affected by the Rio Doce State Park (the largest contiguous area of Atlantic forest in the state, situated in the eastern Vale do Aço region) initiated a movement to claim fiscal compensation. Initially, they sought to share in the parks' revenues by collecting entry fees (Veiga Neto, 2000), but they became interested in the ICMS-E approach on learning of Paraná's experience, divulged locally by the State Forest Institute (Instituto Estadual de Florestas, IEF). With the help of IEF, municipal leaders created a coalition of municipalities hosting CUs – the Mata Viva ('Living Forest') Association – and formulated a proposal to the state legislature to create the ICMS-E. Two successive bills to this effect were passed by the legislature but then vetoed by the governor, on the grounds that a revenue-allocation law favoring some municipalities over others in the state could be unconstitutional. Finally, in December 1995, the ICMS-E was incorporated into Law 12.040/95, known as the 'Robin Hood Law', which was created with the specific objective of overcoming inter-regional and inter-municipal disparities in revenue allocation. The law introduced additional criteria for ICMS allocations, addressing physical area, population density, health, education, agriculture, cultural patrimony, and environment (Veiga Neto, 2000). Under this law, the proportion of ICMS pass-throughs to municipalities allocated based on value-added was reduced in stages, from 94.1 per cent in 1995 to 79.6 per cent in 1998. The proportion based on environmental criteria was gradually increased from 0 in 1995 to 1 per cent in 1998. Other criteria were also added to the formula, such as cultivated area, cultural heritage, education, and health expenses. The phasing-in of the new criteria allowed municipalities to gradually adapt to the law.

Allocation criteria

In Minas Gerais, the two environmental criteria adopted in the ICMS-E were the presence of CUs, as in the Paraná case, and sanitation – more specifically, the final treatment of solid waste and sewage. Each criterion received half of the 1 per cent of ICMS revenues allotted according to environmental criteria. We focus here on the proportion allocated based on the presence of CUs, which is administered by the IEF. The law requires the legal existence (including territorial demarcation and land use restrictions) of federal, state, municipal, or private CUs duly registered with the state Environment and Sustainable Development Secretariat (Secretaria Estadual de Meio Ambiente e Desenvolvimento Sustentável, SEMAD). As in Paraná, the distribution of ICMS-E revenues is based on the proportion of area in CUs in the surface area of the municipality, weighted by a conservation factor related to the degree of protection of the area and to the management category of the CU, and by a quality factor (ranging from 0.1 to 1) related to the physical quality of the area, management plan, infrastructure, protective buffer zone, and access control, among other factors affecting management and protection (Veiga Neto, 2000). However, to date the quality factor remains unregulated in Minas Gerais, and is factored in all cases as 1. Lack of implementation of this measure may substantially weaken the instrument's effectiveness for biodiversity conservation, as shown in the case studies below.

QUANTITATIVE RESULTS

Figure 10.1 presents the revenues allocated according to ICMS-E criteria in Paraná and Minas Gerais. The total values allocated by each state through the ICMS-E are appreciable, averaging over 50 million Brazilian Real (R$) annually in Paraná and about R$15 million annually in Minas Gerais. ICMS-E amounts are higher in Paraná, even though overall ICMS levies are higher in Minas Gerais, due to the substantially higher proportion of overall ICMS revenue allocated according to environmental criterion in Paraná. In Minas Gerais, since its inception, there has been a 100 per cent increase in the number of municipalities that benefit from ICMS-E revenues, while in Paraná the increase has been over 45 per cent. Over half of all municipalities in Paraná and about 30 per cent in Minas Gerais now participate in the program. This growth in interest is both a bane and boon, since additional municipalities dilute the amounts received by municipalities already participating in the program, given the fixed share of ICMS revenues allocated on environmental criteria.

The area dedicated to conservation has also grown significantly in both states since implementation of the ICMS-E, as shown in Table 10.1. In Paraná, the area in CUs grew by over 1 million hectares, a 165 per cent increase, in the nine years since inception of the program in 1992. In Minas Gerais, the area in CUs grew by slightly over 1 million hectares over five years, a 62 per cent increase. The ICMS-E is certainly not the only reason for this growth, however. In Minas Gerais, for example, part of the initial growth observed in the number of CUs was due to efforts by local governments to recognize existing units that had not been regulated by the state (Veiga Neto, 2000).

Intra-state allocations favor municipalities with large proportional areas dedicated to state or federal indirect use CUs (highly weighted by the allocation criteria). But a substantial volume of resources has been allocated to those municipalities that house environmental protection areas (área de proteção ambiental, APAs), which may cover large areas within a municipality with restricted zoning, despite far less rigorous enforcement than other CUs. In both states, the increase in areas dedicated to state and municipal APAs accounts for the vast majority of the incremental area in conservation units. This trend is due to the ease with which APAs can be created and the relatively low level of control exerted over conservation within them. Private natural patrimony reserves (reserva particular do patrimônio natural, RPPNs)[4] have also increased in number

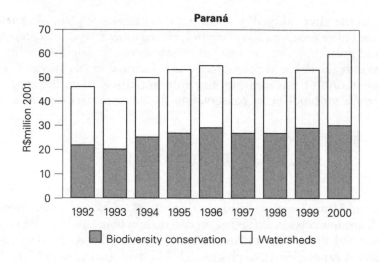

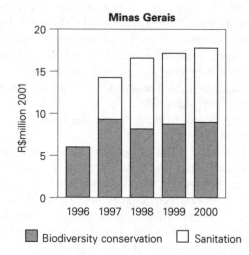

Note: June 2001 R$1 = US$0.42
Sources: Data from Secretaria de Fazenda, Paraná state and Secretaria de Planejamento,
state of Minas Gerais

Figure 10.1 *Amounts passed through to municipalities in Paraná and
Minas Gerais by the ICMS-E, 1992–2000*

and area, particularly in Paraná. Both states have now established state legislation
allowing the creation of RPPNs, and are actively promoting them as part of an
integrated public–private partnership in buffer zones surrounding public protected
areas (Bernardes, 1999).

Table 10.1 *Growth in conservation units in Paraná and Minas Gerais*

	Paraná					Minas Gerais				
	Number		Area (ha)			Number		Area (ha)		
Management Level	To 1991	2000	To 1991	2000	% Change	To 1995	2000	To 1995	2000	% Change
Federal										
Parks and reserves	3	5	218,502	267,603	22.0	6	6	208,453	208,453	0.0
Indigenous lands	12	13	67,255	69,000	3.0	4	4	59,359	59,359	0.0
Forests	2	2	3,825	3,825	0.0	1	1	335	335	0.0
State										
Parks and reserves	34	47	39,859	53,663	35.0	34	49	295,151	491,587	66.5
Municipal										
Parks and reserves	20	90	1,429	4,169	192.0	25	46	3,851	12,927	236.0
Private/mixed										
APAs (federal, state, municipality)	5	17	306,693	1,212,324	295.0	12	61	1,023,566	1,809,460	77.0
RPPNs (federal, state)	0	157	0	26,124		17	54	20,261	34,069	68.0
Other forests[a]			0	38,153						
Faxinais			0	15,454						
Total	**76**	**351**	**637,563**	**1,690,315**	**165.0**	**99**	**221**	**1,610,976**	**2,616,190**	**62.4**

Note: a Streambank reforestation, legal reserves, and other forests are not treated as CUs.
Sources: Paraná: DUC/DIBAP/IAP; Minas Gerais: IEF/MG

MUNICIPAL RESPONSES – PARANÁ

This section and the next describe the responses to pass-throughs received under the conservation criterion of the ICMS-E in a selection of municipalities in both states. The characteristics of the case study municipalities and the ICMS-E pass-throughs they received from the inception of the program to the year 2000 are shown in Table 10.2.

Soybean zone

The soybean zone is part of the principal agricultural region of Paraná. Although it has been occupied for less than 40 years, only 2 per cent of its original forest cover remains. This region was selected so as to study two municipalities with outstanding records in the creation of RPPNs: Campo Mourão and Luiziana. We sought here to understand the means used by municipal governments or the IAP to convince producers to create such reserves in such a highly agricultural region.

Regional characteristics

Campo Mourão and Luiziana are part of a micro-region known as COMCAM (Consortium of Municipalities in the Campo Mourão Region). This micro-region is located in the northwestern area of the state, along the Ivaí tributary of the Paraná River. Due to its fertile soils, agricultural development was intense in this region in the 1960s and the 1970s. The expansion of soybean cultivation in this period practically destroyed its two great forest biomes: the semi-deciduous seasonal forest and the mixed forest (IAP, 2001). According to Alberto Contar, an environmental lawyer from Maringa (personal communication), today there is more forest cover in urban than in rural areas.

Conservation activities

The COMCAM micro-region has the highest number of RPPNs in the state of Paraná: 25 units covering a total area of 2307ha. The creation of the Lago Azul State Park[5] in 1997 is the main reason for the existence of so many RPPNs in the region, as IAP's highest priority had been to stimulate creation of RPPNs in the buffer zone surrounding it to form a protected corridor.[6] Eight of these RPPNs have been created in Luiziana, accounting for the high levels of ICMS-E transfers it has received (see Table 10.2). The average amount received for RPPNs in the region has reached about R$57/ha. According to José Alberto Salvadori, the administrative secretary of Luiziana, the municipality still has many areas with potential to be transformed into RPPNs, that would effectively triple the existing area (personal communication).

Table 10.2 *Characteristics of the case study municipalities and ICMS-E revenues received*

Municipality	Population[a] ('000)	Area[a] ('000 ha)	Area in CUs (% total)		ICMS-E transfers ('000 RS)							ICMS-E as % of total ICMS transfers (2000)	ICMS-E per capita (2000)	ICMS-E as % of municipal budget (1998)
			1995	2000	1995	1996	1997	1998	1999	2000	Total			
Paraná														
Campo Mourão	79.5	75.6	0.0	1.4	10	20	73	95	113	117	**429**	2	2	0.2
Luiziana	8.0	91.2	0.0	1.8			65	97	116	122	**400**	6	16	1.0
Altônia	18.4	96.9	7.0	17.0	697	465	619	810	638	694	**3,923**	28	36	5.3
São Jorge do Patrocínio	6.8	41.3	8.0	38.0	1,554	1,424	1,304	1,478	1,363	1,552	**8,675**	71	136	17.6
Vila Alta	3.6	104.6	7.0	28.0	791	767	654	864	972	1,101	**5,149**	59	291	11.9
Rebouças	13.6	54.4	0.0	3.0	2	0	65	152	142	168	**529**	13	12	1.6
Minas Gerais														
Itamonte	12.0	43.1	75.0	90.0		327	330	217	266	239	**1,379**	13	20	3.3
Alto Caparaó	4.7	10.5	41.0	42.0			575	377	282	253	**1,488**	35	54	12.0
Caparaó	5.0	13.1	2.0	42.0			31	20	15	68	**134**	11	14	0.7

Notes: ICMS-E flows are given in constant June 2001 R$, deflated using IGP-DI (Fundação Getúlio Vargas).
  a Preliminary results of the 2000 Census. Population redistributed according to municipal boundaries in existence on August 1 2000.
Source: Paraná municipalities: IAP, 2001; Minas Gerais municipalities: Based on data from João Pinheiro Foundation and from the state treasury secretariat

Use of ICMS-E resources

Although ICMS-E revenues represent only 1.6 per cent of total ICMS revenues received by Campo Mourão, their impact has been enhanced by strategic investments. According to Ademir Moro Ribas, environmental secretary of this municipality, the ICMS-E resources are used in a number of activities, but particularly in partnership with IAP for the maintenance of Lago Azul Park, including tool purchase and payments to municipal employees who clean the park area (personal communication). The municipality also uses the revenues to pay for the maintenance of the municipal forestry nursery and the municipal park. In Luiziana, where the share of ICMS-E in overall ICMS revenues is somewhat higher, approximately 15 per cent of pass-throughs are used to help in park maintenance; 20 per cent are spent on the municipal forestry nursery (whose seedlings are donated to reforest riversides and RPPN areas and sold to the community at cost); and 55 per cent are spent on services performed with the municipality's machines for current and potential RPPN proprietors (mainly construction and maintenance of roads, drainpipes, and bridges). Neither municipality has formal procedures for deciding on the use of ICMS-E revenues.

Incentives for municipalities

The main incentive to create new CUs, according to local mayors, has been the potential for increased financial flows. According to Campo Mourão's mayor, Tauillo Tezelli, 'in times of crisis, all resources are welcome' (personal communication). Due to the small share of ICMS-E revenues in total revenues, Mayor Tezelli initially did not try to influence the creation of new CUs, nor did he have direct contact with IAP representatives. However, once he was informed of the potential revenues from the creation of new units, he became interested and personally assumed responsibility for contacting owners of the potential areas for creation of new RPPNs.

Incentives for private landowners

For private landowners, the incentives to create RRPNs appear to take several forms, as outlined below.

* **Support from the municipality.** Municipal representatives indicate that the relationship between the municipalities and RPPN owners operates through the services performed on their behalf, especially those involving municipal equipment, such as building drainpipes on the roads and improvements in access to the properties and to the RPPN areas themselves.[7] These services also protect the area against any harm caused by hunting, fishing, and fires. However, the priority given to RPPN owners for machine time has led to a standing complaint from the community that public monies are used to benefit only a few people. This question has been systematically raised by those who oppose the idea of favoring RPPN owners, who perceive this as

an additional instance of the state benefiting larger landowners (Wilson Loureiro, personal communication).

- **Environmental awareness.** As farmers' environmental awareness has increased, especially regarding water resource protection, some farmers have been motivated to protect water sources (Souza, personal communication).
- **Legal forest reserve.** In the Atlantic forest ecosystem, at least 20 per cent of private land must, by law, remain in forest. The possibility of using legal forest reserve areas on private lands to create RPPNs has stimulated their creation in the region. This is particularly notable in Luiziana, where RPPN owners are primarily large farmers (among them, some of the first pioneers in the region or their descendents). The possibility of creating RPPNs also provides options for otherwise idle areas. For example, one Luiziana landowner, Carlos Salonski, created two RPPNs (total area of 411ha), on lands that had been abandoned because they could not feasibly be cultivated mechanically. In his case, besides the desire to protect some of the forest, the motivation to set aside these reserves was to exchange them for other areas that could be cultivated, through the state's system of tradable development rights, SISLEG.[8]
- **Other income from RPPNs.** Another incentive for the creation of RPPNs is the possibility of developing other income-generating activities, notably ecotourism (Artur Cezar Vigillato, personal communication). Although RPPNs earn their proprietors an exemption on the rural land tax due on the area so conserved, landowners do not consider that this provides much of an incentive. The prospects for a link with municipal services and with the landowner's prospects for ecotourism revenue is greater.

Large farmers were prioritized by IAP and the municipal government in the creation of RPPNs because of the ease in operationalizing the resulting CUs, due to their size and the volume of resources that could be generated thereby. Small farmers are sometimes also interested in RPPN creation. However, their lands are not usually eligible due to their small areas of significant remnant forest or other priority biota from a conservation standpoint, which are defining conditions for RPPNs. According to Salvadori, the municipal government is interested in creating more RPPNs, and he believes that a great number of small farmers will ultimately be involved in this process should a means be found to reduce the transactions costs associated with their creation, through reserve condominiums for example.

In this region, which is marked by commercial agriculture, we can observe intense activity by local IAP representatives, supported by the quality evaluation scheme, which favors the creation of RPPNs by generously rewarding these areas with revenue allocations. In Luiziana, we also observed the efficient participation of the municipality in convincing farmers through agreements to perform services with municipal machinery, motivating them to set land aside in RPPNs. Good institutional relationships were found to exist between environmental agencies and the municipal governments, especially in Luiziana, where the two institutions work together in prospecting and convincing the rural proprietors to create new

CUs. Even with these incentives, the area in reserves will in all probability be limited to 20 per cent of the area in the legal forest reserve, due to the potential revenues from agricultural activity on these lands.

Paraná floodplain ('Varjão')

This region was chosen to represent areas where the ICMS-E constitutes a high percentage of municipal revenues. As a consequence, the ICMS-E became an important reference for local people, changing their habits and behavior toward the environment. Action by the public defender (ministério público), reinforced by the possibility of ICMS-E revenues, sparked the creation of municipal APAs. Conservation became a part of the municipal agenda, culminating with the creation of the Ilha Grande National Park by the federal government.[9] To examine this dynamic we visited three municipalities: São Jorge do Patrocínio, Vila Alta, and Altônia.

Regional characteristics

The region is located in the northwestern part of the state, within the Paraná, Paranapanema, and Piquiri watersheds. It is marked by a group of islands that make up the archipelago of Ilha Grande and by lowlands lying along the Paraná river. Although it was the last area in Paraná to be colonized, its forests have been nearly completely exhausted over the past four decades. As the soil is inadequate for annual crops, coffee cultivation dominated initially, and was replaced later by cattle raising and a few mechanized crops due to climate and economic problems. Of the three municipalities, São Jorge do Patrocínio has the best land distribution, with properties averaging around 13ha producing coffee, silk, grapes, oranges, and milk. Cattle ranching is also important in the other municipalities. Land prices in the region are about R$2500/ha for uplands and R$1200/ha for floodplain areas.

Conservation activities

As the only part of the Paraná river that is not dammed for energy supply (Campos, 1999), the Varjão region saw the creation in 1995 of Brazil's first municipal consortium for biodiversity protection (Consórcio Intermunicipal para Conservação do Remanescente do rio Paraná e Áreas de Influência, CORIPA). CORIPA's basic objectives are to represent the municipalities, to plan and execute programs to protect and conserve the ecosystem that borders the Paraná river, and to promote and foster regional social, economic, and environmental development through ecological–economic zoning and APA management. The potential for additional resources from ICMS-E transfer was an important motivation for APA creation in the region. The mechanism also promised to help ameliorate the serious social problems on the island, especially the costs associated with the periodic evacuation of families during floods.

The public defender's role

The public defender's office played an important role in CU creation in this region. Its first measures were aimed at stopping the commercialization of *pfaffia* (Brazilian ginseng), whose extraction resulted in indiscriminate burning in stream-bank areas (Azevedo, 1999). Local cattle ranchers had also exploited the island and floodplain indiscriminately, causing social and environmental harm. The public ministry proposed that cattle be removed from Ilha Grande and from the area alongside the river, in a decision based on the Forest Code, which requires the maintenance of riparian forests. The availability of ICMS-E resources provided the public defender with a carrot to supplement its law enforcement stick. The public defender contacted the mayors of the four municipalities involved and explained the possibility that the ICMS-E could generate revenues linked with environmental protection. The possibility of ecotourism development was also mentioned.

ICMS-E's importance to the municipalities

The impact of ICMS-E resources in the region has been very significant, especially to the municipality of São Jorge, in which 52 per cent of the total area are CUs (see Table 10.2). Differences in ICMS-E pass-throughs between municipalities are mainly due to differences in the proportions of park area compared with the total area of the municipality. The high ICMS-E transfers have become a solution to the financial problems of these municipalities. The local populations also perceive this, and the result has been a change in the behavior of the community toward the environment. The Ilha Grande National Park offers the prospect of greater revenue generation, both from ICMS-E revenues and from ecotourism. This will only be possible when the management plan is implemented, affecting the annual quality evaluation of the park by IAP, and the amounts consequently received by the municipalities.

Use of ICMS-E resources

ICMS-E resources are used for numerous activities in the communities, such as well-drilling (to provide drinking water), acquisition of tractors, maintenance of seedling nurseries, cleaning and landscaping of urban areas, construction of industrial facilities, garbage collection, landfills, environmental education, and enforcement of land use controls in parks and APAs. All these benefits, provided by ICMS-E revenues, are disclosed to the community to make the public aware of the link between environmental protection and day-to-day problems. All the resources required to maintain the Ilha Grande National Park also come from ICMS-E revenues.

Central southern region

This region was selected to explore the incentive created by Paraná's ICMS-E to preserve *faxinais* (common property forest resources). This land use system, characteristic of central southern Paraná, a region primarily colonized by Ukrainian migrants in the 19th century, involves the collective use of land for animal production.[10] It is based on the integration of unfenced, range-fed animal production, using collective breeding sites; agriculture production, based on subsistence polyculture for consumption and commercialization; and low impact forest extraction of erva-mate, araucária (Paraná pine), and other native species. This type of production is important both from the perspective of environmental conservation and from that of maintaining the region's cultural heritage. Recognizing the vulnerability of small farming enterprise in the region, especially the planting of annual crops or exotic forest species, the state government created special regulated-use areas ('*faxinais*') through State Decree 3.446/97, allowing *faxinais* to be included in the state registry of CUs. In this case study, our objective was to understand whether the people living in the *faxinais* – low income producers – and the system itself benefited from the ICMS-E pass-throughs. For the current study, we selected the municipality of Rebouças. This region of Paraná accounts for 48 per cent of the state's tobacco production, 42 per cent of erva-mate tea, 37 per cent of onions, and 33 per cent of black beans (Cerri, 1999). About 25 per cent of the municipality's population lives in areas where *faxinais* are prevalent.

Environmental importance of faxinais

Although generally considered primitive from an agricultural production standpoint, the *faxinal* system allowed protection of large forest areas that otherwise would have been cut down for agricultural purposes. There are important remnants of Paraná pine (*Araucária angustifolia*), which is threatened or nearly extinct, in *faxinais*.

ICMS-E pass-throughs

The low profitability of the *faxinal* system, the impossibility of obtaining authorization for forest clearing from the late 1980s onward, and the needs for improvement of living conditions of the *faxinal* inhabitants were the main reasons that led local mayors to link the *faxinal* and the ICMS-E. After *faxinais* became eligible for ICMS-E transfers, Rebouças started receiving significant amounts, as shown in Table 10.2. The four *faxinais* that account for these transfers total 1349ha, ranging from 61 to 637ha each. They generate municipal revenues of approximately R$100/ha of *faxinal*. According to IAP data, ICMS-E pass-throughs represent approximately 12 per cent of the total amount transferred to the municipalities. The municipality has used these resources for education and health expenditures, road improvements, and the repair of outer fences, whose poor condition is a frequent cause of conflict between ranchers and farmers.

One factor that differentiates *faxinais* from other CUs is that actions taken with the support of ICMS-E resources take into consideration the needs of the *faxinal*'s inhabitants directly. Specific actions are negotiated between the municipal governments and the *faxinal* associations with IAP participation, and are part of the annual targets evaluated by IAP. These include forest maintenance and conservation, improvement in the quality of life of the community, and the organization and participation of the community in decision-making (Márcia Zarpellon, personal communication).

This participatory approach has resulted in a substantial popular perception of the benefits from ICMS-E. Fence installation and reduced in-fighting were clear evidence of improvements resulting from the ICMS-E that could be perceived by the *faxinal* population. The municipality also implemented a project to fumigate the animals raised there, thus overcoming resistance from state agricultural extension technicians who had always opposed this method of animal management.

This example illustrates how the ICMS-E transfer can allow for redistributive effects in favor of low-income and traditional groups that use land in sustainable ways. This support may fortify their capacity to react against the loss of land to commercial agriculture. Another way in which ICMS-E transfers could have redistributive effects is discussed in Box 10.1.

Box 10.1 *ICMS-E POTENTIAL IN LAND-REFORM SETTLEMENTS*

ICMS-E transfers could be used to support poor communities by creating RPPNs in legal reserve areas located in land-reform settlements in Paraná. According to members of the Brazilian Movement of Landless Workers (Movimento dos Sem Terra, MST), 17 settlements are already engaged in the process of creating RPPNs. RPPNs created in land-reform settlements could generate ICMS-E pass-throughs of approximately R$200,000 per month to the municipalities in which they are located. The MST is proposing that this amount be shared equally between settlements and municipalities. The major problem in implementing this proposal is ensuring that any such revenue-sharing commitment continues in subsequent municipal administrations. The MST hopes that the creation of RPPNs and consequent receipt of ICMS-E transfers will generate revenues for settlement maintenance and help improve the movement's environmental image, which has been criticized due to the deforestation that has occurred in some settlements.

MUNICIPAL RESPONSES – MINAS GERAIS

The ICMS-E in Minas Gerais, although it has similar origins, began to be implemented somewhat later than that in Paraná, due to questions of equity and constitutionality. Its criteria were immersed in a much broader bill aimed to redress regional disparities in revenue allocations, and the ecological intent of the program was hence somewhat diluted. Nevertheless, as in Paraná, the ICMS-E has leveraged a movement toward the creation of private reserves, linking conservation more directly to the communities surrounding major parks and protected areas.

Itamonte

Itamonte has always been among the top municipalities in Minas Gerais in ICMS-E transfers. In recent years a new state APA, the Papagaio Mountain State Park, was created there. Itamonte was selected specifically so that municipal involvement in the creation of this new state CU could be studied.

Regional characteristics

Itamonte (which means 'rocky mountain') is located in southern Minas Gerais, and shares a border with São Paulo and Rio de Janeiro states. With steep slopes and abrupt scarps, the area divides the Rio Grande and Paraíba do Sul river basins (Itamonte, 1999). It is a former dairy region in the process of becoming an important ecotourism area.

Conservation activities

Itamonte includes parts of three CUs. The most important in terms of ICMS-E generation is the 30,000ha Itatiaia National Park, of which about 9800ha lie within the municipal borders.[11] The municipality also includes about 22,300ha of the Serra de Mantiqueira APA, an environmental protection area of 23 municipalities in the tri-state region. A third CU, Papagaio Mountain State Park, was created in August 1998, with about 6500ha within municipal lands.[12]

ICMS-E pass-throughs

Itamonte received one of the highest ICMS-E allocations in the first year of the program's implementation in Minas Gerais – as much as 64 per cent of total transfers in 1995, according to Veiga Neto (2000) (see Table 10.2). However, pass-throughs fell substantially in the second year as new CUs were added in other municipalities. With the creation of Papagaio Mountain State Park, ICMS-E revenues began to increase again in 1999. The possibilities for expanding ICMS-E revenues are slim, given that the greater part of the municipality is already protected. A few projects that would allow transfer increases, such as creating a municipal park and a waste recycling plant, were mentioned by interviewees, but none of these has progressed.

Municipal perceptions of the ICMS-E

Even though Itamonte is one of the top recipients of ICMS-E resources, municipal government officials expressed some measure of ignorance about the functioning of the instrument. This ignorance is probably due to the town obtaining most of its tax revenues from a Parmalat milk processing plant. The ICMS-E represents only about 10 per cent of total ICMS transfers to the municipality. The mayor believed, incorrectly, that the municipality was receiving ICMS-E only due to its share of Itatiaia National Park. In fact, ICMS-E pass-throughs also result from the presence of Mantiqueira APA and, since 1998, Papagaio Park. The mayor also incorrectly believed that resources received from the ICMS-E have been diminishing over time (they have actually stabilized in real terms). Local people are also generally uninformed about public administration, and in particular have no knowledge about the ICMS-E and its potential benefits (Isabel de Andrade Pinto, personal communication).

Use of ICMS-E resources

The mayor considers the ICMS-E resources insufficient to allow the municipality to undertake substantial investments. Instead, the municipality has employed the additional resources to maintain its almost 800km of rural roads. Besides improving the local quality of life, this allows tourism expansion, especially rural tourism and ecotourism, activities that have awoken municipal interest as an alternative to traditional cattle ranching.

Our hypothesis that the municipality – one of the greatest ICMS-E beneficiaries in Minas Gerais – played an important role in the creation of Papagaio State Park is far from being corroborated. The initiative for the park's creation was taken by IEF, and predates the creation of the ICMS-E. There was no municipal support, whether official or popular, for its creation. On the contrary, the municipal government appears to be generally ignorant of the instrument, its potential, and even of its present value. The ICMS-E, therefore, appears not to have changed the behavior of either the local government or local producers. This situation would perhaps change if the amounts passed through and the activities undertaken with the additional resources were better publicized.

In contrast, in the neighboring municipality of Alagoas the ICMS-E has stimulated a proactive environmental attitude. According to its administration secretary, the municipality spends more on the environment than it receives from the ICMS-E (approximately R$58,000 per year). He considers the ICMS-E one of the most important laws created in Brazil, responding to the trend toward ecotourism, an activity that is progressively occupying the place of the local dairy industry. But its development also requires attention from public agencies to avoid the predatory exploitation that has been observed in other regions of the Mantiqueira Mountains (personal communication). This response in a neighboring municipality suggests that it is not necessarily the highest revenue recipients that best respond to the instrument's potential, but rather those who have a clearer idea of its potential to complement other resources for environmental protection.

Alto Caparaó

The coffee growing municipalities of Caparaó and Alto Caparaó are situated at the frontier of Minas Gerais and Espírito Santo, in the headwaters of the Itabapoana river basin.

ICMS-E pass-throughs

Alto Caparaó separated from Caparaó in 1996. Alto Caparaó retained the greater part of Caparaó National Park, which explains the substantial difference in ICMS-E pass-throughs received by the two municipalities, as shown in Table 10.2. The new municipality has 4350ha within the park, or 42 per cent of its total area, while the former municipality kept only 292ha within the park, representing 2 per cent of its total area. According to mayor of Alto Caparaó, Delfino Emerich, the main motivation for the separation of the new municipality was the neglect it suffered from the old Caparaó municipal administration, not the potential to receive greater ICMS-E pass-throughs by retaining the greater share of the park in the new municipality. The new administrators had been unaware of the scale of ICMS-E resources they would receive thanks to the park.

In terms of ICMS-E transfers, Alto Caparaó's best year was 1997. Thereafter, the creation of new CUs by a growing number of Minas Gerais municipalities led to a decline in transfers to municipalities with pre-existing CUs. The significant funds received by Alto Caparaó prompted neighboring municipalities to create new reserves to gain access to ICMS-E funds. The principal regional municipality of Manhuaçu, for example, created a municipal park, and Caparaó a municipal APA. Creation of new CUs, whether municipal or private, is impossible in Alto Caparaó, given the absence of available areas. Its relative share of ICMS-E resources thus declined.

Use of ICMS-E resources

Alto Caparaó pays its regular monthly expenses with transfers from the municipal participation fund (a separate mechanism that supports the smallest municipalities; its revenues are smaller than those from the ICMS-E), leaving ICMS-E resources to carry out a number of necessary works. Among the principal works undertaken were rural and urban electrification, construction of flood containment barriers, street paving, the construction and repair of schools, a health center, sewer and drainage networks, and a bridge, and the acquisition of machinery. Few ICMS-E transfers were used for environmental purposes. Alto Caparaó gave priority to general expenses, such as health, education, and waste collection. Indeed, the mayor's office had an unfriendly relationship with the park. Earmarking of ICMS-E resources would without any doubt benefit the environment, but the mayor clearly prefers the funds to be unconstrained: 'for us mayors, suffering with lack of money, it would be better if we could be free to work with the money [as we choose]' (personal communication).

Caparaó fights back

With Alto Caparaó's separation, the original municipality saw a reduction in its prospects for ICMS-E transfers, given the loss of much of its protected area. Since 2000, however, Caparaó has seen a rise in such revenues, thanks to the creation of a municipal APA. Caparaó's mayor, Itair Horst Pinheiro, cites the increasing municipal revenues from the ICMS-E as a primary objective of the APA's creation, along with environmental protection. He considers the ICMS-E's role to be very important, because it is difficult to justify the creation of new CUs on environmental criteria alone (personal communication). During the meetings before the

APA's creation, producers were informed of the benefits it would bring to the municipality, as well as of the possibility of rural land tax exemption for those creating RPPNs. Nevertheless, some municipal producers, who had their areas zoned for wildlife conservation, feel damaged by this, considering the rural land tax exemption to be too small. The environment secretary, Dulio Garcia Sepúlveda, is hoping to use part of the ICMS-E resources to establish and fortify an independent environmental management agency (personal communication). To achieve this, he expects to propose that the city council allocate part of ICMS-E revenues for a recently created municipal environmental fund, following the lead of some Paraná municipalities.

Conclusions

The ecological value-added tax adopted by most Brazilian states provides a valuable fiscal instrument to reward local governments for efforts to protect forests and unique biological resources. It has been associated with a significant increase in the number and size of protected areas in the states where it has been adopted, prompting other states to take it up as a means to encourage natural resource conservation through revenue reallocation, rather than additional expenditure. As the review of the ICMS-E experience in Paraná and Minas Gerais has shown, although the instrument itself is fairly uniform in construction and intent, its operation in practice has differed markedly between municipalities, both within and between states. ICMS-E resources appear to have had a substantial impact on conservation decisions in some areas, while in others their impact has been much more limited. This section reviews some of the main lessons of this experience and provides recommendations for improving this impact in the future.

Compensation alone or a stimulus toward additional conservation?

Much of our work in this study focused on the question of whether the ICMS-E constitutes a simple compensation for past efforts on the part of governments to protect remaining forests and other unique areas, or rather as a mechanism that effectively stimulates stakeholders to take greater conservation initiatives. Although the bulk of resources is still allocated to lands that were either previously committed for conservation, or whose status was quickly registered so as to benefit from the instrument, we conclude that the ICMS-E has indeed been a harbinger of new partnerships between public and private actors for conservation purposes. By recognizing RPPNs, APAs, and *faxinais* as contributors to public conservation efforts, the instrument rewards those municipalities that have promoted their creation or maintenance as part of a mosaic of privately owned reserves and public parks.

Would earmarking reinforce the instrument's benefits?

The challenge ahead will be to reinforce the incentive created by the ICMS-E toward expansion in local and private conservation areas, by providing for transfers between local government and landowners who agree to protect forest remnants, whether through implicit earmarking (as in the case of *faxinais* or the MST proposal for agrarian settlements) or provision of in-kind services to RPPN owners, as in the soybean zone of Paraná. Another important use of such committed resources would be to build capacity for regional management over the loosely regulated land uses within APAs, such as has occurred in the Varjão area of Paraná and, incipiently, in Caparaó, Minas Gerais. Indeed, some municipalities have gone so far as to pass laws requiring that additional revenues derived from the ICMS-E be applied toward specifically ecological purposes, in response to a local environmental agenda.

How important is the quality factor?

The principal aspects that differ between Paraná and Minas Gerais in the implementation of the ICMS-E are the absence of regulation of the quality factor in the latter, and the fact that the instrument has existed longer in the former. State agents have built on their experience in developing and applying the quality evaluation criteria in Paraná, and are now actively prompting mayors to take steps that will enhance the quality of protection in local CUs over time, thus increasing their potential for revenue capture through the instrument. State environmental agents may thereby assume an important role in the definition of municipal public policies toward the environment if they are able to effectively inform local officials of the link between conservation and municipal revenues.

The ICMS-E can thus create a virtuous circle that involves both institutional learning on the part of the state authority and local capacity-building. The availability of additional funds has prompted the establishment of formal agreements between state park managers and municipal governments, providing for a share of these funds to be used to support CU protection and maintenance, adding further points to the quality assessment.

In many cases, on the other hand, the instrument's potential has been reduced due to insufficient information. Municipalities receive ICMS-E transfers along with transfers received under other ICMS criteria. The amount generated by each CU is something of a 'black box', with or without the quality factor. Awareness of the instrument's potential among local officials is mixed, but has been generally greater in Paraná than in Minas Gerais, due both to the instrument's longer time in application there, and considerable effort by the implementing agency to communicate its potential to local governments.

Implementation of the quality factor has been assessed as an important way to promote the instrument's effectiveness. But for the quality factor to be effective it must be treated as a dynamic feature of the instrument, subject to continual reassessment so as to stimulate certain CU categories, reward local actions, fine negligent municipalities, and induce the appropriate use of resources and a local environmental agenda. It is currently often perceived as a subjective 'black box'. Greater transparency is needed so that local governments and communities can see clearly why and how they were ranked, and how they might improve their ranking to receive greater resources.

Can the ICMS-E improve relations between protected areas and surrounding communities?

Improvements in relations between parks and surrounding populations are an important potential benefit by the ICMS-E. Once local communities perceive that CUs lying within their municipalities generate additional revenues, traditional resistance toward environmental protection is replaced by a concern to mobilize greater synergy with local economic development, particularly through eco-tourism. Transfer of ICMS-E revenues has, by and large, been a significant source of support for traditional economic activities in areas where earnings rely on threatened ecosystems, such as *faxinais* and indigenous lands. In addition, some local governments apply ICMS-E resources to provide employment so as to minimize the loss of income from traditional activities that are now repressed, such as palmito harvesting.

Does the ICMS-E promote the creation of new CUs?

The difficulties of creating public CUs, owing to the high financial and, eventually, social costs of expropriations, prevent municipal governments from taking such actions. The ICMS-E brought with it an incentive to form private reserves. Agreements such as those signed between municipal governments and producers in the Paraná soybean region serve as examples of how public authorities can divide the benefits of creating the RPPNs between their owners, with obvious gains for both sides, thus reinforcing the creation of these private reserves, which are still viewed with distrust by a large number of rural landowners.

Does the ICMS-E favor the rich?

There is strong evidence that the ICMS-E can serve as a low cost mechanism to affect private landowner behavior. But it is important to stress that distributional effects will vary, and in the case of RPPNs, it is more likely to favor large landowners, given the relatively high transaction costs involved in registering perpetual conservation areas. The experience with *faxinais* belies this apparent distributional bias, as does the proposal by the MST, which, if implemented, could benefit hundreds of formerly landless rural laborers.

RECOMMENDATIONS

Although the ICMS-E has been shown to be an effective compensatory fiscal transfer, and to stimulate additional efforts toward forest conservation under certain conditions, there are a number of ways to improve it as it is adopted by an increasing number of Brazilian states.

Democratize information and reinforce local environmental agendas

Showing in a clear, consistent, and regular manner to the largest possible number of stakeholders the amounts involved in ICMS-E transfers and how they are used is crucial to the accountability and transparency of this instrument. This inherently governmental role, as well as the regular evaluation of the quality of CUs and their integration with the local community, may be most effectively assumed by non-governmental organizations (NGOs).

Consider earmarking ICMS-E revenues

One aspect of the instrument that remains undefined at the state level, in part because of the need for constitutional amendment, is the adoption of local laws that earmark where and how the ICMS-E is to be spent. Another option to be explored is the direct payment of some of the funds raised to RPPN proprietors, commensurate with their contribution to municipal revenues. This approach has been effective in stimulating the creation of additional private CUs in the soybean zone of Paraná, as well as the preservation of the *faxinais*, and could be formally established at the state level.

Clearly, the desirability of across-the-board earmarking of funds requires broader discussion, since there are many mayors who would resent any meddling in the allocation of local revenues (as indicated in the interviews cited). Furthermore, earmarking could be accused of doubly rewarding conservation, since the areas that benefit will already have been created as a response to environmental concern, and rewarded (at least in Paraná) commensurate with the degree of local conservation effort. But in general in Brazil, fiscal incentives are far more directed toward development purposes than toward conservation, and the vast majority of protected areas are insufficiently enforced and poorly managed. The redirection of revenues from traditional economic activities toward conservation effected by the ICMS-E marks a substantial shift in policy. Reinforcement to improve the sustainability of the areas conserved would be a logical next step.

Increase the ecological share of ICMS allocations

As the number and proportional area of CUs grows, their relative share of ICMS-E revenues shrinks. This fundamental paradox deserves to be reconsidered. Indeed, this is already under consideration in both of the states studied, with proposals to increase the proportionate share of municipal ICMS revenue-sharing allocated on environmental criteria. There is a significant tension generated from such proposals, as those municipalities that were 'losers' in the initial years of the instrument's allocation (primarily major urban centers) lead a fierce backlash that could threaten the instrument's very survival. Yet these measures have great merit and deserve more attention from the national environmental movement, as resources dwindle for traditional parkland acquisitions.

NOTES

1   The authors are grateful to the many municipal and state officials, and other people, who generously devoted their time to interviews for this study. They also acknowledge the financial support of the World Bank research project, Fiscal Incentives for Conservation (No 683-42), under the general direction of Kenneth Chomitz, who contributed to the study design. However, all opinions, interpretations, and conclusions in this study are the sole responsibility of the authors, and are not to be attributed to the World Bank or to any Brazilian agency. The project was ably managed by REDES at the Federal Rural University of Rio de Janeiro, Graduate Program in Development, Agriculture and Society. In the interests of full disclosure, it should be noted that one of the authors, Wilson Loureiro, played an important role in establishing and managing Paraná's ICMS-E system on behalf of IAP.

2   In the state of Paraná, the ICMS-E also benefits those municipalities that protect watersheds; in Minas Gerais, it also benefits those that invest in waste treatment facilities. However, the discussion in this Chapter focuses on the ICMS-E's role in forest conservation.

3   The quality index is assessed by regional officers of the state environmental agency, based on the following variables: physical quality; biological quality (fauna and flora); quality of water resources (within the CU and in its surroundings); physical representativeness; quality of planning, implementation, and maintenance; exceeding compliance with extant agreements with municipalities; development of facilities; supplementary analysis of municipal actions regarding housing and urban planning, agriculture, health, and sanitation; support to producers and local communities; and the number and amount of environmental penalties applied within the municipality by public authorities. This evaluation is expressed as a score used as a quality factor in the calculation of revenue distribution. The bands for each score vary in accordance with the type of CU and the objectives of state environmental policy, giving greater weight to the state's environmental management capacity over that of municipal or federal agencies.

4   RPPNs are properties under private domain in which either the total area or a part are identified as primitive, semi-primitive, recuperated natural conditions, or as possessing characteristics that justify recuperation, for scenic value or for the preservation of the biologic cycle of native Brazilian species of fauna and flora. Properties registered as RPPNs must be conserved in perpetuity, being restricted in use to ecotourism, education, and scientific research

5   The park is 1749ha in size, and comprises the remnants of the two forest biomes mentioned above. The park also has a reservoir (operated by the state power authority, COPEL) with a water surface area of approximately 11km^2 (IAP, 2001).

6   The park manager, Rubens Lei Pereira de Souza, is the chief person in charge of prospecting areas eligible to be transformed into RPPNs. Souza tries at first to demonstrate the environmental importance of the forest to the municipality as a way of persuading landowners to participate (personal communication).

7   For example, rural landowner and hotelier Artur Cezar Vigillato, the owner of an RPPN in Campo Mourão (109ha) and another in Luiziana (71ha), stated that no agreement with municipal governments existed prior to the RPPNs' creation. However, this possibility was in his mind, as he was aware of the financial benefits that would accrue to the municipality. For this reason, he is now able to demand services from the municipal governments. Vigillato says that he received support in the form of machine time to build and maintain roads, allowing the control of predatory hunting and fishing in his reserve.

8   The legal forest reserve of 20 per cent, required by the Forest Code of 1964 in Atlantic forest areas, in practice emulates the conservation benefits of RPPNs. However, the perpetual easement conferred on RPPNs, and their restrictive use, imposes a greater degree of permanent protection on these areas than that conferred by the Forest Code, which allows for extractive resource management in legal reserves.

9   The 78,875ha Ilha Grande National Park was created in 1997, and contains parts of the municipalities of Guairá, Altônia, São Jorge do Patrocínio, Vila Alta, and Icaraíma in Paraná; and parts of the municipalities of Mundo Novo, Eldorado, Naviraí, and Itaquiraí in Mato Grosso do Sul. The park is considered a transitional zone between the seasonal forest of Paraná (*cerrado*) and the *pantanal* of Mato Grosso do Sul, with very significant biodiversity. Besides the typical objectives of a federal park, its objectives also include the implementation of economic and ecological zoning in APAs. For the municipalities, the park also offers the prospect of greater resource generation whether from ICMS-E revenues or from ecotourism. This will only be possible when the management plan is implemented, affecting the annual quality evaluation of the park by IAP, and consequently the amount of ICMS-E resources received by the municipalities.

10 *Faxinais* were created by families settling in forest areas, normally on flat lands close to the water. As they lived close to each other and raised their animals freely, they created collective grazing areas. These areas, some of them extensive, were fenced on the outer limits, beyond which subsistence crops were cultivated (Márcia Zarpellon, personal communication). Normally each family had two pieces of land, one inside the *faxinal* and the other for cultivation outside the *faxinal*. Over the course of the 20th century, this system came under strong pressure from professional farmers, who coveted the flat forest areas. Many *faxinais* were sold or transformed into cultivated areas during the 1980s, when forest clearing was still legally permitted.

11 Itatiaia National Park, created in June 1937, was the first national park in the country. Its initial area of 11,943ha was later enlarged to 30,000ha in 1982. The park includes the highest peak in southeast South America, and has a variety of ecosystems from tropical forest to alpine meadows. Despite its longevity and importance, the land tenure situation in the park has still not been completely regularized, even in its oldest part (Mendes Jr, 1991).

12 Papagaio Mountain State Park was created on August 5 1998 after a ten-year process. The landowner initially intended to donate the area to the state, but after perceiving the state's interest he offered to sell it instead. Although the park is registered for purposes of ICMS-E transfer, no IEF management has yet been designated because the park is still in the planning stage. Cattle raising is still underway in the area as the park has not not in fact been implemented except by decree, and nothing has as yet been paid to the owner.

REFERENCES

Azevedo, R.F. 1999. "A Presença do Ministério Público na Área do Remanescente do Rio Paraná." In J.B. Campos (ed.), *Parque Nacional de Ilha Grande: Re-conquista e Desafios*. Maringá: Instituto Ambiental do Paraná.

Bernardes, A.T. 1999. "Some Mechanisms for Protection of Biodiversity in Brazil with Emphasis on Their Application in the State of Minas Gerais." Brazil Global Overlay Project. Washington: World Bank (processed).

Campos, J B (ed). 1999. "Parque Nacional de Ilha Grande: Re-conquista e Desafios." Maringá: IAP.

Cerri, C. 1999. "De Volta ao Brasil." *Globo Rural*, 14:159, January, pp. 26–33.

Freitas, A. 1999. "ICMS Ecológico: um Instrumento Econômico para a Conservação." Brasília: WWF Brasil.

Grieg-Gran, M. 2000. "Fiscal Incentives for Biodiversity Conservation: the ICMS Ecológico in Brazil." Discussion Paper No.00–01. London: IIED.

Instituto Ambiental do Paraná (IAP). 2001. "Plano de Manejo Parque Estadual Lago Azul." Maringá: IAP.

Instituto Brasileiro de Meio Ambiente e Recursos Naturais Renováveis (IBAMA). 2001. "Floresta Nacional de Irati." Paraná: IBAMA (processed).

Itamonte. 1999. "Terras Altas da Mantiqueira, Itamonte, MG." Itamonte: Galeria Serrana.

Loureiro, W. 1998. "Incentivos Econômicos para Conservação da Biodiversidade no Brasil: ICMS Ecológico." Curitiba: IAP.

Mendes Jr., L.O., 1991. "Relatório Mantiqueira." São Paulo: Frente em Defesa da Mantiqueira.

Veiga Neto, F.C. 2000. "Análise de Incentivos Econômicos nas Políticas Públicas para o Meio Ambiente – O caso do 'ICMS Ecológico' em Minas Gerais." M.A. Dissertation, CPDA. Rio de Janeiro: Universidade Federal Rural do Rio de Janeiro.

PEOPLE INTERVIEWED

Aguiar, R.M. – Mayor's advisor, Alto Caparaó City Hall, Minas Gerais

Alvarenga, R. – Matutu community, Airuoca, Minas Gerais

Andrade, J.A. – Municipal Secretary of Agriculture and Environment, Rebouças, Paraná

Azevedo, R.F. – District Attorney, Altônia, Paraná

Bagão, P. – Municipal Environmental Secretary, Altônia, Paraná

Barbosa, P.L. – Mayor, Ibitirama, Espírito Santo

Battilani, E. – City Councilman, Campo Mourão, Paraná

Bezerra, C.A. – Tourism entrepreneur, Alto Caparaó, Minas Gerais

Contar, A. – President of Brazilian Association for Environmental Defense, Maringá, Paraná

Emerich, D. – Mayor, Alto Caparaó, Minas Gerais

Faria, de Marcos, P. – Mayor, Vila Alta, Paraná

Fumião, R.A. – EMATER technician, Caparaó, Minas Gerais

Guedes Neto, R. – Ex-Secretary of Environment, Caxambu, Minas Gerais
Kepka, Z.A. – Municipal Agriculture Secretary, Fernandes Pinheiro, Paraná
Koch, R. – EMATER technician, Fernandes Pinheiro, Paraná
Loss, E.F. – Mayor, Fernandes Pinheiro, Paraná
Marchezini, E.F. – Manager, Caparaó National Park, Alto Caparaó, Minas Gerais
Maria Jr., J.J. – Manager, Passa Quatro National Forest, Passa Quatro, Minas Gerais
Melo, L.A.N. – IBAMA State Representative, Paraná
Mendes, R.R. – Municipal Secretary of Administration, Alagoa, Minas Gerais
Milhiolo, R.J.I. – Municipal Environmental Secretary, Espera Feliz, Minas Gerais
Motta, M.N.J. – Manager, Ilha Grande National Park, Vila Alta, Paraná
Nilcinei. – Agronomist, Landless Peoples' Movement (MST), Curitiba, Paraná
Oliveira, G.M. – IAP regional office, Umuarama, Paraná
Palozzi, C. – Ex-Mayor, São Jorge do Patrocínio, Paraná
Panceri, S.L. – Vice-President, Mourão Agricultural Cooperative, Campo Mourão, Paraná
Pinheiro, I.H. – Mayor, Caparaó, Minas Gerais
Pinto, I.A. – Colina Community, Itamonte, Minas Gerais
Pitombeiras, M. – Manager, Mantiqueira Federal APA, Passa-Quatro, Minas Gerais
Rezende Neto, J. – Municipal Secretary of Environment, Vila Alta, Paraná
Ribas, A.M. – Municipal Secretary of Infrastruture and Environment, Campo Mourão, Paraná
Ribon Jr, M. – Biodiversity Protection Director, IEF, Belo Horizonte, Minas Gerais
Rodrigues, J.D. – IEF Technician, Carangola, Alto Caparaó, Minas Gerais
Romanelli, N. – Mayor-elect, Itamonte, Minas Gerais
Saloniski, C.A. – Farmer, Campo Mourão, Paraná
Salvadori, J.A. – Administration Secretary, Luiziana, Paraná
Samek, J.L. – Coordinator, ICMS-E for Watersheds, SUDERHSA, Curitiba, Paraná
Santos, V.M.M. – President of the Environmental Guardians Institute, Prudentópolis, Paraná
Sepúlveda, D.G. – Municipal Environmental Secretary, Caparaó, MG
Silva, J.M. – IEF Technician, Itamonte, Minas Gerais
Silva, L.P. – Mayor, Itamonte, Minas Gerais
Simiano, V.R. – IAP, Curitiba, Paraná
Souza, A. – Mayor's office, São Jorge do Patrocínio, Paraná
Souza, R.L.P. – IAP Regional Technician, Campo Mourão, Paraná
Tanahaki, P. – Regional office chief, IAP, Campo Mourão, Paraná
Tezelli, T. – Mayor, Campo Mourão, Paraná
Uchoa, L.A.C. – Manager, Iratí National Forest, Iratí, Paraná

Vigillato, A.C. – Farmer and hotelier, Campo Mourão, Paraná
Witzel, R.M. – Municipal Environmental Secretary, São Jorge do Patrocínio, Paraná
Zak, L.E. – Mayor, Rebouças, Paraná
Zarpellon, M.A.O. – IAP Regional Technician, Irati, Paraná

Chapter 11

Developing a Market for Forest Carbon in British Columbia

Gary Bull, Zoe Harkin, and Ann Wong[1]

The budding market for carbon generated by the Kyoto Protocol process is creating opportunities to supplement income from traditional forestry activities with income from the sale of carbon emission services. The Canadian province of British Columbia (BC), with its vast forest areas and sophisticated forest industry, is well-positioned to take advantage of these new developments. Carbon markets do not just happen, however. Creating new markets for services such as carbon sequestration requires substantial efforts on technical, legal, and commercial fronts. This Chapter examines the progress being made in developing such markets in BC.

BC's FORESTS

BC's forest area covers approximately 59 million hectares. These forests are unique in terms of their ecological diversity, their high level of public ownership (approximately 95 per cent), and their critical role in the provincial economy. The forest sector generates around US$10.6 billion in gross domestic product (GDP) for the province annually, and employs directly and indirectly 14 per cent of the workforce (Council of Forest Industries, 2001). The timber harvest volume for 2000 was 75 million m³ (Natural Resources Canada, 2001).

The forests were originally managed for timber production using the 19th-century principle of sustained yield. The greatest challenge of forest management was generally understood to be engineering in nature: roads had to be built, rivers crossed, and large trees removed with cables. Increasing calls for sustainable forest management (Hoberg, 2001; Wilson, 2001), starting as early as the mid-1970s, have required a different approach to management. Forest management objectives have been broadened significantly to include protected areas, wildlife, aesthetics, fish, water (Council of Forest Industries, 2001), and now, most recently, carbon. Given the vastness of the forest resource and the need to account for carbon, the forest sector in BC has proven to be fertile ground for forest carbon market development.

Markets for carbon

A potential market for forest carbon was first spawned with the signing of the Kyoto Protocol at the third session of the Conference of the Parties (COP) to the United Nations Framework Convention on Climate Change (UNFCCC) in 1997. The Kyoto Protocol gave official recognition to the role of forests as carbon 'sinks' in the mitigation of global climate change by reducing atmospheric concentrations of CO_2, one of the major greenhouse gases (GHGs). The Kyoto Protocol also includes a mechanism allowing trade in emissions to meet GHG reduction targets at least cost. After signing the Kyoto Protocol, the Canadian government expressed interest in establishing markets for forest carbon through planting, conservation, and sustainable management of forests (NCCP, 1999). Clearly, indications are that storing carbon in forests is an attractive, cost-effective, and environmentally-sensitive solution to the climate change problem.

Since signing the Kyoto Protocol in 1997, however, efforts to develop a market for forest carbon have been constrained by the relatively slow progress of international climate change negotiations. Indeed, lack of agreement as to the role of forests in the Kyoto Protocol has been a significant factor contributing to the difficulty in reaching consensus throughout the negotiations. Prior to the Sixth Conference of Parties (COP 6), the only forest-based activities that were included with any degree of certainty within the Kyoto Protocol were afforestation and reforestation under Article 3.3. In the lead-up to the November 2000 COP 6 meeting in The Hague, Canada aligned itself with the so-called 'umbrella group', adopting a controversial position on sinks, hoping to receive credit for both natural and human-induced carbon uptake from all managed forests (Bull and others, 2001). This position was strongly contested by several countries in the European Union (EU), who argued that credit should not be given for 'business-as-usual' carbon uptake (Bull and others, 2001). An intense political debate erupted in April 2001, when the United States announced that it would not ratify the Kyoto Protocol. As a result, the COP 6 negotiations that resumed at Bonn in July 2001 were heavily political in nature (Bull and others, 2001). The EU pushed hard for agreement between the remaining Annex I countries, and the resulting 'Bonn decision' clarified definitions related to forest sinks, and determined that a range of activities under the broad definition of 'forest management' were eligible for inclusion under the Kyoto Protocol (Kopp, 2001). At the COP 7 negotiations in Marrakesh in November 2001, these definitions were officially accepted, and many of the participant Annex I nations have since publicized their intention to ratify the Kyoto Protocol.

The combined efforts of researchers, government, and the business community in BC are helping to explore forest carbon market possibilities. The key players in understanding forest carbon science and markets are scientists/modelers, forest companies, energy companies, auditors/verifiers, and governments. This Chapter investigates the development of a market for forest carbon in terms of three major elements that are essential for a market in environmental services:

1 a credible science-based knowledge of the forest and soil resources;
2 government policy and the development of a market mechanism; and
3 recent action to facilitate forest carbon trade by buyers, sellers, and non-governmental organizations (NGOs).

ELEMENT ONE: APPROPRIATE FOREST DATA AND MODELS

In order to buy or sell a good or service, it has to be quantified (Heal, 2000). An understanding of how to measure forest ecosystem carbon dynamics and carbon budgets is essential, therefore, to the development of carbon markets. In addition it is imperative to have reporting across spatial scales that is consistent with the quantification tools. This can be achieved by directly linking all data and forecasts from the national, regional, and operational levels. This section summarizes the forest data available, the carbon models tools, and the early efforts at developing consistency.

Carbon modeling: national and regional level

At the national level, forest carbon budgets have been estimated using both remote sensing techniques and the carbon budget model of the Canadian forest sector (CBM-CFS).

- The remote sensing techniques have been developed by the Canadian Centre for Remote Sensing. Their model, the integrated terrestrial ecosystem C-budget model (InTEC), estimates the carbon budgets of forests from atmospheric, climatic, and biotic changes (Canada Centre for Remote Sensing, 2000). These changes include CO_2 fertilization, nitrogen deposition, and natural disturbances in forest growth. InTEC also estimates soil carbon and net primary production in stands. Nonetheless, carbon modeling in remote sensing is still immature since it does not measure biomass or carbon directly, but rather other forest characteristics such as crown reflectance (Schroeder and others, 1997). Remote sensing does not predict biomass well in mixed species and closed canopy stands; however, it may be useful in finding areas that have been subject to land use change or natural disturbance.
- The CBM-CFS is a more developed national model used by the Canadian forest service. Using forest inventories, ecosystem classifications, soils surveys, and other government and industry statistics, the CFM-CFS estimates carbon stocks and carbon flows in forest biomass, soils, and wood products. Annual

forest growth and soil decomposition are simulated using empirical relationships. The effects of wildfires, insect attacks, and harvesting on forest age structure and on carbon releases to the atmosphere and forest floor are calculated on a five-year cycle (Price and others, 1997). The initial version of CBM-CFS estimated carbon pools and fluxes for a single year. An updated model, CBM-CFS2, simulates the carbon budget for any time period between 1920–1989 (Kurz and others, 1992; Kurz and Apps, 1999). The CBM-CFS model is based on historical data on forest inventory, management, and disturbances; therefore, the model predicts the carbon budgets that would have occurred in the past, given the historic and present information. However, assumptions about future forest management and forest processes have to be made and used to predict future carbon budgets. To date, the CBM-CFS model has only been used to forecast future forest carbon scenarios at the forest management level and not at the national level.

The Canadian budget model of the forest product sector (CBM-FPS) has been developed to complement the CBM-CFS (Apps and others, 1999). The CBM-FPS accounts for the biomass carbon harvested from the start of the manufacturing process until it is released into the atmosphere. CBM-FPS accounts for changes in carbon stocks in the landfill, pulp and paper, solid-wood products, and fuelwood pools. CBM-FPS also accounts for emissions during product manufacture and use; energy use from purchased electrical energy; self-generated hydroelectric energy; fuelwood and energy from pulp residues or wood waste; and energy production through the combustion of hogfuel, spent liquor, or wood waste in the forest product sector (Apps and others, 1999).

The CBM-CFS2 model has been used at the regional level to estimate the carbon budget for the period of 1920–1989 for four eco-climatic provinces in BC: Boreal, Cordilleran, Interior Cordilleran, and Pacific Cordilleran (Kurz and others, 1996).[2] These eco-climatic provinces range in size from 4.7 million ha to 32.8 million ha. Still using CBM-CFS2, a second approach has also been being tested in BC where carbon budgets are being calculated for each of the province's 14 bio-geoclimatic zones (Kurz, personal communication).[3] Forest sinks and sources of emissions will also be analyzed in these zones under different combinations of potential accounting rules and reforestation definitions and various scenarios of fire, disease, and pest disturbance rates (BC MELP, 2000).

Carbon modeling: management level

An operational approach for carbon budget calculations is also underway in the province for each of the six forest regions. The regions are divided into districts, and in each district there are two different management units classified as a timber supply area (TSA) or a tree farm license (TFL).[4] In BC, there are 37 TSAs, which range in size from 76,751ha to 13.4 million ha, and 34 TFLs, which range in size from 8366ha to 804,000ha (Boyce, personal communication). The CBM-CFS2 model has been used to forecast the carbon budget for the period of 2000–

2032 for all TSAs and most of the TFLs (Kurz, personal communication).[5] The assumptions in the Timber Supply Review 2[6] and the guidelines of the Intergovernmental Panel on Climate Change (IPCC) (Houghton and others, 1997) were applied in the carbon analysis. Preliminary analysis suggests that BC's forests will be a sink of 25.3 million tonnes of carbon per year (tC/year) in the first Kyoto Protocol commitment period (BCMWLAP, 2001). The Canadian forest service (CFS) is currently modifying the CBM-CFS2 to make it user-friendly for operational-level carbon budgeting. In addition, there is communication between the Canadian Model Forest Network and the CFS to do further carbon modeling in the model forests.

In BC, some forest companies consider it important to calculate the forest carbon contributions to the global carbon cycle as part of their environmental responsibility. There are many timber harvest regulation models[7] used by forest companies that could be readily updated to predict forest carbon by incorporating appropriate carbon accounting assumptions and conversion factors. For example, Forest Ecosystem Solutions has applied the volume-to-biomass conversion factors of Penner and others (1997) to their Forest Simulation Optimization System (FSOS) model and calculated carbon balances in wood products. The model developers are now incorporating predictions of below-ground carbon, which represents an additional essential component for forest owners when calculating the carbon budget. Carbon modeling using FSOS has now been applied in two TSAs within BC.

A third model, FORECAST, is under development (Kimmins and others, 1999; Seely and others, 1999; Seely and others, forthcoming). It is a comprehensive ecosystem model of carbon and nitrogen cycling and net primary production in the forest. FORECAST includes carbon pools above the ground and in roots, soils, litter, and dead wood. Pre-determined natural disturbance events can be modeled, as well as a range of management activities such as planting, fertilization, and thinning, and silvicultural systems such as shelterwood and clearcutting. Because FORECAST is a stand-level model, it can simulate stand-level carbon processes at quite a detailed level. However, when addressing larger-scale issues such as wildlife corridors and beetle infestations, a landscape-level model is required. Links have already been made between FORECAST and other landscape level models such as FSOS. FORECAST is being used for the Arrow TSA and the Canadian Forest Products TFL 48.

Carbon accounting and carbon processes in the forest ecosystem are complex. There is still a considerable degree of uncertainty, particularly in below-ground and dead woody debris pools; the dynamics between above and below-ground with aging forests; the soil and future above-ground carbon after harvest, thinning, fertilization, and other silvicultural actions; and the effects of natural disturbances such as insects and fire on forest carbon. Further research is also required in linking stand-level forest carbon modeling with that of landscape management models, as most management issues need to be addressed at the landscape level. Furthermore, most carbon models have not been thoroughly tested or verified. This is a matter of difficulty and cost in measurement as the models are still rather new. However, if a forest carbon project were to be audited to gain carbon credits then a field sampling system would be beneficial in measuring the 'actual' carbon and would also aid in testing the sensitivity of the model. Ideally, a model should indicate a likelihood range of the amount of carbon predicted to be sequestered (with possibly some confidence level) which would help in determining the proportion a carbon owner may want to sell.

Forest and biomass inventories in Canada

In the past, Canada's national forest inventory was based on the summation of forest inventories conducted individually by each province.[8] However, inventory standards and coverage differ by province (Canadian Forest Service, 1999a). In 1997, a plot-based national forest inventory (NFI)[9] was designed in which all provinces report similar data from sample plots identified within a national 4 x 4km network. One of the aims of the NFI is to collect data for international initiatives such as the Kyoto Protocol, FAO forest resource assessments, and the Montreal Process (Canadian Forest Service, 1999b). The NFI will update the last national biomass inventory, conducted in 1985, using existing biomass information and the new NFI plot data on land use, ownership, conversion of forest land, and biomass in tree, stump, shrub, herb, and coarse woody debris. It will be completed in 2004 to 2005. As part of the NFI initiative, the BC Ministry of Forests plans to design and develop a two-year field sampling program that would instal monitoring stations in the bio-geoclimatic zones to update national-scale estimates of soil carbon (BC MELP, 2000). In 1996, BC started the Vegetation Resources Inventory (VRI) program to collect data on shrubs, herbs, and woody debris in addition to the traditional timber and soils data. Together, the national biomass inventory, NFI, and VRI will provide valuable data for carbon accounting in the future. A number of additional biomass and carbon studies have also been undertaken in Canada (Bonnor, 1985; Penner and others, 1997; Siltanen and others, 1997; Stanek and State, 1978).

Analysis

Canada has developed preliminary forest data, forest inventory methods, and carbon models to make better carbon predictions. On-going inventory improvements and the model developments currently underway will greatly improve the estimates.

The carbon accounting rules will require a 'real time' inventory system for all carbon and emission pools, and this has to be linked with all forest management activities. Models are being adapted to allow land managers to explore the relationship between forest management for both timber and carbon budget outputs while still addressing the many other objectives of sustainable forest management. This requires analyzing the 'production possibility frontiers' between carbon and timber, and then generating different scenarios that will meet the broader objectives of forest management in an operational area. It also allows different management scenarios to be explored. For example, if fertilizers are applied to a forest to increase growth for higher harvest levels, what are the implications for the forest as a carbon sink? The combination of good inventories and robust models is an essential basis for the monitoring and verification of carbon budgets.

Forest management with carbon objectives requires that the science behind forest ecosystem carbon dynamics and modeling should be broadly understood by the many stakeholders. It is also necessary to build consensus and standards for linking carbon accounting rules, data collection, carbon modeling, carbon monitoring, and verification at the operational, regional, and national level. Standards development is also particularly important for the broader reporting requirements of forest certification, criteria, and indicators as outlined in the Montreal Process (Montreal Process Working Group, 1998).

ELEMENT 2: GOVERNMENT POLICY AND MARKET MECHANISM DEVELOPMENT

Despite preliminary steps to develop an emissions trading market as early as 1995 (BC MELP, 1995), forest carbon market development in BC has been constrained by the lack of certainty over the rules related to forest carbon sinks and international emissions trade. In spite of this limitation, the provincial and federal governments, as well as private industry, have pushed to develop markets for forest carbon in four main areas:

1   establishment of an emissions trading platform;
2   development of a national carbon registry;
3   incentives to promote implementation of forest carbon projects in BC; and
4   development of the necessary legislation to identify forest carbon ownership in BC.

These areas of carbon market development are discussed further below.

Provincial initiatives to establish an emissions trading platform in BC

In 1995, pioneering work toward establishing an emissions trading platform in BC began with the release of the Greenhouse Action Plan (BC MELP, 1995). The plan suggested that the creation of tradable emission permits was a viable policy option to mitigate climate change, paving the way for a report on emissions trade to the Minister of Environment, Lands and Parks and the Minister of Employment and Investment, which investigated the design options for a provincial emission reduction trading pilot (BC MELP and the MEI, 1997). Two potential models for emissions trade were examined: 'cap and trade'[10] and 'baseline and credit'.[11] The report's authors concluded that the baseline and credit trading system would be more suitable for implementation in BC, since it would: allow for the inclusion of a range of emissions sources; be better suited to a voluntary emissions reduction program; allow compatibility between emission allowances and credits; and provide inherent incentives to buy emissions reductions (BC MELP, 1998). The report on emissions trade also provided rules for the pilot baseline and credit emissions trading program. Work toward developing a provincial emissions trading platform was replaced in 1998, when a larger cooperative arrangement with the federal government was formed to establish a national emissions trading platform.

Federal initiatives to establish an emissions trading platform for Canada

The key elements from the design of BC's Pilot GHG Offsets Program and Ontario's Pilot Emissions Reduction Trading (PERT) project were merged to create a major Canadian pilot emissions trading system, the Greenhouse Emissions Reduction Trading (GERT) pilot (Caton, personal communication). GERT, launched in 1998, has allowed many Canadian businesses to gain valuable experience with emissions trading by meeting their own voluntary GHG reduction commitments without penalty for early abatement activities (Rosenbaum, 2001). Another initiative to provide additional experience in domestic emissions trading is the Pilot Emission Removals, Reductions and Learning initiative (PERRL), currently still in the consultation stage. PERRL is a joint project between the federal and provincial governments, whereby the federal government will distribute funding to approved GHG emission-reduction projects in exchange for the purchase of low-cost carbon credits (PERRL Working Group, 2001). Pilot emissions trading platforms such as GERT, PERT, and PERRL are unlikely to be replaced by a final emissions trading system in Canada until the Kyoto Protocol is ratified (Hasselknippe and Hoibye, 2000).

Private initiatives to establish an emissions trading platform

The slow, albeit steady, development of a national emissions trading system is reflective of a global trend of governmental reticence. In response, private companies have intervened to proceed in partnership with government initiatives. While no corporate-level private emissions trading platforms have emerged in BC,[12] ClimatePartners emulates a commercial-scale emissions trading system by allowing individuals to contribute donations to selected emission-offset projects in BC. ClimatePartners, founded in 1999, has successfully implemented a car-pooling project to reduce vehicular emissions, and is currently raising funding for an afforestation project in northern BC with the potential to sequester up to 1 million tonnes of carbon (ClimatePartners, 2001).

Pending the expansion of a Canadian-based emissions trading system, Canadian companies also have the option of participating in a number of global emissions trading platforms, which have been spawned by large multinational accounting and auditing firms. One of these is CO2e.com, launched by Cantor Fitzgerald and PricewaterhouseCoopers in November 2000 (CO2e.com, 2001). CO2e.com, one of the first online international emissions trading platforms, functions in a range of capacities, including emissions trade, management advice, verification and monitoring, registry services, financial and legal advice, and insurance (CO2e.com, 2001). Approximately 160 million metric tonnes of CO_2 equivalents have already been traded (CO2e.com, 2001).

CO2e.com is representative of the growing trend for streamlining a range of emissions trading services within a single, all-encompassing emissions trading platform. The preference for multi-service emissions trading platforms is evident. Trexler & Associates (TAA) administered its first emission-offset project more than ten years ago, and has recently established ClimateServices.com. Like CO2e.com, ClimateServices.com provides a number of activities, including emissions trading, policy development, monitoring and evaluation, and regulatory representation (ClimateServices.com, 2001). In November 2000, international consulting firm ICF launched EmissionStrategies.com, an online trading platform to facilitate the buying and selling of GHGs as well as nitrogen oxide (NOx) and sulfur dioxide (SO_2). EmissionStrategies.com represents another large all-encompassing trading platform, offering a range of services related to the emerging emissions trading market, including online emissions trading, advice on climate change mitigation strategies, assistance with GHG inventories, monitoring, evaluation and verification, and financial and marketing advice (EmissionsStrategies, 2001). Other large trading platforms include the Chicago Climate Exchange, Ctrade.org, The Universal Carbon Exchange, and the Emissions Market Development Group. While the infrastructure of these online trading platforms is in place, the number of trades that have actually occurred online at this preliminary stage is minimal, with bilateral trades being predominant so far (Donnelly, personal communication).

Development of a carbon registry for Canada

To meet the reporting requirements of the Kyoto Protocol, each Annex B party is required to establish a national registry to document emissions trading (FCCC, 2000). Emission offsets are an intangible commodity, so careful documentation of the sequestration, emission, and buying and selling of carbon via a national registry is crucial to prevent fraudulent activities, such as selling the same emission offset more than once. Canada is well advanced in developing a national registry, with the establishment of the Voluntary Challenge and Registry (VCR) in 1994. The VCR is a non-profit organization that aims to record, track, and provide incentives for voluntary GHG reductions. Despite the fact that the registry is entirely voluntary, VCR has received strong support, with a total of 772 registrants representing over 75 per cent of GHG emissions from business and industrial sources in Canada (Heal, 2000). Primary motivations for registration include the desire to achieve early emission reductions in anticipation of an emissions-constrained future, and for public relations reasons (Russell, 2002). In order to qualify for registration, businesses are required to submit base-year emission inventories and an action plan for GHG reductions. Following registration, businesses must submit annual progress reports. The Baseline Protection Initiative is affiliated with the VCR and offers a means of reporting and documenting emission reductions. The initiative, announced in January 2001 as part of the national climate change process, removes disincentives for early voluntary actions to reduce GHG emissions by allowing registrants to use their 1990 level of emissions as a baseline in the event that allocation of emission allowances is based on the 'grandfathering' approach[13] (Buckley, 2001).

Incentive-based policies in BC

The first major policy statements on climate change in BC were announced in the BC Greenhouse Gas Action plan (BC MELP, 1995). It acknowledged increasing evidence of global warming, and recognized the role of forests in mitigating climate change. As part of its 'no-regrets' climate change policy,[14] the BC government promised to conduct further work in modeling the carbon balance of BC's forests; promote sequestration via the achievement of forest sustainability objectives; and provide incentives for more efficient use of forest harvesting residues (BC MELP, 1995).

In September 1997, a report from the BC Greenhouse Gas Forum stated that 'there are significant, possibly unnecessary costs to early action' (BC MELP, 1997). In 1998, the same group released a series of reports on early action. The potential for carbon sequestration through afforestation programs was recognized, but aggressive action was not recommended until international rules and guidelines around the treatment of sinks was defined (BC MELP, 1998).

In October 2000, the three-year Climate Change Business Plan was released, accompanied by US$8.4 million in new funding for GHG reduction projects. The plan identified forests and agriculture together as one of the five key areas for action, and outlined three major objectives for climate change mitigation in this sector (BC MELP, 2000). The first was to learn more about the science and management of carbon sinks by funding projects focusing on the processes underlying sequestration, carbon modeling procedures, and monitoring, reporting, and verification standards. As described above, this led to the cooperative arrangement with the CFS to develop provincial-level carbon budget estimates using the CBM-CFS2 model. The second objective was to facilitate the implementation of additional forest carbon sequestration activities, including a US$3.7 million grant to implement a large-scale afforestation program.[15] This initiative is still waiting for guidance from the federal government (BC MWLAP, 2001). The third objective outlined in the plan was to examine methods for reducing GHG emissions from the agriculture sector, such as no-till cropping and improved fertilizer management (BC MELP, 2000). The informational materials to prepare for these workshops have already been developed, but only internal (government) workshops have been held so far (BC MWLAP, 2001).

Efforts to implement forest climate-change policy have been delayed by a change in government (NRTEE, 2001). As a result, many of the above-mentioned programs are still under review (Beattie, personal communication).

Forest carbon ownership legislation

The 2000 Climate Change Business Plan for BC recognized that establishment of forest carbon ownership is critical for the successful trade of forest carbon. The theoretical basis for this approach was proposed by Ronald Coase, who said that the problem of depletion of common pool resources[16] can be addressed by assigning property rights to the resource (VanKooten, 1993). This allows the resource to be owned, and therefore bought or sold (Heal, 2000). Assigning property rights to forest carbon allows the atmospheric benefits provided by the forest to be sold separately from the forest and the land itself. Carbon ownership legislation is also required to establish liability in the event of carbon loss. Establishment of carbon ownership rights is a particularly pertinent issue in BC, where forested land is owned by the provincial government, but the forest harvesting company with tenure over the forested land has ownership rights to timber extracted from the forest (BC Ministry of Forests, 1999). Under the current legislation, both parties might legitimately have claim to the atmospheric benefits provided by the forest. Carbon ownership is also complicated by the on-going First Nations negotiations for rights and title (BC Ministry of Attorney General, 2001). A University of British Columbia research team submitted a carbon ownership legislative framework to the provincial government, using the Carbon Rights Amendment Bill introduced by the Australian state of New South Wales as a precedent (Harkin and Bull, 2001b). The legislation recommends the establishment of time-limited forest carbon rights in Canada by adopting trad-itional *profit a prendre* land rights,[17] limited to 100 years. This distinguishes the ownership of carbon sequestration benefits from the forest and land, but provides realistic time frames to encourage investment.

Analysis

The over-riding factor constraining the establishment of government policy and market mechanisms to facilitate trade in forest carbon has been uncertainty in the Kyoto Protocol negotiations. In anticipation of an emissions-constrained future, firms and governments have been attempting to establish a domestic emissions trading platform and a national carbon registry. Participation in the GERT, PERT, and PERRL emissions trading initiatives and the VCR registry is likely to remain voluntary given the uncertainty over Canada's ratification of the Kyoto Protocol. A number of reports detailing GHG-reduction programs have been published by both federal and provincial governments, but a much greater effort is required if Canada is to meet its required 6 per cent reduction from 1990 emissions levels by the conclusion of the first commitment period. Currently, emissions are predicted to rise by more than 20 per cent above the

1990 level (some 770 megatonnes) by 2010 (Russell, 2002). In other words, Canada has to find a 26 per cent solution if it is to meet the Kyoto target.

The development of forest carbon ownership legislation will be a major step toward facilitation of markets for forest carbon in BC. The current system provides few incentives to implement additional carbon-capturing activities.

ELEMENT 3: ACTION TO FACILITATE FOREST CARBON TRADE BY BUYERS, SELLERS, AND NGOS

In the face of ever-tightening profit margins, the forest sector in BC is increasingly looking to diversify sources of income in order to compete in an international timber market (Cashore and others, 2001). The forest sector in BC is therefore keen to generate extra revenue via the establishment of markets for forest carbon. Large power companies, in anticipation of an emissions-constrained future, are also keen to buy emission offsets from the forest sector, as the cost of forest carbon sequestration is often cheaper than reducing emissions at the plant (Climate Change Central, 2001b). Herein lie the fundamental elements of any market: demand and supply. This section examines the actions taken by buyers, sellers, and NGOs to facilitate the forest carbon trade in BC.

Potential buyers

To date, there have been no recorded sales of forest carbon from BC's forests. The market has suffered from the proverbial Catch 22: extreme caution from potential buyers has resulted in insufficient incentive for forest growers to supply forest carbon. There are two main reasons for buyers to be cautious. First, the role of forest carbon sinks in the Kyoto Protocol has been uncertain.[18] Second, forest carbon in BC is currently relatively poorly quantified in terms of legislative ownership and the precision of carbon inventory.

Despite caution on behalf of potential buyers, the demand for fully quantified, verifiable emission offsets in BC far exceeds supply. The lack of domestic supply of forest-based offsets, however, may have forced buyers to seek emission offsets offshore (Donnelly, personal communication). Three organizations that have expressed strong interest in investing in GHG offset projects within BC are GEMCO, Suncor Energy, and BC Hydro.

The Greenhouse Emissions Management Consortium (GEMCO) is an organization of 12 Canadian energy companies whose key objectives include the development of GHG offset projects and least-cost emissions trading. GEMCO has already invested in one biological-sink-based project: an agreement to purchase 2.8 million metric tonnes of CO_2 from farms in Iowa, through implementation of sustainable farm management practices (GEMCO, 1999). GEMCO is also seeking to invest in a forest carbon sink project within Canada (Donnelly, personal communication).

Suncor Energy is a Canadian oil-based energy company that has been particularly proactive in the area of climate change mitigation since first registering with the VCR in 1996 (Suncor, 2000). As well as taking steps to manage its own emissions, Suncor has already taken steps to offset its emissions by purchasing emission offsets from the US power company Niagara Mohawk. Suncor has also expressed particular interest in investing in a forest carbon project within Canada, having already invested in a reforestation project in Australia and a forest protection project in Belize (Suncor, 2000).

BC Hydro has been another major contributor to the evolution of an emissions trading system in BC. BC Hydro was one of the key players in the transition from the BC Pilot Program to GERT (BC MELP, 1997), and has committed to a 50 per cent reduction in emissions from its new power plants by 2010 (BC Hydro, 2001a). In order to meet this target, BC Hydro is committed to the internal reductions of GHGs and to invest in external emissions-reduction projects. To this end, BC Hydro released a call for proposals in early 2000, and again in January 2002, with the aim of investing in Canadian or international climate change mitigation projects to offset 5.5 million tonnes of CO_2 (BC Hydro, 2001b). BC Hydro has also recently released a request for advisory services on the acquisition of credits from afforestation projects (BC Hydro, 2001b).

Canadian companies like GEMCO and Suncor Energy have stated that they are prepared to invest in forest carbon sink projects in BC, providing three criteria are met. First, there must be a recognized and credible forest inventory system in place (McIntosh, 2001). Second, the forest carbon inventory must be subject to verification by an independent, approved third party. Third, the supplier must provide assurances on the duration of forest carbon storage (Donnelly, personal communication).

Potential sellers

It appears that the limited activity in the market for forest carbon may be largely due to the limited supply of forest carbon offsets. Supply of forest carbon offsets in BC has been limited for two main reasons:

1 the recent uncertainty as to the role of forest carbon sinks in the Kyoto Protocol has prevented the forest sector from investing in additional carbon sequestration activities; and
2 the relatively limited forest land base that was eligible for inclusion in the Kyoto Protocol.

This latter constraint resulted from approximately two-thirds of BC being classified as 'forest land' (BC Ministry of Forests, 1999). The only forest that was Kyoto-eligible with any certainty prior to the July 2001 Bonn decision was forest that had been established after 1990 on previously non-forested land (NCCP, 1999). Under this criterion, the scope for the forest industry to mitigate climate change was relatively constricted. Following the Marrakesh Accord in November

2001, however, a range of forest management activities are now eligible for inclusion under the Kyoto Protocol, therefore resulting in a much greater area of Kyoto-eligible forest within BC. In addition, greater certainty regarding the role of forest sinks in the Protocol reduces the risk of investment in incremental forest carbon-capturing activities. This is likely to result in an increased supply of forest-based emission offsets from BC in the near future.

Low market prices for carbon have also constrained the supply, especially since there are significant costs associated with forest inventory, project establishment, and improvement of models and transactions. At this stage of market development, GEMCO is offering to pay around US$3 per ton of carbon. In the past, this has proved too low to offset the additional costs of implementing a forest carbon project in BC (Donnelly, personal communication).

Confusion surrounding the process required to design and implement a forest carbon project may be a major factor preventing smaller forest owners from establishing forest carbon projects in BC. To address this problem, the University of British Columbia has developed a step-by-step carbon accounting framework specifically for BC forests (Harkin and Bull, 2000; Harkin and Bull, 2001a,). It has also taken steps to educate forest owners in the basic science of forest carbon sequestration and in silvicultural activities that can increase carbon storage in forests (Bull and Wong, 2001). General information related to the science of forest carbon sequestration is widely available on the web pages of the Canadian Forest Services' Climate Change Network, the National Climate Change Process, Environment Canada, the Government of Canada's Climate Change division, and the Canadian Centre for Climate Modeling and Analysis.

Input from NGOs

Non-governmental and environmental groups have largely been skeptical about the development of a market for forest carbon. In a report, the David Suzuki Foundation and the West Coast Environmental Law (WCEL) Research Foundation outlined three major issues related to forest carbon sinks: permanence, verifiability, and additionality (Anderson and others, 2001). The issue of permanence refers to the concern that forest carbon storage is reversible, in the event that forest is harvested, burnt, or simply poorly managed. The verifiability issue has been discussed previously: forest carbon is relatively poorly quantified in terms of legislative ownership and the precision of carbon inventory. Concerns about additionality relate to the importance of ensuring that all emission offsets should be generated from forest carbon sequestration that is in excess of business-as-usual sequestration. The Sierra Club of Canada took a similar viewpoint to the David Suzuki Foundation and WCEL, strongly emphasizing the verifiability issue (Corbett and others, 1997). Some Canadian NGOs, such as Greenpeace, are opposed to including forest sinks in the Kyoto Protocol on the basis of the three issues outlined above, in addition to the fear that old-growth forests will be replaced by highly active carbon-sequestering plantations, and that forests have the potential to offset too large a portion of Canada's total GHG reduction commitments.

Analysis

There is significant potential to develop and market forest carbon in BC: the forest sector is avidly seeking new sources of revenue, and a number of high-emission energy companies wish to secure low-cost forest-based emission offsets. Again, progress has been limited largely by the uncertainty over the role of forest carbon sinks in recent climate change negotiations. This uncertainty has locked potential buyers and sellers of forest carbon into a Catch 22 situation: buyers have been extremely cautious about investment in forest-based emission offsets, resulting in a lack of funding to implement forest carbon projects, and therefore a lack of supply. Supply is also limited by the relatively low initial prices for emission offsets. Skepticism on the behalf of some NGOs may have also constrained market expansion. The market for forest carbon in BC is still in its infancy but there are strong expressions of interest from both buyers and sellers.

CONCLUSION

In Canada there is a clear recognition by the private sector that we are facing an emissions-constrained future and that steps have to be taken to find market-based solutions that will include forests as carbon sinks. From a science point of view it is clear that measuring, modeling, and accounting for all carbon pools are indeed complex processes, but thanks to some outstanding research in the last two decades and the rapid development of new information technology tools to compile and disseminate information, we can provide credible answers to the very complex problems associated with the storage of carbon. From a policy point of view, there is still a need to define the property rights, develop appropriate measurement, modeling, and verification standards, and allocate permits for emissions and carbon storage. The key at this point is to learn by doing, and already government and industry have embarked on pilot projects to gain a further understanding of the policy and economic challenges that have to be addressed. There is also a series of policy and market initiatives across Canada and these are now being used to work with a wide range of stakeholders, but there is clearly a need to build much more capacity in the scientific, governmental, non-governmental, and industrial sectors.

Perhaps the most exciting part of forest carbon market development is that an environmental service provided by forests – carbon sequestration – will become an integral part of forest planning. This new forest product is clearly a practical expression of the broadening of management objectives in keeping with the concept of sustainable forest management.

Notes

1   We wish to thank Forest Renewal British Columbia for their financial support. We would also like to acknowledge the enthusiastic cooperation of the following: Forest Ecosystem Solutions Inc, the BC Ministry of Forest, Lignum Ltd, the Forest Ecosystem Simulation Group at the University of British Columbia, and the Canadian Forest Service.

2   The CBM-CFS2 used the 1989 eco-climatic classification of Canada, which contained the four above-mentioned eco-climatic provinces in BC. The classification has since been revised and the eco-climatic provinces are similar to the eco-zones in the current eco-climatic framework.

3   The Biogeoclimatic Ecosystem Classification (BEC) is a hierarchical system that uses climate, soil, and characteristic vegetation to group ecosystems at various levels, including regionally, locally, and chronologically (BC Ministry of Forests, 2001a).

4   A timber supply area (TSA) is an area of Crown land defined in accordance with the Forest Act, primarily based on an established pattern of wood flow from the forest to the primary timber-using industries (BC Ministry of Forests, 1999). A tree farm licence (TFL) is an agreement entered into with the provincial government, which provides for the establishment, management, and harvesting of timber by a private interest on a defined area of Crown land in accordance with the Forest Act (BC Ministry of Forests, 1999).

5   The CBM-CFS2 model has also been applied to the Foothills Model Forest in the neighboring province of Alberta (Price and others, 1997). Seventeen carbon budget scenarios that differ in the levels of management, harvesting, protection from fires and insects, and natural disturbance cycles, were compared for the simulation period 1958–2238.

6   The Timber Supply Review program updates and assesses the timber that may be available for harvesting over the short and long term for each TSA and TFL. By law in BC, the annual allowable cut must be pre-determined at least once every five years (BC Ministry of Forests, 1999). The assumptions in the Timber Supply Review 2 differ for each TSA and TFL. They encompass assumptions about growth and yield curves and management constraints due to factors such as biodiversity, water quality, and recreation. Further information can be found in individual reports or 'data packages' on http://www.for.gov.bc.ca/tsb/tsr2/tsr2.htm.

7   Forest resource planning models that are available and have been used in BC include: COMPLAN (Olympic Resource Management, 2001), Forest Simulation Optimization System (Forest Ecosystems Solutions, 2001), and various simulation programs by Timberline Forest Inventory Consultants (TFIC, 2001).

8   The most recent national forest inventory (and the last conducted under the old national inventory process) was the inventory for 2001 (Gillis, personal communication).

9   Air photos, satellite imagery, and field plot data will be used to determine the NFI. The goal is to survey a minimum of 1 per cent of Canada's landmass, or approximately 22,000 sample plots. Remeasurement will occur over a ten-year period in which one-tenth of all sample units will be remeasured each year (Canadian Forest Service, 1999b).

10 The 'cap and trade' system involves strictly limiting or 'capping' emissions allowances, and allowing them to be traded. The cap, which is assigned to parties in the

form of 'allowable emission permits', is usually set at a fraction of historic emissions levels (CO2e.com, 2001). At the end of the compliance period, the actual emissions of the company are compared to their quantity of allowable emission permits. Parties whose emissions are lower than their cap may choose to sell excess allowances, and likewise parties whose emissions are greater than their cap will be required to purchase additional permits, or risk a fine for non-compliance (CO2e.com, 2001). The main advantage of this approach is that there is a quantifiable schedule of emission reductions for each company, and therefore this approach is compatible with the allocated emission-reduction targets specified in the Kyoto Protocol (Russell, 2002).

11   Under the 'baseline and credit' trading system, each company is allocated a baseline schedule of allowable emissions that is equivalent to their business-as-usual emissions. If a company produces fewer emissions (or sequesters more carbon) than their allocated baseline, they can sell these excess emissions as carbon credits on the market. The system differs from the cap and trade system in that there is no constraint on the amount of emissions each party can emit, as long as they have enough permits to offset their emissions (Harkin and Bull, 2000). The main disadvantage of this approach is that there is no pre-determined emission-reduction target, and therefore the baseline and credit system is less compatible with the Kyoto Protocol (Russell, 2002).

12   Canada's first commercial-scale emissions trading platform is being established in the province of Alberta. Climate Change Central was established in November 1999 and represents a private–public partnership, among whose key responsibilities are to act as a broker and clearing house for climate change mitigation projects (Climate Change Central, 2001a). To fulfil this role, a call for proposals was released in April 2001, to establish Canada's first online emissions trading simulation. The simulation, conducted in partnership with CO2e.com, took place in early September 2001.

13   Under the grandfathering approach, the initial allocation of allowable emissions is based on levels of emissions in the past (NCCP, 2001).

14   A no-regrets climate change policy generally has a range of other benefits in addition to climate change mitigation. For example, a climate change policy might also improve economic efficiency, improve local air quality, and promote sustainable development (BC MELP 1995).

15   It was also recognized that the Ministry of Forests was investigating the legislative changes required in order to facilitate the trade of forest carbon (BC MELP, 2000).

16   Common pool resources (CPRs) are goods and services that are owned by the general public, and are openly accessible for use by all citizens (Heal, 2000).

17   *Profit a prendre* rights allow an individual to enter land owned by somebody else and take something off the land – in this case, carbon (Findlay and Hillyer, 1994).

18   Following the consensus regarding the role of forest sinks at the COP 7 negotiations at Marrakesh in November 2001, the confidence of buyers about using forest carbon credits as emission offsets in the future is likely to increase.

REFERENCES

Australian Greenhouse Office (AGO). 1999. "National Emissions Trading: Crediting the Carbon." Discussion Paper No.3. Canberra: AGO.

Anderson, D., R. Grant, and C. Rolfe. 2001. "Taking Credit: Canada and the Role of Sinks in International Climate Negotiations." Vancouver: David Suzuki Foundation and West Coast Environmental Law.

Apps, M.J., W.A. Kurz, S.J. Beukema, and J.S. Bhatti, 1999. "Carbon Budget of the Canadian Forest Product Sector." *Environmental Science and Policy,* 2, pp.25–41.

BC Hydro. 2001a. "Request for Greenhouse Gas Offset Proposals." Vancouver: BC Hydro (processed).

BC Hydro. 2001b. "BC Hydro: GHG Offsets." Invitation for Proposals (Consulting Services) BC Hydro – Corporate Sustainability Group. Hydro Reference No.GHG-2002-01. Vancouver: BC Hydro (processed).

BC Ministry of Attorney General. 2001. "The BC Treaty Commission Process." Victoria: Treaty Negotiations Office.

BC Ministry of Environment, Lands and Parks (MELP). 1995. "British Columbia Greenhouse Gas Action Plan." Victoria: BC Ministry of Environment, Land and Parks.

BC Ministry of Environment, Lands and Parks (MELP). 1997. "British Columbia Greenhouse Gas Forum: Report to the British Columbia Ministers of Environment, Lands and Parks and the Minister of Employment and Investment on the Elements of the Kyoto International Climate Change Protocol." Victoria: BC Ministry of Environment, Land and Parks.

BC Ministry of Environment, Lands and Parks (MELP). 1998. "British Columbia Greenhouse Gas Forum: Plan For Early Action." Victoria: BC Ministry of Environment, Land and Parks.

BC Ministry of Environment, Land and Parks (MELP). 2000. "British Columbia Climate Change Business Plan 2000–2003." Victoria: BC Ministry of Environment, Land and Parks.

BC Ministry of Environment, Land and Parks (MELP) and the Ministry of Employment and Investment (MEI). 1997. "GHG Emission Reduction Pilot: Backgrounder." Victoria: BC Ministry of Environment, Land and Parks.

BC Ministry of Forests (MF). 1999. "Timber Supply Review: Backgrounder." Victoria: BC Ministry of Forests (processed).

BC Ministry of Forests (MF). 2000. "Forest Act." Victoria: BC Ministry of Forests.

BC Ministry of Forests (MF). 2001a. "Biogeoclimatic Ecosystem Classification." Victoria: BC Ministry of Forests.

BC Ministry of Forests (MF). 2001b. "Determining an Area Harvest Level Using Optimum Rotation Length." Victoria: BC Ministry of Forests.

BC Ministry of Water, Land and Air Protection (MWLAP). 2001. "British Columbia Climate Change Measures (Forestry and Agriculture Sectors): Status Report." Victoria: BC Ministry of Water, Land and Air Protection.

Bonnor, G.M. 1985. "Inventory of Forest Biomass in Canada." Ottawa: Canadian Forest Service.

Buckley, C. 2001. "Baseline Protection Initiative." Paper presented at the BC Greenhouse Gas Forum workshop on Greenhouse Gas Emission Trading, Vancouver, BC, June 20, 2001.

Bull, G.Q., Z.E. Harkin, and A. Wong. 2001. "What Role Should Forest Management Play in the Global Climate Change Regime?" Vancouver: University of British Columbia (processed).

Bull, G.Q., and A. Wong. 2001. "Carbon Accounting for Small Woodlot Owners." Paper presented at the British Columbia's Small Woodlands Conference – Steps to Sustainability, Richmond, BC, February 15–16.

Canada Centre for Remote Sensing (CCRS). 2000. "BEPS – Net Carbon Absorption/ Release by Plants and Soils: Net Ecosystem Productivity (NEP)." Ottawa: Canada Centre for Remote Sensing.

Canadian Forest Service. 1999a. "Overview: The Forest Inventory." Ottawa: Canadian Forest Service.

Canadian Forest Service. 1999b. "A Plot-based National Forest Inventory Design for Canada." Ottawa: Canadian Forest Service.

Cashore, B., G. Hoberg, M. Howlett, J. Rayner, and J. Wilson. 2001. *In Search of Sustainability – British Columbia Forest Policy in the 1990's.* Vancouver: UBC Press.

Climate Change Central. 2001a. "Strategic Plan 2000–2010." Calgary: Climate Change Central.

Climate Change Central. 2001b. "Alberta Emissions Trading Simulation: Final Report." Calgary: Climate Change Central.

ClimatePartners. 2001. "Welcome to Climate Partners." Website: http://www.climatepartners. com/. Victoria: Climate Partners Network Inc.

ClimateServices.com. 2001. "Climate Services." Website: http://www.climateservices.com/ . Portland: Trexler and Associates.

CO2e.com. 2001. "CO2e.com." Website: http://www.co2e.com/. Toronto: CO2e.com Canada.

Corbett, L., R. Hornung, and C. Rolfe. 1997. "Third meeting of the Conference of the Parties to the United Nations Framework Convention on Climate Change." Delegation report. Ottawa: Sierra Club of Canada (processed).

Council of Forest Industries. 2001. "Report: Forestry Facts." Vancouver: Council of Forest Industries.

Emission Strategies. 2001. "Emission Strategies." Website: http://www.emissionstrategies. com/. Fairfax: ICF Consulting.

Environment Canada and Agriculture and Agri-Food Canada. 2000. "A National Ecological Framework for Canada." Hull: Environment Canada.

Framework Convention on Climate Change (FCCC). 2000. "Mechanisms Pursuant to Articles 6, 12 and 17 of the Kyoto Protocol – Registries." Presented at COP6, The Hague, Netherlands. FCCC Subsidiary Body for Scientific and Technological Advice and Subsidiary Body for Implementation. Bonn: FCCC Secretariat (processed).

Findlay, B., and A. Hillyer. 1994. "Here Today, Here Tomorrow: Legal Tools for the Voluntary Protection of Private Land in British Columbia." Vancouver: West Coast Environmental Law Research Foundation.

Forest Ecosystem Solutions Ltd. 2001. "Forest ecosystem solutions Ltd." Website: http:/ /www.forestecosystem.com/. North Vancouver: Forest Ecosystem Solutions.

GEMCO. 2001. "BC Greenhouse Gas Forum Workshop on Greenhouse Gas Emission Trading." Victoria: GEMCO (processed).

GEMCO. 1999. "GEMCo Members Agree to Buy Emission Reduction Credits From Iowa Farmers." Press release, October 19. Victoria: GEMCO (processed).

Harkin, Z.E., and G.Q. Bull. 2000. "Development of a Forest Carbon Accounting Framework for Forests in British Columbia." Paper No.IR-00-46. Laxenburg: International Institute for Applied Systems Analysis (processed).

Harkin, Z.E., and G.Q. Bull. 2001a. "An International Forest Carbon Accounting Framework: A System for Managing, Measuring, Reporting and Trading Forest Carbon from an Operational to an International Scale." In B. Schlamadinger, S. Woess-Gallasch, and A. Cowie (eds.)., *Greenhouse Gas Balances of Biomass and Bioenergy Systems.* Proceedings of the Workshop on carbon accounting and emissions trading related to bioenergy, wood products, and carbon sequestration, Canberra, March 26–31. Graz: IEA Bioenergy Task 38.

Harkin, Z.E., and G.Q. Bull. 2001b. "Development of a Legislative Framework in Anticipation of Forest Carbon Trade in Canada." Draft. Vancouver: University of British Columbia (processed).

Hasselknippe, H., and G. Hoibye. 2000. "Meeting the Kyoto Protocol Commitments. Summary – Domestic Emissions Trading Schemes." Oslo: Confederation of Norwegian Business and Industry (processed).

Heal, G.M. 2000. *Nature and the Marketplace. Capturing the Value of Ecosystem Services.* Washington: Island Press.

Hoberg, G. 2001. "Don't Forget the Government Can Do Anything: Policies Toward Jobs in the BC Forest Sector." In B. Cashore, G. Hoberg, M. Howlett, J. Rayner, and J. Wilson (eds.), *In Search of Sustainability.* Vancouver: UBC Press.

Houghton, J.T., L.J. Meira Filho, B. Lim, K. Treanton, I. Mamaty, Y. Bonduki, D.J. Griggs, and B.A. Callender (eds.). 1997. *Revised 1996 IPCC Guidelines for National Greenhouse Gas Inventories.* IPCC/OECD/IEA. Bracknell: UK Meteorological Office.

Kimmins, J.P., D. Mailly, and B. Seely. 1999. "Modelling Forest Ecosystem Net Primary Production: the Hybrid Simulation Approach used in FORECAST." *Ecological Modelling,* 122:3, pp.195–224.

Kopp, R.J. 2001. "An Analysis of the Bonn Agreement." *Weathervane,* Feature No.134. Washington: Resources for the Future (processed).

Kurz, W.A., and M.J. Apps. 1999. "A 70-year Retrospective Analysis of Carbon Fluxes in the Canadian Forest Sector." *Ecological Applications,* 9:2, pp.526–547.

Kurz, W.A., M.J. Apps, P.G. Comeau, and J.A. Trofymow. 1996. *The Carbon Budget of British Columbia's Forests, 1920–1989: Preliminary Analysis and Recommendations for Refinements.* FRDA report: 0835-0752. Victoria: BC Ministry of Forests.

Kurz, W.A., M.J. Apps, T.M. Webb, and P.J. McNamee. 1992. *The Carbon Budget of the Canadian Forest Sector: Phase I.* Information Report No.NOR-X-326. Edmonton: Canadian Forest Service.

McIntosh, E. 2001. "Carbon Trading and the Small Woodlands Program." Prince George: Small Woodlands Program of BC (processed).

Ministry of Attorney General. 2001. "The BC Treaty Commission Process." Victoria: Treaty Negotiations Office.

Montréal Process Working Group. 1998. "Criteria and Indicators for the Conservation and Sustainable Management of Temperate and Boreal Forests." Ottawa: Montréal Process Liaison Office.

National Climate Change Process. 1999. " Sinks Table Options Paper: Land Use, Land Use Change and Forestry in Canada and the Kyoto Protocol." Ottawa: National Climate Change Secretariat (processed).

National Climate Change Process. 2001. "Baseline Protection: Opening of the Baseline Protection Registries." Ottawa: National Climate Change Secretariat (processed)

National Round Table on Environment and Economy (NRTEE). 2001. "Canada's Options for a Domestic Greenhouse Gas Emissions Trading Program." Ottawa: NRTEE.

Natural Resources Canada. 2001. *The State of Canada's Forests 2001.* Ottawa: Canadian Forest Service.

Olympic Resource Management. 2001. "SOFTWARE – COMPLAN." Vancouver: ORM Canada.

Penner, M., K. Power, C. Muhairwe, R. Tellier, and Y. Wang. 1997. *Canada's Forest Biomass Resources: Deriving Estimates from Canada's Forest Inventory.* Information Report No.BC-X-370. Victoria: Canadian Forest Service.

PERRL Working Group. 2001. "Pilot Emission Removals, Reductions and Learnings (PERRL) Initiative." Consultation Document, PERRL Working Group; 2001 May 16.

Price, D.T., D.H. Halliwell, M.J. Apps, W.A. Kurz, and S.R. Curry. 1997. "Comprehensive Assessment of Carbon Stocks and Fluxes in a Boreal-Cordilleran Forest Management Unit." *Canadian Journal of Forest Research,* 27: 12, pp.2005–2016.

Rosenbaum, K.L. 2001. "Climate Change and the Forestry Sector: Possible Legislative Responses for National and Subnational Governments." FAO Legal Papers Online No.14. Rome: FAO.

Russell, D. 2002. "Emissions Trading: The Basics." Paper presented at the National Round Table on Environment and the Economy seminar, 'The ABC's of Emissions Trading: An overview', January 24, 2002. Vancouver, BC.

Schroeder, P., S. Brown, J. Mo, R. Birdsey, and C. Cieszewski. 1997. "Biomass Estimation for Temperate Broadleaf Forests of the United States using Inventory Data." *Forest Science,* 43:3, pp.424–434.

Seely, B., J.P. Kimmins, C. Welham, and K. Scoullar. 1999. "Defining Stand-level Sustainability and Exploring Stand-level Stewardship." *Journal of Forestry,* 97:6, pp.4–10.

Seely, B., C. Welham, and H. Kimmins. Forthcoming. "Carbon Sequestration in a Boreal Forest Ecosystem: Results from the Ecosystem Simulation Model, FORECAST." *Forest Ecology and Management.*

Siltanen, R.M, M.J. Apps, R.M. Zoltai, and W.L. Strong. 1997. "A Soil Profile and Organic Carbon Data Base For Canadian Forest and Tundra Mineral Soils." Edmonton: Natural Resource Canada, Canadian Forest Service.

Stanek, W., and D. State. 1978. *Equations Predicting Primary Productivity (Biomass) of Trees, Shrubs and Lesser Vegetation Based on Current Literature.* Report No.BC X-183. Victoria: Pacific Forest Research Centre.

Suncor. 2000. "Taking Action on Global Climate Change." Calgary: Suncor Energy (processed).

Timberline Forest Inventory Consultants. 2001. "Resource Planning and Analysis." Vancoucer: TFIC (processed).

Van Kooten, G.C. 1993. *Land Resource Economics and Sustainable Development: Economic Policies and the Common Good.* Vancouver: UBC Press.

Wilson, J. 2001. "Experimentation on a Leash: Forest Use Planning in the 1990's." In B. Cashore, G. Hoberg, M. Howlett, J. Rayner, and J. Wilson (eds.), *In Search of Sustainability.* Vancouver: UBC Press.

Chapter 12

Helping Indigenous Farmers to Participate in the International Market for Carbon Services: The Case of Scolel Té

Richard Tipper[1]

Over the past decade there has been significant progress in developing markets for carbon offsets, as part of efforts to implement the United Nations Framework Convention on Climate Change (UNFCCC), signed in Rio in 1992 during the United Nations Conference on Environment and Development (UNCED). The market is still in its very early stages, but recent initiatives around the world suggest that forestry offsets could play an increasingly important role in achieving the emission-reduction targets agreed by signatories to the 1997 Kyoto Protocol. Discussion of the potential role of forests in carbon services has tended to focus on large-scale forest industry projects, with relatively little attention being paid to the potential role of small farmers. This neglects their potential contribution to addressing global climate change problems, while cutting them out of a potentially valuable source of additional income. Involving small farmers in the emerging international market for carbon services is not an easy task, however. This Chapter examines an effort to do so: the Scolel Té project in southern Mexico.

THE INTERNATIONAL MARKET FOR CARBON SERVICES

The Intergovernmental Panel on Climate Change (IPCC) has identified a likely gap of around 800 million tonnes of carbon (tC) per year between the greenhouse gas (GHG) emissions of industrialized (Annex 1) countries under a business-as-usual scenario, and the commitments that these countries have made for the first commitment period (2008–2012) under the Kyoto Protocol (Watson and others, 2000). Part of this gap is likely to be covered by emission reductions derived from projects undertaken in developing countries through an instrument known as the Clean Development Mechanism (CDM). Afforestation and reforestation are among the activities that are eligible under the CDM.

In addition to official carbon markets regulated by the institutions of the UNFCCC, there is also a growing market based on the voluntary commitments of private companies and individuals wishing to offset some of their environmental impacts, such as GHG emissions. For example, the International Automobile Federation (FIA) wishes to offset the direct emissions associated with Formula 1 and the World Rally Championship.

Both the CDM and the voluntary carbon-offset market have objectives that go beyond sequestering carbon. According to Article 12 of the Kyoto Protocol, CDM projects are also supposed to contribute to the sustainable development objectives of host countries. In many cases, this includes poverty reduction or livelihood improvement in rural areas. Several of the voluntary initiatives have gone even further, seeking to identify projects that will sequester carbon in forestry projects 'with a human face'.

These evolving international markets for carbon services give rise to a number of important questions regarding the options open to farmers and communities about how, when, and under what terms they should engage in these markets.

- How should CDM land use projects engage rural communities in ways that enhance rural livelihoods and reduce poverty?
- What are individual and communal rights vis-à-vis the generation and transfer of carbon assets?[2]
- Will small farmers and communities be able to compete with large-scale forest industry projects?
- What types of monitoring, administrative, and support activities meet the needs of local people and the requirements for generating carbon credits under the CDM regulations?

THE SCOLEL TÉ PROJECT

The Scolel Té project in southern Mexico is one of the first projects to address these questions through practical engagement with small farmers and communities who are potential carbon service providers. The project began in 1996, following a six-month feasibility study by Mexican and British researchers in collaboration with representatives of indigenous farmers from the northern highlands of the state of Chiapas.

From the start, the approach adopted by the Scolel Té project differed from that of previous studies, which had focused on broad estimates of the biological or economic potential of carbon sequestration in tropical regions from the industrial country perspective. Rather than asking how much carbon could be sequestered at a given cost, the Scolel Té project took as its point of departure the land use activities that communities and individual farmers were seeking to implement and then asked how the carbon benefits could be packaged and marketed in order to provide capital to finance their implementation.

The project is currently active in over 20 communities in the central and northern highlands of Chiapas, and is expanding to other areas in the eastern lowlands.

The project site

Chiapas is the southernmost state of Mexico. It has an area of 7.5 million ha and a population of 3.6 million. The majority of the rural population consists of small-scale indigenous farmers, most of whom live in and operate under communal land ownership of various forms. Individual families farm most of the agricultural land while forests and rangelands are managed by communal authorities. Subsistence agriculture, based on the *milpa* system, provides maize and beans. Coffee, cattle, artisanal work, and itinerant laboring provide supplementary income. The state was chosen as a site for the research project because of existing links between the researchers and local farmers organizations and because of the availability of data on carbon storage within a number of the key vegetation types found within the state.

Over the past 20 years there has been rapid population growth in most rural areas (around 4 per cent per annum). This growth appears to be one of the factors responsible for widespread degradation of forest resources (de Jong and others, 1999). Highland areas have experienced thinning-out of pine-oak forests, with extraction of the timber-quality pine trees, cutting of oak for charcoal and firewood, and grazing by sheep. Lowland areas have suffered from significant wholesale clearance of moist tropical forest for cattle pasture. The resultant landscape is a complex patchwork of secondary vegetation and agriculture at various stages of regeneration and cultivation.

A recent study of the CO_2 emissions associated with land use change from the 2.5 million ha in the Scolel Té project area estimated that around 140 million tC were emitted between 1974 and 1996. This is roughly comparable to the total current emissions generated by the United Kingdom in a single year (Hellier and others, 2002).

Development

The project has its origins in 1994, when researchers from the University of Edinburgh and El Colegio de la Frontera Sur in Chiapas received funding from the European Union (EU) and the Mexican government to conduct an initial appraisal of the technical options for sequestering carbon in agroforestry systems (de Jong and others, 1995). The researchers established a stakeholder group of interested farmers, drawn mainly from one of the farmers unions operating in the region – the Union de Crédito Pajal Ya Kac' Tic.

The specific objective of the first phase, which ran from 1996 to 1999, was to study the requirements of a system for planning and administering the production and sale of carbon services from small-scale landowners in a way that would be consistent with the improvement of rural livelihoods, and develop appropriate solutions. The research project was financed by United Kingdom Department For International Development's (DFID) Forestry Research Programme and Mexico's National Ecology Institute (Instituto Nacional de Ecología, INE).

During the short study the researcher and the stakeholder group identified four key principles that were to inform the design of the subsequent project, and the planning system that evolved during the first four years of operation.

- **Transparency.** Both producers and purchasers of carbon services require a clear understanding of their roles, rights, and responsibilities.
- **Simplicity.** Producers of small quantities of carbon assets require simple, standardized procedures for planning, registering, implementing, and monitoring carbon sequestration activities
- **Flexibility.** Producers wish to provide different amounts of carbon services from different types of forestry systems at different times. The capacity for implementation may take time to scale up.
- **Evidence-based.** Overall quality and credibility of the system should be based on verifiable, documented evidence in the form of field data, accounting records, published literature, and official statistics.

These principles are thought to be of equal importance to participating farmers and purchasers of carbon services.

The feasibility study also quantified the carbon sequestration benefits of a number of agroforestry and forest management practices that were identified by participating farmers as potentially attractive and useful for communities in the areas studied. Some of these systems are listed in Table 12.1.

In parallel with research effort in the field, the Edinburgh Centre for Carbon Management (ECCM) has been working to develop real carbon trading on a pilot voluntary basis with sales of 'prototype emission reduction credits' to the FIA and other organizations. These efforts created a demand for carbon credits in these pre-CDM days.

THE MECHANISM AND ITS INSTITUTIONS

Having identified some of the main technical opportunities and conditions for acceptable operation, the project team set about establishing a pilot project that could begin to undertake carbon trading on an experimental basis, learning by experience. The name 'Scolel Té' was chosen by the initial participants – farmers from six Tzeltal communities and four Tojolobal communities in the municipalities of Chilón and Comitán. Scolel Té is a Tzeltal expression (also understood by most Tojolobals) meaning 'the tree that grows'.

A trust fund, the Fondo Bioclimatico, was established to act as the project bank account and as a clearing house for the carbon credits generated by the

Table 12.1 *Carbon sequestration potential of selected forest restoration and agroforestry systems in Chiapas, Mexico*

System	Summary description	Long-term additional carbon storage (tC/ha)[a]
Lowland areas (below 1,500 meters above sea level)		
Taungya	Cultivation of small plantations of high value hardwood trees such as Spanish cedar, intercropped with maize for the first four years	120–150
Enhanced regeneration of damaged forest	Liberation thinning and interplanting of secondary vegetation to encourage the restoration of valuable forest trees	80–120
Highland areas (above 1,500 meters above sea level)		
Pine-oak restoration	Regeneration of degraded pine-oak forests through stock control, selective interplanting	70–100
Pine plantations	Establishment of plantations of pine on disused pastures	70–120

Note: a Calculated as the average increase in above-ground and harvested product carbon stocks over a 100-year period, relative to the pre-existing vegetation.
Source: de Jong and others, 1995

farming systems. At present, the Fondo is a non-incorporated entity overseen by a management committee that includes representatives of farmers' organizations, a local research institute, and the ECCM. A local company of foresters, agronomists, community advisers, and administrators known as Ambio carries out day-to-day administration and technical work.

A set of initial operating procedures covering administrative, planning, monitoring, and transaction functions was devised and put into action. After some initial trials, these procedures were consolidated into a management system named Plan Vivo.

Under the Plan Vivo system, most contacts between the Fondo team and local communities are arranged through the numerous farmers' organizations and other organizations that operate in the region. Following preliminary discussions with the contacts in these organizations, meetings with communities or groups are arranged. Frequently, the groups participating in the initial meetings are composed of self-selected farmers who are either active in the local organization or have a specific interest in the carbon project. At these initial meetings, the basic concepts of climate change, carbon sequestration by vegetation, and carbon service provision are introduced, and the terms and conditions associated with carbon transactions through the Fondo are explained.

Only once sufficient understanding and consensus have been reached will the community be accepted onto the active program of the Fondo. Working either individually or in groups, farmers produce simple plans describing the type of forestry or agroforestry systems that they wish to develop, where they will be situated, what vegetation and current practices will be modified, and how much labor and materials they will need. The Fondo provides training and support during this planning process to help farmers consider the various options that may be possible within the area and to ensure that the relevant information is included on the plan. This level of detailed planning is meant to ensure that farmers develop forestry systems that will be beneficial and sustainable in the long run but also feasible to implement in the short term.

Completed plans are submitted to the Fondo Bioclimatico, usually via a village representative, who by this time will have received some training to ensure that the basic details have been properly completed. The Fondo's technical team then reviews these plans, judging whether the proposed activities are technically feasible and estimating the carbon sequestration benefits of each plan. This evaluation is facilitated by grouping plans according to 'technical specification': detailed descriptions of the ecological and technical requirements for the most common agroforestry systems implemented in the project area. Technical specifications also include estimates of carbon sequestration potential and guidelines for monitoring. The maintenance and improvement of technical specifications is a task that runs parallel to the mainstream process of the Fondo and involves scientific and technical input as well as information gleaned from the monitoring and internal review of activities.

Once a plan has been approved, an offer letter is issued to the applicant setting out the results of the evaluation, the amount of carbon they are expected to sequester, and the terms and conditions for receiving payment for the delivery of carbon services. At the current time, the main conditions are as follows:

- Applicants should implement the activities as set out in the plan.
- The applicant agrees to make 'reasonable efforts' to ensure the permanence of the forestry or agroforestry system proposed (permanence is defined as a 100-year time frame).
- 5 per cent of the value of timber products will be ceded to the Fondo in the event of the non-continuation of the scheme.
- Any changes to the plan have to be approved by the technical team.
- Applicants are to facilitate and assist in the monitoring procedures of the Fondo.
- Any problems with implementation should be reported to the technical team.

If applicants agree with the terms and conditions, they are given 'active status'.

To try to match the supply and demand for carbon services, the Fondo has structured its transactions as follows. Activation of a Plan Vivo triggers the creation of an individual or group 'carbon account', and a corresponding money account in the Fondo. The account owners are issued with a passbook, in which the following types of transactions are logged:

- forward agreements, whereby the Fondo agrees to purchase a specific quantity of carbon from the account holder within a certain time frame at a specific price. If this carbon is generated by the account holder within the agreed time frame, then the seller is committed to sell and the purchaser is committed to buy; and
- actual transactions, which include the crediting of carbon to the account following the completion of monitoring and debits of carbon associated with sales. When carbon is debited from the account, the money account of the farmer is credited and the farmer may withdraw cash from the Fondo.

Figure 12.1 illustrates the information contained in the passbooks, which are issued to all new participants in the Fondo.

Similar passbooks are used by some farmers in the area for deposit accounts at the local banks. However, many farmers find it difficult to understand the details of the current accounting system and the administrative team is still working on ways to make this simpler. The issue of carbon accounting is one area of the project where we are still exploring the trade-offs between allowing maximum flexibility for the participants and making the system transparent and understandable.

Name of owner:									
Zone:									
Code:									
Forward purchase agreement									
Amount of C (t)	Price ($/tC)	Buyer	Date of delivery	Signed and dated					
65.4	8	FIA	1998–2003						
Account transactions									

date	type of transaction	Carbon account (tC)				Money account ($)			
		C added	C sold	buyer	balance	Price of C US$/tC	$ added	$ withdrawn	balance
	C sale		21.8	FIA	−21.8	8	175	0	175
	$ withdawal							175	0
	C monitoring	38			16.2				
	C sale		21.8	FIA	−5.6	8	175		175
	$ withdrawal							175	0
	C monitoring	38			32.4				
	C sale		21.8	FIA	10.6	8	175		175
	$ withdrawal						175	175	0

Figure 12.1 *Example of information contained in passbooks for the Plan Vivo system*

As a risk control measure, the owners of accounts are required to keep a positive carbon credit on their books amounting to 10 per cent of the total amount sold. This 'risk buffer' is likely to be reviewed over time.

The current system of crediting of carbon to the accounts of producers is designed for the voluntary market, which generally claims the carbon benefit at the time of forest establishment (as opposed to following carbon uptake).[3] These ex ante credits are assigned to the producer's carbon account in three stages over the first ten years of management. In general, 20 per cent of the carbon credits expected to accrue from a plan is allocated to participating farmers once the plan has been activated, so that the payments they receive for these credits provide a source of working capital. Typically, about 50 per cent of the total effort for the establishment and maintenance of forestry systems is concentrated in the first 18 months, creating an important need for up-front financing. Once a system reaches ten years of age the benefits, in terms of production of fuelwood, poles, and non-timber products, typically exceed the annual costs of maintenance.

Further credits of carbon to account holders are made following annual monitoring exercises. Monitoring is structured as follows:

- Annual monitoring is conducted in all the sites by local teams drawn from participants in the Fondo. Monitoring team members are given short (one to two days) training on the specific indicators to be monitored and are allocated to a series of sites. It has become common practice for participants in one village to monitor sites in a neighboring village. Labor costs for monitoring are paid for from the technical and administrative budget of the Fondo.
- The Fondo's own technical staff sample 10–20 per cent of sites, depending on the experience of the local team, to check the consistency and accuracy of measurements.
- Procedures for independent verification of the monitoring system are currently being developed on the basis of recommendations arising from a recent study of the Plan Vivo system by SGS verification services.

Developments and refinements of the planning and administration systems are discussed at stakeholder meetings, held every six months. These meetings are also used to discuss strategic issues such as the supply and demand for carbon credits, international policy developments, and local events.

DEVELOPMENT OF THE PROJECT

Over the past six years, the Scolel Té project has steadily expanded from a rather vague concept to a small but viable business based on the development and commercialization of carbon assets. There are currently over 400 individual participants from about 30 communities, representing four different ethnic groups and a wide range of agro-ecosystems. The dropout rate has been under 5 per cent for the past three years.

The Fondo is currently selling carbon at US$12 per tC (US$3.3 per tCO_2). The expected income from the sale of carbon services for 2002 is expected to be around US$180,000. This sale price broadly reflects the start-up costs of most of the forestry systems being established by the participants, but also takes account of carbon prices quoted by other projects in the forest sector (these range from US$1–4 per tCO_2).

While the project is recognized by the Mexican and US governments under their respective pilot programs for 'activities implemented jointly for the mitigation of climate change', in legal terms the units being exchanged are non-statutory papers on a par with the gift vouchers, tokens, or loan notes that can be issued by any company. There is no corresponding change of sovereignty of carbon credits between governments (as would occur under the mechanisms of the Kyoto Protocol).

Of the US$12 sale price, 60 per cent (US$8) goes directly to farmers and communities to invest in implementing the forestry and agroforestry activities set out in their plans. The remaining 40 per cent of the sale price is used to cover the costs of technical support for farmers (including training, assessment of management plans, identification of seed sources, supervision of preparatory work, and liaison with regulatory institutions), administration of individual carbon accounts and Fondo accounts, liaison with purchasers, and monitoring and reporting. There is some scope for increasing the percentage going direct to farmers as the business increases in scale. However, comparisons of administrative costs between projects should be drawn with some caution, since social forestry/agroforestry activities require considerable cost allocations to offer technical support to small, often dispersed groups of farmers.

An independent economic assessment of the benefits of the forestry systems encouraged by the project conducted by consulting firm DTZ Pieda (DTZ Pieda, 2000) found that discounted benefits for most participants lie in the range of about –US$110 to +US$1700/ha. These estimates take into account all labor inputs and carbon credit sales, but do not include other possible associated benefits such as soil conservation, income diversification, and the availability of secondary forest products (for example, bromeliads for ceremonial use, medicinal plants, and fenceposts). On average, this represents a modest but significant improvement on local incomes (these range from US$300 to US$1800 per year, per family).

All purchasers of carbon from the Fondo are currently acting on a voluntary basis, with no tax or legal incentives available. The largest purchasers of carbon credits are the FIA. Other purchasers include the World Economic Forum, the rock group Pink Floyd, and the carbon trading company Future Forests.

The Plan Vivo system employed by the Fondo BioClimatico is currently being tested in two other pilot projects, one in southern India and one in Mozambique. One advantage of this approach is the ability to initiate an active carbon trading system at a very small scale. The system appears to be robust enough to function on minimal resources; each project functions with a core administrative and technical staff of between two and four people, with periodic support and advice from the coordinating agency (ECCM). In Chiapas, the system was developed during a time of considerable rural tension and conflict yet appears to have been accepted by a wide range of political and ethnic groupings.

At present it is still too early to make a judgment as to the long-term sustainability of the systems initiated by the Scolel Té project. However, the experience to date gives some grounds for optimism: there is a significant and growing willingness on the part of communities and organizations within the region (as well as in neighboring states and countries) to participate in the project or to replicate its systems. We are also confident that the farmers and communities who have participated in the project have put much more effort into planning their forestry activities than was the case with previous state- or aid-funded afforestation and forest management programmers.

An important by-product of the project has been the level of training and empowerment produced by exposure to the ideas associated with trading in environmental services. Many farmers have learned specific technical skills, such as surveying, mapping, financial planning, and silviculture. Some of the farmers' representatives have had the chance to engage in international conferences and workshops on climate change mitigation, and have gained a deeper understanding of the linkages between international policies and local development issues.

Within local NGOs, there is now a far greater understanding of the implications of international instruments such as the CDM, and there is a growing awareness that rural stakeholders need to think strategically about how they should develop and use potential carbon assets arising from the management of agricultural and forestry ecosystems.

Comments from individual participating farmers can also give an indication of the kind of benefits arising from the project, which are difficult to analyze in quantitative terms:

> *Restoring this woodland means that my family will not have to walk so far to collect wood for cooking. We will also have a good supply of fenceposts and beams, which are getting very difficult to find these days. (Farmer in Jusnajáb, near Comitán)*

> *If these cedros grow as well as the ones in the next village then by the time my son is old enough to go to college, they should be worth enough to pay for his fees and upkeep. (Farmer in Muquenal, near Palanque)*

NOTES

1   This publication results from a research project funded by the DFID for the benefit of developing countries (DFID Forestry Research Programme Project 7274). The views expressed are not necessarily those of the United Kingdom government.
2   A carbon asset is defined as any quantifiable, verifiable reduction in GHG emissions that can be owned by a legal entity.
3   The ECCM is currently developing a system for converting ex ante carbon credits to ex post credits which should be compatible with the carbon accounting framework of the CDM.

REFERENCES

de Jong, B.H., M.A. Cairns, N. Ramírez-Marcial, S. Ochoa-Gaona, J. Mendoza-Vega, P.K. Haggerty, M. González-Espinosa, and I. March-Mifsut. 1999. "Land-use Change and Carbon Flux between the 1970s and 1990s in the Central Highlands of Chiapas, Mexico." *Environmental Management*, 23:3, pp.373–385.

de Jong, B.H.J., G. Montoya-Gómez, K. Nelson, L. Soto-Pinto, J. Taylor , and R. Tipper. 1995. "Community forest Management and Carbon Sequestration: A Feasibility Study from Chiapas, Mexico." *Interciencia,* 20:6, pp.409–416.

DTZ Pieda. 2000. "An Evaluation of FRP's Carbon Sequestration Project in Southern Mexico." Consulting Report for Department for International Development. London: DTZ Pieda (processed).

Hellier, G., M.H. Castillo, and R. Tipper. 2002. "The Causes of Land Use Change and CO_2 Emissions from Chiapas, Southern Mexico." Submitted to *Mitigation and Adaptation Strategies for Global Change.*

Watson, R.T., I.R. Noble, B. Bolin, N.H. Ravindranath, D.J. Verardo, and D.J. Dokken (eds.). 2000. *Land Use, Land-Use Change, and Forestry.* Special Report of the Intergovernmental Panel on Climate Change. Cambridge: Cambridge University Press.

Chapter 13

Investing in the Environmental Services of Australian Forests

David Brand

There is a growing recognition that forests have a key role to play in addressing the environmental challenges of the 21st century – global climate change, the conservation of biodiversity, and the reversal of land and water resource degradation. Yet forests continue to be lost and degraded, and opportunities for reforestation to address these key environmental issues are unrealized, largely because the value of environmental services provided by forests are not remunerated (Brand, 2001). However, the multilateral international negotiations on the Kyoto Protocol to the United Nations Framework Convention on Climate Change (UNFCCC) have provided a major opportunity to price and trade an important environmental service from forests: carbon sequestration.

This Chapter discusses work being undertaken by the Hancock Natural Resource Group's (HNRG) New Forests Program to develop new instruments that will contribute to addressing this problem. These instruments respond to the growing demand for tools to assist business in managing greenhouse gas (GHG) emissions. In particular, corporations in the energy, minerals, transport, construction, and manufacturing sectors have an identified need for strategic investments to assist them in managing their emissions of GHGs. The New Forests Program aims to provide investors with a portfolio of reforestation projects that will systematically and cost-effectively sequester carbon dioxide (CO_2) from the atmosphere. The investments can be seen as 'natural infrastructure funds', as they seek to re-establish forests that will contribute to climate change, biodiversity conservation, and the reversal of land degradation, as well as providing long-term wood or bio-energy products. The design of these investments is important, as the future conservation of the world's ecosystems is heavily reliant on our ability to establish forms of investment that replenish or conserve the environment, rather than degrading it. The focus of this Chapter is the Australian situation, in which the commercial opportunity and environmental imperative for this type of investment are particularly significant.

ENVIRONMENTAL SERVICES FROM AUSTRALIAN FORESTS

Australia is a biologically unique continent, having evolved in isolation over approximately 60 million years. It represents the 'Gondwanan' flora and fauna, including a range of approximately 700 eucalyptus tree species, kangaroos, wombats, platypuses, kookaburras, and many other well-known endemic species. The continent is generally dry and subject to substantial cyclical climatic variation including the El Niño Southern Oscillation (ENSO).

The establishment of permanent European settlements in Australia beginning in 1788 led to the introduction of large-scale European forms of agriculture as a dominant land management system. Over the past 200 years, approximately 95 million ha of forest and woodland vegetation have been cleared for pastoral grazing and agricultural cropping. Even in recent times, Australia has continued to clear native vegetation in order to expand agricultural production. As a result, Australia's forest and land use sector was a net emitter of CO_2 in 1990, the baseline year of the Kyoto Protocol. About 15–20 per cent of Australia's GHG emissions arise from the on-going clearance of forests and woodlands (Australian Greenhouse Office, 2001). Dryland salinity, caused by this deforestation, continues to threaten millions of hectares of productive farmland (Murray–Darling Basin Commission, 1999).

The result of these trends is a continent facing major environmental challenges, including the following:

- a depleted carbon pool, where huge quantities of vegetation have been oxidized into the atmosphere;
- a destabilized hydrological system, where the loss of vegetation transpiration in the landscape is leading to rising water tables and the leaching of salts, brought from deep in the soil profile into rivers and other freshwater supplies (AFFA, 2001); and
- a substantial colonization of the Australian biota by exotic plants and animals, including cane toads, rabbits, cats, pigs, camels, horses, foxes, dogs, camphor laurel, scotch broom, bitou brush, lantana, and willows, leading to the disruption of native ecosystems and threatening biological diversity.

In the past these issues were either ignored or simply accepted as an undesirable but inevitable consequence of development. However, these problems are growing, together with public recognition of their significance.

DEVELOPING MARKETS FOR FOREST ENVIRONMENTAL SERVICES IN AUSTRALIA

Despite the urgency of the problems, Australian federal and state governments are patently unable to allocate sufficient funding to the task of addressing them, given competing priorities such as public health and education, and public reluctance to accept major tax increases. A more promising option is to mobilize private capital. Private investment in forests has previously been difficult to justify in Australia, as the long rotation periods required and relatively low internal rates of return made it hard for forestry to compete with alternative assets. However, investments that can provide a cash flow from environmental services and still offer long-term, stable timber revenues may be much more attractive.

The HNRG New Forests Program has been a pioneer in efforts to meet the challenge of creating new positive incentives for vegetation conservation and reforestation in Australia. HRNG undertook market research to assess market demand for financial products related to carbon sequestration. Based on the results of that research, HNRG announced its intention to establish the New Forests Program and to design investment products related to carbon sequestration and other environmental services of forests.

The ultimate goal is to establish investment products that will assemble a portfolio of different forests with varying profiles of carbon sequestration, land and water rehabilitation benefits, timber production, and other returns. These investments can pool the carbon credits and establish multiple cash or benefit flows for the investor.

Several recent projects have invested directly in reforestation in Australia as a basis for enhancing carbon sequestration. These projects are significant, as they may point toward a different model of forestry investment in which carbon sequestration provides a benefit stream during the years when the forest is growing, while periodic timber revenue carries the forest investment into the future.

The Kyoto Protocol rules, particularly the provisions of Article 3.3, are an important stimulus to this new financial mechanism. Article 3.3 requires national governments in the industrialized Annex 1 countries to account for afforestation, reforestation, and deforestation events occurring since 1990. The Bonn agreement in 2001 confirmed that projects eligible for credits against agreed national CO_2 emission targets would include those where a land use change from non-forest to forest had occurred.

While these rules create the possibility of using forests to sequester carbon, they also impose restrictions. The accounting methodology to be used is based on the stock change approach, in which carbon stocks increase with forest growth but are reduced by timber harvesting (see Figure 13.1). The chart shows cumulative tonnes of CO_2 equivalents sequestered per hectare in each year (1997–2007). Note the relative contribution of the stem, crown, and roots to the overall carbon budget and the effect of thinning and final harvest on sequestered carbon stocks. This means that while forests are growing, they act as net carbon sinks. Harvesting timber, on the other hand, will reduce carbon stocks and is therefore treated as a re-emission to the atmosphere.

To account for this cyclical pattern of carbon uptake and emission, carbon stock management will probably be pooled across several reforestation projects

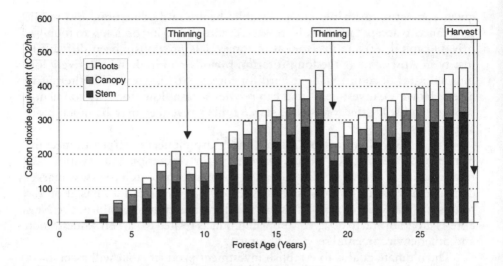

Source: data provided by State Forests of NSW

Figure 13.1 *Illustration of the carbon stock change accounting method for a typical eucalyptus reforestation project*

characterized by varying cycles and silvicultural regimes. This is illustrated in Figure 13.2, which shows how a carbon pool can integrate the various types of forests and silvicultural regimes into an integrated carbon accounting system. On the righthand side the carbon accounts are converted to stock change accounting, and can be smoothed through the banking of excess credits (expressed here in tonnes of CO_2 equivalents).

Pioneering efforts have been made in Australia to support the commercialization of these environmental services from forests. In late 1998, the New South Wales (NSW) state parliament passed carbon rights legislation that allows investors to record ownership of the rights to carbon sequestration in forests on land titles. This then allows separate ownership of the land, the trees, and the carbon rights. Most recently, in January 2002, the NSW government indicated that, as part of its goal of reducing net greenhouse gas emissions by 5 per cent per capita from 1989–1990 levels, it would impose a penalty of 10–20 Australian dollars (A\$) per tonne of excess CO_2 emissions. The NSW government also indicated that carbon sequestration credits could be used as offsets against this commitment and released a detailed position paper on the carbon credit accounting, registry, and trading systems (Ministry of Energy and Utilities, 2001).

It is also important from a socioeconomic perspective that land use changes take place in areas where marginal cropping or grazing activities are currently occurring. Changing these areas back into forestry can help to diversify regional economies and will increase the long-term economic product in many areas.

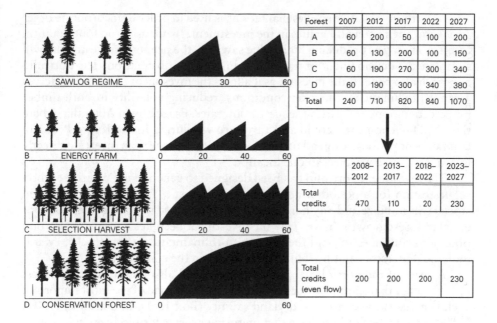

Forest	2007	2012	2017	2022	2027
A	60	200	50	100	200
B	60	130	200	100	150
C	60	190	270	300	340
D	60	190	300	340	380
Total	240	710	820	840	1070

	2008–2012	2013–2017	2018–2022	2023–2027
Total credits	470	110	20	230

Total credits (even flow)	200	200	200	230

Figure 13.2 *Constructing a carbon pool*

THE HANCOCK NEW FORESTS PROGRAM: OVERVIEW

The Hancock New Forests Program is an early attempt to introduce this new class of 'natural infrastructure investments'. The program is based on the premise that we can structure investment products that combine carbon sequestration and other environmental credit streams with traditional wood product or bio-energy markets. An Australian fund illustrates how the new investments operate.

Hancock New Forests Australia (HNFA) was publicly announced in July 2001. The fund is structured as an unlisted company and shares are offered to sophisticated investors such as corporations or institutional investors. The fund is being marketed at the time of writing and has not yet been closed to subscription.

HNFA is designed to use the equity raised in the company to invest in a portfolio of native species reforestation projects across Australia. Its objectives are to establish or acquire reforestation projects that systematically sequester CO_2 from the atmosphere, and which have the additional potential for long-term appreciation in the value of the forests. The appreciation in value is based on the discounted future cash-flow from sustainable timber or energy revenues. As the forests grow and approach the point at which wood products may be harvested, their value increases.

A portfolio of native species plantations is used in order to incorporate other social and environmental values in the investment. By focusing on long rotation forestry, aiming at producing high value sawlogs, the proposed investments will stimulate the development of regional industry and job creation. The portfolio approach also benefits the investor, as it allows the investment to be spread across a range of climatic and market conditions, reducing volatility in both timber market conditions and carbon sequestration rates. Especially in Australia, where the ENSO phenomenon could affect tree growth during future Kyoto Protocol commitment periods, a spread of assets is a better strategy than investing directly in a single forestry project in one location.

The investment portfolio has been designed to generate net positive carbon sequestration for a period of approximately 20 years. After this point carbon stocks will stabilize and any harvest will be constrained so that it is less than or equal to forest growth. In this way the investment becomes a perpetual carbon pool, and continues to hold the obligation to maintain carbon stocks, even if individual investors exit by selling their shares in the company.

As part of the portfolio approach, HNFA will also seek to include forest benefits other than carbon sequestration. In Australia, one of the most important such benefits is the control of dryland salinity (Box 13.1). In addition, HNFA will seek to establish a baseline and monitoring process for biodiversity conservation and will work toward the development of a tradable biodiversity index. The ultimate goal is to have systems to benchmark carbon sequestration, water quality, and biodiversity conservation values at a landscape scale.

To manage the carbon sequestration credits, and potentially other environmental credits, HNFA will create a pooling mechanism. Carbon accounting will occur across all projects and balance future growth with timber harvesting. The aim is to create a relatively consistent yield of carbon credits on an annual basis. Current projections indicate that the carbon yield will be in the order of 43,000 tonnes per annum over 20 years, for every A$10 million invested (US$5 million).

The HNFA will contract with local forestry service providers to establish and manage the forests. The local service providers will be expected to work with the surrounding community to establish a framework of performance measures for each project. The goal is to achieve investments that are environmentally, socially, and commercially sustainable.

The HNFA will have all the features of a well-structured institutional investment. Investors will receive quarterly statements of expenditure and fully audited annual accounts. In addition, the forests will be subject to independent third party evaluation each year, so that investors can book the value of the investment over time. The carbon credit price will also be marked to market conditions each year to facilitate booking the carbon credit value. This should lead toward the concept of full environmental accounting, allowing businesses to measure and report on liabilities and assets related to GHG emissions and other environmental issues. Pricing of these environmental commodities ultimately leads to environmental management becoming part of the corporate bottom line.

Box 13.1 MARKETS FOR SALINITY CONTROL

The HNFA also intends to establish reforestation projects in the Murray–Darling Basin region that will assist with a rebalancing of hydrological conditions in key areas. These projects will be designed to pilot the concept of salinity credits, in which private investors may be paid for the environmental services provided by reforestation in areas previously cleared of trees.

A market-based approach to revegetation for dryland salinity will require a more regional approach. Australian state and federal governments have agreed that dryland salinity is a national issue (AFFA, 2001). Significant resources are needed to reverse the trend toward rising water tables and associated soil salinity and leaching of salt into watercourses. It has been estimated that anywhere between 1 million and 9 million hectares would need to be reforested in the Murray–Darling Basin region alone in order to stop the spread of salinity. This would cost somewhere in the order of A\$6–60 billion (US\$3–31 billion). A recent press release by the Australian Conservation Foundation and the National Farmers Federation called on the Australian government to provide A\$60 billion (US\$31 billion) to combat dryland salinity over the next ten years (Australian Conservation Foundation, 2002).

Precipitation rates in the Murray–Darling Basin range from over 1000mm per annum in the headwaters down to as little as 50mm in western NSW (near Broken Hill). Reforestation programs should be targeted to areas of medium rainfall, between 500–800mm per annum. In these areas the deep-rooted trees will reduce recharge of groundwater levels, but not transpire the potential runoff needed by downstream water users. Yet there is limited experience with forestry below 700mm of rainfall, and even less experience with commercial reforestation in these regions. The ENSO cycle also means that there will be periods of crippling drought during the life of any tree plantation, and therefore species with good drought tolerance must be used.

PROJECT DESIGN

HNFA will seek to comply with Article 3.3 of the Kyoto Protocol as a basis for investment decisions. While the ultimate ratification and entry into force of the Protocol remains uncertain at the time of writing, there is relatively widespread support for reforestation activities as a credit against emissions. In particular, where the revenue provided by carbon credits can encourage reforestation of degraded land, it creates additional environmental benefits.

The provisions of Article 3.3 will require each property to be assessed in terms of its land use in 1990. Only areas of land that were clear of forest can contribute to the stock-change accounting. Areas that were forested in 1990 and subsequently cleared can be determined by aerial photography or high-resolution satellite imagery from 1990 and removed from the accounting. Remaining areas can then be identified in a geographic information system and linked to models that will project carbon stocks over time for each plantation area.

The modeling of carbon stocks for each area will be carried out using simulation models linked to traditional forest inventory. Forest mensuration has developed methods to project the growth and yield of the bole of the tree. Allometric equations can expand these models to address the growth in whole tree biomass. Finally these biomass estimates can be converted to carbon stocks by the use of specific gravity measures and knowledge of the molecular carbon content of trees. Specific gravity can range from as low as 300kg per cubic meter (m^3) for species like aspen to 1000kg/m^3 for heavier species, such as the dry zone Eucalyptus species (River red gum or Ironbark, for example). Molecular carbon content is relatively constant, varying between about 47 and 53 per cent of the dry weight of the tree.

Once areas have been reforested, a regular inventory system will be used to measure the growth of the trees and to confirm and update the carbon accounting models on a regular basis. It will be necessary to undertake detailed inventory and third party verification at the beginning and end of each commitment period, in the event that the Kyoto Protocol comes into force. These inventories allow the establishment of baselines for the stock-change accounting in each commitment period.

At this point there is no officially sanctioned registry of carbon stocks anywhere in the world. However, as governments pursue policies to encourage voluntary action on climate change and ultimately to regulate GHG emissions, the legal aspects of carbon sequestration must be addressed. The key aspects of creating a homogenous and fungible carbon credit include:

- definition of the product, including the ability to own legal title or rights to sequestration;
- standardized methods of measuring and accounting for carbon stocks;
- independent processes for verifying carbon accounts and accrediting verifiers; and
- mechanisms to serialize (uniquely number), vintage (identify the year in which a tonne of carbon becomes active and usable), register (track the ownership and status of each credit), and certificate (provide a tradable instrument) individual tonnes as tradable credits.

The HNRG has been active in contributing to the design and implementation of public policy in this area. In implementing programs like the HNFA, many of the issues relating to carbon sequestration can be identified and addressed in a practical way. In this sense there is an expectation that the projects being established in the fund will contribute to the development of national and international policy related to carbon sequestration.

FINANCIAL PERFORMANCE

As an equity investment, the HNRG does not guarantee the financial returns or yield of HNFA carbon sequestration investments. However, to provide assistance to potential investors evaluating the fund, a financial model has been constructed to illustrate the financial and carbon credit returns from a hypothetical portfolio of Australian reforestation projects. The model uses a set of projects based in Queensland, NSW, Victoria, and South Australia to assess the potential performance of a set of forestry investments in the future.

Each project being modeled is based on data from local forestry service providers, including land costs, reforestation costs, growth rates, management fees, and timber market prices. From the growth and yield models, the HNRG has also calculated the potential carbon sequestration rates. The model also provides a profit-and-loss and tax calculation, so that potential investors can see the potential internal rates of return after tax.

The overall fund performance will depend on the nature of the portfolio of investments actually achieved. The nominal internal rate of return is forecast at 10.6 per cent per annum after tax, calculated over a 50-year time frame. However, this rate of return assumes a zero value of carbon credits. If carbon credits, calculated as tonnes of CO_2 equivalent, traded at a price of about US$5 per tonne, the nominal internal rate of return would increase to 12 per cent per annum after tax (assuming future inflation rates of approximately 3 per cent per annum in Australia).

The carbon credit yield from the fund is expected to be in the order of 40,000–45,000 tonnes of CO_2 equivalent per annum for 20 years, for every A$10 million investment (US$5.2 million). The carbon credit distribution will occur from years 3 to 23 in the life of the fund and then be stabilized. Again, the carbon models indicate that this is a sustainable level of carbon stocks in the pool, but it will depend on the particular mix of projects acquired or established by HNFA.

The concept of the HNFA is that over time the nature of the investors is likely to change. As the fund ceases to distribute further carbon credits, corporate investors may exit and institutional investors may purchase blocks of shares to gain the cash-flow from timber harvesting. It is important to note, however, that the HNFA is structured as a perpetual entity and will continue to be managed on a sustainable basis, protecting the carbon stocks into the future. In the event of the company being wound up and the assets liquidated, there would be an assumed liability to discharge or replace the carbon credits that had been distributed.

How the fund is managed in the future will ultimately depend on the relative market values of timber, energy products, carbon sequestration, and other environmental services. The manager will in all cases seek to act in the interest of the investors. In this regard, the HNRG has a fiduciary responsibility to investors in the HNFA and will provide annually audited financial statements and independently assessed annual valuations of the assets. This assists investors in evaluating the performance of their investments and provides transparency in the quality of management by HNRG.

FUTURE DIRECTIONS

There is a growing acceptance that natural environmental services must be priced to be effectively protected. While governments can undertake regulation to protect forests or create additional protected areas, the sheer size and scope of human impacts on forests will inevitably lead to a continued impact on the environment, whether through atmospheric change, land and water degradation, or continued homogenization of ecosystems through weeds and feral animals.

One of the key impediments to the commercialization of environmental services is the lack of definition, accreditation, and registration of these goods and services. It is often difficult to decide whether there should be a market first and a product second, or vice versa; but in this case, there cannot be a market without a definition of the product. In the case of environmental services, it is not enough to define the service; it must also be structured into a product that can be brought effectively to the market.

There is widespread optimism that carbon sequestration may be the first of these international environmental commodities. Significant work has occurred to define the nature of the product, and there is growing agreement on the procedure for carbon accounting. Financial products developed by the Hancock New Forests Program will also provide mechanisms to attract investment in enhancing these environmental services. However, more work by governments is needed to facilitate continued progress in this area. Governments can establish legislation to regulate and register the trade in these new products. Governmental endorsement will increase the security of the buyer and will raise the value to the seller.

Once these markets are functioning and price signals and forward price curves are established, we will see institutional capital take a lead role in providing services such as carbon sequestration, watershed management, and biodiversity enhancement. If these funds can compete with investments that draw down or degrade natural capital to provide returns, then our environmental problems will begin to diminish. Ultimately, however, we will probably see an integration of these environmental investments with the traditional provision of raw materials and public services like energy, water, and consumer goods.

REFERENCES

Agriculture, Fisheries and Forestry Australia (AFFA). 2001. *Our Vital Resources. A National Action Plan for Salinity and Water Quality in Australia.* Canberra: Agriculture, Fisheries and Forestry Australia.

Australian Conservation Foundation. 2002. "Conservationists, Fishers and Scientists Unite to Stop Truckloads of Salt." Press Release. Melbourne: Australian Conservation Foundation.

Australian Greenhouse Office (AGO). 2001. *National Carbon Accounting System: A Progress Report.* Canberra: AGO.

Brand, D.G. 2001. "Mechanisms to Encourage Private Capital Investment in the Environmental Services of Forests." Paper presented at the International Workshop on financing sustainable forest management, Oslo, Norway, 22–25 January, 2001.

Ministry of Energy and Utilities. 2001. "Greenhouse Gas Emissions from Electricity Supplied in NSW. Framework for the Use of Carbon Sequestration to Offset Emissions." Sydney: Ministry of Energy and Utilities.

Murray-Darling Basin Commission. 1999. *The Salinity Audit of the Murray–Darling Basin: A 100-year Perspective.* Canberra: Murray–Darling Basin Commission.

Chapter 14

Insuring Forest Sinks

Phil Cottle and Charles Crosthwaite-Eyre[1]

For forestry to participate in the emerging global carbon market, new investment is needed in projects that demonstrate rigorous principles of carbon management. Such initiatives will require investment that can only be justified on the basis of long-term financial returns competitive with alternative uses of capital. Forestry projects have unusual and longer-term risk management requirements compared with most other insurance business. But while there is well-developed market for conventional forestry insurance, the insurance of long-term projects involving carbon offsets poses a more difficult challenge. This Chapter outlines some of the issues involved in managing and insuring risk in forest-based carbon projects, and illustrates these issues in the context of the Noel Kempff Mercado Climate Action Project in Bolivia.

Risk management is a critical issue for all aspects of the forest sector. Clearsighted efforts to alleviate risk can confer a wide range of economic, environmental, and social benefits. In the same way that the forest sector is developing innovative mechanisms for carbon management, the insurance and financial sectors are generating new products to manage risk in a competitive and cost-efficient way.

Forest projects developed under the rules of the Kyoto Protocol will need to produce greenhouse gas (GHG) mitigation benefits that are real, measurable, additional, verifiable, and consistent with sustainable development. Moreover, the cost of emission reductions in forestry must be competitive with alternative means of achieving such reductions – for example, through improvements in industrial processes. These projects will demand a new level of financial and project security if additional revenue is to be realized from the sale of carbon offsets. While the increased management requirements of existing forest certification systems reduce the risks associated with forestry operations, they are unable to shield projects against some risks, which could threaten environmental integrity as well as their financial viability. Where carbon offsets are to be sold under one of the flexible mechanisms envisaged under the Kyoto Protocol, such as the Clean Development Mechanism (CDM) or Joint Implementation (JI), and particularly where these offsets are sold forward (banked in advance), the potential benefits of risk transfer and insurance may be considerable.

INSURANCE MARKETS AND FOREST CARBON

To our knowledge there are no insurance products currently available to investors that specifically cover the risks associated with sequestration of carbon dioxide (CO_2) as a source of tradable emissions reductions. While there has been limited trade in emission reductions, no insurance products guaranteeing delivery or providing financial indemnity on forward transactions of emission reductions have been developed. Financial indemnity covers are occasionally available in other sectors. Generic physical loss or damage policies are being written to include specific national emissions trading issues, as international and national emission trading policy emerges. Insurance covers and solutions are also likely to be developed on a project-by-project basis. Consequently, risk is currently borne by project sponsors or their financiers (to the extent that such risk is taken into account by banks in determining debt provisions).

Since the Kyoto Protocol was signed at the third Conference of the Parties (COP 3) to the United Nations Framework Convention on Climate Change (UNFCCC) in 1997, the insurance industry has been working to develop risk transfer instruments for the different kinds of climate change projects that may be eligible under the Protocol. However, inter-governmental negotiations on national emission reduction targets, timetables, and eligible activities have proved extremely contentious. The uncertainty increased with the failure of countries to reach agreement at COP 6 in November 2000, followed by the United States' outright rejection of the Kyoto Protocol.

As a result of this uncertainty about the eventual eligibility of forest-based carbon sequestration projects, many investors shelved plans to develop projects in which a key revenue source was expected to be the sale of forest carbon offsets. The insurance sector also found it increasingly difficult to justify major investments of time and personnel, especially where forest carbon was concerned.

More recent agreements, in Bonn in July 2001 and subsequently in Marrakesh in November 2001, have revitalized the process and encouraged developers and insurers to renew their interest, although the role of forestry in the CDM still remains uncertain.

WHAT ARE THE RISKS OF FOREST CARBON PROJECTS?

All economic activity confronts risk. In general, the risks facing forest-based carbon projects can be grouped into political, institutional, trading, and project risks. Figure 14.1 summarizes the different types of risk associated with forest carbon projects. It is widely recognized that the institutional and political risk

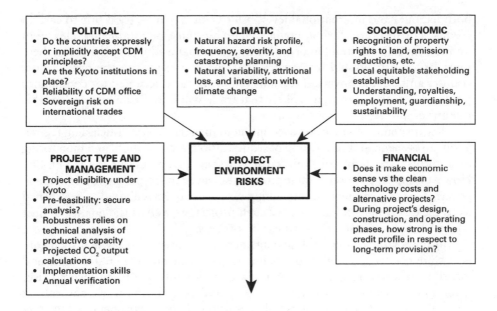

Figure 14.1 *Risks facing forest carbon projects*

element of climate projects is common to all investment within the carbon sector, while trading and project risk are specific to particular initiatives.

Political risk

Political risk encompasses the uncertainties related to the ratification of the Kyoto Protocol as well as individual nations' reputation in the financial world for governmental stability, consistency in respect of international obligations, legal structures, and the domestic financial frameworks in which investors operate. Political risk insurance is a relatively mature sector. Several specialist agencies generate political risk ratings for individual countries. However, such ratings do not normally reflect the risks associated with ratification of the Kyoto Protocol, which are not generally insurable as they are either 'off' or 'on'. Political risk premiums reflect national credit ratings and the likelihood of governments altering or acting outside the law with respect to property rights and repatriation of profits. National political and financial stability has a significant impact on the ability and appetite of insurers to enter into long-term contracts. Conventional political insurance policies are therefore often limited to a few months' duration.

Institutional risk

Forestry activities linked to GHG trading require a long-term commitment. They also require supportive legislative and economic frameworks for investors, at both national and international levels. One critical issue is legal title to carbon credits. For insurers, carbon credit ownership must be established clearly in domestic law. In addition, in order for international trading to take place, there must be an institutional framework that encompasses both the project host country and foreign buyers, if carbon credits are to be accepted for compliance purposes. For this reason, it is likely that trade will initially be bilateral, as this minimizes uncertainties for the buyer.

The procedures for carbon accounting in forestry projects (including registration, assessment, and verification of sequestration, accreditation, and monitoring of auditors) are defined by specialist working groups under the UNFCCC. However, implementation of these procedures will be the responsibility of national governments. Governments representing potential buyers will need to be satisfied as to the environmental integrity of each project, as well as the quality of host country institutions and the verification process.

Insurers will consider risk management and transfer only when such core issues are resolved. Where projects intend to sell carbon credits forward, and insurers are asked to guarantee to replace credits lost due to an insured risk, insurers will need to be satisfied that they understand the precise nature of a replacement credit, in terms of its utility as a compliance instrument and the prevailing accounting standards and practices. The greater the fungibility between different sources of carbon credit replacement, the greater the likelihood that such a guarantee will be offered by insurers.

Trading risk

Much of the anticipated emissions trading will be conducted as forward contracts enabling companies with emission constraints and obligations to lock in the costs of compliance. Depending on the contract structures, there may be significant differences in contract liability between forward trading of emission allowances (that is, corporate caps) and project-related emission reductions. It may be assumed that trading of allowances (government allocations) has a lower risk of non-delivery than emission reductions. In forward trading of emission reductions, buyers carry the risks associated with non-delivery of reductions due to sponsor insolvency, project failure, or under-performance. Regional and geographic risk profiles, financial strength, and creditworthiness of project sponsors, along with performance risk associated with the technology and project design, will need to be part of the pricing process and buyer risk assessment. Risk for non-delivery of emission reductions due to poor project performance should be allocated in the sale and purchase contract and reflected in the price. Buyers will naturally favor competitive emission reductions with relatively attractive risk-adjusted prices.

The overall risk of non-compliance to which the company remains exposed after entering trading agreements involving allowances or emission reductions (that is, residual corporate compliance risk) will be reflected in the strength of their emission-reduction strategy and their trading portfolio. These risks can be mitigated by having a spread of reliable suppliers of allowances and project partners, increasing the probability that contracted emission allowances or reductions will be delivered as contracted.

Project risk

On a global scale natural hazards are a constant threat. Fire, wind, pest, disease, animals, earthquakes, and socioeconomic factors are the main causes of forest loss worldwide. Forest managers and sector professionals understand the nature of forest risk very well, but this is not the same as being able to quantify the severity and frequency of such risks.

- Fire is the dominant cause of loss to insurers in most forest zones throughout the world. Although the impact of fire on large forestry operations is not necessarily catastrophic, it can be devastating for small forestry projects. Thus while average loss rates appear to be low, a single event can deal a fatal blow to an unprotected business.
- Wind is a catastrophic peril with very different frequency and severity to fire. Losses due to wind vary greatly from country to country, with mid- to high-latitude regions more risk-prone. Wind can lead to major losses of standing timber, which can represent significant emissions of GHG under carbon accounting rules. Moreover, in addition to the immediate impact of lost timber, dry windblown wood presents ideal conditions for fires and insect outbreaks, threatening forests that are not affected by the storms themselves.

CASE STUDY: NOEL KEMPFF MERCADO CLIMATE ACTION PROJECT

In 1997 a unique partnership was forged between the Government of Bolivia, the Friends of Nature Foundation (FAN) in Bolivia, The Nature Conservancy (TNC), two US-based electric utility companies (American Electric Power and PacifiCorp), and a major international petroleum company (BP Amoco). They agreed to work together to protect nearly 4 million acres of threatened tropical forests in the department of Santa Cruz, Bolivia, for at least 30 years. The main purpose of the project – which is located in the Noel Kempff Mercado National Park – is to sequester CO_2 and store carbon that would otherwise be released as a result of logging activities in the area. At the same time, the project preserves one of the richest and most biologically diverse ecosystems in the world and fosters sustainable development in local communities. It is the largest project of its kind in the world and serves as a showcase for an innovative and cost-effective approach to abating GHG emissions. In this section, we describe how this forestry carbon project was analyzed in terms of potential risk management and insurance.

The Noel Kempff Mercado Climate Action Project (NKMCAP) aims to avoid emissions of 7–10 millions tons of carbon, or 25–36 million tons of CO_2, during its 30-year life. Prior to the project, the park was under imminent and demonstrable threat from logging and conversion to agriculture. The key generator of carbon offsets within the project is thus the termination of existing logging concessions, together with measures to ensure that logging is not simply displaced to other areas.

The project has several different components, including park expansion and protection, ecotourism, local community development, a for-profit venture to generate revenue for the park (Canopy Botanicals), monitoring and verification activities, and support to the Government of Bolivia's climate change program. Direct cash contributions from industry and grants from the TNC and other sponsors totaled US$10 million for the project life, with an agreed annual contribution from the GOB of US$250,000. The project has been approved by the governments of both the United States and Bolivia. The major partners and their involvement are summarized in Table 14.1.

The role of insurance in NKMCAP

In order to be commercially and politically viable over the long term, the NKMCAP project needs to achieve a minimum output of carbon offsets. Insurance could help to guarantee this objective.[2] One potential benefit of insuring carbon output is the increased market value of certified carbon offsets that are guaranteed for delivery by insurance. Another is that insurance enables managers to set aside a smaller buffer to allow for uncertain risks, thereby reducing costs and maximizing income in the short term.

Appropriate insurance for NKMCAP would not need to cover every potential event that could reduce carbon offsets on an annual basis. This would be prohibitively expensive, probably impossible, and not very useful, since maximum annual performance (the volume of carbon offset production) is not the critical issue. What is critical is performance over time.

Identifying perils

In order to meet the project objectives, NKMCAP managers need to consider all significant risks that could affect carbon output. These include: fire and allied perils; pest and disease; wind; drought (accumulated water/soil moisture deficits); theft of timber; earthquakes; malicious damage; strikes, riots, and civil commotion; political and socioeconomic risks (action by government or local peoples); and credit risk.

Hypothetical scenarios can be used to determine how success may be thwarted, and where further management or resources are required to reduce this exposure. Where there is an economic or practical limit to what can be done by the project to mitigate risk, external risk transfer through insurance may be a feasible

Table 14.1 *Noel Kempff Mercado Climate Action Project*

Partner	Activity/interest	Project investment	Project benefit
American Electric Power System (AEPS)	Power generation with the United States. Participant in the United States Department of Energy Voluntary Climate Challenge Program	AEPS and TNC undertook to raise the bulk of US$7 million CDM project registration and verification costs shared	5% carbon offset over-rider as recompense for its contribution to the project. Of the remaining 95%, the split is given below (as 100% of the 95%)
BP AmericaPacifiCorp	Public relations benefits Experience in this type of project	Contributed to the US$7 million total required	2% carbon offsets 49% carbon offsets
The Nature Conservancy (TNC)	To identify, protect, and maintain the best examples of communities, ecosystems and endangered species in the natural world	Establish effective park management system. US$0.8 million grants; US$1 million to be raised from sponsors	Achievement of mission Cost-effective use of funds Credibility
Fundacion Amigos de la Naturaleza (FAN)	Assist the GOB in preserving national biological diversity Management and administrative authority over park for 10 years granted by GOB	Establish effective park management system	Operational costs paid plus successful outcome of the project Income from ecotourism
Government of Bolivia	Experience in this type of project International recognition of environmental activities Socioeconomic development of remote peoples of Bolivia Development of appropriate carbon institutions	Provides the forest Provides US$2.5 million annually	49% carbon offsets Political benefits of participation Socioeconomic development of remote communities
Bolivians living in or near the park	Continued economic development and ability to make a living based on the park or its products	Possible termination of logging and other activities in the park	Improved economic and social standard of living

alternative solution. A key decision criterion will be the relative costs of external risk transfer versus internal actions to achieve the same level of protection. Project managers also need to consider whether in-house measures can provide protection against low probability but potentially catastrophic risks.

NKMCAP documents provide some estimates of the probability of different risks on an annual basis, and their likely impact on carbon output. This information feeds into an estimate of the total carbon output of the project over its lifetime. Interestingly, while in 1998 the project was expected to provide 18 million tonnes of sequestered carbon, by 2001 the figure published on the project website had been reduced to about 10 million tonnes. This reflects a reassessment of the risk profile of the project.

One of the major risks facing NKMCAP is that illegal logging continues within or outside the project boundaries and that consequently timber is lost to the project. This risk may be summarized as theft, and the loss measured in terms of a reduced yield of carbon offsets. Theft is unlikely to result in major losses unless there is no internal protection whatsoever. However, project documents reveal that the felling of a given volume of timber leads to the destruction of 2.48 times that volume among adjacent biomass. Hence unrestrained theft could affect annual production of carbon credits by several percentage points.

A related concern is that logging may simply be transferred to other locations outside the project area. Such 'leakage' would imply a loss of carbon credits to NKMCAP. Similarly, there may be some loss of forestland to agriculture in surrounding areas. The project's socioeconomic programs and improved monitoring of forest boundaries are designed to prevent the latter, while control of external logging will require the cooperation of local government agencies.

Another major risk confronting NKMCAP is the loss of timber due to forest fire. In other parts of the world, fire affects native forest at annual rates of between 0.1 per cent and 0.5 per cent of total area, on average. The risk of drought is also considered potentially significant but more difficult to assess. One approach would be to analyze the long-term effects of drought in terms of reduced biomass growth rates or higher than average tree mortality, leading to increased carbon emissions. Other natural hazards were considered to pose smaller risks to the project.

Note that with many perils, while mean annual losses may be small, catastrophic events do occur. Consultation with local people or a review of historical records may indicate just how extensive major loss events can be. In respect of tree mortality due to forest fires, wind, pests, or disease, it is important to avoid further losses when salvaging dead trees (if this is permitted to generate a mitigating source of income). Salvage must be conducted in such a way that the rapid recovery of the flora through natural regeneration is not hampered.

In addition to natural hazards, there is a measure of political risk associated with NKMCAP. Changes in the government's attitude to the project could be catastrophic if, for example, licenses, concessions, or central funding are restricted or revoked. While the Government of Bolivia has undertaken to fund the running costs of the original park area during the life of the project, this funding could be reduced or terminated unless the project is seen to be making progress toward its aims. The likelihood of such funding cuts may increase when project management reverts to the Government of Bolivia after ten years.

Finally, there is the possibility that buyers of carbon offsets will become insolvent and fail to pay the contracted price on delivery. This trading risk must also be managed.

Insuring the perils of NKMCAP

In order for a particular risk to be insurable, it must be a measurable event, unaffected by the behavior of the insured, which may or may not occur, and the likelihood of which can be predicted with some accuracy. The accuracy with which specific risks can be predicted is highly variable. While it may be possible to insure against certain events using information about their frequency in similar environments elsewhere, the resulting estimates of risk may be incorrect, leading to inefficient pricing of risk transfer.

Certain risks can only be insured when well-defined 'triggers' are agreed with the insured beforehand. A trigger is an agreed and specified set of circumstances which, when they occur, become an insurable event. Triggers are often used for policies covering political or credit risk, pest, disease, or drought, which are otherwise difficult to insure. For instance, political 'events' tend not to happen suddenly, but instead develop over a period of time, during which risk-reduction activities (negotiations) must occur in order to minimize potential losses. In general, it is not possible to insure against long-term changes in government policy and there is little that forest managers can do to mitigate such risks. One practical option is to seek partial risk guarantees, which are offered by certain global financial institutions.[3] To give another example of triggers, pest and disease are always present in a forest, but may only cause losses when certain thresholds are exceeded. Such a threshold event may be caused by special climatic conditions, such as high humidity, high temperatures, or excessive and/or prolonged rainfall. In the latter case, climatic conditions could themselves be used as quantitative triggers agreed with insurers as a precursor to subsequent pest and disease losses.

Defining insurable interests

The 'insured interest' is the subject of an insurance contract. In the case of NKMCAP, this would represent a measure of performance of the project that determines the financial outcome for the insured entity (policy holder). Setting aside, for the present, who or what would be the insured entity for NKMCAP, we can identify a number of potential insured interests. In respect of carbon sequestration, these might include:

- volume of timber and/or carbon offset yield;
- value of the timber and/or carbon offsets;

- amortized cost of carbon credits per tonne over the project life (investment costs); or
- net present value of sales of carbon credits over the coming 30 years.

Other insured interests are beyond the scope of this Chapter, but include several environmental products and services, such as:

- start-up capital (investment costs to establish a legal foundation for the project);
- annual management budget;
- the forest timber itself;
- lost tourist income from ecotourism;
- loss of any downstream benefits such as water quality and flooding control;
- loss of biodiversity and genetic value;
- replacement value of amenities and equipment destroyed by an insured peril;
- costs of restoration of the project following a destructive event; and
- direct fire-fighting costs (over and above the annual protection budget).

Detailed consideration of different project performance measures is required to determine which of them best represent the interests of investors and hence need to be insured (that is, 'the insured interest'). Some of the items listed above are variations on a theme and any insurance would need to apply to just one, as double indemnity is not permitted. However, other items are complementary and could be the subject of separate sections within a single policy.

For example, insuring fire-fighting costs may be an effective way of protecting the forest once an adequate fire protection and warning system is in place. On spotting a fire such cover would enable project managers to call up the necessary extra resources without worrying about the size of the fire-fighting budget. This cover could sit alongside carbon offset insurance.

If the insured interest is carbon offset yield, losses may not be immediately measurable. Normally one would have to wait for annual monitoring and verification to determine whether there was a reduction in the carbon offsets created, any shortfall was due to the peril event, and if so the nature and magnitude of the loss.

Insured values

Insurers are normally flexible with respect to the method used to value clients' forestry enterprises. The key to valuation is that it follows a logical process, which can be explained, audited, and repeated. In the case of carbon credits it may be possible to adapt the methods commonly used to value timber, for instance:

- cumulative investment (production) costs up to the point of loss;
- current market value less the costs of marketing;

- net present value of future carbon credit sales; or
- estimated replacement costs.

Two of the methods listed above require information about the value of a carbon offset. This value is currently impossible to estimate, as there is no reliable carbon futures or spot market to enable price setting or risk hedging. While it may be possible to agree a price with an insurer, this price could turn out to be too low to compensate the project for potential loss, or too high, leading to a risk of perverse incentives ('moral hazard' and insurance fraud). The latter possibility would make any insurer uncomfortable, out of fear that losses would not be minimized in circumstances where the potential value of an insurance claim exceeds the market value of the underlying carbon offsets.

An alternative is to set artificial prices based on some known alternative, such as a carbon tax or penalties (fines) for non-compliance. In the US market for sulfur dioxide emissions permits, fines were US$2000/tonne for non-compliance with mandated emission limits. In the case of carbon offsets, however, penalties remain to be resolved. At COP 7 in Marrakesh, the penalties for non-compliance with Kyoto commitments were agreed at 130 per cent of the national non-compliance volume for participating Annex 1 countries. Unfortunately this does not answer the valuation issue.

In the absence of logically derived or known market prices, insured values may have to be based on the costs of production or replacement of carbon credits, or the means to produce them. Costs of production should include management and set-up costs as well as marginal costs, if true indemnity is to be obtained.

A CONCEPTUAL CARBON INSURANCE PRODUCT

The above discussion illustrates the difficulties of quantifying potential losses and identifying the insurable risks of forest carbon sinks. Moreover, NKMCAP also needs to consider the risk of non-payment by contracted purchasers of carbon offsets.

In the present circumstances, a practical insurance product would avoid the need to establish a value for carbon offsets. One approach would be to insure the volume of carbon offsets to be delivered to a buyer who has signed a forward contract, or who has bought a futures option. As the seller, NKMCAP has to guarantee such carbon deliveries at some specified date in the future. An insurance policy issued by a reputable insurer could add considerable value to the carbon offsets being sold by standardizing both risk and price.

Where precise risk cannot be quantified, it is especially important that insurers manage their exposure by pooling risks from a high quality, geographically dispersed portfolio. In this way they can spread political, credit, and natural hazard risks across a range of different environments. All projects in such an insurance portfolio should adhere (more or less) to the same technical and audit standards. Carbon baselines and sequestration rates need to be measured in a standard way to ensure that they are acceptable to buyers as compliance instruments. It follows that any guaranteed replacement offsets must have the same utility as compliance instruments to the insured. Unfortunately, until the international and national rules on emission trading are finalized this will be an insuperable problem, as it is not yet clear whether forestry offsets will be acceptable everywhere for compliance purposes.

Ultimately, insurers will need to manage their portfolio exposure to potential loss through the replacement of tradable emission reductions and offsets. An insurer may require that insured projects provide physical cover by reserving a proportion of total potential carbon offset yield to reflect aggregate project risk. In this way the insurer could replace carbon offsets claimed through insured losses from other projects. In time, the insurer may acquire a climate project fund itself and use its own carbon offsets to cover losses. Over many years, insurer liability would decline (total exposure falling as offsets are delivered) and it could allow a reduction in reserves and further sales of offsets. The number and selection of participants in any such facility will be critical to its performance and cost.

Most insurance contracts run for one year. In the case of political or credit risk, insurance may operate for only a few months. For other risks, a series of one-year contracts may be agreed, with cancellation or 'break' clauses to prevent either party being severely disadvantaged if conditions change dramatically. Occasionally insurers will agree to issue three-, five-, or eight-year continuous contracts.

An insurance contract effectively makes the insurance company liable for the whole contract period. For climate projects that seek to sell carbon offsets in the years 2008–2012, contracts written today will need to guarantee future delivery dates. Such long-term commitments are a concern not only to insurers but also for potential purchasers, politicians, and project managers. Which of the many parties to a contract will still be in existence by the end of the project? Current economic conditions show that even the most highly credit-rated corporations can fall from grace. High quality corporate debt can sink to junk-bond status almost overnight.

Following the World Trade Center disaster in September 2001, many insurers are even less inclined to accept long-term liabilities. However, rising premiums and more cautious risk rating, increased capitalization, possibly improved returns on equity, and changed or reduced obligations in other areas may soon begin to restore confidence to global insurers and reinsurers. Thus the current hard insurance market conditions may improve just at the time that new projects come on-stream, following ratification of the Kyoto Protocol in 2002.

CONCLUSION

Forest carbon sinks are risky projects that need insurance no less than any other human endeavor. As we have seen in this Chapter, the performance of forestry carbon projects depends not only on physical risks but also on a range of other factors. No forestry investor, carbon buyer, or insurer considering a carbon sequestration project can afford to ignore these risks. With the right information and open dialogue, however, cost-effective insurance or other financial risk management solutions can be designed and implemented.

NOTES

1   The authors' comments are based on their personal professional experiences and do not necessarily reflect the corporate policy or strategy of their respective employers.
2   To the authors' knowledge the NKMCAP did not approach any insurers at the inception of the concept nor at anytime prior to project start-up. However, the authors were invited by TNC to comment on the project in 1999.
3   Partial risk guarantees are provided to cover specific risk arising from non-performance of government contractual obligations that are critical to the viability of projects. Partial risk guarantees mitigate specific risks that private financiers generally find difficult to absorb or manage. Such guarantees typically cover risks arising from government actions, non-delivery of inputs, and/or non-payment for output by state-owned entities, changes in the agreed-upon regulatory framework, and political force majeure. Foreign exchange transfer risk in projects that do generate foreign exchange may also be covered. The World Bank's guarantee in favor of the private sector strengthens the credibility of governmental contractual undertakings. A government counter-guarantee may also be provided to reaffirm the government's acceptance of their obligations, backed by the Bank.

Chapter 15

Making Market-based Mechanisms Work for Forests and People

Stefano Pagiola, Natasha Landell-Mills, and Joshua Bishop

Forest destruction throughout the world poses significant risks. Not only are forests a source of valuable timber and non-timber products, but they also provide important environmental services that help sustain life on Earth. However, only rarely do beneficiaries pay for the services they receive, resulting in low incentives to conserve forests, and limiting opportunities for rural development. Market-based approaches are thought to offer considerable promise as a means to address these problems.[1] The case studies described in this book testify to the tremendous innovation all around the world in the use of market-based mechanisms to secure valuable forest environmental services, while at the same time highlighting what must be done to ensure that market-based forest conservation also supports rural livelihoods.

Making market-based mechanisms work for both forests and people is not easy. Designing and implementing the necessary rules and institutions is a daunting task under the best conditions. Policy-makers and potential investors need guidance on what kind of approaches are appropriate, when and where, and how to develop and manage them. While it is far too early to provide a blueprint for effective, sustainable, and equitable markets, some initial lessons are discernible from the case study chapters on emerging markets for watershed protection, biodiversity conservation, and carbon sequestration. Given the very early stage of market development, in most cases, we focus here on the conditions required to make market mechanisms work. In addition, we offer some preliminary reflections on the effectiveness of markets for forest environmental services, while recognizing that a definitive assessment must await further experience.

Table 15.1 *Summary of case study mechanisms*

Project (country)	Main service sold	Jointly provided services	Beneficiaries (service buyers)	Benefit capture mechanism	Providers	Provider payment mechanism	Chapter, authors
FONAFIFO (Costa Rica)	Water (mainly improved dry-season flow)	Biodiversity, carbon, scenic beauty	HEP producers, others	Individual contracts with beneficiaries	Landowners	Payment for service	3 Pagiola
Sukhomajri (India)	Reduced sedimentation		Lake used by downstream city dwellers	None[a]	Upstream village residents	Access to irrigation water	4 Kerr
Wetland banking (US)	Wetlands and associated benefits		Water users, ecosystems	Cap-and-trade[b]	Private sector investors	Payments from land developers	5 Salzman and Ruhl
FONAG (Quito, Ecuador)	Water (miscellaneous)	Biodiversity, scenic beauty	Domestic water users, HEP producers	Redirection of part of water and electricity user fees	Protected areas	Not yet decided	6 Echevarria
Shade-grown coffee (Chiapas, Mexico and El Salvador)	Biodiversity	Water, carbon	Consumers with existence value for biodiversity	Premium on coffee price	Coffee producers	Premium on coffee price	7 Pagiola and Ruthenberg
Private protected areas (Chile)	Biodiversity, scenic beauty	Water, carbon	Park owners[c]	Land acquisition	Park owners[c]	Land acquisition	8 Corcuera, Sepúlveda, and Geisse
Bioprospecting (worldwide)	Biodiversity		Pharmaceutical companies	Fees for access, royalties	Protected areas	Fees for access, royalties	9 Laird and ten Kate

Project (country)	Main service sold	Jointly provided services	Beneficiaries (service buyers)	Benefit capture mechanism	Providers	Provider payment mechanism	Chapter, authors
Ecological VAT (Paraná and Minas Gerais, Brazil)	Biodiversity	Water	Brazilian society	Earmarked portion of VAT	Municipalities, conservation unit managers	VAT pass-throughs to municipalities	10 May, Veiga Neto, Denardin, and Loureiro
Carbon market (BC, Canada)	Carbon	Biodiversity, water	Buyers of Kyoto-eligible C credits	Carbon emissions trading industry (effectively cap-and-trade)	BC forest trading	Carbon emissions	11 Bull, Harkin, and Wong
Scolel Té (Chiapas, Mexico)	Carbon		Non-Kyoto carbon buyers	Carbon emissions trading	Small farmers	Carbon emissions trading	12 Tipper
Carbon investment fund (Australia)	Carbon	Biodiversity conservation, salinity reduction	Buyers of Kyoto-eligible C credits	Carbon emissions trading	Australia forest sector	Carbon emissions trading	13 Brand
Carbon insurance Eyre (worldwide)	Carbon		Buyers of Kyoto-eligible C credits	Insurance premiums	Investors in projects to supply Kyoto-eligible C credits	Insurance premiums	14 Cottle and Crosthwaite-

Notes: a City channeled efforts by government agencies (soil conservation service, forest service) to Sukhomajri.
 b Law imposes no net loss of wetlands.
 c By buying the land, investors supply its services to themselves.

How do market-based mechanisms work?

The major features of the case studies described in this book are summarized in Table 15.1. As with any other market, there needs to be a product (the services the forest is providing) as well as buyers (the beneficiaries of the service) and sellers (the land users who make decisions on forest management and thus supply environmental services).

The product: which forest services does the mechanism provide?

The mechanisms described in this book seek to provide a wide variety of forest benefits. Particularly within the broad rubrics of water and biodiversity services, there is considerable diversity in the services provided. Thus the water services required by residents of the city of Quito are not the same as those that matter to run-of-the-river hydroelectric power (HEP) producers in Costa Rica; the biodiversity of interest to pharmaceutical companies is not the same as that sought by consumers paying a premium for shade-grown coffee. In most cases, what is sold is not the desired service itself but a proxy – not improved water quality but reforestation of the watershed; not genetic information but rights to search for it. Only in the case of carbon markets do the mechanisms examined come close to selling the desired service itself, namely carbon sequestration.

Water

Markets for watershed protection generally do not involve directly trading water quantity or quality. Rather, they usually involve 'selling' land uses that are thought to generate the desired water services. Costa Rica's FONAFIFO, for example, sells reforestation and conservation in existing forest areas, and Quito's FONAG pays for conservation in the protected areas from which it derives its water supply.

The Achilles' heel of most markets for watershed protection (and indeed of most other forms of watershed management) is a lack of good information on the relation between land use and water services. None of the cases reviewed devote much attention to clarifying these relationships, despite the uncertainties outlined in Chapter 2. Instead, all rely on the conventional wisdom that forests protect water supplies. This may pose problems for their long-term sustainability.

Biodiversity

The economic benefits of biological diversity are even more varied than those of watershed protection, but they too are generally proxied by land uses thought to contain or protect that biodiversity. For example, shade-grown coffee involves a production system that provides habitat for a range of wild species, particularly birds. Likewise, the Brazilian ecological value-added tax (ICMS-E) redistributes tax revenue to municipalities based in large part on the extent of protected areas on their territory. An important exception to the use of such proxies is biodiversity prospecting, which sells either rights to search for samples of genetic information or the samples themselves.

In general, the relationship between the land uses being sold and biodiversity are better documented than those between forests and water services. There have been many studies on the biodiversity contained in shade-grown coffee areas, for example. These studies consider various aspects of biodiversity but generally focus on species counts, with particular emphasis on endemic or endangered species. While such studies may not satisfy a specialist's definition of biodiversity, they appear to satisfy potential buyers.

Carbon

Markets for carbon sequestration come closest to the direct sale of an environmental service, in the form of certificates of emission reduction or carbon credits. Carbon sequestration is achieved by absorbing and storing atmospheric carbon in vegetation, through activities such as reforestation (as in Australia), agroforestry (as in the Scolel Té project), or reduced-impact forest management (as in British Columbia). Because carbon in the atmosphere is a global 'bad', it makes no difference where carbon sequestration services are generated. Carbon sequestration through reforestation in Africa, for instance, generates the same benefit as sequestration in Australia.[2]

The links between forests and atmospheric carbon dioxide (CO_2) levels are well documented. They have had to be in order to satisfy the political objections to counting forests as carbon sinks in the Kyoto Protocol. The case study of British Columbia's efforts in the field of carbon sequestration underlines the hard work needed to achieve an acceptable level of scientific evidence. Nevertheless, the biggest stumbling block has not been the measurement of carbon stocks or how they change, but rather the continuing uncertainty about whether and when changes in forest carbon stocks will be counted toward a nation's efforts to meet its obligations under the Kyoto Protocol. A focus of contention has been whether forest conservation (that is, avoided deforestation) should be considered an eligible approach for generating carbon credits.[3]

Multiple services

Whatever specific environmental service buyers may be interested in, it is almost never supplied alone. Protecting a forest by selling its biodiversity services, for example, also protects related hydrological services and maintains sequestered carbon. Even within a given category of services, there is some inevitable 'bundling'. Using forests to reduce flood risks may also improve water quality, while protecting forests for their ecotourism potential may also preserve genetic diversity, and vice versa. In some cases multiple services can be sold together as a bundle; in other cases it may be possible to sell each service separately (Landell-Mills and Porras, 2002).

The demand: who benefits from forest environmental services?

Efforts to sell forest environmental services must begin by considering the potential markets for them. That a given forest provides a service does not mean there is a market for it. The old saw asks whether a tree that falls in the forest makes a noise if no one is there to hear it. The question here is whether water purification is a service if no one is there to drink the water. From the perspective of being able to sell the service, the answer is clearly 'no'.[4] Without demand, there can be no market. The value of forest services depends not only on their nature and magnitude, but also on the uses to which they are put, as well as the number and preferences of the people using them.

Market-based initiatives that pay insufficient attention to demand tend to run into problems. In the case of shade-grown coffee, early efforts to organize the supply by certifying producers were not adequately supported by efforts to market biodiversity-friendly coffee, with disappointing results to date. Costa Rica's FONAFIFO may be a counter-example; it has thrived despite introducing a system of payments to suppliers before mechanisms for capturing consumer willingness to pay were established. However, FONAFIFO was only able to do this because revenues from a fuel tax were earmarked for its use, allowing payments to landowners to be made before any income was received from service beneficiaries. Worryingly, only a small portion of the area enrolled in the Payments for Environmental Services (PSA) program has proved to be of interest to service buyers – of the 200,000ha enrolled in the program, only some 2000ha receive payments from water service buyers. The lack of payments by beneficiaries is storing up problems for the future, particularly in light of recent failures to guarantee the continued transfer of income from Costa Rica's fuel tax to the PSA scheme. Starting from the supply side can also cause problems beyond cash-flow: it can lead to the provision of undesired services by the 'wrong' suppliers. In Costa Rica, an additional 35,000ha or so will need to be added to the PSA system to fulfil agreements with water service buyers.

The demand for forest environmental services may be local, national, or global in scope. At one extreme, the demand for watershed protection arises primarily from local and national beneficiaries buying very site-specific services. At the other extreme, demand for carbon sequestration may come from anywhere in the world. Demand for biodiversity services can lie anywhere within this spectrum, depending on the service being sought. The nature of the demand has important implications for the type of market-based mechanism that will work in each case.

Water

Demand for water services tends to be both site-specific and user-specific. Services provided in one watershed are usually of no interest to users located in a different watershed, and two users in the same watershed may be interested in different services. Moreover, users in a given watershed seldom have the option of switching suppliers: they can only receive their water services from existing upstream providers.[5] Hence markets for most water services need to be developed on an ad hoc basis, depending on the specific technical and institutional characteristics of each case. This means in turn that lessons from any one case are unlikely to be directly transferable to another.

Carbon

Carbon services are the opposite of water services. A tonne of carbon sequestered in one place or in one way has the same mitigating impact on global warming as a tonne of carbon sequestered in any other place or in any other way.[6] Indeed, it is precisely this equivalence that allows forests to be used to satisfy the demand for emission reductions. Consequently, there are a large number of potential buyers all over the world. The primary potential customers are firms in Annex 1 countries, which are committed to reducing their carbon emissions under the terms of the Kyoto Protocol. Under current multilateral agreements (or at least until the United States comes back into the market) the demand for carbon sequestration will arise mainly in Europe and Japan, where governments are committed to reducing national carbon emissions. Multinational companies with operations in these countries may also be major buyers. To serve this market, costs and risks must be minimized. Forest owners seeking to provide carbon sequestration services compete with each other and with alternative ways to provide these services.

Biodiversity

Both the form of biodiversity services and the demand for them are very diverse. Some biodiversity services mainly benefit local populations, such as habitat for game and gathered wild plants, or pollination services. In contrast, the demand for other services may be national or global in scope. Genetic information and chemical compounds available only from wild species are of considerable interest to biotechnology and cosmetic industries in many countries, while the presence of charismatic wild species attracts both national and international tourists. Hence in some cases markets for biodiversity services are like those for water services (site-specific, requiring ad hoc approaches) while in others they are more like those for carbon services (generic), or a mixture of both. Shade-grown coffee producers, for example, are selling a generic commodity: one kilogram of shade-grown coffee from one area may be indistinguishable from a kilogram produced elsewhere. Indeed, different certification schemes appear to be counter-productive, as they can confuse consumers. On the other hand, investors in Chile's private protected areas (PPAs) clearly do not consider a hectare of wild land in Region I to be interchangeable with a hectare in Region X. Their investments focus on a few areas of great scenic beauty and recreational potential.

In some cases, buyers are interested in more than one service and are content to pay for a bundle. In the case of shade-grown coffee, the main attraction is 'bird-friendly' coffee, but the certification mechanism also includes social and other objectives. Indeed, the tendency is toward a 'super-seal' that encompasses shade-grown, organic, and fair trade criteria. On the other hand, some buyers are only interested in a narrow range of services. In such cases it may be possible to sell the additional services separately to other buyers. Costa Rica's FONAFIFO, for example, sells the carbon emission credits arising from forest conservation separately from the watershed, landscape beauty, and biodiversity benefits provided by the same forest areas. Similarly, efforts are underway in both Chiapas and El Salvador to find buyers for the hydrological benefits that shade-grown coffee is thought to provide.

How can the willingness to pay for environmental services be turned into cash-flow?

The mere existence of beneficiaries who are willing to pay is insufficient to ensure the success of market-based mechanisms. Mechanisms must be devised to capture at least part of the benefits generated by forest services and convey these benefits in the form of payments to encourage forest conservation.

Water

One of the many challenges of developing markets for water services is that the use of water flowing in a river, or in an underground aquifer, cannot easily be confined to those who pay to protect that flow. Hence non-payers ('free riders') may benefit from the expenditure of others, undermining the incentive to pay, particularly where there are many beneficiaries. There may also be problems of coordination between different types of users. In Quito, for example, only the two largest water users have so far been persuaded to participate in FONAG. It is also significant that almost all of the agreements that FONAFIFO has reached with water users are in watersheds where those users are the sole or dominant users.

Water benefits are easiest to capture when users are already organized (as in the case of municipal water supply, irrigation systems, and HEP producers) and when payment mechanisms are already in place. Payments for the water service can then simply be added to existing channels: domestic water users can be charged an additional fee for conservation as in the case of Heredia, or part of the revenue from water fees can be allocated to conservation as with Quito's FONAG. Where users are not already organized or lack a payment mechanism, the costs of capturing benefits are likely to be substantial.

Carbon

In order to tap the emerging global market in carbon emission reductions, the main requirement is a product that satisfies the elaborate rules of the Kyoto Protocol. As described in Chapter 2, mechanisms such as Joint Implementation (JI) and the Clean Development Mechanism (CDM) create opportunities for land managers to sell carbon sequestration services. However, continuing uncertainty over the rules has been a major constraint. This has caused many efforts to fall by the wayside, such as a plan by the Sydney Futures Exchange to create the world's first exchange-traded market for carbon credits. Even after the Bonn and Marrakesh meetings in 2001, significant details remain undecided. While it seems clear that forest conservation in developing countries will not be eligible, there are a number of unresolved issues surrounding the eligibility of afforestation and reforestation activities.[7]

Even once the rules are finalized, considerable work will be needed to create a suitable product, as illustrated by the efforts in British Columbia and Australia. The inherent characteristics of forests – with their regular cycles of growth and harvest and their vulnerability to natural disasters such as fires – create particular challenges for those attempting to develop standardized carbon offsets that are attractive to a range of investors. Australia's Hancock Natural Resource Group (HNRG) aims to overcome these difficulties by pooling several Kyoto-eligible activities, so as to smooth the flow of carbon sequestration from individual projects while at the same time spreading the risk. Similarly, the insurance industry is grappling with the challenges of insuring carbon sinks, which are unusually long-lived compared to most other assets.

Biodiversity

Biodiversity benefits may be the hardest to capture, if only because of the difficulty of defining what is being sold. Corresponding to the diversity of biological benefits is an equally wide range of potential buyers: pharmaceutical and other companies looking for access to genetic materials, individual consumers willing to pay a premium for biodiversity-friendly products, and land buyers seeking scenic beauty and recreational opportunities, among many others. This very diversity makes it difficult to generalize about how best to capture willingness to pay. As with water and carbon services, the first step in capturing benefits is to identify the needs of beneficiaries. The fact that different groups may be seeking different benefits makes this task all the more complex.

Selling biodiversity often involves creating markets for new products. The example of shade-grown coffee illustrates the difficulties of generating a new market where none previously existed, even if it is based on solid evidence of consumer demand. Converting a preference for a hypothetical commodity into a payment at the cash register is not easy. Both organic and fair trade coffee have, to different degrees, succeeded in doing so. Shade-grown coffee, to date, has not. In such cases, it may be easier if the mechanism can 'piggy-back' on an existing market, at least initially, as shade-grown coffee producers in Chiapas have done by marketing their product as organic. By taking advantage of the premium paid for organic coffee, farmers in Chiapas have obtained higher prices than producers in El Salvador, who focused on shade-grown certification alone.

Significant hopes have been placed on biodiversity prospecting (bioprospecting) as a means of generating income for biodiversity conservation. To date these hopes have largely been disappointed. Although pharmaceutical companies remain interested in genetic material from forests, their willingness to pay is far lower than the optimistic forecasts of the early 1990s. Developing countries are learning how to ensure that they receive a fair share of the benefits generated by products based on genetic material from forests, but they have also learned to be more realistic about the magnitude of these benefits.

The supply: who generates forest services and how can payments enhance supply?

Turning to the supply of environmental services, a key step in setting up a market-based mechanism is to identify the actors who generate these services, or make decisions that affect the level and quality of the services provided. Depending on local circumstances, these may be private land owners, tenant farmers, logging companies, or public land agencies, among others. Equally important is the need to understand what currently motivates these actors to choose particular land uses or land use practices. In most cases they will be motivated by the constraints and opportunities of producing specific commodities for the market, such as timber or livestock, with little regard for the impact of their decisions on the magnitude and quality of the environmental services they also provide. Hence another crucial stage in developing markets for environmental services is to determine how the changes in land use or management that are required to secure or enhance them will affect the costs, risks, and returns to forest users (or other actors). Finally, based on such information, one can begin to devise a system of incentives that satisfies both the aims of land users and the needs of service users. Simply having money available will not, by itself, help to ensure the provision of forest services. That money must be used to modify the incentives of land users in appropriate ways.[8] To date, this issue has received much less attention than that of collecting payments (Pagiola and Platais, forthcoming).

The cases described in this book illustrate the range of actors involved in supplying forest environmental services. Government agencies are often major suppliers, due to their large landholdings. The national parks surrounding Quito and the municipal protected areas in Brazil are examples of publicly managed forest areas delivering services in the cases reviewed here. However, private firms and individuals also play important roles, and increasingly so as government budgets are squeezed. Costa Rica's PSA scheme is specifically targeted at private landholders, while in Chile private individuals are purchasing their own forest areas to protect. Even where government formally owns lands, non-governmental actors are often responsible for managing the land and delivering services.

Different market mechanisms will be appropriate to different types of suppliers. Where individual decision-makers are concerned, be they smallholder farmers or timber companies, market-based mechanisms need to channel the payments collected from beneficiaries to suppliers in ways that create appropriate incentives to adopt land use practices that are associated with forest environmental services. Where the state manages supply, however, a different set of incentives may be required. The size of some government agencies means that incentives need to be carefully targeted at those responsible for forest management. It is particularly important to guard against the governmental reallocation of funds paid by service beneficiaries to uses other than conservation. Only a small fraction of the funds generated by bioprospecting arrangements has been used for conservation, for example. Most have remained in the hands of central government, urban-based companies, and research institutions.

Turning to the incentive effect of payments for environmental services, we see a range of different mechanisms and results in the cases described in this volume. In the case of shade-grown coffee, the payment takes the form of a price premium, increasing its profitability relative to alternative land uses. The impact on behavior is direct, and depends mainly on the magnitude of the premium received by the producer. In Costa Rica's PSA program, direct payments are also made to land-owners for adopting (or maintaining) a specified land use. However, to date these payments have been poorly targeted. Payments are fixed for specified land management practices such as forest management and reforestation, and no account is taken of variations in the conservation value of different parcels of land. Thus, while they may be encouraging conservation, they are not necessarily encouraging it where it is most useful. In Brazil, ICMS-E payments for conservation flow to municipal governments rather than to land users. Municipalities in turn use a variety of mechanisms to induce local land users or other agencies to create new conservation areas that would further enhance the flow of funds. But the latter mechanisms have not always been very effective, as documented in Chapter 10.

The complexity of changing behavior is well illustrated in the case of Sukhomajri. There, two problems were intertwined. First, there was an externality problem, in which upstream land use practices threatened Sukhna Lake. This problem was addressed not through direct payments to upstream land users, but by providing them with a valuable service (irrigation water) which happened to be vulnerable to the same problem that threatened the lake (sedimentation). This approach ensured that the interests of people upstream and downstream coincided. Second, there was a collective action problem within the village of Sukhomajri itself. Land users in the lower part of the watershed, who stood to gain most from irrigation, lacked control over land use practices in the upper part of the watershed, which had the greatest impacts both on the lake and on the irrigation system in the watershed itself. If the collective action problem within the community had not been solved, efforts to address the upstream–downstream externality would have failed. In this case, an elegant solution was found to share the benefits of the irrigation system among all community members, thus aligning their interests.[9]

Pagiola and Platais (forthcoming; see also Chapter 3) stress that payments need to be on-going rather than short term because leverage over land users' behavior ends as soon as payments cease. All the mechanisms examined in this book envisage the establishment of long-standing payment systems. Shade-grown coffee producers will in principle receive a price premium every year. Brazilian municipalities that house conservation areas will likewise receive annual payments of value-added tax funds through the ICMS-E. While Costa Rica's PSA scheme involves five-year contracts, they are renewable. In Sukhomajri regular payments are made to all villagers based on revenue from water users, as well as from the sale of *bhabber* grass from the protected forest areas. Perhaps the main exception is biodiversity prospectors, who pay a lump sum for access to forest genetic material and then only provide regular payments if research leads to the development of a successful drug.

An alternative to regular payments is for beneficiaries to become suppliers themselves. This is what individuals who create PPAs in Chile are doing through the acquisition of areas that provide the services they desire (such as scenic beauty and recreational opportunities). In Ecuador, the city of Cuenca is also following this approach. Unlike Quito, Cuenca's water supply comes mainly from privately-owned areas. The city's water utility, ETAPA, has been acquiring land in the upper parts of the watershed and placing it under conservation. Such an approach is expensive, however, and requires considerable up-front financing.[10]

What institutional structure is needed to create a market?

Figure 15.1 summarizes the functions that must be performed by market-based mechanisms. A portion of the benefits received by environmental service beneficiaries must be captured and channeled to land users to provide incentives to protect forests. These systems depend on several prerequisites. Market participants must have access to information on the value and volume of services being exchanged. Participants must have opportunities for finding and negotiating payments. Property rights over service commodities need to be clearly defined and ownership assigned. Monitoring and enforcement mechanisms are required. A network of supporting regulatory and institutional arrangements may be necessary for markets to function effectively. Establishing such market infrastructure is not easy and is rarely cheap.

Of the many institutions that underpin successful market mechanisms, property rights deserve special mention. Property rights define who owns the

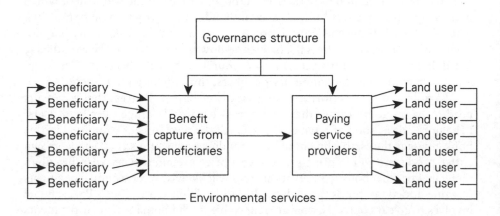

Figure 15.1 *Markets for environmental services: institutional functions*

carbon sequestered in forests, the genetic information contained in biodiversity, or the water flowing in a stream. Without clear ownership of these services, or at least the underlying land, they cannot be bought and sold. The difficulties posed by uncertain property rights are highlighted in the case of carbon sequestration in British Columbia. Here, the provincial government owns forest land, while forest harvesting companies own the timber under legal concessions. Thus both parties have a plausible claim to the carbon storage benefits provided by the forest. On-going negotiations with First Nations for rights and title to lands further complicate matters.

Ownership is partly determined by law, but governments cannot act alone in determining property rights. Local custom and practice are also important. In many countries the law awards forest ownership to the state, but in practice forest lands may be managed by non-governmental local actors. In these cases assigning de jure ownership over forest services may be insufficient to create credible property rights. Asserting that the state owns genetic information is of little use if individual decision-makers continue to destroy the habitats that contain that information. Likewise, asserting the 'polluter pays' principle (which implicitly assigns ownership of clean water to users) is likely to be ineffective when the polluters are a multitude of non-point sources, such as farms managed by smallholders.

Cooperative institutions can also play a role in supporting market-based mechanisms. For example, Sukhomajri's erosion problem could not have been solved if the village had not acted together to protect common areas. The village's Hill Resource Management Society was instrumental in achieving consensus and subsequently enforcing the agreed rules. Similarly, cooperation is often necessary on the demand side if multiple beneficiaries need to coordinate their actions. Quito's FONAG is an example of a cooperative institution representing local government, national park authorities, non-governmental agencies, and water-user groups. Cooperative institutions can also help to reduce transaction costs; thus collective certification was instrumental to the development of shade-grown coffee, as certification would have been too onerous for individual farmers to undertake. Collective certification was also used by the PSA program in small-holder areas. Village and producer organizations similarly help to keep down the (already high) costs of operating the Scolel Té program.

Building supportive regulatory or cooperative institutions can require significant time and financial resources. Establishing FONAG in Quito, for instance, required investments in background scientific and policy research, proposal development, and consultation exercises with key stakeholder groups in and around the city, as well as practical activities such as recruiting staff and renting office space. Where appropriate institutional structures already exist, the task is much easier. Thus Costa Rica was able to develop its PSA program relatively quickly by building on existing institutions created for the previous timber support program. This had disadvantages, however, as the PSA inherited some features of the previous program – such as a lack of targeting – that are not suited to its new purpose.

Who are the main actors in market mechanisms?

Commercial enterprises, various levels of government, local and international non-governmental organizations (NGOs), donors, community groups, and individual land users all participate in markets for forest environmental services as buyers, sellers, intermediaries, brokers, and providers of support services. It is difficult to pigeonhole participants according to their main function, since most play different roles depending on the case.

Commercial companies stand out as increasingly important buyers of the services considered in this book. Thus bioprospecting is dominated by private biotechnology companies while shade-grown coffee is chiefly of interest to coffee retailers. Payments for water services may come from a broader group, but private hydropower and water supply companies are frequent participants. In Costa Rica, several private HEP producers agreed to participate in the PSA program long before the state-owned power producer CNFL came on board. In some cases, companies participate voluntarily. For example, Costa Rican HEP producers see watershed protection as essential to their commercial interests. In other cases, enterprise demand may depend on government regulations. The Clean Water Act in the United States, for instance, is the principal reason for growing payments for wetland conservation by real estate developers.

Private companies are not only buyers; they are also intermediaries and providers of ancillary services. Sometimes the role is a minor one (which is not to say unimportant). For example, a commercial investment bank manages FONAG funds. In other cases the role is central, as with the many brokers and distributors who handle shade-grown coffee. A striking feature of private sector involvement is the dynamic way in which companies respond to new market opportunities. Thus Chilean real estate companies responded to growing consumer interest in private conservation by developing new eco-real estate projects. Similarly, as forest-based carbon sequestration develops into a profitable business, investment bankers have begun packaging it for investors, while insurers figure out how to insure it. Likewise entrepreneurs have developed wetland banks in response to the need of US real estate developers to mitigate damage to wetlands. These reactions are not always entirely benign; some Chilean eco-real estate developers, for example, have sold many more lots in their conservation areas than they had promised, diluting the environmental benefit received by all buyers.

Governments also play important roles in market-based mechanisms. In addition to developing policy and regulatory frameworks, governments may be significant buyers and sellers of services and they are frequently active intermediaries as well.

- **Government as buyer.** Municipal water suppliers and government-owned HEP producers are notable public-sector buyers of watershed services.[11] Brazil's ICMS-E system offers an interesting example of how state governments buy environmental services such as biodiversity conservation and watershed protection from municipalities. ICMS-E allocation rules act as an implicit price list for the environmental services that the government wishes to buy, and municipalities have responded by supplying them. Government participation in market-based mechanisms is frequently limited, however, by regulations governing their ability to introduce new resource user fees, or by restrictions on the use of public funds. In Costa Rica, for example, public moneys cannot be used to contract landowners who lack land titles. Changing these restrictions may be complicated and politically sensitive.

- **Government as seller.** Forests are often publicly owned. Government agencies that manage these forests often suffer from chronic budget shortfalls and they increasingly view market mechanisms as a key component of long-term financing strategies. Ecuador's Ministry of Environment, for instance, has been a major driver of Quito's emerging water fund, which it expects will fund the management of the Cayambe Coca and Antisana Ecological Reserves. In a similar vein, Costa Rica has sought to extract payments from bioprospectors via the National Biodiversity Institute (INBio) to help finance its national system of conservation areas.

- **Government as intermediary.** Governments can catalyze market mechanisms not only through regulatory action (as in the case of cap-and-trade schemes to control pollution) but also by offering intermediary services that link buyers with sellers. Costa Rica's FONAFIFO is a good example of the latter. Governments may also stimulate market payments through the provision of information, advice, and training. For example, the Central Soil and Water Conservation Research and Training Institute (CSWCRTI) provided these services in Sukhomajri to support the development of a benefit-sharing system for watershed protection.

Local NGOs and community groups often play crucial roles by working with smallholders to deliver service supplies, or by organizing service buyers. For example, local NGOs have organized participation by smallholders in Costa Rica's PSA program and in shade-grown coffee certification in Chiapas and El Salvador. In Quito, FONAG will rely on local environmental NGOs to implement watershed protection activities. On the demand side, community user groups are expected to help bring small-scale water consumers into the market for Quito's watershed services. In Sukhomajri, the Hill Resources Management Society played a central role in collecting payments from water users and distributing revenues.

Donor organizations and international NGOs have likewise contributed in different ways to the development of markets for environmental services. Some have been important buyers of global environmental services, such as carbon sequestration and biodiversity protection. Thus the Global Environment Facility (GEF) was established to compensate developing countries for the incremental cost of undertaking investments that generate global environmental services as well as local development benefits: in essence, they are buying global environmental services (Dixon and Pagiola, 2001). Donor agencies and international NGOs have also facilitated the establishment and management of market mechanisms, helping to overcome problems posed by start-up costs and technical constraints. For instance, the World Bank has provided technical expertise, finance, and capacity-building on establishing payments for environmental services in a number of countries, especially in Latin America (Pagiola and Platais, forthcoming). Similarly, the World Bank's Prototype Carbon Fund (PCF) was established to kick-start the market in carbon offsets. The Nature Conservancy's input into the development of FONAG and the Rainforest Alliance's design of the Eco-OK seal for biodiversity-friendly products provided similar stimulus at key junctures.

How did market-based mechanisms emerge?

Markets for environmental services do not emerge fully-grown from an analyst's drawing board or computer. Rather, they evolve over time according to local circumstances. Understanding how and why different initiatives have developed in the way they have can help shed light on the key determinants or drivers of successful market-based mechanisms.

Demand-side drivers

These reflect the growing appreciation of forest environmental services by consumers, alongside the heightened awareness of threats to these services. Thus the successful watershed protection scheme in Sukhomajri emerged from growing concern in the city of Chandigarh over the sedimentation of Sukhna Lake. Similarly, Quito's electricity and water utilities helped set up FONAG in response to the degradation of the protected areas from which they draw their water. Likewise, investors in Chile's PPAs were responding to the degradation of natural forests.

The desire of some companies to be green – or to be seen to be green – for public relations reasons and to ward off criticism from NGOs has played an important role in the development of many mechanisms. The brewery Cervecería Costa Rica signed a watershed protection contract with FONAFIFO partly for such reasons.[12] Similarly, in the case of Scolel Té, buyers of carbon sequestration credits appear to be motivated by personal ethical concerns as well as public relations objectives. Such motives may even help to overcome defects in emerging market-based mechanisms, such as the limited understanding of forest–hydrology links. The number of customers motivated primarily by ethical considerations is likely to be limited, however. Attempts to replicate these or similar mechanisms, or indeed to expand the reach of existing mechanisms, might well encounter more demanding customers.[13]

Supply-side drivers

These reflect the desire of land users, planners and owners to obtain more income from their forest management activities. Many large forestry companies, for example, are well aware of the potential carbon value of the lands they manage. Where suppliers are uninformed about markets for environmental services, however, or are poorly organized, the impetus for developing market-based mechanisms has usually come from NGOs and other groups working on their behalf.

Regulatory drivers

These are often critical factors in the emergence of market-based mechanisms. Most governments impose quantitative environmental standards, but increasingly these are accompanied by market-based mechanisms to reduce the costs of compliance. The flexibility mechanisms under the Kyoto Protocol and the system of wetland banking in the United States are both examples of regulatory systems bringing forth market mechanisms.

Intermediaries and ancillary service providers

These have been important drivers in some cases. In the carbon market in particular, ancillary service providers such as insurers and certifiers have taken on a catalytic role, pushing for increased use of the flexibility mechanisms which they expect to generate more business. Similarly, wetland banks in the United States pushed for flexibility in meeting mitigation goals.

The structure and performance of market-based mechanisms are also heavily influenced by the distribution of political and financial power between buyers, sellers, and intermediaries. In some cases vested interests may block the introduction of payment systems altogether, as illustrated by the difficulties of replicating the Sukhomajri success story in other watersheds. In many villages, powerful landowners have resisted the introduction of similar benefit-sharing systems. Some public utilities have likewise resisted the introduction of payments for water services, preferring instead to pass the burden of conservation to other agencies. Powerful groups can also exert influence over the structure of payment mechanisms, as seen for example in the design of FONAG in Quito.

Once created, market-based mechanisms can create a vested interest in their success. Although this is generally positive, it can also lead to rigidities. Current participants in Costa Rica's PSA program, for example, are opposed to moves toward greater targeting, as many of them would likely be dropped from the program as a result. In the emerging market for carbon sequestration, there is a danger that short-sighted rules which limit access to the market (through restrictions on eligible land use activities) may create a vested interest on the part of early entrants to keep new suppliers out, for fear of depressing asset prices.

What are the transaction costs?

All the mechanisms described in this book involve two sets of costs: the initial costs of establishment, and the costs of operating the mechanism once it is in place.[14] These costs include both financial expenditures and non-monetary costs (such as time inputs) borne by various participants.

Up-front costs

The costs of establishing the mechanism include the costs of clarifying technical factors (for example, understanding hydrological linkages), establishing appropriate organizations, and ensuring that a supportive legal framework is in place.

- **Technical.** Market-based mechanisms require a clear understanding of the role of forests in service delivery. The preparatory work underway in British Columbia on carbon sequestration in forests provides an example of what is involved. Skimping on research may reduce costs in the short term, but is likely to undermine the long-term sustainability of the market.
- **Organizational.** Market-based mechanisms often require an elaborate network of supporting organizations to manage, monitor, and enforce payments. In Chiapas, considerable efforts were devoted to strengthening the capacity of local organizations to undertake tasks such as extension. El Salvador already had reasonably strong organizations supporting coffee producers, and so was able to move faster to certify shade-grown coffee producers. Organizational costs will clearly be higher the greater the numbers of beneficiaries and/or suppliers involved, and the more diverse each group.
- **Legal.** One of the most important legal requirements is to ensure that property rights over land and environmental benefits are clearly defined – a task that is often politically sensitive and costly. In addition, where government agencies are involved as buyers or sellers of environmental services, changes in their mandates or responsibilities may be necessary. For example, water companies such as Costa Rica's AyA need regulatory approval in order to charge additional fees. Costa Rica had to pass a special law establishing the principle of payments for environmental services, creating FONAFIFO, and allocating funds. However, such a comprehensive approach is not always necessary. El Salvador's Environment Law, for example, gives the Ministry of Environment authority to implement payments for environmental services, although in general terms only. While some additional laws may be needed (for example, to ensure that electric and water utilities can participate), in this case the law already provides a basis on which to build.

The up-front costs imposed on participants can also be significant, and are not always visible. Land users applying to Costa Rica's PSA program, for example, must draw up a detailed management plan. Similarly, coffee producers seeking certification for their coffee as shade-grown must adapt their production systems to meet a variety of criteria. Ignoring these requirements can lead to significant underestimation of the cost of the mechanism, and overestimation of the incentives to participate.

External organizations such as bilateral and multilateral donors and NGOs often play a catalytic role during start-up, providing essential financial assistance or technical know-how to help mechanisms get underway. Thus the GEF has supported the establishment of certification mechanisms for shade-grown coffee and other biodiversity-friendly crops, with the expectation that this would lead to a self-sustaining market that would help to preserve biodiversity. Outside agencies can also help to ensure that small farmers and other marginal groups are not excluded from market-based mechanisms. For example, the United Kingdom's Department For International Development (DFID) provides support to the Scolel Té project in an effort to ensure that poor groups gain access to the emerging carbon market.

Operating costs

Once a mechanism is in place, there will be on-going costs associated with monit-oring performance, enforcing rules, and of course renegotiation when the original contract expires, or if it is judged unsatisfactory by one or both parties. Ideally, operating costs will be covered by the mechanism itself. Where this cannot be achieved, the mechanism is unlikely to be sustainable.

The magnitude of set-up and operating costs are partly a function of the level of market maturity; teething problems in nascent markets are to be expected. As market-based mechanisms for forest environmental services spread and mature, more sophisticated payment systems are evolving to help control costs. Examples include the formation of producer associations and user groups, standardized contracts, more sophisticated intermediaries such as FONAG in Ecuador, and new risk management tools such as carbon offset insurance.

There may be trade-offs between transaction costs and how efficiently a mechanism provides the desired service. Systems of payments for environmental services are most likely to be efficient in providing the desired services when they are targeted. At the limit, this might mean a different payment, for a different land use, for every participating plot of land. Such an approach would clearly be impractical; the transaction costs of operating such a system would rapidly swamp its benefits. At the other extreme, a system of untargeted, undifferentiated payments for a single, homogeneous set of land uses would be cheap to implement but probably very inefficient. A middle ground needs to be found. Costa Rica's PSA program has tended to emphasize low transaction costs, although recent years have seen moves toward increased targeting. El Salvador is planning to pay more attention to targeting, accepting that this may entail higher transaction costs.

How effective are market-based mechanisms?

This Chapter has sought to identify some key questions that must be addressed in order to develop markets for forest environmental services. Of course, market-based mechanisms are not ends in themselves. They are designed to achieve certain objectives and ultimately must be judged on the extent to which they succeed in doing so.[15] These objectives include forest conservation as well as broader aims of rural development and poverty alleviation. Experience with market-based mechanisms is still relatively limited and it remains to be seen to what extent such diverse expectations can be met by the kind of initiatives described in this book. With this in mind, we attempt to draw some initial conclusions on the effectiveness of alternative market mechanisms, and the factors that appear to influence their performance. We then discuss the factors that are likely to affect their sustainability.

How well do market-based mechanisms promote conservation?

The broad range of mechanisms and the problems they address means that their effectiveness in promoting forest conservation cannot be assessed in a uniform way. Some mechanisms seek to conserve existing forest areas, some to expand them, others to modify the way they are managed, and yet others to reduce the cost of complying with regulations. Nevertheless, two basic criteria can be used to examine the effectiveness of these mechanisms: the extent to which they attract participants and influence their behavior, and the extent and nature of the forest that is ultimately conserved. Clearly, the second will only apply if the first is met.

Most of the mechanisms reviewed in this book appear to have been quite successful in attracting participants. Among water-oriented mechanisms, Sukhomajri has successfully involved the entire population of its target watershed, while Costa Rica's FONAFIFO has attracted five times more participants than it can pay for. Among biodiversity-oriented mechanisms, the Chiapas coffee project has surpassed its certification objectives by 20 per cent, despite difficult institutional conditions (albeit thanks primarily to organic rather than shade-grown price premiums); the ICMS-E in Brazil has spurred a considerable expansion of the conservation area in Paraná and Minas Gerais; and a variety of new approaches to PPAs have developed to meet demand in Chile. Most carbon-oriented mechanisms are still in the planning stage, but the Scolel Té project has attracted substantial participation in its target areas. The sole exception to this generally successful picture is biodiversity prospecting. Once thought to be a major new source of finance for forest conservation, biodiversity prospecting is now generally considered to offer no more than a modest supplement to other sources of financing.[16] Shade-grown coffee has also been disappointing so far, although the success of organic and fair trade coffees and moves toward the creation of a super-seal encompassing all the sustainable coffee criteria are causes for optimism.

Closer examination of the cases in this book yields a more nuanced picture, together with indications of the conditions under which different mechanisms are likely to provide attractive incentives to forest managers. In particular, it must be noted that the extent to which a specific mechanism provides incentives to forest managers to undertake conservation depends not only on the extent and form of payments but also on the opportunity costs of conservation. Thus, while Costa Rica's PSA system is vastly oversubscribed, the town of Heredia had to create a parallel system in its watershed. The US$40/ha/year payments that have attracted applications covering a million hectares of forest are insufficient in Heredia's watershed, where the opportunity cost of land is high due to profitable agricultural opportunities. Likewise, most PPAs in Chile have been created in relatively remote areas with limited agricultural potential. Although some local authorities grumble that PPAs limit local development opportunities, the truth is that such potential is generally limited, otherwise most buyers would not have been able to afford to buy the land. In Brazil, the ICMS-E has induced a greater expansion of conservation areas in municipalities with limited alternative land uses.

Figure 15.2 illustrates the interaction between downstream benefits and upstream opportunity costs in the case of payments for watershed protection. Such systems are most likely to be effective when downstream benefits are high (resulting in high willingness to pay) and upstream opportunity costs are low. Most participants in Costa Rica's PSA program are landowners in areas with limited alternative land uses, for example. It may be possible to implement such systems in situations when both downstream benefits and upstream opportunity costs are high, but it will be more difficult to do so because the margins will be small. Whether Heredia will succeed in attracting landowners to its program, even with its higher payments, remains to be seen. When downstream benefits are low, in general there is little scope to use such mechanisms, even if upstream opportunity costs are also low. Although this latter case is unlikely to justify the creation of an ad hoc mechanism, if a mechanism already exists it may be possible to apply it effectively. Large parts of Costa Rica's PSA program are in fact in such areas, as a result of the program's initial lack of targeting.

| | | Upstream opportunity costs | |
		Low	High
Downstream benefits	High	Yes	Possibly, but difficult to make work
	Low	Possibly, but not very useful	No

Source: Pagiola and Platais, forthcoming

Figure 15.2 *Applicability of systems of payment for water services*

One of the main attractions of market-based mechanisms, at least in theory, is that they are sensitive to regional variation in the demand for environmental services and the costs of supply. Hence most market-based mechanisms tend to focus on forests that provide relatively high levels of specific services. Chile's PPAs are concentrated in areas of great scenic beauty and recreational potential. Payments for water services in Costa Rica's PSA program are likewise concentrated in a few specific watersheds, covering less than 1 per cent of the system's current area (rising to 10–20 per cent as current agreements are implemented). Nevertheless, the areas protected by these mechanisms may not always have the highest priority from a pure conservation perspective. Shade-grown coffee, for example, protects agricultural areas that are rich in biodiversity, but not as rich as primary forest. This problem is discussed extensively in the Chile case study. Most PPAs have been created in areas that were already reasonably well represented in the public protected area system, leaving many valuable ecosystems unprotected. Moreover, most PPAs are of insufficient size to sustain long-term, genetically viable populations of most species.

Even if a mechanism does not conserve the highest-priority areas, however, it can still play an important role by allowing other efforts to be focused on highest-priority areas. Moreover, it may be possible to channel the mechanism so as to increase its conservation benefits. The ICMS-E in Paraná and Minas Gerais, for example, contains elaborate criteria related to the effort to direct conservation to desired activities – including, in the case of Paraná, an effort to assess the quality of the resulting conservation.

In this context, it is also important to guard against the possibility of perverse incentives. Kyoto rules on carbon sinks as currently defined may exacerbate the growing competitive advantage of intensively managed plantations over natural forests in global timber markets. While plantations created after 1990 are potentially eligible to receive carbon credits, natural forests are not. This may further undermine the competitive position of natural forests in global timber supply, following a decade of NGO boycotts, logging bans, demands for certification, and other regulatory pressures. Likewise, higher returns to shade-grown coffee might encourage farmers to convert primary forest to coffee. To guard against this eventuality, neither the Chiapas nor the El Salvador programs will certify recently converted forests.

How well does the mechanism contribute to rural development and poverty reduction?

Market-based mechanisms are predicated on voluntary exchange between buyers and sellers, and should in theory benefit all of those involved. Buyers of services pay only as much as the service is worth to them, while sellers need only accept compensation if it covers all of their costs, including the opportunity costs of forgone land uses. Intermediaries get involved to the extent that they can capture a share of the benefits of trade to reward their inputs.

The distribution of costs and benefits has crucial implications for stakeholder support for market mechanisms and, thus, their long-term sustainability. Where key groups or individuals feel that they are net losers from market mechanisms, they can be expected to resist implementation and may threaten the mechanism's success. Beyond these practical considerations, however, the potential impact of market-based mechanisms on the poor is of particular interest for ethical reasons.

Market-based mechanisms can be powerful tools for poverty alleviation and rural development. First, they offer a means to increase the income of the rural poor. Payments for environmental services can likewise help to diversify household income sources, thereby reducing risk and vulnerability. In Chiapas, one of

Mexico's poorest states, both the Scolel Té carbon project and the El Triunfo shade-grown coffee project appear to have significantly boosted the income of poor farmers. Second, where market mechanisms are associated with investments in local institutions, education, and health, additional positive spin-offs may be expected. The importance of social capital has been increasingly recognized throughout the world. The institutions and strengthened local community capacity developed for the purposes of the mechanism may thus prove useful in a number of ways.

The extent to which poor producers are able to participate in market-based mechanisms is closely linked to the structure of the resulting market. In the case of carbon services and shade-grown coffee, for example, buyers have a wide range of potential suppliers to choose from. The high transaction costs incurred in dealing with many small, dispersed producers place them at a competitive disadvantage in bidding to supply these services. Proactive interventions by outside actors may be needed if the poor are to participate at all. Without the assistance of the DFID and the GEF, for example, it is unlikely that smallholders in Chiapas would have been able to participate in carbon sequestration and shade-grown coffee markets. Conversely, in the case of watershed protection, buyers typically have no choice but to deal with whomever is managing land in the watershed, and that often includes poor smallholders. Indeed, this necessity is so strong that it can drive institutional innovation. In Sukhomajri, for instance, the pivotal role played by landless villagers in protecting common lands led to the design of a mechanism that ensured their participation. In Costa Rica a new PSA contract had to be designed to protect the Platanar watershed, as most landowners there had no legal title to their land and so were precluded from participating in the standard PSA contract.

Experiences in Sukhomajri, the Scolel Té project, and Latin America's shade-grown coffee initiatives offer some early lessons about the factors that affect the impact of market mechanisms on the poor, and on how mechanisms might be designed to maximize their positive impact. These include:

- **Property rights.** Poorer households are more likely to have insecure property rights over land and the associated environmental services. Special efforts may be needed to clarify property rights and to allocate them appropriately, to ensure that relatively deprived groups are not excluded. A related priority is to consider the potential impact of market-based mechanisms on the landless poor, including tenant farmers and agricultural laborers.
- **Cooperative institutions.** Because poorer groups will tend to hold smaller parcels of land (if any), be less well educated, and have fewer contacts with potential buyers, they face significant obstacles in accessing market mechanisms. Cooperative arrangements are a valuable mechanism for overcoming such hurdles and, in the cases described in this book, have been most valuable where smallholders need to coordinate land management and the supply of services. In the Scolel Té carbon project, for instance, farmer cooperation has

been essential for meeting demand for carbon offsets. Cooperative mechanisms can also help overcome conflicts between landowners and landless households, as seen in the case of Sukhomajri.

- **Product definition.** Care needs to be taken in designing the markets so that the poor are not precluded from participating. Introducing commodities that fit with short-term and flexible livelihood strategies will increase their accessibility to poorer households. Considerable effort was devoted to designing shade-grown coffee certification criteria that smallholders in Chiapas could implement, for example – not an easy task, as consumer preferences tend to impose more stringent and onerous criteria. Likewise, the Scolel Té carbon project workers labored to design carbon offsets that are transparent, simple, and flexible to suit local community needs. In this regard, existing restrictions under the CDM on the eligibility of avoided deforestation and some other carbon storage activities that are relatively accessible to the poor are especially worrying.

- **Access to start-up finance.** Participants in market mechanisms often need to bear initial costs. Financial support, through direct subsidies or technical assistance, may be necessary to allow poor producers to participate. This is particularly true in more competitive markets, such as those for carbon credits and shade-grown coffee.

How sustainable is the mechanism?

The sustainability of the mechanisms studied in this book is even harder to assess than their effectiveness, as most are relatively new. Three dimensions of sustainability can be distinguished: a continued demand for the environmental services being sold; a continued ability to supply these services; and the sustainability of the institutional structure created to make the mechanism work.

Continued demand for the services being sold is partly exogenous, depending on factors such as population growth, economic growth, and so on. For some services, such as drinking water, it is likely that demand will continue to grow for the foreseeable future. Demand for other services may be more variable. The demand for biodiversity protection, for example, may be highly sensitive to changing economic conditions. Will consumers be as willing to pay a premium for biodiversity-friendly coffee in a recession as they are in times of rapid growth? Another important exogenous factor is the risk of competition from low-cost alternative technologies. This has been most evident in the case of biodiversity prospecting, where competition from synthetic chemistry has undermined the value of supply from natural areas.

Continued demand through a particular mechanism also depends on the track record of that mechanism in delivering the services it promises. If services fail to materialize, buyers are likely to abandon payments quickly. The greatest risk of such a backlash appears to be in the watershed service market, where scientific understanding of forest–hydrology links is weakest, creating a risk that service delivery may not be forthcoming. Careful monitoring is important, both to document service delivery to buyers and in order to improve the mechanism's operation. Designers of carbon mechanisms have devoted considerable efforts to the issue of monitoring, including the need for independent verification. Biodiversity mechanisms have also usually included monitoring efforts, although these sometimes take the form of one-off surveys rather than on-going monitoring. Water mechanisms have devoted the least effort to monitoring, if any. The PSA program in Costa Rica, for example, only monitors the implementation of agreed reforestation and forest conservation activities, but not the resulting impact on water supplies.

The sustainability of the institutional framework in which markets evolve is closely intertwined with demand- and supply-side sustainability. For the most part, none of these are likely to be static. Rather, institutions – be they market, regulatory, or cooperative – are constantly evolving in response to changing preferences and power balances. Where market mechanisms gain support from more powerful groups and generate greater payments, it is likely that they will be associated with increased investment in supporting institutions and that they will become more sophisticated. However, where market mechanisms are rejected by key stakeholders and fail to generate the desired financial transfers, they may be abandoned.

CONCLUSIONS

There is an urgent need for new measures to finance forest conservation, and more generally to encourage land users to provide important environmental services. There is likewise a need for new economic opportunities to sustain and improve livelihoods, especially in hard-pressed rural areas. Market-based mechanisms appear to offer many advantages over conventional approaches to forest conservation, including the possibility of mobilizing new funding from consumers of environmental services, a better match of funding to supply and thus more cost-effective provision of environmental services, and additional and diversified income for rural development.

Market-based mechanisms are still in their infancy, and much remains to be learned. There is a significant danger of over-enthusiasm. Interest in market-based mechanisms in recent years has led to a proliferation of sometimes poorly prepared schemes. There is a great potential for disillusionment. Avoiding this danger and successfully implementing market-based mechanisms requires considerable care. Though the principles are simple, putting them into practice is not. The detailed case studies collected in this book seek to advance this learning process by illustrating how these mechanisms are being applied in a wide range of situations.

Throughout this review, we have emphasized the questions that need to be asked to develop and implement market-based mechanisms. We are still far from understanding these mechanisms sufficiently to be able to answer all these questions. Nevertheless, the case studies in this book do suggest some broad initial lessons:

- **One size does not fit all.** None of the mechanisms described in this book are universally applicable. Even when mechanisms are similar, the details of their application are likely to differ substantially in the light of local technical, economic, and institutional conditions.
- **Identify the services being provided clearly.** Potential buyers are not interested in generic forest services, nor even in water services or biodiversity services. Rather, they are interested in clean water, a reliable dry-season water supply, or access to genetic information. Without a clear understanding of which specific services a given forest is providing, and to whom, developing market-based mechanisms will be difficult.
- **Understand and document the links between forests and services.** Just as important as identifying the services is understanding how these services are generated. Too often, mechanisms rely on conventional wisdom that forests provide services such as improved water supply. Sometimes this conventional wisdom is wrong, leading to the wrong actions being taken. But even when the conventional wisdom is right, it is often insufficiently precise to allow effective mechanisms to be designed. What kind of forest is most effective in improving water supplies, for example, and where should it be located? How compatible are other uses? Without answers to questions such as these, the mechanism is unlikely to work effectively.
- **Begin from the demand side, not the supply side.** By focusing on the demand for services and asking how best to meet it, it is more likely that an effective and sustainable mechanism will be developed. Without demand, there can be no market. Beginning from the supply side risks developing mechanisms that supply the wrong services in the wrong places, or at prices that buyers are unwilling to pay. We predict that supply-driven mechanisms will have a higher mortality rate than demand-driven ones.
- **Monitor effectiveness.** Monitoring effectiveness is essential if one is to provide documentation to buyers confirming that they are getting what they are paying for, and adjust the functioning of the mechanism should problems arise. At the same time, excessively burdensome monitoring requirements can discourage potential suppliers without necessarily providing more reassurance to buyers. Finding the right balance of information and compliance costs is an on-going concern, as seen in the case of markets for certified timber and agricultural products.
- **Design flexible mechanisms.** Market-based mechanisms must also be sufficiently flexible to respond to changing demand and supply conditions and improvements in knowledge about how forests generate services. They should reward efforts to expand and improve service delivery and to reduce costs, while minimizing the incentives for destructive rent-seeking or free-riding.
- **Ensure that the poor can participate.** Market-based mechanisms have great potential to provide additional income sources to rural land users, as well as

reduced risk through diversification and other indirect benefits. However, realizing this potential often requires particular efforts to be made to ensure that the poor are not excluded, such as securing land tenure for marginalized groups, supporting cooperative institutions for bundling and bargaining, facilitating access to training and start-up capital, and of course designing the market itself.

The cases described in this book suggest that carefully designed markets for forest environmental services can make an important contribution to environmental improvement and rural development. While most initiatives are still in the early stages of development, they all provide useful lessons and inspiration for further innovation in this rapidly changing area, for the benefit of both forests and people.

NOTES

1   It should also be borne in mind that market failures are not the sole source of threats to forests. Policy failures also play an important role (Barbier and others, 1994; Binswanger, 1991; Browder, 1985; Mahar, 1988; Repetto and Gillis, 1988; Schneider, 1994). Reducing or removing subsidies that encourage forest destruction, including government support for extensive agriculture or road building in environmentally sensitive areas, can be equally or more important. Similarly, much may be achieved by strengthening liability laws governing environmental damage claims, or by introducing more comprehensive environmental reporting requirements for private companies. Such reforms lie outside the scope of this book, but can create powerful incentives for conservation.
2   While carbon sequestration is in many ways a pure public good, being both non-excludable and non-rival in consumption, the market for carbon sequestration service is in fact for an excludable private good: certificates of emissions reduction (see Chapter 2).
3   Most of these uncertainties were resolved by the political agreements reached in Bonn (July 2001) and Marrakesh (November 2001), although key details remain undecided. Under the agreements, only reforestation and afforestation are eligible in non-Annex 1 countries, and even these are subject to specific rules. However, definitions for afforestation and reforestation have yet to be clarified and there is uncertainty surrounding activities such as enrichment planting or agroforestry. Policy-makers also left the door open to changes in eligibility rules in the next commitment period, after 2012.
4   This is obviously a decidedly anthropocentric view. For a discussion of the different philosophical approaches to valuing ecosystem services, see Goulder and Kennedy (1997).
5   When inter-basin water transfers are possible, as is the case with many water supply systems for large cities, it makes sense to define the catchment area of interest to include all watersheds from which the system draws its supplies. Even then, the system may not consider water services provided in different parts of the catchment area to be interchangeable, given differences in transport costs.

6   While carbon sequestered in different ways and places may contribute equally to slowing global warming, buyers can be expected to discriminate between alternative carbon assets on the basis of both price and security (risk), as discussed in Chapter 14.

7   Some carbon buyers (such as those in the Scolel Té example) have been motivated by ethical or public relations considerations, rather than by any need to meet emission-reduction targets under the Kyoto Protocol. These buyers are obviously not constrained by Kyoto rules, so the main requirement is simply to provide them with a product that they find acceptable. Such buyers are likely to be fewer in number than those who need to meet Kyoto emission limits, however. Moreover, as the market develops and more Kyoto-compliant carbon sequestration products become available, it is likely that non-Kyoto buyers will also turn to them. The market for non-Kyoto-compliant carbon sequestration products, therefore, is likely to be quite limited.

8   Payments will not always involve direct financial transfers, but may use a range of in-kind and financial benefit-sharing mechanisms designed to suit the local context, as in the case of Sukhomajri. Moreover, in some cases there may be a need for punitive measures as well, as part of market-based enforcement mechanisms.

9   Murray (1994) describes a similar arrangement in the Dominican Republic.

10   To reduce this burden, considerable effort has been devoted to exploring the possibility of acquiring easements rather than ownership of the land (Gustanski and Squires, 1999). A landowner who sells an easement sells some of the rights he has over land – for example, the right to cut down the forest – but retains others, such as the right to harvest non-timber products provided that they are compatible with the easement. The Nature Conservancy has been particularly active in this area.

11   Of course, payments are ultimately passed on to customers, either as explicit additional fees or by earmarking part of the fees they pay. Heredia, for instance, charges an 'environmentally-adjusted water tariff', while Quito's FONAG allocates part of its existing income from water fees to conservation.

12   FONAFIFO is exploring ways to capitalize on similar willingness to pay for the public relations benefits of the PSA program by introducing a logo that participants would be able to use.

13   Efforts to expand the use of 'triple bottom line' accounting (Elkington, 1997), in which firms supplement their traditional financial accounts with accounts of their performance on social and environmental indicators, may make firms more receptive to participation in market-based instruments for environmental conservation.

14   Ostrom and others (1993) add a third category of cost, namely the strategic costs associated with shirking, free-riding, and corruption. Strategic costs tend to be higher where service delivery is difficult to measure. We include these costs in either up-front or operational costs, as appropriate.

15   Market-based approaches to providing forest environmental services must also be compared to non-market approaches, such as the creation of protected areas by government or regulations requiring the adoption of low-impact timber harvesting methods. Such a comparison is beyond the scope of this volume.

16   It may be that science and industry have yet to realize the full potential of natural biological diversity, in which case an important value of forest conservation is simply the continued opportunity to investigate natural genetic and biochemical richness (option value). Creating a market for such a pure public good is a major challenge.

REFERENCES

Barbier, E.B., J.C. Burgess, J. Bishop, and B. Aylward. 1994. *The Economics of the Tropical Timber Trade*. London: Earthscan.

Binswanger, H. 1991. "Brazilian Policies that Encourage Deforestation in the Amazon." *World Development*, 19, pp.821-829.

Browder, J. 1985. *Subsidies, Deforestation, and the Forest Sector of the Brazilian Amazon*. Washington: World Resources Institute.

Dixon, J.A., and S. Pagiola. 2001. "Local Costs, Global Benefits: Valuing Biodiversity in Developing Countries." In OECD, *Valuation of Biodiversity Benefits: Selected Studies*. Paris: OECD.

Elkington, J. 1997. *Cannibals With Forks: The Triple Bottom Line of 21st Century Business*. Oxford: Capstone Publishing Limited.

Goulder, L.H., and D. Kennedy. 1997. "Valuing Ecosystem Services: Philosophical Bases and Empirical Methods." In G.C. Daily (ed.), *Nature's Services: Societal Dependence on Natural Ecosystems*. Washington: Island Press.

Gustanski, J.A., and R.H. Squires (eds.). 1999. *Protecting Land: Conservation Easements Past, Present, and Future*. Washington: Island Press.

Johnson, N., A. White, and D. Perrot-Maître. 2001. "Financial Incentives for Watershed Management: Issues and Lessons for Innovators." Washington: Forest Trends.

Landell-Mills, N., and I. Porras. 2002. *Silver Bullet or Fools' Gold? A Global Review of Markets for Forest Environmental Services and Their Impact on the Poor*. London: IIED.

Mahar, D. 1988. "Government Policies and Deforestation in Brazil's Amazon Region." Environment Department Working Paper No.7. Washington: World Bank.

Murray, G. 1994. "Technoeconomic, Organizational, and Ideational Factors as Determinants of Soil Conservation in the Dominican Republic." In E. Lutz, S. Pagiola, and C. Reiche (eds.), *Economic and Institutional Analyses of Soil Conservation Projects in Central America and the Caribbean*. Environment Paper No.8. Washington: World Bank.

Ostrom, E., L. Schroeder, and S. Wynne. 1993. *Institutional Incentives and Sustainable Development: Infrastructure Policies in Perspective*. Boulder: Westview Press.

Pagiola, S., and G. Platais. Forthcoming. *Payments for Environmental Services*. Washington: World Bank.

Poteete, A., and E. Ostrom. Forthcoming. "An Institutional Approach to the Study of Forest Resources." In J. Poulsen (ed.), *Human Impacts on Tropical Forest Biodiversity and Genetic Resources*. New York: CABI Publishing.

Repetto, R., and M. Gillis (eds.). 1988. *Government Policies and the Misuse of Forest Resources*. Cambridge: Cambridge University Press.

Schneider, R. 1994. "Government and the Economy on the Amazon Frontier." LAC Regional Studies Program Report No.34. Washington: World Bank.

Index